VALUES: Assemblies for

VALUES: Assemblies for the 1990s

Roy Blatchford

SIMON & SCHUSTER
EDUCATION

For my parents and their values.

First published in 1992 in Great Britain by
Simon & Schuster Education
Campus 400, Maylands Avenue
Hemel Hempstead, Herts HP2 7EZ

Reprinted in 1993, 1994

A catalogue record for this book is available from the British Library

ISBN 0 7501 0217 9

Typeset in 9½ on 11pt Times Roman
by Graphicraft Typesetters Ltd., Hong Kong
Printed in Great Britain by T.J. Press (Padstow) Ltd.

Contents

Introduction

Why assemble?

The short answer to this question is that the law requires that: all pupils in attendance at a maintained school shall on each school day take part in an act of Collective Worship – an assembly. It is important to note that the term *Collective* Worship is used, not *Corporate*, a recognition that pupils in schools come from a variety of backgrounds.

We cannot assume that our students constitute a body of worshippers. Our responsibility is to provide the *opportunity* for worship. Individuals will respond and react at different levels and in different ways, which may include

- awareness
- appreciation
- respect
- preference
- commitment
- devotion/dedication
- adoration

Expanding the range of responses is the only way to deal effectively and sensitively with the spectrum of religious and non-religious stances held by staff and pupils.

Within a school setting a broad definition of worship makes sense. Something like this works well for pupils, parents, staff and governors alike:

Worship has to do with worth and worthiness. It is the recognition, affirmation and celebration of the 'worth'ship of certain realities and values, held to be of central importance to the community which worships. The act of worshipping renews the meaning of these realities and values for the community, helping each of its members to grasp them personally. The community focuses on what it knows to be of great or supreme worth, hence worthy of preservation and promotion, and of its members' dedication.

If the law didn't require assemblies, would we hold them? This is an open question, and one to which I would reply in the affirmative. Assemblies provide an opportunity for a group of people who have a common daily goal and many common interests to come together and celebrate their community values. When school's out, where else in life – outside our places of worship, sports stadia and concert halls – is this opportunity on offer? All too rarely.

Ask a group of 15-year-olds the question 'Why assemblies?' and they'll probably answer 'Don't bother'. Anyone regularly presenting school assemblies must do so in the certain knowledge that only some of what is being said will register some of the time with some of those gathered.

Yet the opportunity to promote the 'spiritual' aspect of our lives is vital. Assemblies, thoughts-for-the-day, collective acts of worship, reflections – call them what you will – afford a much-needed alternative prospectus to that of the material values which so dominate young people's contemporary society.

Taking assemblies

A few tried and tested tips:

1 The visible support of all teaching colleagues helps secure the status of assemblies in pupils' eyes.
2 The form of worship and routine of gathering should be the same throughout a school.
3 Multi-faith schools should seek to hold on to corporate, rather than separate assemblies.
4 Dignity, comfort and safety are given to the occasion if everyone can be properly seated.
5 If worship is to be respectful, then disciplined calm is needed, established through custom, practice and quiet exhortation.
6 Music before and after the collective worship helps set the appropriate atmosphere.
7 Due reverence should be shown when prayers are used.
8 Singing? Yes, if not achieved by haranguing!
9 Pupil accompaniment and participation in an assembly rota is essential – but contributions must be well organised and rehearsed.
10 Outside speakers should be encouraged – and carefully briefed.
11 Use assemblies to give out important notices and champion (past and present) pupils' achievements.
12 Keep some kind of record in a log-book of subjects/themes used in Collective Worship – it saves embarrassing repetition!
13 Don't take assemblies unless you *enjoy* taking them.

Using this collection

My own experience in education over the past 20 years has encompassed middle-size and large comprehensives in London and Oxfordshire, with assembly gatherings ranging from 150 to 600, comprising both mono-ethnic and multi-faith audiences. From years of taking assemblies I have a fair idea of what works with young people, what risks might be taken, and which staff, parental and governor sensibilities to watch out for. But these, of course, vary from one school to the next, and will be judged accordingly.

Assemblies for the 1990s works on the premise that it is possible to make most subjects relevant to any age group (within the 11–19 age range) given good preparation and delivery of the material. That said, certain readings included here are more challenging in language and subject matter. The presenter may wish to adapt or judiciously edit these as s/he goes along. Some of the assemblies will be more appropriate for a 16+ audience. Those assemblies are marked * in the Contents list.

The collection is simply organised around 12 core themes. Within each thematic section are 12 assemblies, organised to a common pattern:

- subject title
- introduction
- reading
- reflections

Each assembly is planned to take around 15 minutes.

The *Readings* have been chosen first and foremost as a good read in any hands. If you use this volume in no other way, you are guaranteed around 150 items – story, anecdote, quotation, humour – that have proved successful with young people.

The *Introduction* and *Reflections* provide a context for each reading. This material is drafted in a personal and colloquial style which the presenter can adapt to suit the audience and the topicality of the occasion. There are clear links between assemblies within and across thematic sections.

This collection seeks to broaden young people's horizons and aspirations, to express optimism in today's school students and to offer them alternative values to those of the 'me-generation' where so many know 'the cost of everything and the value of nothing'.

I would like to thank the many staff and pupils who have both heard and listened to me over the years and told me, through their body language, whether what I've been saying is of value to them. Just occasionally I have heard a pin drop . . .

Roy Blatchford,
Oxford 1992

Being Human: One

1 Wealth and possessions

Introduction

In today's world we are surrounded by material wealth. There are many pressures on all of us to want more things, particularly money. Many people work hard all their lives, save, and in their later years find they have built up personal wealth. Others – criminals for example – try to take short cuts to securing wealth. Others still – like winners of the football pools – suddenly find themselves with a fortune. But there is often a price to pay for 'instant riches'. The following short story has an interesting phrase at its heart:

'When the gods wish to punish us, they answer our prayers'

Reading

The outside chance

It's a funny thing about money. If you haven't got it, you think it's the most important thing in the world. That's what I used to think, too. I don't any more, though, and I learned the hard way.

When I was at school, we had this English master. He was always quoting to us from famous writers. I wasn't very interested, and I don't remember much about it now. But it's funny how things come back to you. He used to say:

'When the gods wish to punish us, they answer our prayers.'

Sounds a bit daft, doesn't it? Well, I didn't understand it then, either, but I can tell you what it means now. It means if you want something really badly, you'll probably get it. But you'll probably get it in a way you don't expect.

I mean, you might have to pay a price you didn't bargain for.

It started one rainy day, when I was coming home from work.

I'm a motor mechanic, and I liked working in the garage. But, I was restless. I'd always had this dream of owning my own business. Nothing big – just something I could build up. I don't mind hard work, you see, if I'm working for myself. That's why I'd left my mum and dad in the North, and come to London. I thought I'd make more money that way.

We'd had arguments about it. My dad and me. He didn't see why I should want to leave home when I had enough to live on.

Enough! Enough for what? I used to ask him. To live as he had in a council house all his life, with nothing to look forward to but a gold watch and a pension?

Oh, I was fond of him, you see, and it annoyed me to see him so content. He had nothing to show for all those years of work in that noisy factory.

Anyway, all this was on my mind, as I walked home that night. The rain didn't help, either. I remember thinking, if only I could get out of the rut, if only I could get a thousand quid – just that, just a thousand.

I stopped and bought a newspaper outside the Tube. I thought it would take my mind off things on the way home. I could read about other people's troubles for a change. See what films were on.

I don't know when I first realised there was something wrong with the paper. It looked ordinary enough. But there was something about it that didn't seem quite right. As if there was a gap in the news. As if it was a jump ahead. So, in the end, I looked at the front page, and instead of Tuesday 22nd November, it said Wednesday 23rd November.

'My God,' I thought, 'it's tomorrow's paper!'

I didn't believe it to start with. But it did explain why all the news was different. There couldn't be any other explanation. Somehow, I had bought tomorrow's paper – today!

And that was the moment I realised it. The moment I realised that all my prayers could be answered. My hands were shaking so much that I could hardly turn the pages. But they *were* there. The results of tomorrow's races!

I looked at the winners, and chose from them carefully. I picked only the outsiders that had won at prices like 30–1.

There was even one at 50–1! A horse I would never have thought of betting on.

Next morning, I went to the bank, and drew out just about all I had – £150. I laid my bets during my lunch hour. I went to several shops. I didn't want anyone to become suspicious.

It's a funny thing, but I just knew they'd come up. And – God forgive me – I never stopped to think *why* I had been given this chance to see into the future.

They *did* come up – every one of them. All I had to do was to go round and collect, and I couldn't wait to get home and count my money. A cool £4,000!!

Well, nothing could stop me now! I'd give in my notice at work the next day, and look for a place of my own. Wait till I told Mum and Dad! They'd hardly be able to believe it.

I switched on the television, but I couldn't concentrate on it. I kept thinking what I'd do with the money. I hardly heard a word of the programme.

Then the news came on.

The announcer mentioned Selby. That was where my parents lived. I began to listen.

There had been an explosion up there, that afternoon, followed by a fire in a factory. Twenty-two people had been killed, and many more were in hospital. I don't remember the rest – something about a government enquiry.

I stopped listening, but I couldn't move out of the chair. I think I must've known then that my dad was dead – even before the telegram came.

The newspaper had fallen on the floor. I picked it up, not realising what I was doing. Then, I saw it – in the 'Stop Press'. FACTORY DISASTER IN SELBY. MANY FEARED DEAD. I hadn't seen it before. I'd been too busy picking winners. I could've saved my dad's life, but I'd been too busy picking bloody winners. I don't often cry, but the words swam in front of me then.

There isn't much more to tell. I got my own business, and I'm doing well. As for my mum, she was paid insurance by the firm that owned the factory, so she's better off than she ever was. The only thing is, she doesn't care if she's alive or dead now my dad's gone.

When the gods wish to punish us, they make a damn good job of it.

'The Outside Chance' by Jan Carew

Reflections

* What are your reactions to this slightly fantastic tale? Is it possible to find sudden wealth without some kind of 'price'? Do families suffer when someone within the family pursues money at any cost? What 'price' would you be prepared to pay to be a very rich person? We need, don't we, to balance wealth and *quantity* of things alongside *quality* of life. There is, then, *spiritual* as well as *material* wealth that we need to think about.

* *Matthew 6: 19–24*
  Do not store up for yourselves treasures on earth, where moth and rust destroy, and where thieves break in and steal. But store up for yourself treasures in heaven, where moth and rust do not destroy, and where thieves do not break in and steal. For where your treasure is, there your heart will be also. The eye is the lamp of the body. If your eyes are good, your whole body will be full of light. But if your eyes are bad, your whole body will be full of darkness. If then the light within you is darkness, how great is that darkness!

  No-one can serve two masters. Either he will hate the one and love the other, or he will be devoted to the one and despise the other. You cannot serve both God and Money.

2 Accidents and personal tragedy

Introduction
It is a fact of our lives that accidents do happen. Sometimes they are minor mishaps. But sometimes they involve loss and death within a family or a whole community. If we lose someone close to us we feel it very deeply.

How do we react to loss and tragedy? How do we come to terms with it? How can we help others cope with loss or personal tragedy? The following passage offers some interesting thoughts on the subject.

Reading

When disaster strikes

A SURVIVOR of the Zeebrugge ferry disaster told how she and an eight-year-old girl, Clare, sat in the watery darkness and talked as they waited to be rescued. Again and again Clare would say: 'But I've always been good. I've never told lies.'

What Clare was trying to deal with was the great confusion which faces us all when we, or those near to us, are struck by disaster.

After a disaster we face two questions. *How did this happen*? and *Why did this happen*?

How looks for causes. The causes may be technically difficult to find but psychologically the answer is easy to find. It is the subject of an inquiry, and usually the events leading to the disaster are revealed. The bow doors were left open, the man fired a gun, an oil pipe burst, a signal wire was misplaced, the plane burst apart.

But *why* something happened is a much more difficult question to answer, for whichever way we do, we can find no peace. The fabric of our lives has been irreparably torn. *Why* looks for reasons, and reasons lay blame on somebody. *Why* can give us only three kinds of answers. It was somebody else's fault. Or, it was my fault. Or, it happened by chance.

When disaster happens to people far away from us, answering the *why* question gives us no problems at all. Obviously it is not our fault, almost certainly it was somebody else's fault, and even if it happened by chance, nothing like that could ever happen to us.

We can blame the people who ought to have prevented the tragedy.

However, when disaster happens close by or to us, the protective devices of blaming other people and congratulating ourselves do not work. We are compelled to go beyond the question *Why* to those of why we exist and why anything happens.

The answers to the question *Why* which lay blame on ourselves or somebody else rest on the assumption of some causal pattern. Whatever it is, this causal pattern gives us a way of understanding our life and guarding against danger.

Some of us see this causal pattern as being that of science, which says that every event has a cause, and which promises that if we know enough about the causes of events, we can protect ourselves from danger.

Most of us see the causal pattern as being some kind of Grand Design, presided over and infused by a great Power. For some of us this Power is clear and specific – God – and for some of us the Power is amorphous and generalised, a force with which we should live in harmony.

Whichever way the Grand Design is seen, human beings occupy a special place in it. It does not just explain our place in the order of things, it defines good and evil, and shows us how to keep ourselves safe by being good. All of us, as children, were taught that if we were bad we would be punished and if we were good we would be safe and rewarded for our goodness. Jesus, or God, or Allah was watching over us. We lived, we were told, in a just world.

However, when disaster strikes us, we, like Clare, at first protest that we have tried to be good, and then, like Clare, we begin to suspect that we have been taught a lie. Being good does not mean that we are safe. Whether our goodness is that of being rational and scientific or of being morally good, it is no protection against disaster.

Such a discovery throws into question our assumption of a Grand Design where the good are rewarded and the bad punished. Thus, when disaster strikes us, the underpinnings of our life shatter and dissolve and we are in danger of being overwhelmed by the most tremendous fear. To keep this fear at bay we can cling to our belief in the Grand Design by insisting that the disaster was the outcome of negligence or a conspiracy by others, or of our own moral failure. Similarly many people prefer to blame themselves for the disaster that befalls them and their family, rather than recognise our own helplessness always to keep ourselves and our loved ones safe.

But such solutions are costly. The people that we can blame are the people on whom we depend, people in positions of responsibility, and we find ourselves afraid and resentful. If we blame ourselves, we destroy our self confidence and put ourselves in the prison of depression.

However, some people, often as a result of being shaken by the closeness of a disaster, contemplate the third explanation, that events can happen by chance. Out of such a contemplation they can discover that, frightening though such a thought can be, it is also joyous, for they are now free. No longer are they trapped in the system of scientific cause or the system of rewards and punishments which, because they make everything secure, deny hope.

Bad things which we do not deserve and for which there is no recompense can happen to us, and, equally, good things for which we pay no price can happen to us. All we need is the courage to face such uncertainty.

By recognising that disasters happen by chance, we assume responsibility for ourselves. We recognise that if we want to be safe, we cannot rely on the infallibility and incorruptibility of people who assume authority and power. Nor can we cling to the belief of a just world. Instead, we can help and support one another, recognising our own weaknesses, and our own courage. For us all to make such a discovery would in no way compensate for the tragedies which have befallen us, but it would prevent us from repeating our own tragic history.

From 'The Successful Self' by Dorothy Rowe, quoted
in the 'Independent' 3.1.89

Reflections

* 'By recognising that disasters happen by chance, we assume responsibility for ourselves.'

  The writer here is trying to suggest that when disaster occurs we should not immediately seek to *blame* either ourselves or someone else. Chance or 'fate' are a part of our lives.

  Many people believe in a God, who determines life and death. These people often find that their faith helps them when accidents and tragedies occur.

* Death is nothing at all. I have only slipped away into the next room. I am I and you are you, whatever we were to each other we are still.

  Call me by my old familiar name, speak to me in the easy way we always used. Put no difference in your tone; wear no forced air of solemnity or sorrow. Laugh as we always laughed at the little jokes together.

  Smile, think of me, pray for me.

  Let my name be ever the household word that it always was, let it be spoken without an effort, without a trace of a shadow in it.

  Life means all that it ever meant, it is the same as it ever was; there is absolute unbroken continuity.

  Why should I be out of mind because I am out of sight? I am but waiting for you, for an interval, somewhere very near, just around the corner.

  All is well.

Canon Henry Scott Holland

3 Values

Introduction

Basic to human existence is our value system: what we believe to be good or bad, right or wrong, honest or dishonest, worthwhile or worthless.

Each of us has a personal value system, framed by our upbringing. But we also share values with others around us in society. Some values you would find common to all peoples of the world; some would vary from country to country.

Think about these questions:

What do I value in my life? People? Time? Ideas? Other?
Is 'a value' the same as 'something valuable'?
Are 'values' the same as 'beliefs'?

The following two well-known stories from the Christian Bible throw an interesting light on this subject of *values*.

Reading

The Parable of the Lost Son

¹¹Jesus continued: 'There was a man who had two sons. ¹²The younger one said to his father, "Father, give me my share of the estate." So he divided his property between them.

¹³'Not long after that, the younger son got together all he had, set off for a distant country and there squandered his wealth in wild living. ¹⁴After he had spent everything, there was a severe famine in that whole country, and he began to be in need. ¹⁵So he went and hired himself out to a citizen of that country, who sent him to his fields to feed pigs. ¹⁶He longed to fill his stomach with the pods that the pigs were eating, but no-one gave him anything.

¹⁷'When he came to his senses, he said, "How many of my father's hired men have food to spare, and here I am starving to death! ¹⁸I will set out and go back to my father and say to him: Father, I have sinned against heaven and against you. ¹⁹I am no longer worthy to be called your son; make me like one of your hired men." ²⁰So he got up and went to his father.

'But while he was still a long way off, his father saw him and was filled with compassion for him; he ran to his son, threw his arms around him and kissed him.

²¹'The son said to him, "Father, I have sinned against heaven and against you. I am no longer worthy to be called your son."

²²'But the father said to his servants, "Quick! Bring the best robe and put it on him. Put a ring on his finger and sandals on his feet. ²³Bring the fattened calf and kill it. Let's have a feast and celebrate. ²⁴For this son of mine was dead and is alive again; he was lost and is found." So they began to celebrate.

²⁵'Meanwhile, the older son was in the field. When he came near the house, he heard music and dancing. ²⁶So he called one of the servants and asked him what was going on. ²⁷"Your brother has come," he replied, "and your father has killed the fattened calf because he has him back safe and sound."

²⁸'The older brother became angry and refused to go in. So his father went out and pleaded with him. ²⁹But he answered his father, "Look! All these years I've been slaving for you and never disobeyed your orders. Yet you never gave me even a young goat so I could celebrate with my friends. ³⁰But when this son of yours who has squandered your property with prostitutes comes home, you kill the fattened calf for him!"

³¹' "My son," the father said, "you are always with me, and everything I have is yours. ³²But we had to celebrate and be glad, because this brother of yours was dead and is alive again; he was lost and is found." '

Luke 16: 11–32

The Parable of the Good Samaritan

²⁵On one occasion an expert in the law stood up to test Jesus. 'Teacher,' he asked, 'what must I do to inherit eternal life?'

²⁶'What is written in the Law?' he replied. 'How do you read it?'

²⁷He answered: '"Love the Lord your God with all your heart and with all your soul and with all your strength and with all your mind"; and, "Love your neighbour as yourself."'

²⁸'You have answered correctly,' Jesus replied. 'Do this and you will live.'

²⁹But he wanted to justify himself, so he asked Jesus, 'And who is my neighbour?'

³⁰In reply Jesus said: 'A man was going down from Jerusalem to Jericho, when he fell into the hands of robbers. They stripped him of his clothes, beat him and went away, leaving him half-dead. ³¹A priest happened to be going down the same road, and when he saw the man, he passed by on the other side. ³²So too, a Levite, when he came to the place and saw him, passed by on the other side. ³³But a Samaritan, as he travelled, came where the man was; and when he saw him, he took pity on him. ³⁴He went to him and bandaged his wounds, pouring on oil and wine. Then he put the man on his own donkey, brought him to an inn and took care of him. ³⁵The next day he took out two silver coins and gave them to the innkeeper. 'Look after him,' he said, 'and when I return, I will reimburse you for any extra expense you may have.'

³⁶'Which of these three do you think was a neighbour to the man who fell into the hands of robbers?'

³⁷The expert in the law replied, 'The one who had mercy on him.'
Jesus told him, 'Go and do likewise.'

Luke 10: 25–37

Reflections

* In their different narratives, these two tales have much to tell us about universal value systems.
  In the first, the father values the *life* of his son as being more important than money and material wealth.
  The second emphasises the value of caring for others. This point is made all the more strongly because two neighbours turned their back on the man in the road before a third 'stranger' helped him.
  It is important to reflect on our values, as individuals, as families, as groups of friends, and as a school community.
  Each school has its own value system which all who work in it need to share and celebrate if it is to be a flourishing community.

* This mini-saga (a story of just 50 words) offers another angle on the subject of values. Think about its moral!

Different Values, Or Who Got The Best of The Bargain?   R S Ferm
Harris boasts he gave an African a cheap watch for an uncut diamond. Sold it and gambled the proceeds for more.
Abukali tells of the tiktik he swapped for a wife and two goats.
Harris chases further millions.
Abukali sleeps in the shade while his children tend his 20 goats.

4 Death and bereavement

Introduction

One of the most difficult things we face in life is the fact of death. The sudden death of someone else can throw our own emotions into turmoil.

If the death is within our own family or within our own community then the effect on everybody within that circle can be quite devastating.

How can we deal with death?

What can we say to someone to comfort them, if they have lost a close friend or member of the family?

We are often lost for words.

The following is an extract from a fascinating short story. This is how the story begins:

Reading

Fireflies

Yesterday I met a man on a train. Two months ago, he told me, his only daughter had taken the elevator up to the top of a tall building in Japan. She was holding a firework in her hand. A Roman candle. She had struck a match and lit the touch-paper, then she had raised the firework high above her head like a torch. It had started to crackle and splutter. Broken lines of white heat had shot out into the night sky – thin darts of light being fired into the blackness, just as a snake might flick out its tongue. Then a fountain of stars had showered down over her head and into her hair, drenching her in brightness. And then she had jumped. She and the firework hit the pavement together, both of them extinguished in the same split second. The rescue workers clearing up afterwards complained very bitterly about the mess.

'They sent us a photograph,' he said emptily. 'But it wasn't the same. It could have been anyone. So then we asked to have the body flown home. And they said that would cost fourteen thousand pounds. We couldn't believe it at first. Fourteen thousand! It seemed so incredible. But there was nothing we could do, of course. So we just had to let them cremate her.' He half-smiled, 'Did you know that there are seven different grades of cremation in Japan? They all cost different amounts of money.' I shook my head and said nothing. I didn't trust myself to speak.

'It cost seven hundred pounds,' he continued. 'That was the cheapest. And then I went through to Heathrow to pick up the ashes. They were in a metal urn. And the metal urn itself was in a polythene container that said Human Remains. The taxi-driver gave me a queer look. 'What you got in there mister,' he said. 'A dead dog?' When I got home I took the urn up to her bedroom, and we didn't open it for two weeks. And all the time in between, I just couldn't stop thinking about her. Wondering why she did it. Wondering if it hurt. Imagining her falling over and over again, that firework in her hand like a shooting star . . .'

I saw that he was crying quietly.

'In the end, we went upstairs and lit a candle in the room and said a sort of prayer, and took her down from the shelf. There was a plaque screwed down on the outside. Her date of birth, and the date she died. Only they'd got the first date wrong. They put 1960. But really she was just twenty-five. Then we lifted the lid and looked inside. It seemed so easy at first. It was as if it wasn't really her. Just ash and bits of flaky stuff. But then my wife saw something glittering, and put her hand in and lifted it out. It was the steel plate she had put in her knee after the biking accident. That was all there was left of her.'

I didn't know what to say. There we were, in a tin box in the middle of nowhere. I looked at our reflections in the window. Two ghostly heads – facing each other, yet always apart – fixed by the glass in a strange limbo that was neither inside nor out of the train. 'I'm so sorry,' I said hopelessly.

From 'Fireflies' by Linda Cookson

Reflections

* The extract reveals the important of *listening* to someone else if they want to talk about their own grief.
  You may not be able to *say* much but you can always offer your time to *listen*. When you face loss or sadness, you will need others to comfort and understand you. Remember always to give someone else your *time* and your *ear*.

* *Romans 14: 7–9*
  For none of us lives to himself alone and none of us dies to himself alone.
  If we live, we live to the Lord; and if we die, we die to the Lord. So, whether we live or die we belong to the Lord.
  For this very reason, Christ died and returned to life so that he might be the Lord of both the dead and the living.

* Peace, peace! He is not dead, he doth not sleep –
  He has awakened from the dream of life –
  'Tis we, who lost in stormy visions, keep
  With phantoms an unprofitable strife,
  And in mad trance, strike with our spirit's knife
  Invulnerable nothings – We decay
  Like corpses in a charnel; fear and grief
  Convulse us and consume us day by day,
  And cold hopes swarm like worms within our living clay.

  . . . . . .

  The One remains, the many change and pass;
  Heaven's light forever shines, Earth's shadows fly;
  Life, like a dome of many-coloured glass,
  Stains the white radiance of Eternity,
  Until Death tramples it to fragments. – Die,
  If thou wouldst be that which thou dost seek!

  From 'Adonais' by Shelley

5 Showing off? Telling the truth?

Introduction

Most of us, at one time or another, find ourselves boasting about something – 'showing off'. There can be positive reasons: sometimes we feel proud of an achievement we've worked hard for, like winning a sports medal or passing a music exam. Or we might want to show off a special present from our parents or friends. But sometimes we boast about things just to impress other people. That's what happens in this extract from the novel *Three Men in a Boat*.

Three men are sitting in a pub as this extract opens. What does the passage say to you about 'showing off' or boasting? Or do you think it is lying?

Reading

The trout

Then a pause ensued in the conversation, during which our eyes wandered round the room. They finally rested upon a dusty old glass-case, fixed very high up above the chimney-piece, and containing a trout. It rather fascinated me, that trout; it was such a monstrous fish. In fact, at first glance, I thought it was a cod.

'Ah!' said the old gentleman, following the direction of my gaze, 'fine fellow that, ain't he?'

'Quite uncommon,' I murmured; and George asked the old man how much he thought it weighed.

'Eighteen pounds six ounces,' said our friend, rising and taking down his coat. 'Yes,' he continued, 'it wur sixteen year ago, come the third o' next month, that I landed him. I caught him just below the bridge with a minnow. They told me he wur in the river, and I said I'd have him, and so I did. You don't see many fish that size about here now, I'm thinking. Good night, gentlemen, good night.'

And out he went, and left us alone.

We could not take our eyes off the fish after that. It really was a remarkably fine fish. We were still looking at it, when the local carrier, who had just stopped at the inn, came to the door of the room with a pot of beer in his hand, and he also looked at the fish.

'Good-sized trout, that,' said George, turning round to him.

'Ah! you may well say that, sir,' replied the man; and then, after a pull at his beer, he added, 'Maybe you wasn't here, sir, when that fish was caught?'

'No,' we told him. We were strangers in the neighbourhood.

'Ah!' said the carrier, 'then, of course, how should you? It was nearly five years ago that I caught that trout.'

'Oh! Was it you who caught it, then?' said I.

'Yes, sir,' replied the genial old fellow. 'I caught him just below the lock one Friday afternoon; and the remarkable thing about it is that I caught him with a fly. I'd gone out pike fishing, bless you, never thinking of trout, and when I saw that whopper on the end of my line, blest if it didn't quite take me aback. Well, you see, he weighed twenty-six pound. Good night, gentlemen, good night.'

Five minutes afterwards a third man came in, and described how *he* had caught it early one morning, with bleak; and then he left, and a stolid, solemn-looking, middle-aged individual came in, and sat down over by the window.

None of us spoke for a while; but, at length, George turned to the new-comer, and said:

'I beg your pardon, I hope you will forgive the liberty that we – perfect strangers in the neighbourhood – are taking, but my friend here and myself would be so much obliged if you would tell us how you caught that trout up there.'

'Why, who told you I caught that trout!' was the surprised query.

We said that nobody had told us so, but somehow or other we felt instinctively that it was he who had done it.

'Well, it's a most remarkable thing – most remarkable,' answered the stolid stranger, laughing; 'because, as a matter of fact, you are quite right. I did catch it. But fancy your guessing it like that. Dear me, it's really a most remarkable thing.'

And then he went on, and told us how it had taken him half an hour to land it, and how it had broken his rod. He said he had weighed it carefully when he reached home, and it had turned the scale at thirty-four pounds.

He went in his turn, and when he was gone, the landlord came in to us. We told him the various histories we had heard about his trout, and he was immensely amused, and we all laughed very heartily.

'Fancy Jim Bates and Joe Muggles and Mr Jones and old Billy Maunders all telling you that they had caught it. Ha! ha! ha! Well, that is good,' said the honest old fellow, laughing heartily. 'Yes, they are the sort to give it *me*, to put up in *my* parlour, if *they* had caught it, they are! Ha! ha! ha!'

And then he told us the real history of the fish. It seemed that he had caught it himself, years ago, when he was quite a lad; not by any art or skill, but by that unaccountable luck that appears to always wait upon a boy when he plays the wag from school and goes out fishing on a sunny afternoon, with a bit of string tied on to the end of a tree.

He said that bringing home that trout had saved him from a whacking, and that even his schoolmaster had said it was worth the rule-of-three and practice put together.

He was called out of the room at this point, and George and I turned our gaze upon the fish.

It really was a most astonishing trout. The more we looked at it, the more we marvelled at it.

It excited George so much that he climbed up on the back of a chair to get a better view of it.

And then the chair slipped, and George clutched wildly at the trout-case to save himself, and down it came with a crash, George and the chair on top of it.

'You haven't injured the fish, have you?' I cried in alarm, rushing up.

'I hope not,' said George, rising cautiously and looking about.

But he had. That trout lay shattered into a thousand fragments – I say a thousand, but they may have only been nine hundred. I did not count them.

We thought it strange and unaccountable that a stuffed trout should break up into little pieces like that.

And so it would have been strange and unaccountable, if it had been a stuffed trout, but it was not.

That trout was plaster of Paris.

From 'Three Men in a Boat' by Jerome K Jerome

Reflections

* In this passage we meet people boasting about an achievement that they would like to have experienced, but never quite did. The author paints a humorous picture of boasting.

   But it *can* have an unpleasant effect – both on the person who boasts and on those who have to listen to someone showing off in an unpleasant or aggressive way.

* There is sometimes a fine line between not clearly remembering what you saw, exaggerating facts, and telling a lie. Remember the following when you next find yourself in a situation where different accounts of the same 'facts' are being given.

Where does 'the truth' lie?
What kind of a liar are you?
People lie because they don't remember clear what they saw.
People lie because they can't help making a story better than it was the way it happened.
People tell 'white lies' so as to be decent to others.
People lie in a pinch, hating to do it, but lying on because it might be worse.
And people lie just to be liars for a crooked personal gain.
What sort of a liar are you?
Which of these liars are you?

Carl Sandburg

6 Under pressure

Introduction

We all feel pressure from time to time. Some people positively enjoy and thrive on it – you will hear someone say, 'I only work well under pressure'. For other people, pressures can build up and cause tension and stress.

Young people – at home, in school, among friends – experience all kinds of pressures. Learning to cope with pressure – turning it into something positive – is part of growing up.

The following passage was written by George Orwell. It is a piece of auto-biographical writing, about his years spent in India. As the person in authority he finds himself having to do something he would rather not do; but he is under great pressure to meet the expectations of those who surround him.

Reading

Shooting an elephant

As soon as I saw the elephant I knew with perfect certainty that I ought not to shoot him. It is a serious matter to shoot a working elephant – it is comparable to destroying a huge and costly piece of machinery – and obviously one ought not to do it if it can possibly be avoided. And at that distance, peacefully eating, the elephant looked no more dangerous than a cow. I thought then and I think now that his attack of 'must' was already passing off; in which case he would merely wander harmlessly about until the mahout came back and caught him, Moreover, I did not in the least want to shoot him. I decided that I would watch him for a little while to make sure that he did not turn savage again, and then go home.

But at that moment I glanced round at the crowd that had followed me. It was an immense crowd, two thousand at the least and growing every minute. It blocked the road for a long distance on either side. I looked at the sea of yellow faces above the garish clothes – faces all happy and excited over this bit of fun, all certain that the elephant was going to be shot. They were watching me as they would watch a conjurer about to perform a trick. They did not like me, but with the magical rifle in my hands I was momentarily worth watching. And suddenly I realized that I should have to shoot the elephant after all. The people expected it of me and I had got to do it; I could feel their two thousand wills pressing me forward, irresistibly. And it was at this moment, as I stood there with the rifle in my hands, that I first grasped the hollowness, the futility of the white man's dominion in the East. Here was I, the white man with his gun, standing in front of the unarmed native crowd – seemingly the leading actor of the piece; but in reality I was only an absurd puppet pushed to and fro by the will of those yellow faces behind.

. . . For it is the condition of his rule that he shall spend his life in trying to impress the 'natives', and so in every crisis he has got to do what the 'natives' expect of him. He wears a mask, and his face grows to fit it. I had got to shoot the elephant. I had committed myself to doing it when I sent for the rifle.

But I did not want to shoot the elephant. I watched him beating his bunch of grass against his knees, with that preoccupied grandmotherly air that elephants have. It seemed to me that it would be murder to shoot him. At that age I was not squeamish about killing animals, but I had never shot an elephant and never wanted to. Besides, there was the beast's owner to be considered. Alive, the elephant was worth at least a hundred pounds; dead, he would only be worth the value of his tusks, five pounds, possibly. But I had got to act quickly. I turned to some experienced-looking Burmans who had been there when we arrived, and asked them how the elephant had been behaving. They all said the same thing: he took no notice of you if you left him alone, but he might charge if you went too close to him.

The crowd grew very still, and a deep, happy sigh, as of people who see the theatre curtain go up at last, breathed from innumerable throats. They were going to have their bit of fun after all. The rifle was a beautiful German thing with cross-hair sights. I did not then know that in shooting an elephant one should shoot to cut an imaginary bar running from ear-hole to ear-hole. I ought, therefore, as the elephant was sideways on, to have aimed straight at his ear-hole; actually I aimed several inches in front of this, thinking the brain would be further forward.

When I pulled the trigger I did not hear the bang or feel the kick – one never does when a shot goes home – but I heard the devilish roar of glee that went up from the crowd. In that instant, in too short a time, one would have thought, even for the bullet to get there, a mysterious, terrible change had come over the elephant. He neither stirred nor fell, but every line of his body had altered. He looked suddenly stricken, shrunken, immensely old, as though the frightful impact of the bullet had paralysed him without knocking him down. At last, after what seemed a long time – it might have been five seconds, I dare say – he sagged flabbily to his knees. His mouth slobbered. An enormous senility seemed to have settled upon him. One could have imagined him thousands of years old. I fired again into the same spot. At the second shot he did not collapse but climbed with desperate slowness to his feet and stood weakly upright, with legs sagging and head drooping. I fired a third time. That was the shot that did for him. You could see the agony of it jolt his whole body and knock the last remnant of strength from his legs. But in falling he seemed for a moment to rise, for as his hind legs collapsed beneath him he seemed to tower upwards like a huge rock toppling, his trunk reaching skywards like a tree. He trumpeted, for the first and only time. And then down he came, his belly towards me, with a crash that seemed to shake the ground even where I lay.

Finally I fired my two remaining shots into the spot where I thought his heart must be. The thick blood welled out of him like red velvet, but still he did not die. His body did not even jerk when the shots hit him, the tortured breathing continued without a pause. He was dying, very slowly and in great agony, but in some world remote from me where not even a bullet could damage him further. I felt that I had got to put an end to that dreadful noise. It seemed dreadful to see the great beast lying there, powerless to move and yet powerless to die, and not even to be able to finish him. I sent back for my small rifle and poured shot after shot into his heart and down his throat. They seemed to make no impression. The tortured gasps continued as steadily as the ticking of a clock.

In the end I could not stand it any longer and went away. I heard later that it took him half an hour to die. Burmans were bringing dahs and baskets even before I left, and I was told they had stripped his body almost to the bones by the afternoon.

From 'Shooting an Elephant' by George Orwell

Reflections

* In this incident the writer succumbs to the pressures from those around him, against his better judgement. He fails to resist their expectations of him and has to do something which he is not proud of.
There are many circumstances in which we need to stay true to our own values – what we believe to be right or wrong – and not be swayed by others. Sometimes we have to compromise.

* Being able to recognise when pressure is positive or negative is important. Otherwise we end up feeling like this young woman:

As soon as I could speak – I was told to listen
As soon as I could play – they taught me to work
As soon as I found a job – I married
As soon as I married – came the children
As soon as I understood them – they left me
As soon as I had learned to live – life was gone

Debbie Carnegie

7 Time

Introduction
Something we all take for granted – rather like good health – is time. Adults tend to say that young people don't think about time – for them, the present is far more important than the past or the future. Yet time is not something we should take for granted.

Many people throughout history have written about time, and the passing of time. One very thought-provoking passage concerning time is to be found in the autobiographical novel *Portrait of the Artist as a Young Man* by the Irish writer James Joyce. In order to place the time-span of human life in a wider perspective, he describes how long we are dead for – eternity!

Reading

Eternity

For all eternity! Not for a year or for an age but for ever. Try to imagine the awful meaning of this. You have often seen the sand on the sea-shore. How fine are its tiny grains! And how many of those tiny little grains go to make up the small handful which a child grasps in its play. Now imagine a mountain of that sand, a million miles high, reaching from the earth to the farthest heavens, and a million miles broad, extending to remotest space, and a million miles in thickness: and imagine such an enormous mass of countless particles of sand multiplied as often as there are leaves in the forest, drops of water in the mighty ocean, feathers on birds, scales on fish, hairs on animals, atoms in the vast expanse of the air: and imagine that at the end of every million years a little bird came to that mountain and carried away in its beak a tiny grain of that sand. How many millions upon millions of centuries would pass before that bird had carried away even a square foot of that mountain, how many eons upon eons of ages before it had carried away all? Yet at the end of that immense stretch of time not even one instant of eternity could be said to have ended. At the end of all those billions and trillions of years eternity would have scarcely begun. And if that mountain rose again after it had been all carried away and if the bird came again and carried it all away again grain by grain: and if it so rose and sank as many times as there are stars in the sky, atoms in the air, drops of water in the sea, leaves on the trees, feathers upon birds, scales upon fish, hairs upon animals, at the end of all those innumerable risings and sinkings of that immeasurably vast mountain not one single instant of eternity could be said to have ended; even then, at the end of such a period, after that eon of time the mere thought of which makes our very brain reel dizzily, eternity would scarcely have begun.

From 'Portrait of the Artist as a Young Man' by James Joyce

Reflections

* Such a passage surely makes us think hard about how we make use of our time on this earth. We need to make sure that we use time profitably and wisely. Indeed, many people say that the greatest gift you can give to any one else is your time.
'Use your time wisely' is not an empty phrase.

* Here are some more comments about time that might help our reflections on this enormously complex topic:

'Tomorrow is a long time'
'Live every day as if it were your last; because one day it will be'
'Some people spend money to save time; some spend time to save money.'
'The future is tomorrow, not some place out there.'
'A lifetime is more than sufficiently long
For people to get what there is of it wrong.'

'As eternity is reckoned
There's a lifetime in a second'
'Time present and time past
Are both perhaps present in time future,
And time future contained in time past.'

8 Change

Introduction

Change can be seen as positive or negative. Some people see change as a force for good; others as something unnecessary and undesirable. It is perhaps rather like asking someone whether they describe a glass of liquid as 'half-empty' or 'half-full' – are they a pessimist or an optimist?

Change is an irresistible part of human life. In most cases we need to accept and adapt to change if we are to lead happy and successful lives. Of course, change for change's-sake is not necessarily desirable and needs to be viewed with caution. The irresistibility of gradual or sudden change is well summed up in the following lyrics of American songwriter Bob Dylan.

Reading

'The Times They Are A-Changin''

Come gather 'round people
Wherever you roam
And admit that the waters
Around you have grown
And accept it that soon
You'll be drenched to the bone.
If your time to you
Is worth savin'
Then you better start swimmin'
Or you'll sink like a stone
For the times they are a-changin'.

Come writers and critics
Who prophesize with your pen
And keep your eyes wide
The chance won't come again
And don't speak too soon
For the wheel's still in spin
And there's no tellin' who
That it's namin'.
For the loser now
Will be later to win
For the times they are a-changin'.

Come senators, congressmen
Please heed the call
Don't stand in the doorway
Don't block up the hall
For he that gets hurt
Will be he who has stalled
There's a battle outside
And it is ragin'.
It'll soon shake your windows
And rattle your walls
For the times they are a-changin'.

Come mothers and fathers
Throughout the land
And don't criticize
What you can't understand
Your sons and your daughters
Are beyond your command
Your old road is
Rapidly agin'.
Please get out of the new one
If you can't lend your hand
For the times they are a-changin'.

The line it is drawn
The curse it is cast
The slow one now
Will later be fast
As the present now
Will later be past
The order is
Rapidly fadin'.
And the first one now
Will later be last
For the times they are a-changin'.

Bob Dylan

Reflections

* This song was written in the 1960s, a time of great social change in America. But its message rings true for human beings in any period in history: each generation takes over from the previous one and remoulds laws, attitudes and values to suit itself and its period. We need to understand this because it helps us to respect the views and viewpoints of people younger and older than ourselves.

  There isn't always a simple 'right' or 'wrong' answer to a question. As Bob Dylan says:

  As the present now
  Will later be past
  The order is
  Rapidly fadin'
  And the first one now

Will later be last
For the times they are a-changin.

We need to face up to change, and make the most of it.
Change is a *constant* in human lives.

* Give me serenity to accept the things I cannot change, give me courage to change those things which I can, and grant me wisdom to know the difference.

9 Courage and bravery

Introduction
When we think of the words 'courage' and 'bravery' we tend to link them to tales of adventure and brave deeds. Of course courage can take many forms: a person fighting for years against an incurable disease; a pilot struggling to land a plane which has caught fire; a climber scaling a mountain she has never tried before; or – for any of us – simply summoning up the courage to say you are in the wrong and wish to say sorry to someone.

Throughout history there have been countless tales of outstanding bravery. Today's account stands out in terms of personal courage. It is the story of 'Scott of the Antarctic'.

Captain Robert Falcon Scott and his party: Edward Wilson, Henry Bowers, Captain Oates and Seaman Evans, arrived in their race to the South Pole on the 17th January 1912. The temperature was 22° below zero. As they came within sight of the Pole, they could see the fluttering Norwegian flag left by their rival, Amundsen, and his party. Using husky dogs, Amundsen had arrived more than a month earlier.

After the failure of his chosen means of transport – ponies – Scott had had to rely on manhauling. One can imagine the bitter disappointment of being beaten to the Pole, which must have had a depressing effect on Scott's party in their titanic struggle to overcome the terrible blizzard and sub-zero conditions (–40° at times) as they returned.

'Had we lived, I should have had a tale to tell of the hardihood, endurance and courage of my companions which would have stirred the heart of every Englishman. These rough notes and our dead bodies must tell the tale.'

So runs the final entry in Scott's diary.

Reading

Scott's diary

Friday, 16 March or Saturday, 17. Lost track of dates, but think the last correct. Tragedy all along the line. At lunch, the day before yesterday, poor Titus Oates said he couldn't go on; he proposed we should leave him in his sleeping-bag. That we could not do, and induced him to come on, on the afternoon march. In spite of its awful nature for him he struggled on and we made a few miles. At night he was worse and we knew the end had come.

Should this be found I want these facts recorded. Oates's last thoughts were of his Mother, but immediately before he took pride in thinking that his regiment would be pleased with the bold way in which he met his death. We can testify to his bravery. He has borne intense suffering for weeks without complaint, and to the very last was able and willing to discuss outside subjects. He did not – would not – give up hope to the very end. He was a brave soul. This was the end. He slept through the night before last, hoping not to wake; but he woke in the morning – yesterday. It was blowing a blizzard. He said, 'I am just going outside and may be some time.' He went out into the blizzard and we have not seen him since.

I take this opportunity of saying that we have stuck to our sick companions to the last. In case of Edgar Evans, when absolutely out of food and he lay insensible, the safety of the remainder seemed to demand his abandonment, but Providence mercifully removed him at this critical moment. He died a natural death, and we did not leave him till two hours after his death. We knew that poor Oates was walking to his death, but though we tried to dissuade him, we knew it was the act of a brave man and an English gentleman. We all hope to meet the end with a similar spirit, and assuredly the end is not far.

I can only write at lunch and then only occasionally. The cold is intense, –40° at midday. My companions are unendingly cheerful, but we are all on the verge of serious frostbites, and though we constantly talk of fetching through I don't think any one of us believes it in his heart.

Sunday, 18 March. Today, lunch, we are 21 miles from the depot. Ill fortune presses, but better may come. We have had more wind and drift from ahead yesterday; had to stop marching; wind N.W., force 4, temp. –35°. No human being could face it, and we are worn out *nearly*.

My right foot has gone, nearly all the toes – two days ago I was proud possessor of best feet. These are the steps of my downfall. Like an ass I mixed a small spoonful of curry powder with my melted pemmican – it gave me violent indigestion. I lay awake and in pain all night; woke and felt done on the march; foot went and I didn't know it. A very small measure of neglect and have a foot which is not pleasant to contemplate. Bowers takes first place in condition, but there is not much to choose after all. The others are still confident of getting through – or pretend to be – I don't know! We have the last *half* fill of oil in our primus and a very small quantity of spirit – this alone between us and thirst. The wind is fair for the moment, and that is perhaps a fact to help. The mileage would have seemed ridiculously small on our outward journey.

Monday, 19 March. Lunch. We camped with difficulty last night and were dreadfully cold till after our supper of cold pemmican and biscuit and a half a pannikin of cocoa cooked over the spirit. Then, contrary to expectation, we got warm and all slept well. Today we started in the usual dragging manner. Sledge dreadfully heavy. We are 15½ miles from the depot and ought to get there in three days. What progress! We have two days' food but barely a day's fuel. All our feet are getting bad – Wilson's best, my right foot worse, left all right. There is no chance to nurse one's feet till we can get hot food into us. Amputation is the least I can hope for now, but will the trouble spread? That is the serious question. The weather doesn't give us a chance – the wind from N. to N.W. and –40° temp. today.

Wednesday, 21 March. Got within 11 miles of depot Monday night; had to lay up all yesterday in severe blizzard. Today forlorn hope, Wilson and Bowers going to depot for fuel.

Thursday, 22 and 23 March. Blizzard bad as ever – Wilson and Bowers unable to start – tomorrow last chance – no fuel and only one or two of food left – must be near the end. Have decided it shall be natural – we shall march for the depot with or without our effects and die in our tracks.

Thursday, 29 March. Since the 21st we have had a continuous gale from W.S.W. and S.W. We had fuel to make two cups of tea apiece and bare food for two days on the 20th. Every day we have been ready to start for our depot *11 miles* away, but outside the door of the tent it remains a scene of whirling drift. I do not think we can hope for any better things now. We shall stick it out to the end, but we are getting weaker, of course, and the end cannot be far.

It seems a pity, but I do not think I can write more.

R SCOTT

For God's sake look after our people.

From 'South Polar Expedition; Captain Scott's Diary, March 1912'

Reflections

* Captain Oates made a supreme personal sacrifice, thinking that his own death would help his companions to survive.

   Of course it is very unlikely that any of us would be in a position to sacrifice our life for someone else's. Captain Oates's story is an extreme one – but it is an example of courage. In our daily lives, courage can mean putting someone else's needs before our own, particularly when the natural human instinct is often to put our own needs and wants first.

   A happy community needs people to be courageous and brave in the way Captain Oates was – sometimes putting the wider needs of the community before personal interests.

* *John 15: 12–14*

   My command is this: Love each other as I have loved you. Greater love has no-one than this, that he lay down his life for his friends. You are my friends if you do what I command.

10 Language and speaking

Introduction

The ability to speak a developed language system is something that singles out human beings from all other living things. Every one of us is born with an ability to speak a language, whether born in Britain, Peru, Greenland or Bangladesh.

Language is something we take for granted. And like so many things, language can be used well or it can be abused. The following short story shows how language can be misinterpreted, in this case with rather amusing – and perhaps evil – results.

Reading

A lot to learn

The Materializer was completed.

Ned Quinn stood back, wiped his hands, and admired the huge bank of dials, lights and switches. Several years and many fortunes had gone into his project. Finally it was ready.

Ned placed the metal skullcap on his head and plugged the wires into the control panel. He turned the switch to ON and spoke: 'Pound note.'

There was a whirring sound. In the Receiver a piece of paper appeared. Ned inspected it. Real.

'Martini,' he said.

A whirring sound. A puddle formed in the Receiver. Ned cursed silently. He had a lot to learn.

'A bottle of beer,' he said.

The whirring sound was followed by the appearance of the familiar brown bottle. Ned tasted the contents and grinned.

Chuckling, he experimented further.

Ned enlarged the Receiver and prepared for his greatest experiment. He switched on the Materializer, took a deep breath and said, 'Girl'.

The whirring sound swelled and faded. In the Receiver stood a lovely girl. She was naked. Ned had not asked for clothing.

She had freckles, a brace and pigtails. She was eight years old.

'Hell!' said Quinn.

Whirr.

The fireman found two charred skeletons in the smouldering rubble.

'A Lot to Learn' by R T Kurosaka

Reflections

* The story has a message about how we use words; unless they are used precisely words can be lethal! Words can praise or offend. Words can be instructive or destructive.

  When you are speaking, choose your words carefully – don't use language thoughtlessly. This is particularly important if you are talking about people's beliefs, race and sex. Using language unthinkingly can lead to unnecessary arguments and ill-feeling in a community.

* The real power of language is also evident in the Christian Bible Story of the Tower of Babel:

  Now the whole world had one language and a common speech. As men moved eastward, they found a plain in Shinar and settled there.

  They said to each other, 'Come, let's make bricks and bake them thoroughly.' They used brick instead of stone, and bitumen for mortar. Then they said, 'Come, let us build ourselves a city, with a tower that reaches to the heavens, so that we may make a name for ourselves and not be scattered over the face of the whole earth'.

  But the Lord came down to see the city and the tower that the men were building. The Lord said, 'If as one people speaking the same language they have begun to do this, then nothing they plan to do will be impossible for them. Come, let us go down and confuse their language so they will not understand each other.' So the Lord scattered them from there over all the earth, and they stopped building the city. That is why it was called Babel – because there the Lord confused the language of the whole world. From there the Lord scattered them over the face of the whole earth.

  Genesis: 11

11   Listening and imagination

Introduction

In the same way that language, the ability to communicate, is a key part of being a human being, *listening* and *imagining* are also two human faculties worth reflecting on. Many of us find it more difficult to *listen* than to speak; of course everyone's voice is important at the right moment and freedom of speech is an aspect of society we all value. But sometimes 'silence is golden'; silence *is* better than words; silence allows us to both listen and use our imaginations.

The following two poems place *listening* and *imagination* side by side.

Reading

Silence

Silence in London is generally a word that a teacher
uses to make a class quiet.
But in the country,
It is a word that explains the country.
The first thing you notice in the country,
Is the silence.
Happy singing of birds and creaking of branches,
Dont seem to be noticed.
All the noises of the country,
Seem to blend together like an orchestra,
Playing a woodland melody.
A funny echo fills the country.
There seems to be a breeze in my mouth.
My voice seems travelless.
My voice does not travel in the country,
for the trees grab it,
And make it a part of their symphony.
The trees rustle greedily when they clutch my voice,
Proud that my noise has become part of their song.
Sounds in London are jerky and bumpy,
My voice is full of stuffiness,
My voice travels far in London,
Not anybody bothers to take it,
My voice is too small to be important.

Trevor Dawson Aged 9

A boy's head

In it there is a space-ship
and a project
for doing away with piano lessons.

And there is
Noah's ark,
which shall be first.

And there is
an entirely new bird,
an entirely new hare,
an entirely new bumble-bee.

There is a river
that flows upwards.

There is a multiplication table.

There is anti-matter.

And it just cannot be trimmed.

I believe
that only what cannot be trimmed
is a head.

There is much promise
in the circumstance
that so many people have heads.

Miroslav Holub

Reflections

* Trevor Dawson's poem – written when he was 9 – makes us think about all the empty noise that surrounds us, and puts speech in perspective: sometimes listening to silence has a place.

* Miroslav Holub's poem challenges us to think more widely about human imagination. Each one of us is a unique human being whose ability to think and imagine makes the world a rich and unpredictable place. In his final lines he suggests that it is the human capacity to imagine and invent that will ensure our survival as human beings and our continuing development as inventors and pioneers of knowledge.
  In summary, speech and using language properly are very important. Equally, *listening* to what others have to say and listening to what others have thought and imagined is vital in our lives and communities.

* 'Hear no evil, speak no evil.'

12 Human needs

Introduction

If you were asked the question: 'What do you need to survive?' what would you put on your shopping list? If the question were asked of a girl living in the Australian desert or a boy living in the slums of Bombay, would their lists be the same as yours?

Thinking about that question helps us distinguish between *needs* and *wants*. This is a difference worth reflecting on in our own society which is so rich in consumer goods – expensive cars, designer clothes, camcorders, microwaves, CDs, etc.

In the following passage, taken from a book called *The Needs of Strangers*, Michael Ignatieff considers his responsibilities towards those members of society less well-off than himself.

Reading

The needs of strangers

I live in a market street in north London. Every Tuesday morning there is a barrow outside my door and a cluster of old age pensioners rummage through the torn curtains, buttonless shirts, stained vests, torn jackets, frayed trousers and faded dresses that the barrow man has on offer. They make a cheerful chatter outside my door, beating down the barrow man's prices, scrabbling for bargains like crows pecking among the stubble.

They are not destitute, just respectably poor. The old men seem more neglected than the women: their faces are grey and unshaven and their necks hang loose inside yellowed shirt collars. Their old bodies must be thin and white beneath their clothes. The women seem more self-possessed, as if old age were something their mothers had prepared them for. They also have the skills for poverty: the hems of their coats are neatly darned, their buttons are still in place.

These people give the impression of having buried their wives and husbands long ago and having watched their children decamp to the suburbs. I imagine them living alone in small dark rooms lit by the glow of electric heaters. I came upon one old man once doing his shopping alone, weighed down in a queue at a potato stall and nearly fainting from tiredness. I made him sit down in a pub while I did the rest of his shopping. But if he needed my help, he certainly didn't want it. He was clinging on to his life, gasping for breath, but he stared straight ahead when we talked and his fingers would not be pried from his burdens. All these old people seem like that, cut adrift from family, slipping away into the dwindling realm of their inner voices, clinging to the old barrow as if it were a raft carrying them out to sea.

My encounters with them are a parable of moral relations between strangers in the welfare state. They have needs, and because they live within a welfare state, these needs confer entitlements – rights – to the resources of people like me. Their needs and their entitlements establish a silent relation between us. As we stand together in line at the post office, while they cash their pension cheques, some tiny portion of my income is transferred into their pockets through the numberless capillaries of the state. They are dependent on the state, not upon me, and we are both glad of it. We are responsible *for* each other, but we are not responsible *to* each other.

My responsibilities towards them are mediated through a vast division of labour. In my name a social worker climbs the stairs to their rooms and makes sure they are as warm and as clean as they can be persuaded to be. When they get too old to go out, a volunteer will bring them a hot meal, make up their beds, and if the volunteer is a compassionate person, listen to their whispering streams of memory. When they can't go on, an ambulance will take them to the hospital, and when they die, a nurse will be there to listen to the ebbing of their breath. It is this solidarity among strangers, this transformation through the division of labour of needs into rights and rights into care that gives us whatever fragile basis we have for saying that we live in a moral community.

Modern welfare may not be generous by any standard other than a comparison with the nineteenth-century workhouse, but it does attempt to satisfy a wide range of basic needs for food, shelter, clothing, warmth and medical care. The question is whether that is all a human being needs. When we talk about needs we mean something more than just the basic necessities of human survival. We also use the word to describe what a person needs in order to live to their full potential. What we need in order to survive, and what we need in order to flourish are two different things. The aged poor on my street get just enough to survive. The question is whether they get what they need in order to live a human life.

From 'The Needs of Strangers' by Michael Ignatieff

Reflections

* The writer, then, makes us think about two important issues:

    1 'What we need in order to *survive*, and what we need in order to *flourish* are two different things.'
    2 Who decides what *needs* are, and what *wants* are?

* We are all part of a local community. But we are also part of a wider national and international community in which, though we are not responsible *to* each other, we are responsible *for* each other.
  As members of a *school* community we are, however, responsible both *to* and *for* each other. We need to remember this each day: it is an important point.
  And at an international level, living in a global village, we should think about the question: 'Is life more than mere survival?'

* *Matthew 7: 1–6 – Judging others*
  Do not judge, or you too will be judged. For in the same way as you judge others, you will be judged, and with the measure you use, it will be measured to you.
  Why do you look at the speck of sawdust in your brother's eye and pay no attention to the plank in your own eye? How can you say to your brother, 'Let me take the speck out of your eye,' when all the time there is a plank in your own eye? You hypocrite, first take the plank out of your own eye, and then you will see clearly to remove the speck from your brother's eye.
  Do not give dogs what is sacred; do not throw your pearls to pigs. If you do, they may trample them under their feet, and then turn and tear you to pieces.

Education: School Days

1 A new school (1)

Introduction

Starting a new school is always going to be a new experience for children, even if they've visited the building many times before. Settling into the new environment, with new teachers and new timings for lessons – we all experience different emotions at such a time.

But it's not only pupils who start school. Teachers do as well – and feel equally strange in their new place of work. Can you imagine what it might be like to be the very first person in a new school?

Back in 1924 in a small town in Oxfordshire a new school was opened by a Headmaster called Mr Howson. Here is what he wrote about his early days and months in the town of Bicester.

Reading

Recollections

My recollections of Bicester date back to June 20th, 1924, when I first came to Bicester to meet the Governors. It was a hot, blazing midsummer's day; my wife and I had just arrived from London at the (L.M.S.) station and walked up the road trying to find Bicester Hall, for that was where I was going to meet the governors and that was the name of the School before it was a school. Three were no people about to direct us; dogs were asleep on the side-walk outside Layton's shop, a solitary black cat picked its way gingerly across the empty Market Square and all Bicester was enveloped in a deep and slumbrous peace. London seemed a thousand miles away. Eventually the sound of a distant door closing broke the stillness and I saw a man just emerging from a shop some hundred yards away; he kindly directed us.

I was given what was to me the truly delightful job of starting the school from the very beginning. I felt like Noah, coming out of the ark with his family and animals and beginning the world anew – a world where there were to be no more floods and no more wars. During July and August I was busy ordering chalk, blotting-paper, grass-clippers, soap, geometry text-books and all the hundred and one things essential to the school of a civilized community. I thought I was getting on well; I had made a most exhaustive list of everything necessary for a school and, when my list was completed, I realized that the sum of money allowed by the Committee for the equipment of the school must be fully exhausted. However, I felt quite pleased with myself, for I had spent the money thriftily only on essentials and had not forgotten anything; and then one morning I awoke, thinking, I don't know why, about pianos. Yes, that was it; I had forgotten all about the school piano. As soon as I had had my breakfast, I wrote to Oxford requisitioning a school piano. My letter caused quite a commotion at Oxford, for at a time when all monies had been allocated already £40 odd for a piano had to be found somewhere, and somehow. Subsequently, it was rumoured that the inhabitants of Stanton St. John, in the south of the county, were growing restive, as they feared the expenditure on the new school at Bicester was going to increase their rates. I resolved never again in the future to forget about pianos.

The school was opened for the first time on September 14th, 1924, with 43 scholars, 15 girls and 28 boys. The staff consisted of Miss H M Bell, B.Sc., the Senior Mistress, Miss M L Alden, B.Sc., Assistant, and Mr W R Bray, B A. Only one pupil, Leslie Evans, had ever been to a secondary school before; so far as the others were concerned, they felt that anything might happen there and so, though resolving to do their best, they appeared on the first morning quiet, subdued, and highly apprehensive of the strange experiences to which they might be subjected. Had I told them that it was usual in secondary schools to pass the first five minutes of the morning assembly by standing on their heads, I believe that with more cheerfulness than skill they would have attempted to do so.

Noisy as the school may have been at other times since then, it was at its noisiest during the first term. There had been a building strike during the summer of 1924; consequently, when the school opened in September, the builders, who had been unable to begin earlier, were hard at work on the necessary elevations and the heating engineers were also busy running their pipes and installing radiators. Teachers had to raise their voices high to surmount the combined noise of hammers, saws and files. Mr T O Willson, the Director of Education, often came over at this time and was always ready to modify the building plans when such alterations were seen to be of benefit to the school. The building foreman in charge of the operations did not approve of any deviations from the plan originally delivered to him. In a moment of gloom he confided to me his belief that Noah, when engaged in building the Ark, would never have completed it before the deluge, had he been working at the instructions of a committee. However, the work was all finished during the autumn term, and I have never had reason to share the foreman's gloom with regard to the efficiency of committees.

Strange as the School was to its first pupils, it was equally strange, I am inclined to think, to older members of the Bicester community. Some parents were very hesitant about entrusting their children to this new thing that was growing up in their midst; it seemed to them eminently safer to allow other parents first to make the hazardous experiment of sending their children to the new school. Rumour, which even now on fleet wings carries its conflicting stories of fallen bombs, gave its frequent comments on the School and sometimes these were accepted as the truth. Thus one parent, who happened to be a fervent Socialist, refused to send his child to a school which stood for class distinctions. I think he meant the girls' brown school uniform. Another parent, a staunch Conservative, asserted that all the Staff of the School were Socialists, that it was the aim of the School to turn out all its pupils as Socialists, and, accordingly, it was no fit place for his son. Cordial as have been my subsequent relations with parents and much as I owe to their encouragement and support, it was at this time I first began to entertain the suspicion that it was impossible to please every parent. Further experience has not allayed this first suspicion.

From 'Recollections' by Mr Howson, published in 'The Bicestrian'.

Reflections

* So you see that not only was the new school *new* to the children it was also a little strange to teachers, local residents, parents and officials. Probably the most important thing to remember when you go anywhere for the first time is that you're probably not alone in being new.

  Mr Howson says that he felt like Noah in the Christian Bible – but Noah soon filled his Ark, you will remember.

  Starting school will be strange in many ways but there are plenty of others to share the experience with you. There will be moments when you're happy and times when you'll be worried. Just remember to *share* any problems you have, in the way that Mr Howson shared his concerns with those in the community around him, when he started Bicester School.

* *Psalm 46*

  God is our refuge and strength,
  an ever-present help in trouble.
  Therefore we will not fear, though the earth give way
  and the mountains fall into the heart of the sea,
  though its waters roar and foam and the mountains
  quake with their surging.

2 A new school (2)

Introduction

Your first steps in a new school – whether you are 5, 11, 16 or any age – are going to be hesitant ones.

The one thing you can be sure of is that you are not alone in your feelings. Parents and teachers have all had similar experiences before you: expectations, fears, excitements – they are there to be shared.

The following extract comes from an autobiography called *A Comprehensive Education* by Roger Mills, in which he describes the move from primary to secondary school. See which parts ring true for you as you listen.

Reading

First day

I was waiting in the school's reception area. Teachers and boys alike passed and looked down their noses at me inquisitively. I had only been here once before, with my parents while awaiting my interview. It had gone pretty smoothly. I had read from a book, tried my best to get a few sums right and answered questions on general knowledge.

I could never see the point of the interview with its questions and everything, as the purpose of the school was to teach you all the answers you didn't know anyway.

A tearless farewell from primary school and a long hot six weeks holiday culminating in a sleepless last night had resulted in my sitting outside the administrative offices of Effingham Road Comprehensive School. Actually, due to a previously booked holiday, I missed the first week at Effingham Road and for ever after wondered if I had missed some vital explanation during that week, some single phrase or few words which would have made everything add up, made everything clear and given some meaning and reason for the next five years I would spend here.

All I had actually missed was a guided tour on the first day. The first year boys, without the hindrance of the other years, who started the nest day, were shown the wonders of the premises. The school was just five years old. It was the Phoenix out of the flames of a couple of old mixed schools which lost the girls on the way.

Now I was alone with my brand new briefcase, empty save for a fountain pen. There was no group of boys to hide behind and no friends to share my worries with. I was awaiting the man whom a kind voiced secretary told me would take me to join my class. My heart pumped. The man was the Deputy Headmaster, an old man who spoke to me only briefly, very formally, in a squeaky voice.

He led me up to the first floor, head down as if deep in thought, not looking to check if I was still here behind him. In the long corridor, through the small glass panels by the classroom doors, I could see teachers taking registers. All the boys were clothed in the school uniform of black trousers and blazers, white shirts and school ties.

The six classes in the first year were given the initials of the tutor master, the one who marked the register morning and afternoon. I was in 1M: Miss Munroe.

Looking around the class I saw that nearly all the boys were as well turned out as I was. A few of the boy's blazers were obviously hand-me-downs years old. Doubtless if I had had an elder brother my uniform would not have been as brand new as it was.

On being accepted to the school my family had received a list of clothes required and a choice of just two places to get them. Besides the basic uniform I was told I must have a sports vest, shorts and plimsolls, a cap that nobody ever wore, a regulation pullover and an apron for technical work.

The very uniforms themselves gave the boys a frightening anonymity. No more short trousers and woollies that you always got milk on. We all looked like young bankers. There was just one boy wearing short trousers, a very small boy who made up in cunning what he lacked in physique. He had already made friends with Sammy Johnson, a ginger haired boy and at eleven one of the school's tallest inhabitants, pupil or teacher. At five feet eleven he was the only first year not to get picked on in the playground.

The boy next to me explained the tutor groups. Shortly we would be going to assembly and then straight on to our various lessons. Every lesson a change of room, a change of teacher, not at all like primary school. Besides now and early afternoon we would not see Miss Munroe again except for French. I could tell she was a French teacher because of the corny posters of Paris on the back wall and the hand written sign 'Bibliotheque' above a row of two books on a shelf.

Suddenly, and to nobody's surprise but mine, a box on the wall began to talk. It had a plummy middle aged voice which told teachers to prepare the classes and bring them down to assembly. The box on the wall, one of which lived in every room, also let out three bleeps or pips every time we had to change lessons.

Sometimes if we were lucky we could hear the people inside it discussing the school when they forgot to switch off.

As we banged our desks and scraped our chairs along the floor to line up by the door in twos, I noticed with instant nausea what the first lesson of my whole secondary school career was to be, according to the timetable:

Maths.
There in plain black and white.
Maths.
No argument.
Maths.
No mistake.

Assembly? I didn't notice that for worry. In no time at all I found myself in an orderly if nervous queue outside room 101 right on the top floor. I was hot and then cold. Ever since I could remember I had had a sort of mental block where Arithmetic was concerned. I never got past the two times table. In primary school the other children would confidently rattle all the tables off in unison while I mimed them. I was terrified that any moment I would be stood up on a chair and commanded to perform them solo.

The teacher turned out to be short and fat and apart from providing me with a text and exercise book made no acknowledgement of my previous absence. To my horror I was placed just a row from the front, too close for comfort. I don't know if the division sums he gave me were easy or hard, my mind was a thick fog and I could not even begin to work them out. It was all just numbers, it made no sense.

A glance at the boy's book beside me made him cup his hand over the page. I felt like shouting for help. To my great relief the small boy told the teacher he didn't know how to do the work, something I was afraid to do. After tutting and making a few chalk marks on the board however the short fat teacher still made me none the wiser. I merely wrote the questions out as neatly as possible in the hope of leniency. I did the elementary parts I knew how to do and even made a wild guess at some of the answers. None was correct.

Whatever my punishment was to be I was consoled in the thought that it would be postponed for a few days until the books were marked. It was not to be. At about ten minutes from the end of the forty minute period everybody began to line up either side of the teacher's desk to have their books marked. I was hot again now and actually felt a little sick. I stood last in the line hoping those funny pips would save me. They didn't, and being the last made it all the worse. The teacher was jibing and complaining about the boys' work and the state of their books and when I put my one down he exploded. There was not one complete sum and after all my neat setting out I had smudged the lot with my sleeve.

'What do you call this?' he asked.

'I'm not very well, sir,' I lied.

'I'm not very well either,' he lied back, 'But I do what's expected of me. If your couldn't do the work why the devil didn't you tell me?'

I felt my face go bright red and heard some sniggering from behind me.

'If you come here next time and sit there doing nothing then I'll do something about you. As it's your first time here however I'll let it pass. You make sure you do your homework though, and that goes for all of you,' he said, thankfully taking the attention from me at the end.

'It's everything on page twelve of your text book.'

Homework? I had never had any of that before at my primary school. I figured at least I could get my father to help me on that one though, so I was not worried. I crammed my books into my briefcase and was pleased to get out of that room.

From 'A comprehensive education' by Roger Mills

Reflections

* The change of *scale* and of *routine* clearly made a big impression on the writer. There are many myths and stories about what will happen to 'small' children as they enter 'the big school'. 'Myth' is the right word to use because it means a story that is fictitious, not based on real facts.

   Parents and teachers always try to reassure children that joining a new school will be quite a simple thing to do – but of course only once you've experienced it yourself are you in a position to agree, or disagree.

* Another interesting and amusing account of first impressions and confusions at a new school is in this poem by Roger McGough:

First Day at School

A millionbillionwillion miles from home
Waiting for the bell to go. (To go where?)
Why are they all so big, other children?
So noisy? So much at home they
must have been born in uniform.
Lived all their lives in playgrounds.
Spent the years inventing games
that don't let me in. Games
that are rough, that swallow you up.

And the railings
All around, the railings.
Are they to keep out wolves and monsters?
Things that carry off and eat children?
Things you don't take sweets from?
Perhaps they're to stop us getting out.
Running away from the lessins. Lessin.
What does a lessin look like?
Sounds small and slimy.
They keep them in glassrooms.
Whole rooms made out of glass. Imagine.

I wish I could remember my name.
Mummy said it would come in useful.
Like wellies. When there's puddles.
Yellowwellies. I wish she was here.
I think my name is sewn on somewhere.
Perhaps the teacher will read it for me.
Tea-cher. The one who makes the tea.

Roger McGough

3 Teaching

Introduction

Teaching someone else to do something is a privilege. It my be teaching someone to be a pilot or a jockey, to play music, use a tennis racket, sew a hem, design an ornamental garden or build a model railway. All these require knowledge, skill and patience from the teacher.

Particular skills are required when a teacher is working with a group of people, as school teachers do with classes of pupils and students. Because teachers are human beings, they can feel frustrated when pupils don't listen or learn as quickly and easily as the teacher might like. It is always important – as a learner – to understand the teacher's feelings and point of view.

The following two poems offer challenging perspectives on the important role of the teacher in any community.

Reading

Last Lesson of the Afternoon

When will the bell ring, and end this weariness?
How long have they tugged the leash, and strained apart
My pack of unruly hounds! I cannot start
Them again on a quarry of knowledge they hate to hunt,
I can haul them and urge them no more.

No longer now can I endure the brunt
Of the books that lie out on the desks; a full threescore
Of several insults of blotted pages, and scrawl
Of slovenly work that they have offered me.
I am sick, and what on earth is the good of it all?
What good to them or me, I cannot see!

        So, shall I take
My last dear fuel of life to heap on my soul
And kindle my will to a flame that shall consume
Their dross of indifference; and take the toll
Of their insults in punishment? – I will not! –

I will not waste my soul and my strength for this.
What do I care for all that they do amiss!
What is the point of this teaching of mine, and of this
Learning of theirs? It all goes down the same abyss.

What does it matter to me, if they can write
A description of a dog, or if they can't?
What is the point? To us both, it is all my aunt!
And yet I'm supposed to care, with all my might.

I do not, and will not; they won't and they don't; and that's all!
I shall keep my strength for myself; they can keep theirs as well.
Why should we beat our heads against the wall
Of each other? I shall sit and wait for the bell.

D H Lawrence

Lies

Telling lies to the young is wrong.
Proving to them that lies are true is wrong.
Telling them that God's in his heaven
and all's well with the world is wrong.
The young know what you mean. The young are people.
Tell them the difficulties can't be counted,
and let them see not only what will be
but see with clarity these present times.
Say obstacles exist they must encounter
sorrow happens, hardship happens.
The hell with it. Who never knew
the price of happiness will not be happy.
Forgive no error you recognize,
it will repeat itself, increase,
and afterwards our pupils
will not forgive in us what we forgave.

Yevgeny Yevtushenko
(translated from the Russian by
Robin Milner-Gulland and Peter Levi)

Reflections

* D H Lawrence's poem concentrates on the 'quarry of knowledge they hate to hunt', and the frustrations felt by all teachers at some time or another in the pursuit of their aims.
  Yevtushenko focuses on the more problematic topic of the older generation needing to be honest with the younger generation, even when the truth might hurt:

'Telling them that God's in his heaven
and all's well with the world is wrong.'

Teaching anyone anything also involves selecting knowledge and information – and this can prove difficult for the teacher. In the end it is the teacher's responsibility to be honest, fair and balanced in what they say in the classroom.
Equally the teacher has a right to be listened to carefully by the learner, and questioned thoughtfully.
The following mini-saga (a short story of just 50 words) offers a thought-provoking reflection on the difference between *teaching* and *educating*.

The Interrogation

'What's your occupation?'
    'I am a teacher.'
'Whom and what do you teach?'
    'I teach people to shoot.'
Mental note – may be useful.
    'Next'

'What's your occupation?'
  'I educate people.'
Another bloody intellectual.
  'What's the difference?'
'I show them where to point
    the gun.'
  Dangerous.
The guards took him away.

D Wilby

4 Learning

Introduction

Learning is what schools are all about. A well-ordered and well-resourced environment is vital if true learning is to take place. When groups of pupils are together in a classroom it is important that people *listen* to what the teacher is saying, and listen to other pupils' points of view. Understanding knowledge and ideas frequently comes from discussing them with other learners.

Sometimes it will seem that we are learning facts which appear quite useless at the time we are learning them. Only later in our days as students and in the course of our adult lives do we come to see the connections between what we learnt in one lesson and a situation we subsequently find ourselves in.

One of the other hard facts of life is that human beings do lots of learning – but still go on making mistakes.

The following two poems make this important point in different ways. Tom Paxton's work was originally a folk song.

Reading

What Did You Learn in School Today

What did you learn in school today,
Dear little boy of mine?
What did you learn in school today,
Dear little boy of mine?
I learned that Washington never told a lie,
I learned that soldiers seldom die,
I learned that everybody's free,
That's what the teacher said to me,
And that's what I learned in school today,
That's what I learned in school.

What did you learn in school today,
Dear little boy of mine?
What did you learn in school today,
Dear little boy of mine?
I learned that policemen are my friends,

I learned that justice never ends,
I learned that murderers die for their crimes,
Even if we make a mistake sometimes,
And that's what I learned in school today,
That's what I learned in school.

What did you learn in school today,
Dear little boy of mine?
What did you learn in school today,
Dear little boy of mine?
I learned our government must be strong,
It's always right and never wrong,
Our leaders are the finest men,
And we elect them again and again,
And that's what I learned in school today,
That's what I learned in school.

What did you learn in school today,
Dear little boy of mine?
What did you learn in school today,
Dear little boy of mine?
I learned that war is not so bad,
I learned about the great ones we have had,
We fought in Germany and in France,
And someday I might get my chance,
And that's what I learned in school today,
That's what I learned in school.

Tom Paxton

To David, about His Education

The world is full of mostly invisible things,
And there is no way but putting the mind's eye,
Or its nose, in a book, to find them out,
Things like the square root of Everest
Or how many times Byron goes into Texas,
Or whether the law of the excluded middle
Applies west of the Rockies. For these
And the like reasons, you have to go to school
And study books and listen to what you are told,
And sometimes try to remember. Thought I don't know
What you will do with the mean annual rainfall
Of Plato's Republic, or the calorie content
Of the Diet of Worms, such things are said to be
Good for you, and you will have to learn them
In order to become one of the grown-ups
Who sees invisible things neither steadily nor whole,
But keeps gravely the grand confusion of the world
Under his hat, which is where it belongs,
And teaches small children to do this in their turn.

Howard Nemerov

Reflections

* Both writers remind us, in a way, that learning is essentially about moving from a position of not knowing into the known. And with knowledge comes a loss of innocence, and a discovery that what is presented to us as the truth is, sadly, sometimes not the *whole* truth.

  One of the important lessons for all learners is to question what you are taught, and to try to develop the ability to be critical – in a thoughtful way – of information presented in text-books, on television and by teachers.

  Howard Nemerov's words are worth remembering:

  > 'such things are said to be
  > Good for you, and you will have to learn them
  > In order to become one of the grown-ups
  > Who sees invisible things neither steadily nor whole . . .'

  Learners and teachers never have all the answers. What is important is that there is mutual respect.

5 Bullying

Introduction

Bullying is a fact of life – of family and school life. A lot of research has shown that many children from the age of three to 16 suffer some kind of bullying.

Bullying can take many forms: physical and mental.

Bullying can involve older sisters and younger brothers, or vice-versa. It is often difficult to uncover bullying. For children, mothers and fathers, and teachers – it is not an easy subject to deal with.

And among adults it doesn't stop – sometimes it can be much more subtle than just playground name-calling or the odd punch.

Have you thought why people bully others?

Reading

The Rescue of Karen Arscott

Karen is different. Worse. Worse that anything you can imagine. She looks like that creature from the Black Lagoon, or out of the depths of the Id or whatever it was in those old movies. Get out of my way, she snarls. So I do. We all do. I've been getting out of her way for the past ten years since she flattened me in the Infants' playground and took my lunch and my new pencil case. Next day I brought my Mum into the playground. After she'd gone, Karen flattened me again. After that I gave up saying anything about Karen – just learnt to move very fast in the opposite direction whenever I saw her. And the boys learnt to move even faster. On one of her bad days she could clear the playground quicker than the school dentist arriving. When we left the Primary we hoped she'd go to a different Comprehensive. We kept saying all the good things we knew about the others very loudly when she was about. But it was hopeless, as we realized when we heard her Mom telling our teacher that Karen didn't want to leave her form mates. Her Mom looked like Giant Haystacks, the wrestler, so our teacher agreed, nodding up and down a lot.

But practice had made me very nippy, and there was a good crowd of us – Angie, Tamsin, Jackie and Pat. So we managed without too much aggro even when she turned up in our class despite there being four streams to each year.

No, the one who copped it all was Lindy, fresh from another school and a born loser from the start. We did try to stop it, to help, but Lindy was so wet and Karen so tough that by our year it was more or less the thing that those two paired off and Karen was The Boss.

And then, there in the hall one gloomy February morning stood this girl in between the two of them. And she was beautiful. Her hair was long and black, her face was pale, her eyes misty. Even Angie looked ordinary beside her.

Back in the classroom everyone crowded round her as they always do with anyone new till the novelty wears off. I tried to join in but there was no room so I thought I might just as well get on with the homework I hadn't finished the night before. Then I made out a beauty programme wondering if Mum would let me dye my hair.

Why bother? Never, never in a million light years was I going to look like that new girl. What was her name? Harriet, Mrs Conway was saying, Harriet Carter.

She turned out to be a very quiet girl. Her work was good and she didn't put a foot wrong with the teachers or anyone, being friendly to everyone but not too friendly and going straight home after school. She seemed to live some distance away, no one knew where. In fact Harriet was a bit of a mystery, and rumours soon ran round the school that a) she was a South American millionairess in hiding because of kidnapping threats, b) she was a refugee from Eastern Europe, c) her mother was dead and she had to get home to cook for her Dad. Somehow the last seemed the most likely. In the end she just became another one of the class.

It was a very wet spring term. Every day it rained. Karen developed boils on her face which didn't do much for her looks and even less for her temper. Lindy actually appeared in new PE kit. Miss Johnson had gone on at her so much I suppose she was driven to it. Karen threw it down the loo so that it was soaking wet for the lesson. For once Lindy complained and for once we backed her, and Karen caught it in the neck, detentions for a week, etc. But Lindy appeared with a bruise on her face. Walked into a door she said quietly, my own silly fault, I ought to wear my glasses.

We stayed indoors at lunchtime, it was always so wet, and we had access to the library, to the hall for badminton, and to other rooms for things like chess, stamp club and so on. I went to the Art Room, where I was painting Harriet. I'd asked if I could for my Art continuous assessment . . . I got to know her face well, but what went on behind it was still a mystery.

Someone who also came to the Art Room was Lindy. And without Karen who was forbidden to go in there because she'd wrecked it on three occasions.

This day we came out together, Harriet, Lindy and me, and Lindy was quite pink and human and chatty. Her leaf and tree prints were really good and she was always better when she was doing something Arty, seemed to have more confidence. Besides, Harriet, though she hardly said anything herself, always got Lindy to chat away merrily.

Karen Arscott sat in the middle of the corridor blocking the way to the class-room. Lindy turned pale, the bruise on her face showing up clearly.

'Whatcher bin doing, then?' said Karen to Lindy.

Without a word Lindy handed over her folder.

'Load o' crap, ain't it?' said Karen and threw Lindy's collection on the floor and stamped on it.

'Any objections?' she went on.

Like a shadow Harriet slipped between her and Lindy, pushed Karen back on to the floor then tipped the chair and Karen up. A bellow of rage echoed down the corridor as Karen lumbered to her feet. A crowd gathered. They were all coming but no one was going to interfere, least of all the boys, though cries of, 'Let her have it, Harriet,' were heard. Karen charged at Harriet, who waited almost carelessly till the last possible minute, then moved to one side, and Karen crashed heavily into the wall, the picture on the rail above descending on to her head and putting paid to her. A cheer went up. Until,

'Just what is going on here?' said Mr Keithley, the Headmaster.

But Lindy went on her knees beside Karen and lifted her head on to her lap. Harriet, paler than ever, looked at them, then turned and walked through the crowd, who just melted away before her.

I never saw her again.

Mr Keithley, who always seemed to know everything that went on in the school, said Karen had got her deserts at last, and would we please pack up Harriet's things for her as she would be moving on. So we did. Lindy looked after Karen like a mother hen with its chick, and there was no more trouble in that direction. Karen was a changed person. She depended on Lindy a lot.

About three years later I went to Art School, and moved my gear into a bedsit for term time. As I was clearing out a drawer, a photo in the old newspaper-lining caught my eye, I don't know why. I looked more closely and saw that it resembled Harriet. But an older Harriet with shorter hair. I realized it was her mother.

Underneath the caption read: Mrs Adrienne Carter was today convicted of the manslaughter of her husband, Frederick Herbert Carter. She attacked and killed him with a heavy stick after he had severely beaten their daughter, Harriet, aged nine years.

Oh, Harriet, Harriet.

From 'The Rescue of Karen Arscott' by Gene Kemp, in 'School's OK'

Reflections

* This story helps us to reflect on why people bully others. Part of preventing bullying is understanding *why* someone does it. What would you have done in Karen's situation? Or that of her mates?

  If you find yourself being bullied, or knowing that someone else is suffering, talk about it with a friend or teacher. No community likes or wants bullies. To make the bully feel the odd person out is a good way forward.

  Pupils, parents and teachers need to act together to remove bullying from spoiling a community's values and spirit.

* *Matthew 16: 15–20*

  If your brother sins against you, go and show him his fault, just between the two of you. If he listens to you, you have won your brother over. But if he will not listen, take one or two others along, so that 'every matter may be established by the testimony of two or three witnesses'. If he refuses to listen to them, tell it to the church; and if he refuses to listen even to the church, treat him as you would a pagan or a tax collector . . . I tell you that if two of you on earth agree about anything you ask for, it will be done for you by my father in heaven. For where two or three come together in my name, there am I with them.

6 Schools as institutions

Introduction

What did you think about coming to school today? You probably didn't think much about it – going to school, or to work, is something we take for granted. Our schools are a product of our history and culture; it's hard to imagine they could be very different. But are our schools and classrooms the most effective way to organise group learning?

With changes in technology, might we see the sort of 'school' envisaged in the following story, set in the year 2155?

Reading

The fun they had

Margie even wrote about it that night in her diary. On the page headed 17 May, 2155, she wrote, 'Today Tommy found a real book!'

It was a very old book. Margie's grandfather once said that when he was a little boy *his* grandfather told him that there was a time when all stories were printed on paper.

They turned the pages, which were yellow and crinkly, and it was awfully funny to read words that stood still instead of moving the way they were supposed to – on a screen, you know. And then, when they turned back to the page before, it had the same words on it that it had had when they read it the first time.

'Gee,' said Tommy, 'what a waste. When you're through with the book, you just throw it away, I guess. Our television screen must have had a million books on it and it's good for plenty more. I wouldn't throw *it* away.'

'Same with mine,' said Margie. She was eleven and hadn't seen as many telebooks as Tommy had. He was thirteen.

She said, 'Where did you find it?'

'In my house.' He pointed without looking, because he was busy reading. 'In the attic.'

'What's it about?'

'School.'

Margie was scornful. 'School? What's there to write about school? I hate school.' Margie always hated school, but now she hated it more than ever. The mechanical teacher had been giving her test after test in geography and she had been doing worse and worse until her mother had shaken her head sorrowfully and sent for the County Inspector.

He was a round little man with a red face and a whole box of tools with dials and wires. He smiled at her and gave her an apple, then took the teacher apart.

Margie had hoped he wouldn't know how to put it together again, but he knew how all right and after an hour or so, there it was again, large and black and ugly with a big screen on which all the lessons were shown and the questions were asked. That wasn't so bad. The part she hated most was the slot where she had to put homework and test papers. She always had to write them out in a punch code they made her learn when she was six years old, and the mechanical teacher calculated the mark in no time.

The Inspector had smiled after he was finished and patted her head. He said to her mother, 'It's not the little girl's fault, Mrs Jones. I think the geography sector was geared a little too quick. Those things happen sometimes. I've slowed it up to an average ten-year level. Actually, the overall pattern of her progress is quite satisfactory.' And he patted Margie's head again.

Margie was disappointed. She had been hoping they would take the teacher away altogether. They had once taken Tommy's teacher away for nearly a month because the history sector had blanked out completely.

So she said to Tommy, 'Why would anyone write about school?'

Tommy looked at her with very superior eyes. 'Because it's not our kind of school, stupid. This is the old kind of school that they had hundreds and hundreds of years ago.' He added loftily, pronouncing the word carefully, '*Centuries* ago.'

Margie was hurt. 'Well, I don't know what kind of school they had all that time ago.' She read the book over his shoulder for a while, then said, 'Anyway, they had a teacher.'

'Sure they had a teacher, but it wasn't a *regular* teacher. It was a man.'

'A man? How could a man be a teacher?'

'Well, he just told the boys and girls things and gave them homework and asked them questions.'

'A man isn't smart enough.'

'Sure he is. My father knows as much as my teacher.'

'He can't. A man can't know as much as a teacher.'

'He knows almost as much I betcha.'

Margie wasn't prepared to dispute that. She said, 'I wouldn't want a strange man in my house to teach me.'

Tommy screamed with laughter, 'You don't know much, Margie. The teachers didn't live in the house. They had a special building and all the kids went there.'

'And all the kids learned the same thing?'

'Sure, if they were the same age.'

'But my mother says a teacher had to be adjusted to fit the mind of each boy and girl it teaches and that each kid has to be taught differently.'

'Just the same they didn't do it that way then. If you don't like it, you don't have to read the book.'

'I didn't say I didn't like it,' Margie said quickly. She wanted to read about those funny schools.

They weren't even half finished when Margie's mother called, 'Margie! School!'

Margie looked up. 'Not yet, mamma.'

'Now,' said Mrs Jones. 'And it's probably time for Tommy, too.'

Margie said to Tommy. 'Can I read the book some more with you after school?'

'Maybe,' he said, nonchalantly. He walked away whistling, the dusty old book tucked beneath his arm.

Margie went into the schoolroom. It was right next to her bedroom, and the mechanical teacher was on and waiting for her. It was always on at the same time every day except Saturday and Sunday, because her mother said little girls learned better if they learned at regular hours.

The screen was lit up, and it said: 'Today's arithmetic lesson is on the addition of proper fractions. Please insert yesterday's homework in the proper slot.'

Margie did so with a sigh. She was thinking about the old schools they had when her grandfather's grandfather was a little boy. All the kids from the whole neighbourhood came, laughing and shouting in the school-yard, sitting together in the school-room, going home together at the end of the day. They learned the same things so they could help one another on the homework and talk about it.

And the teachers were people . . .

the mechanical teacher was flashing on the screen: 'When we add the fractions ½ and ¼ –'

Margie was thinking about how the kids must have loved it in the old days. She was thinking about the fun they had.

'The Fun They Had' by Isaac Asimov

Reflections

* Can you imagine a time when 'school' might be like that? Isaac Asimov, one of the 20th century's great science-fiction writers, is clearly thinking that machines might replace people. And yet Margie longs for an age when 'teachers were people' and children came together to learn.

This reminds us that school is much more than a place for learning formal lessons. The daily coming together of people from different backgrounds and with different interests is a vital part of 'schooling'.

Friendship, community and shared values lie at the heart of the effective and happy school. We should not forget this – even in the face of strong pressures to introduce more technology into our world. There is no substitute for people meeting and interacting.

* *Peter 2: 13–17*

Submit yourselves for the Lord's sake to every authority instituted among men: whether to the king, as the supreme authority, or to governors, who are sent by him to punish those who do wrong and to commend those who do right. For it is God's will that by doing good you should silence the ignorant talk of foolish men. Live as free men, but do not use your freedom as a cover-up for evil; live as servants of God. Show proper respect to everyone: Love the brotherhood of believers, fear God, honour the king.

7 Achievement

Introduction

'If something is worth doing, it's worth doing well'.

This saying lies at the heart of striving for achievement. What do we mean by achievement in the school setting? We might identify:

* oral skills
* written examinations

- personal and social skills
- sporting success
- artistic achievement
- leadership qualities

All of these are aspects of achievement which schools need to value. The following short passages are worth reflecting on in relation to this topic of Achievement.

Reading

(1) John Holt, a writer on education:

'Some will say that we should not do anything in a class to encourage competition of any kind. To me this is foolish and unrealistic. Children are naturally and healthily competitive. They are interested in knowing who does things best, and they are all deeply interested in doing whatever they do today a little better than they did it yesterday.... What is wrong with most schools is that we honour only a very few skills out of the great many that children possess.'

(2) The second reading is a reminder that teachers don't always get it right. The following is about ... guess!

'My end-of-term reports from this school are of some interest. Here are just four of them, copied out word for word from the original documents;

Summer Term 1930 (aged 14). English Composition. *I have never met a boy who so persistently writes the exact opposite of what he means. He seems incapable of marshalling his thoughts on paper.*

Easter Term 1931 (aged 15). English Composition. *This boy is an indolent and illiterate member of the class.*

Autumn Term 1932 (aged 17). English Composition. *Consistently idle. Ideas limited.* (And underneath this one, the future Archbishop of Canterbury had written in red ink, 'He must correct the blemishes on this sheet'.)

Little wonder that it never entered my head to become a writer in those days.

Roald Dahl

Reflections

* As we all know Roald Dahl went on to become one of Britain's best-selling children's writers. Presumably this achievement only came along after years of application and striving for perfection.

Underpinning all achievement are two things:

1 motivation
2 enjoyment in learning

Like all human beings, we will fail again and again, but we should always try to give of our best.

* A key aspect of achievement in school is to ask yourself – at intervals of a week, a half–term, or a term – 'What have I achieved?'

There are two kinds of targets worth thinking about:

First, the targets and deadline that are set *for* you by teachers.

In many ways, these are the easy targets to meet, mainly because you'll be told if you don't meet them.

Second, there are targets which you set for *yourself* – these are always the difficult ones to meet, but perhaps the most satisfying when you achieve them. As Roald Dahl writes elsewhere in his autobiography about being a writer:

'You must have stamina. In other words, you must be able to stick to what you are doing and never give up, for hour after hour, day after day, week after week, month after month.

You must be a perfectionist. That means you must never be satisfied with what you have written until you have re-written it again and again, making it as good as you possibly can.

You must have strong self-discipline. You are working alone. No one is employing you. No one is around to give you the sack if you don't turn up for work, or to tick you off if you start slacking.'

Once again, motivation, 'stickability' and enjoyment in learning are identified as being at the heart of achievement.

8 Rules and expectations

Introduction

From the earliest times human beings have felt the need to set down rules to help them organise their lives, their homes, their hobbies and sports, their factories, their schools, etc. Without some kind of code or set of expectations, we find it difficult to organise our society – and this is as true in London or Glasgow as it is in Cairo, Sydney or Tokyo.

Schools set down rules and expectations for the good of all those working within them: pupils and students, teachers and support staff. The way we *all* respond to the expectations set down for us will determine whether the school thrives and flourishes as a community.

The following poems offer us some witty observations on school rules.

Reading

The Lesson

A poem that raises the question:
Should there be capital punishment in schools?

Chaos ruled OK in the classroom
as bravely the teacher walked in
the nooligans ignored him
his voice was lost in the din

'The theme for today is violence
and homework will be set
I'm going to teach you a lesson
one that you'll never forget'

He picked on a boy who was shouting
and throttled him then and there

then garotted the girl behind him
(the one with grotty hair)

Then sword in hand he hacked his way
between the chattering rows
'First come, first severed' he declared
'fingers, feet, or toes'

He threw that sword at a latecomer
it struck with deadly aim
then pulling out a shotgun
he continued with his game

The first blast cleared the backrow
(where those who skive hang out)
they collapsed like rubber dinghies
when the plug's pulled out

'Please may I leave the room sir?'
a trembling vandal enquired
'Of course you may' said teacher
put the gun to his temple and fired

The Head popped a head round the doorway
to see why a din was being made
nodded understandingly
then tossed in a grenade

And when the ammo was well spent
with blood on every chair
Silence shuffled forward
with its hands up in the air

The teacher surveyed the carnage
the dying and the dead
he waggled a finger severely
'Now let that be a lesson' he said

Roger McGough

Dumb insolence

I'm big for ten years old
Maybe that's why they get at me

Teachers, parents, cops
Always getting at me

When they get at me

I don't hit em
They can do you for that

I don't swear at em
They can do you for that

I stick my hands in my pockets
And stare at them

And while I stare at them
I think about sick

They call it dumb insolence

They don't like it
But they can't do you for it

I've been done before
They say if I get done again

They'll put me in a home
So I do dumb insolence

Adrian Mitchell

Late

You're late, said miss.
The bell has gone,
dinner numbers done
and work begun.

What have you got to say for yourself?

Well, it's like this, miss.
Me mum was sick,
me dad fell down the stairs,
the wheel fell off me bike
and then we lost our Billy's snake
behind the kitchen chairs. Earache
struck down me grampy, me gran
took quite a funny turn.
Then on the way I met this man
whose dog attacked me shin –
look, miss, you can see the blood
it doesn't look too good,
does it?

Yes, yes, sit down –
and next time say you're sorry
for disturbing all the class.
Now get on with your story,
fast!

Please miss, I've got nothing to write about.

Judith Nicholls

Reflections

* 'The Lesson' reminds us firmly but humorously, why we need rules to protect
  both teachers and pupils. Without them there would be anarchy.

'Dumb insolence' reminds us that rules can feel oppressive to children – they feel 'got at' and thus need to find ways of expressing their frustration. 'Dumb insolence' is not recommended, but experienced teachers recognise it!

'Late' has a more serious moral. It is that when you break school rules you are usually disturbing the learning and well-being of others. This is what school expectations are all about. They exist to secure a well-ordered and happy learning environment, and to ensure that the actions of one thoughtless person do not hinder the learning or health and safety of everyone else.

* 'Wisdom is
  the booby prize
  given when you've been
  unwise.'

* *Ecclesiastes* 7
  Wisdom, like an inheritance, is a good thing
  and benefits those who see the sun.
  Wisdom is a shelter as money is a shelter,
  but the advantage of knowledge is this:
  that wisdom preserves the life of its possessor.

9 Reputation

Introduction

One thing we all know about reputation is that it is very hard to build up a good reputation, but very easy to lose one. We can all think of examples of this in public life – such as famous athletes who are found to have taken drugs and lose their medals and their reputation overnight.

People work hard to secure a fine reputation. As a school we need to remember that our reputation depends on the way we *all* behave in the local community, pupils and teachers alike.

Throughout history reputations have been won and lost – and the reputations of those who have achieved success live on. The following passage is a celebrated one on this subject.

Reading

Let us now praise famous men

44 Let us now praise famous men,
   and our fathers in their generations.
²The Lord apportioned to them great glory,
   his majesty from the beginning.
³There were those who ruled in their kingdoms,
   and were men renowned for their power,
   giving counsel by their understanding,
   and proclaiming prophecies;

⁴leaders of the people in their deliberations
  and in understanding of learning for the people
  wise in their words of instruction;
⁵those who composed musical tunes,
  and set forth verses in writing;
⁶rich men furnished with resources,
  liveing peaceably in their habitations–
⁷all these were honored in their generations,
  and were the glory of their times.
⁸There are some of them who have left a name,
  so that men declare their praise.
⁹And there are some who have no memorial,
  who have perished as though they had not lived;
they have become as though they had not been born,
  and so have their children after them.
¹⁰But these were men of mercy,
  whose righteous deeds have not been forgotten;
¹¹their prosperity will remain with their descendants,
  and their inheritance to their children's children.
¹²Their descendants stand by the covenants;
  their children also, for their sake.
¹³Their posterity will continue for ever,
  and their glory will not be blotted out.
¹⁴Their bodies were buried in peace,
  and their name lives to all generations.

Ecclesiasticus 44: 1–14

Reflections

* This famous passage reminds us that achievements and reputations are often
  won quietly, without great fanfares. Sometimes these achievements can be
  forgotten in the glare of more publicity-seeking figures and events.
  In our school context, we need to think carefully about how reputations are lost
  and won.
  The outstanding achievements of individuals will always attract publicity and
  public recognition – and, usually, enhance reputation. Equally, in terms of how
  the local community will judge a school over a period of time, it is often the
  everyday, unsung actions by pupils that matter most.
  And we should always remember that the thoughtless actions of one or two
  members of a community can bring blame and criticism upon everyone else. We
  are as strong as the weakest link in our chain!

* *Proverbs 27*
  Do not boast about tomorrow,
  for you do not know what a day may bring forth.
  Let another praise you, and not your own mouth;
  someone else, and not your own lips.

10 Examinations (1)

Introduction

Imagine school life with no exams.

Some people actually thrive on the thought of exams – But most of us experience at least mild butterflies, and at worst sheer panic! The easy, reassuring thing for teachers to say to students is 'revise carefully', though we all know this is easier said than done.

The following account comes from a 16-year-old. It has some good advice and a clear sense of perspective about the exam season.

Reading

In the land of the pink exam paper, the elephant's memory is king

PASSING old landmarks in the calendar is usually a pleasurable experience but, sensing a buzz around the school and with fateful dates springing up at me, it is with a faint feeling of apprehension that I note that the run-in starts here. Last year I sat my 16+ achieving satisfactory results but at the cost of much sweat and a huge, irreplaceable slice of summer weather.

The GCSE examination is by far the most demanding and influential test of its kind since the eleven plus, and with the increasing demand for paper qualifications from our troubled industries, the stature of a GCSE certificate as a careers watershed is growing all the time. Apart from being an example of dictatorial efficiency on a grand scale, the exams are a marathon of recall, and it is soon impressed upon one that the bloodthirsty examiners are after facts, facts and true facts. In the land of the pink exam paper, the elephant's memory is king.

The first signs of hysteria to the hardened exam watcher are when teachers begin handing out a welter of these very same pink past papers, a deceptive change from the chilling ice blue of the A level scripts. One young entrepreneur of the chemistry labs ran a most profitable racket by hiring out past papers at 50p a go. There was a rush of takers but no one actually dared read them.

Within days, the Deputy Head had called us together and, commencing with the words 'mentioning no names,' fixed us with a fierce and remarkably accurate stare. He explained to us that during the last two years, some young reprobates had not been keeping up with their classwork and did not possess a full set of notes – oohs from the front row. Not only this but the same ruffians might be tempted to procure notes from more conscientious pupils – a general expression of horror – so would we please be on the look out. He then went on to suggest that we revise each day for some totally impracticable length of time, but that we could, within reason, enjoy ourselves as long as we didn't make a habit of it.

An examination timetable had been up outside the Head's office for some time and we had all checked that the actual exams did not impinge upon any outstanding cricket fixtures. Then we received a personal copy of the same inscrutable sheet which was to be deciphered, cut up and boiled down into a personal timetable to go up on the bedroom wall.

The first steps in the revision campaign are a careful collecting and cataloguing of increasingly familiar exercise books and the longhand copying of equations. At about this time, the school produces one of the most cruel twists of the exam screw. Cards are handed out on which must be written name, number, subject, etc. These are then hastily taken back in and not seen again until they appear leering at one from the examination desk in June, a death warrant in one's own handwriting.

A few days later, a house master asks us for a frank appraisal of our chances. After a moment's thought, we predict for ourselves a total of 6.37 passes each.

The master promises that if we achieve this goal, he will leap from the top of the sixth form centre and dash himself on the rocks below. We laugh sheepishly and review our prospects, possibly with job requirements in mind.

Thanks to our personal timetables, the examination period is a clearly defined island at an uncertain distance from the shore. But suddenly the intervention of oral examinations gives us an uncomfortable feeling of reality, and a proximity to the unthinkable. From now on, the number of weeks remaining takes on a more definite air, and in thousands of diaries, the countdown is on.

Meanwhile lessons continue with an air of desperation as teachers scribble notes on the board long into break time (and are roundly ignored once the bell has gone), all in an effort to get through the syllabus. Having frantically taught at a hitherto unheard of rate in the preceding weeks, they may suddenly, in a fit of extravagance, spend whole periods handing out pink papers.

Room timetables are circulated, withdrawn, amended, recirculated, deemed provisional and then scrapped. There is a purge in the secretary's office and the school is in chaos. Many hardened rugby players take advantage of this to escape lessons on the pretext of sitting a needle-work oral.

Finally the Headmaster himself called us all together, scratching his neck with the air of a man in control, and told us that the main examination hall faces north west and will therefore be very cool in the summer months. We all breathed a hearty sigh of relief and revision continued apace.

The last few weeks passed in a daze, confused by our new-found intelligence and the freedom afforded by study leave. The day arrived amidst frenzied cramming, pencil sharpening and half-hearted bravado. A teacher with an exquisitely mournful expression, obviously thoroughly enjoying himself, informed us that we were not to use red or green ink, nor was liquid paper permitted. The time was 9 45 am, we should write our names, the examination would finish at a quarter past twelve, silence would be maintained, and would we care to commence. A few desperate dissidents whisper, 'Sod off,' as a last gesture of independence, the teacher in question turns majestically towards his elevated console and trips over the bottom step. A titter runs through the hall and we're off.

About three weeks later, I walked out of school with a spring in my step and a pile of physics exercise books under my arm. With a gesture of carefree abandon, I threw one over a nearby wall. Upon a thought, a figure retraced its steps, scaled the wall, and hunted about in a nettle patch until it had reclaimed its prize.

'Just in case of re-sits,' it explained to itself. It was a long summer.

Bruce Railton

Reflections

* So much for the serious side of examinations. The following is a selection of 'exam howlers'. Although they are funny, they are a cautionary warning about thinking *before* you write, and *checking* over your exam paper before you hand it in.

Selection of exam howlers

■The pelvis protects the gentiles.

■Q. What is an animal with a backbone called?

A. A vibrator.

■Q. How can people conserve the environment?

A. Shoot trespassers.

■Q. Give an example where the expansion of a solid causes problems and say how it is overcome?

A. Your fingernails grow and need cutting.

■Q. Why can a bird sit on a high voltage cable without getting an electric shock?

A. The bird's feet are coated with rubber.

■The difference between the North and the South is that they are totally different.

■Q. What does the sickle on the Russian flag stand for?

A. Chopping people's heads off.

■There is no plague in Britain because we have a cure and rats are not popular and people are much cleaner and sterile.

■Sir Francis Drake played with his bowels while the Armada sailed up the Channel.

■Magellan circumcised the world in his 40-foot clipper.

■The Pope could not marry Henry VIII and Catherine of Aragon so Henry started the Protestant religion and married his self.

■Joan of Arc was condomed to death.

■An Arab is a man with a turbine on his head.

■Q. State one change in boys at puberty?

A. There vice deepens.

■Q. What is migration?

A. It is a headache that birds get when they fly south for winter.

■North Sea Gas has been found in Morecambe Bay.

■As he grew older Wordsworth went out one evening because he felt the call of nature.

■Q. Write down some way in which radioactive materials can be useful to humans beings.

A. Atomic bombs.

11 Examinations (2)

Introduction

Examinations are important 'rites of passage' in our society. To pass is to achieve success and congratulation; to fail is to feel depressed and receive consoling comments from others.

The following story casts a rather different – albeit futuristic – eye on 'pass' and 'failure'.

Reading

Examination day

The Jordans never spoke of the exam, not until their son, Dickie, was 12 years old. It was on his birthday that Mrs Jordan first mentioned the subject in his presence, and the anxious manner of her speech caused her husband to answer sharply.

'Forget about it,' he said. 'He'll do all right.'

They were at the breakfast table, and the boy looked up from his plate curiously. 'What exam?' he asked.

His mother looked at the tablecloth. 'It's just a sort of Government intelligence test they give children at the age of 12. You'll be taking it next week. It's nothing to worry about.'

'You mean a test like in school?'

'Something like that,' his father said, getting up from the table. 'Go and read your comics, Dickie.' The boy rose and wandered towards that part of the living room which had been 'his' corner since infancy. He fingered the topmost comic of the stack, but seemed uninterested in the colourful squares of fast-paced action. He wandered towards the window, and peered gloomily at the veil of mist that shrouded the glass.

'Why did it have to rain today?' he said. Why couldn't it rain tomorrow?'

His father, now slumped into an armchair with the Government newspaper, rattled the sheets in vexation. 'Because it just did, that's all. Rain makes the grass grow.'

'Why, Dad?'

'Because it does, that's all.'

Dickie puckered his brow. 'What makes it green, though? The grass?'

'Nobody knows,' his father snapped, then immediately regretted his abruptness.

An hour later, seated by the window he watched the sun force its way between the clouds.

'Dad' he said, 'how far away is the sun?'

'Five thousand miles,' his father said.

Dickie sat at the breakfast table and again saw moisture in his mother's eyes. He didn't connect her tears with the exam until his father suddenly brought the subject to light again.

'Well, Dickie,' he said, with a manly frown. 'You've got an appointment today.'

'I know Dad. I hope –'

'Now, it's nothing to worry about. Thousands of children take this test every day. The Government wants to know how smart you are, Dickie. That's all there is to it.'

'I get good marks in school,' he said hesitantly.

'This is different. This is a – special kind of test. They give you this stuff to drink, you see, and then you go into a room where there's a sort of machine –'

'What stuff to drink?' Dickie said.

'It's nothing. It tastes like peppermint. It's just to make sure you answer the questions truthfully. Not that the Government thinks you won't tell the truth, but this stuff makes *sure*.'

Dickie's face showed puzzlement, and a touch of fright. He looked at his mother, and she composed her face into a misty smile.

'Everything will be all right,' she said.

'Of course it will,' his father agreed. 'You're a good boy, Dickie; you'll make out fine. Then we'll come home and celebrate. All right?'

'Yes, sir,' Dickie said.

They entered the Government Educational Building fifteen minutes before the appointed hour. They crossed the marble floors of the great pillared lobby, passed beneath an archway and entered an automatic lift that brought them to the fourth floor.

There was a young man wearing an insignia-less tunic, seated at a polished desk in front of Room 404. He held a clipboard in his hand, and he checked the list down to the Js and permitted the Jordans to enter.

The room was as cold and official as a courtroom, with long benches flanking metal tables. There were several fathers and sons already there, and a thin-lipped woman with cropped black hair was passing out sheets of paper.

Mr Jordan filled out the form, and returned it to the clerk. Then he told Dickie: 'It won't be long now. When they call your name, you just go through the doorway at that end of the room.' He indicated the portal with his finger.

A concealed loudspeaker crackled and called off the first name. Dickie saw a boy leave his father's side reluctantly and walk slowly towards the door.

At five minutes to eleven, they called the name of Jordan.

'Good luck, son,' his father said, without looking at him. 'I'll call for you when the test is over.'

Dickie walked to the door and turned the knob. The room inside was dim, and he could barely make out the features of the grey-tunicked attendant who greeted him.

'Sit down,' the man said softly. He indicated a high stool beside his desk. 'Your name's Richard Jordan?'

'Yes, sir.'

'Your classification number is 600 – 115. Drink this, Richard.'

He lifted a plastic cup from the desk and handed it to the boy. The liquid inside had the consistency of buttermilk, tasted only vaguely of the promised peppermint. Dickie downed it, and handed the man the empty cup.

He sat in silence, feeling drowsy, while the man wrote busily on a sheet of paper. Then the attendant looked at his watch, and rose to stand only inches from Dickie's face. He unclipped a penlike object from the pocket of his tunic, and flashed a tiny light into the boy's eyes.

'All right,' he said. 'Come with me, Richard.'

He led Dickie to the end of the room, where a single wooden armchair faced a multi-dialled computing machine. There was a microphone on the left arm of the chair, and when the boy sat down, he found its pinpoint head conveniently at his mouth.

'Now just relax, Richard. You'll be asked some questions, and you think them over carefully. Then give your answers into the microphone. The machine will take care of the rest.'

'Yes, sir.'

'I'll leave you alone now. Whenever you want to start, just say 'ready' into the microphone.'

'Yes, sir.'

The man squeezed his shoulder, and left.

Dickie said, 'Ready.'

Lights appeared on the machine, and a mechanism whirred. A voice said:
'Complete this sequence. One, four, seven, ten . . .'
Mr and Mrs Jordan were in the living room, not speaking, not even speculating.
It was almost four o'clock when the telephone rang. The woman tried to reach
it first, but her husband was quicker.
'Mr Jordan?'
The voice was clipped; a brisk, official voice.
'Yes, speaking.'
This is the Government Educational Service. Your son, Richard M Jordan,
Classification 600 – 115, has completed the Government examination. We regret to
inform you that his intelligence quotient is above the Government regulation,
according to Rule 84, Section 5, of the New Code.'
Across the room, the woman cried out, knowing nothing except the emotion she
read on her husband's face.
'You may specify by telephone,' the voice droned on, 'whether you wish his
body interred by the Government, or would you prefer a private burial place? The
fee for Government burial is ten dollars.'

'Examination Day' by Henry Sleaser

Reflections

* Of course we all need to take examinations seriously – they do *count*. But this
  tale is perhaps a cautionary one about whether passing an examination is necessarily a good thing. Equally, it has a rather chilling message about society
  controlling intelligence.

* And what about this recent newspaper story, from another culture and country?

Fight to cheat
Dhaka – Nearly 70 people were injured when Bangladeshi students, demanding
the right to cheat during final exams, fought teachers and police with stones and
home-made bombs. Students defend cheating by saying they must compete with
colleagues who get help from powerful relatives.

Yes, examinations matter – we need to prepare for them carefully and take them
seriously. But we must not feel failure to the point of giving up.
Examinations exist to test our knowledge and our application. If we fail the first
or second time around, we need to have the strength of purpose to try to succeed
the third time.

12 Leaving school

Introduction

Coming to the end of 11 or 12 years of compulsory education is an important
moment. Many students continue into post-16 or post-18 education, and this trend
is increasing. But finishing the compulsory stage inevitably makes us think back –
affectionately, we hope – on the many, many experiences we have had since starting
school at four or five.

Schools exist to promote learning and enjoyment in learning. The pursuit of knowledge for its own sake is very worthwhile. Equally, schools have a responsibility to prepare young people for the next phase of their lives. The following imaginary letter comes from a student who has recently left school. It raises some thought-provoking questions for pupils, parents and teachers.

Reading

To the headteacher

DEAR MR TRAYNOR – I write to thank you and your staff for five happy and hardworking years at school. The teachers worked themselves and me without stint and I am proud to have upheld their faith in me by passing a decent number of exams. It was all very worth-while.

You will remember that I took economics and business studies in case there was a vacancy in the world of commerce. French and German were to help me if I got a job involving foreign travel. My science and engineering courses were to fit me for a career in technology, as was my computer studies. English and maths are, of course, useful in all careers. All the courses were calculated to be of the greatest value to me in my future career and the teachers by their drive and enthusiasm ensured that I did well. Thank you all.

There is only one snag. I am unable to obtain a job of any kind. It seems that where I am best qualified there are no vacancies, and that where there are vacancies I am too well qualified. The careers people tell me that I am not alone in this and that I may be unemployed for some time. I find myself, therefore, in great difficulties. All my education has been geared towards work and there is no work. I have unlimited leisure time, but I have not been educated for leisure – only for work.

The career officer informs me that even when the recession is past there will not be a five-day week for anyone, because computers will be taking more and more of the strain of industrial production, and he advises me to find some ways of using my intelligence and skills in this increased leisure time. Can you or any of your excellent staff help or advise me please? I am sure that the education you gave me at school was splendid and I am sorry to trouble you with problems which have only arisen because of a change in the world outside school.

Thank you again for all you have done for me.

Yours sincerely. . . .

Reflections

* This is a sobering reminder that schools don't have all the answers. An effective school should prepare its students academically and socially for the world beyond the classroom, recognising that change is a constant force in today's society.

Examination success, learning to enjoy learning – these are a key part of a good education. Over and above these, developing in people the personal and social skills to lead a satisfying and fulfilling adult life must be an important aspect of a school's educational role.

* The following is a '17th Century Nun's Prayer' which says a lot about the *really* important lessons for life.

Lord thou knowest better than I know myself that I am growing older and will some day be old. Keep me from the fatal habit of thinking I must say something on every subject and on every occasion. Release me from craving to straighten out everybody's affairs. Make me thoughtful but not moody: helpful but not bossy. With my vast store of wisdom, it seems a pity not to use it all, but Thou knowest Lord that I want a few friends at the end.

Keep my mind free from the recital of endless details; give me wings to get to the point. Seal my lips on my aches and pains.

They are increasing and love of rehearsing them is becoming sweeter as the years go by. I dare not ask for grace enough to enjoy the tales of others' pains, but help me to endure them with patience.

I dare not ask for improved memory, but for a growing humility and a lessing cocksureness when my memory seems to clash with the memories of others. Teach me the glorious lesson that occasionally I may be mistaken.

Keep me reasonably sweet; I do not want to be a Saint – some of them are so hard to live with – but a sour old person is one of the crowning works of the devil. Give me the ability to see good things in unexpected places, and talents in unexpected people. And, give me, O Lord, the grace to tell them so.

AMEN

(The title of this prayer is traditional, the source is unknown.)

Faith and Religion

1 Creation stories

Introduction

From the beginning of human life on earth, people have felt the need to explain the creation of their world. There are as many different creation myths and stories as there are peoples on the earth.

It is interesting to see what these stories have in common, and how they differ. The following creation stories are taken from five different cultures.

Readings

1. The Chinese creation story

O listener, let it be told of a time when there was nothing but chaos, and that chaos was like a mist and full of emptiness. Suddenly, into the midst of this mist, into this chaos of emptiness, came a great, colourful light. From this light all things that exist came to be. The mist shook and separated. That which was light rose up to form heaven, and that which was heavy sank, and formed the earth.

Now from heaven and earth came forth strong forces. These two forces combined to produce **yin** and **yang**. Picture, O listener, this yang like a dragon – hot, fiery, male, full of energy. Imagine, O listener, this yin as a cloud – moist, cool, female, drifting slowly. Each of these forces is full of great power. Left alone, they would destroy the world with their might, and chaos would return. Together, they balance each other, and keep the world in harmony.

This then is yin and yang, and from them came forth everything. The sun is of yang, and the moon, yin. The four seasons and the five elements – water, earth, metal, fire and wood – sprang from them. So did all kinds of living creatures.

So now there was the earth, floating like a jellyfish on water. But the earth was just a ball, without features. Then the forces of yin and yang created the giant figure P'an Ku, the Ancient One. P'an Ku, who never stopped growing every year of his great, long life, set to work to put the earth in order. He dug the river valleys and piled up the mountains. Over many thousands of years he shaped and created the flow and folds of our earth.

But such work took its toll. Even mighty P'an Ku could not escape death, and worn out by his struggle he collapsed and died. His body was now so vast that when he fell to the ground, dead, his body became the five sacred mountains. His flesh became the soil, his bones the rocks, his hair the plants and his blood the rivers. From his sweat came the rain, and from the parasites – the tiny creatures living on his body – came forth human beings.

The people at first lived in caves, but soon Heavenly Emperors came to teach them how to make tools and houses. The people also learned how to build boats, to fish, to plough and plant, and to prepare food. O listener, this is how it all began.

2. The Greeks' creation story

To begin with, there were no shapes. Nothing existed; there were no forms of things. All the elements and atoms that would one day make matter, swirled and seethed in endless, meaningless movement. If a mortal had existed and been able to watch the dance of the elements, it would have seemed as beautiful as dust dancing in a sunshaft. But there was no dust, no sun, no mortal: only the endless dance. The name of the swirling elements was Chaos.

From time to time as things seethed and whirled in Chaos, in the dance of the elements, patterns were formed. For a fleeting moment, in one place or another, shapes appeared: circles, ridges, humps and hollows in the elemental flow. Most of them vanished as quickly as a mirage; but some repeated themselves, growing ever stronger and more permanent. The heavy atoms began to make patterns separately from the light atoms, gradually the patterns of each grew fixed and purposeful, until the first shapes of things were formed. The heavy atoms made the shape called Gaia (Earth): a living organism with clefts, folds and hills like gigantic limbs. The light atoms made Ouranos (Sky): quick-moving, always changing, as restless as breath itself.

Turning and twisting in the swirl of Chaos, Gaia and Ouranos danced a slow dance of love. Sky embraced Earth; Earth opened herself to Sky and grew fertile. Life-giving rain from Sky sought out Earth's cracks and crevices; streams, rivers and oceans formed; the ground produced trees, green plants and flowers, and soon there were birds, animals and insects of every kind. These were the first children of Earth and Sky.

So they floated peacefully in the space made by their own creation. Earth was like a huge flat dish, hillocked and humped by mountain ranges, river-valleys, lakes and seas; Sky soared above like an umbrella of clouds and light. All round, at Earth's circumference, they touched. The touching point, the horizon, was marked by a fast flowing river called Ocean; it whirled round in an endless circle and held everything in place. At the eastern edge of Earth, the Sun rose each morning to begin its journey across the dome of Sky; each evening it plunged into Ocean at the western edge and began its night's voyage to the east, ready to emerge again next morning. Below Earth lay the Underworld, so far below that a dropped object would take nine days to reach it. The entrances to the Underworld were at the edge of the circle of Ocean; there were also cracks and openings in Earth's floor itself. The shortest distance between Earth and Sky was at Ocean's edge, the dome of Sky at the centre, its highest point, rose above Earth to the height of three great mountains piled on top of one another, Mount Olympus, Mount Pelion and Mount Ossa.

The Christian Bible creation story

The Beginning

1 In the beginning God created the heavens and the earth. [2]Now the earth was formless and empty, darkness was over the surface of the deep, and the Spirit of God was hovering over the waters.

[3]And God said, 'Let there be light,' and there was light. [4]God saw that the light

was good, and he separated the light from the darkness. [5]God called the light 'day', and the darkness he called 'night'. And there was evening, and there was morning – the first day.

[6]And God said, 'Let there be an expanse between the waters to separate water from water.' [7]So God made the expanse and separated the water under the expanse from the water above it. And it was so. [8]God called the expanse 'sky'. And there was evening, and there was morning – the second day.

[9]And God said, 'Let the water under the sky be gathered to one place, and let dry ground appear.' And it was so. [10]God called the dry ground 'land', and the gathered waters he called 'seas'. And God saw that it was good.

[11]Then God said, 'Let the land produce vegetation: seed-bearing plants and trees on the land that bear fruit with seed in it, according to their various kinds.' And it was so. [12]The land produced vegetation: plants bearing seed according to their kinds and trees bearing fruit with seed in it according to their kinds. And God saw that it was good. [13]And there was evening, and there was morning – the third day.

[14]And God said, 'Let there be lights in the expanse of the sky to separate the day from the night, and let them serve as signs to mark seasons and days and years, [15]and let them be lights in the expanse of the sky to give light on the earth.' And it was so. [16]God made two great lights – the greater light to govern the day and the lesser light to govern the night. He also made the stars. [17]God set them in the expanse of the sky to give light on the earth, [18]to govern the day and the night, and to separate light from darkness. And God saw that it was good. [19]And there was evening, and there was morning – the fourth day.

[20]And God said, 'Let the water teem with living creatures, and let birds fly above the earth across the expanse of the sky.' [21]So God created the great creatures of the sea and every living and moving thing with which the water teems, according to their kinds, and every winged bird according to its kind. And God saw that it was good. [22]God blessed them and said, 'Be fruitful and increase in number and fill the water in the seas, and let the birds increase on the earth.' [23]And there was evening, and there was morning – the fifth day.

[24]And God said, 'Let the land produce living creatures according to their kinds: livestock, creatures that move along the ground, and wild animals, each according to its kind.' And it was so. [25]God made the wild animals according to their kinds, the livestock according to their kinds, and all the creatures that move along the ground according to their kinds. And God saw that it was good.

[26]Then God said, 'Let us make man in our image, in our likeness, and let them rule over the fish of the sea and the birds of the air, over the livestock, over all the earth, and over all the creatures that move along the ground.'

[27]So God created man in his own image, in the image of God he created him: male and female he created them.

[28]God blessed them and said to them, 'Be fruitful and increase in number; fill the earth and subdue it. Rule over the fish of the sea and the birds of the air and over every living creature that moves on the ground.'

[29]'Then God said, 'I give you every seed-bearing plant on the face of the whole earth and every tree that has fruit with seed in it. They will be yours for food. [30]And to all the beasts of the earth and all the birds of the air and all the creatures that move on the ground – everything that has the breath of life in it – I give every green plant for food.' And it was so.

[31]God saw all that he had made, and it was very good. And there was evening, and there was morning – the sixth day.

2 Thus the heavens and the earth were completed in all their vast array.

[2]By the seventh day God had finished the work he had been doing; so on the seventh day he rested from all his work. [3]And God blessed the seventh day and made it holy, because on it he rested from all the work of creating that he had done.

Genesis 1: 1–24; 2: 1–3

A Cheyenne Indian creation myth

In the beginning there was nothing, a Great Void, where lived Makeo, the All Spirit. From his great Power, Makeo made salt water. 'We will make water beings,' Makeo told his Power, and there were fishes, and mussels, and water snails.

'We will make creatures to live on the water,' said Makeo, and there were snow geese and coots and terns, and many other water birds. Then Makeo made light, so that he could see what his Power had created.

The snow goose called to Makeo, 'This is good water, but we would sometimes like to leave it.'

'Then fly,' said Makeo, and the birds flew up from the lake into the new light, their wings beautiful against the sky.

Then the birds asked Makeo for a dry place to land and build their nests. 'My Power will only let me make four things,' said Makeo, 'and I have made water, light, air, and the creatures of the water. You must help me now.'

So the birds tried to help Makeo, diving into the water to seek for earth, but none was successful. Finally the little coot, the best of the swimmers, brought a little ball of mud to the surface.

Makeo took the shape of a man, and the coot dropped the ball of mud into his hand. Makeo rolled the mud ball, and it became larger and larger until Makeo could no longer hold it, but there was no place to put the mud. He called to the water creatures to help him, but not one was the right shape to carry the mud.

Only the turtle was left. 'Grandmother Turtle.' asked Makeo. 'Can you help me?' The old turtle swam to Makeo, and the piled the mud on her back, and made a hill, which was the Earth.

'We will call the earth our grandmother,' said Makeo, 'and the turtle which carries the earth will be the only creature at home in the water, or in the earth, or on the earth'. And that is why turtles walk slowly, for Grandmother Turtle carries the weight of the earth on her back.

Then Makeo made the earth beautiful with trees and grasses and flowers, and Makeo thought it was the most beautiful thing he had made. He then took a bone from his right side, and made the first man, and one from his left side and made the first woman. He made the animals, to feed and clothe them and their children, and he still watches and guards everything that he made.

A Fulani story 'Mali': West Africa

At the beginning there was a huge drop of milk.
Then Doondari came and he created the stone.
Then the stone created iron:
The iron created fire:
And fire created air:
Then Doondari descended the second time. And he took the five elements
And he shaped them into man.

But man was proud.
Then Doondari created blindness and blindness defeated man.
But when blindness became too proud,
Doondari created sleep, and sleep created blindness;
But when sleep became too proud,
Doondari created worry, and worry defeated sleep;
But when worry became too proud
Doondari created death, and death defeated worry.
But when death became too proud,
Doondari decended for the third time
and he came as Guena, the eternal one,
And Guena defeated death.

Reflections

* It seems that we have a fundamental human need to be able to explain the world's creation and, in particular, how humans came to exist.
  For the Chinese, central to their vision are the forces of yin and yang.
  For the Greeks, there are Chaos, Gaia and Ouranos.
  For the Christians, the Bible tells of God's work over six days, until he rested on the seventh.
  For the Native American Indians, there is Makeo, the All Spirit from whose power everything was created.
  For the people of Mali (in West Africa) omnipotence (all-powerfulness) and omniscience (all-seeingness) came in the shape of Doondari and Guena.

* Over the centuries, human beings have come to understand much about the biology, physics and chemistry of the earth and the life forms that share it. For ancient peoples, lacking this 'scientific' knowledge, it was important to believe in some kind of explanation of the creation of the world in which they lived, and the 'rules' that governed it. The many and varied creation stories around the world are a testament to the basic human need for belief and faith. Do you think we still have this need, in the modern scientific and technological age?

2 Origins of the species (1)

Introduction

'Animal life is precious.' This is an easy phrase to say but one which we humans are all-too-quick to forget. As humans we are part of the enormous animal kingdom; each one of us is unique – were we to die today there would never be another human being like us again. This thought helps us, perhaps, to realise the *sanctity* of life.

The following passage is taken from the writings of David Attenborough, a man who has done much through his television programmes to highlight the colourful and endless variety of the animal kingdom.

Here David Attenborough describes Charles Darwin's ideas about the origins of the species.

Reading

The endless variety

It is not difficult to discover an unknown animal. Spend a day in a tropical jungle and you can collect hundreds of different kinds of small creatures. Moths, spiders, beetles, butterflies disguised as wasps, wasps shaped like ants, sticks that walk, leaves that open wings and fly. One of these creatures may well be new to science – though only a specialist could tell you which one.

The variety of animal and plant life is indeed vast and bewildering and ever since the beginning of science, people have wondered why this should be so. Over the centuries, many reasons have been suggested; one most widely accepted today was made by an English naturalist, Charles Darwin. In 1832 he was visiting Brazil. In a single day there he collected 68 different species of small beetles. He was astounded that there should be so many. An explanation of why this was so occurred to him three years later when his expedition arrived in the Galapagos Islands. These islands lie 1,000 km from the coast of Ecuador, out in the Pacific. The Galapagos creatures Darwin saw looked very like those he had seen on the mainland, but they were slightly different. There were cormorants – black, long-necked diving birds like those that fly along Brazilian rivers, but their wings were so small that they were unable to fly. There were also large lizards called iguanas. Those on the continent climbed trees and ate leaves. Here on the islands, where there was little vegetation, one species fed on seaweed and clung to rocks among the waves with unusually long claws. There were tortoises, very similar to the mainland ones, except that these were many times bigger. Moreover, the tortoises on each island were slightly different. Those that lived on well-watered islands, where there was ground vegetation, had a front edge to their shells that curved gently upwards above their necks. But those that came from dry islands, where the only food was branches of cactus or leaves of trees, had a high peak to the front of their shells so that they could stretch their necks almost vertically upwards.

Darwin began to wonder if one species might, in time, change into another. Maybe, thousands of years ago, birds and reptiles from South America had reached the Galapagos on the rafts of vegetation that often float down the rivers and out to sea. Once there, they had changed, as generation followed generation, to suit their new homes.

The differences between them and their mainland cousins were only small, but if such changes had taken place, was it not possible that over many millions of years, many could add up to big changes. Maybe fish had developed muscular fins and crawled onto land to become amphibians. Maybe amphibians, in their turn, had developed watertight skins and become reptiles. But how did these changes come about? Darwin suggested that they were caused by a process he called 'natural selection'.

His argument was this. All individuals of the same species are not the same. For example, in one clutch of eggs from a giant tortoise, there may be some hatchlings which will develop longer necks than others because of factors inherited from their parents. In times of drought they will be able to reach leaves and so survive. Their brothers and sisters with shorter necks will starve and die. So those best fitted to their surroundings will be selected and survive. In turn, they will pass on their characteristics to their offspring. After a great number of generations, tortoises on the dry islands will have longer necks than those on the watered islands. And so one species will have given rise to another.

David Attenborough

Reflections

* This reading begins with the arresting line: 'It is not difficult to discover an unknown animal'. David Attenborough reminds us that the animal kingdom is of such endless variety that scientists go on discovering new forms of life all the time.

  For many centuries human beings made up stories and myths to explain their own creation. Religious books offer alternative accounts of the genesis of our world. Charles Darwin offers yet another explanation, one which scientists generally accept as the most probable argument about how one species gives rise to another.

* Whichever account of how life began you believe in, what remains fascinating is just how many different species exist in the animal kingdom. And within the animal kingdom as a whole, human beings comprise a species of truly endless variety.

  This fact should always bring home to us the sanctity of human life in a world which so often witnesses wars between people because of their different faiths and beliefs.

3 Origins of the species (2)*

Introduction

All known religions seek to explain how we as human beings – and the natural world around us – came into being. People across the world who have faith in a particular religion believe in a given account of the world's genesis.

Equally, many scientists throughout history have sought to offer their explanations of our natural world. Probably the best known is Charles Darwin who published in 1859 the now celebrated book *Origin of Species*.

The following passage is taken from a fascinating study of our origins titled 'The Blind Watchmaker'. Its author, Richard Dawkins, is a botanist working and writing in Oxford today. In the passage he tries to offer his own interpretation of Darwin's famous theory. He also mentions the work of a writer called William Paley.

The argument he offers needs to be followed carefully if it is to be understood.

Reading

The Blind Watchmaker

We wanted to know why we, and all other complicated things, exist. And we can now answer that question in general terms, even without being able to comprehend the details of the complexity itself. To take an analogy, most of us don't understand in detail how an airliner works. Probably its builders don't comprehend it fully either: engine specialists don't in detail understand wings, and wing specialists understand engines only vaguely. Wing specialists don't even understand wings with full mathematical precision: they can predict how a wing will behave in turbulent conditions, only by examining a model in a wind tunnel or a computer simulation – the sort of thing a biologist might do to understand an animal. But however incompletely we understand how an airliner works, we all understand by what general process it came into existence. It was designed by humans on drawing boards. Then other humans made the bits from the drawings, then lots more humans screwed, rivetted, welded or glued the bits together, each in its right place. The process by which an airliner came into existence is not fundamentally mysterious to us, because humans built it. The systematic putting together of parts to a purposeful design is something we know and understand, for we have experienced it at first hand, even if only with our childhood Meccano or Erector set.

What about our own bodies? Each one of us is a machine, like an airliner only much more complicated. Were we designed on a drawing board too, and were our parts assembled by a skilled engineer? The answer is no. It is a surprising answer, and we have known and understood it for only a century or so. When Charles Darwin first explained the matter, many people either wouldn't or couldn't grasp it. I myself flatly refused to believe Darwin's theory when I first heard about it as a child. Almost everybody throughout history, up to the second half of the nineteenth century, has firmly believed in the opposite – the Conscious Designer theory. Many people still do, perhaps because the true, Darwinian explanation of our own existence is still, remarkably, not a routine part of the curriculum of a general education. It is certainly very widely misunderstood.

The watchmaker of my title is borrowed from a famous treatise by the eighteenth-century theologian William Paley. His Natural Theology, published in 1802, is the best-known exposition of the 'Argument from Design', always the most influential of the arguments for the existence of a God. It is a book that I greatly admire, for in his own time its author succeeded in doing what I am struggling to do now. He had a point to make, he passionately believed in it, and he spared no effort to ram it home clearly. He had a proper reverence for the complexity of the living world and he saw that it demands a very special kind of explanation. The only thing he got wrong – admittedly quite a big thing! – was the explanation itself. He gave the traditional religious answer to the riddle, but he articulated it more clearly and convincingly than anybody had before. The true explanation is utterly different, and it had to wait for one of the most revolutionary thinkers of all time, Charles Darwin.

Paley begins Natural Theology with a famous passage:

In crossing a heath, suppose I pitched my foot against a stone, and were asked how the stone came to be there; I might possibly answer, that, for anything I knew to the contrary, it had lain there for ever: nor would it perhaps be very easy to show the absurdity of this answer. But suppose I had found a watch upon the ground, and it should be inquired how the watch happened to be in that place; I should hardly think of the answer which I had before given, that for anything I knew, the watch might have always been there.

Paley here appreciates the difference between natural physical objects like stones, and designed and manufactured objects like watches. He goes on to expound the precision with which the cogs and springs of a watch are fashioned, and the intricacy with which they are put together. If we found an object such as a watch upon a heath, even if we didn't know how it had come into existence, its own precision and intricacy of design would force us to conclude that the watch must have had a maker: that there must have existed, at some time, and at some place or other, an artificer or artificers, who formed it for the purpose which we find it actually to answer; who comprehended its construction, and designed its use.

Nobody could reasonably dissent from this conclusion, Paley insists, yet that is just what the atheist, in effect, does when he contemplates the works of nature, for:

every indication of contrivance, every manifestation of design, which existed in the watch, exists in the works of nature; with the difference, on the side of nature, of being greater or more, and that in a degree which exceeds all computation.

Paley drives his point home with beautiful and reverent descriptions of the dissected machinery of life, beginning with the human eye, a favourite example which Darwin was later to use. Paley compares the eye with a designed instrument such as a telescope, and concludes that 'there is precisely the same proof that the eye was made for vision, as there is that the telescope was made for assisting it'. The eye must have had a designer, just as the telescope had.

Paley's arguments is made with passionate sincerity and is informed by the best biological scholarship of his day, but it is wrong, gloriously and utterly wrong. The analogy between telescope and eye, between watch and living organism, is false. All appearances to the contrary, the only watchmaker in nature is the blind forces of physics, albeit deployed in a very special way. A true watchmaker has foresight: he designs his cogs and springs, and plans their interconnections, with a future purpose in his mind's eye. Natural selection, the blind, unconscious, automatic process which Darwin discovered, and which we now know is the explanation for the existence and apparently purposeful form of all life, has no purpose in mind. It has no mind and no mind's eye. It does not plan for the future. It has no vision, no foresight, no sight at all. If it can be said to play the role of watchmaker in nature, it is the blind watchmaker.

From 'The Blind Watchmaker' by Richard Dawkins

Reflections

* Clearly, the work of Charles Darwin and Richard Dawkins challenges many religious accounts of the origins of our natural world. This is a difficult subject to explain. For many people, *how* and *why* our natural world came into being remains one of the great, unsolved mysteries.

* As we grow up and learn at school and college we need to make up our own minds on this subject. What is always important to remember is that no-one knows the absolute truth – there will always be debate and argument on this topic. Equally, it is important to form your own opinions, through study and discussion, and to respect the viewpoints and beliefs of others.

4 The Berlin Wall

Introduction

History has many examples of the unthinkable becoming reality. Imagine waking up one morning to find that the road you live in is suddenly – overnight – divided by a wall that you are not allowed to cross. That was the experience of the

Hildebrandt family in August 1961. It was the month that the Berlin Wall, dividing East and West Berlin, was built by the East German authorities.

For the next 30 years the Hildebrandts were cut off from friends and family. But they always believed that one day the Wall would be toppled and that the people of Berlin would be united. At last, in 1989, the people of Berlin tore down the wall. The following is an interview between a journalist and Regine and Jorg Hildebrandt, conducted shortly after the fall of the Berlin Wall.

Reading

Dancing on the ghost of the infamous Wall

WHEN the Berlin Wall was built, Regine Hildebrandt was 20. At the time, she and her future husband Jörg lived in the Bernauer Strasse in the north of the city, right on the East-West divide. Like most Berliners, they have never been able to forget Sunday 13 August 1961.

'At first, everything seemed normal,' recalled Mr Hildebrandt. 'I got up at about 7am to collect my morning paper. The border ran across our front door, so as soon as I stepped into the street I was in the French sector. It was only when I got to the first side street that I realised something was wrong. I saw a crowd of people on the eastern side. They were standing behind some barbed wire and staring over into the West. There had been a lot of speculation about sealing off Berlin, but no one was talking about a wall yet. Technically, it seemed impossible to divide the city – especially our street. We thought the barriers would only last a few days.'

Living in Bernauer Strasse, the Hildebrants enjoyed, fleetingly, a unique privilege: continued access to West Berlin after 13 August 1961. One day later, they attended their god-child's birthday party in the West. Over the next few days, they astonished their many West Berlin friends with surprise visits. Most of East Berlin had by then been cut off: for many, Bernauer Strasse was the final escape route. It was a loophole the authorities were keen to close.

'After about a week, we got a visit from the so-called *Kampfgruppen* – the fighting squads – who told us we were being moved from our ground-floor flat to a first-floor flat down the street,' said Mrs Hildebrandt. 'They wanted to brick over all the front doors and ground-floor windows. We knew they were serious about a wall, but we decided to stay. We felt we belonged in the East.'

Others did not. Over the next few days, Bernauer Strasse witnessed many dramatic escapes as people jumped from as high as the fourth floor into safetynets held by West Berliners below. Four people missed the nets and died. 'It was dreadful,' said Mrs Hildebrandt, recoiling at the recollection. 'My brother and his wife escaped from our flat using a rope. One day, the police burst in and ran to our window like wild men to yell at the people jumping out. They were not allowed into the street because it was in the West. Thank God they didn't use their guns.'

By early September, the East German authorities decided to seal off Bernauer Strasse altogether, prior to demolishing it. The knock on the door came at 5am. 'It was the *kampfgruppen* again,' said Mrs Hildebrandt. 'They told us we had four hours to get our things packed as we were moving to another part of town.'

The Wall spelled an abrupt end to the Hildebrandts normal family life and completely destroyed the close church community in which they had grown up. 'The human suffering caused by the Wall was indescribable,' said Mrs Hildebrandt, now 49, in the living room of the couple's home near East Berlin's Alexanderplatz.

'When my aunt lay dying we were unable to visit her even though she was only half an hour's drive away. There were no exceptions . . . I did not see my brother for 10 years.'

Reaching for the family albums, Mrs Hildebrandt points to black-and-white photographs of her old school friends standing on the pavement during their last days in Bernauer Strasse. 'By this time we could only talk to them out of the window. We could no longer shake hands, but we were able to haul up their little parcels of chocolates and magazines. It was the last contact we had.'

Taking off her glasses and rubbing her eyes, Mrs Hildebrandt shudders: 'Terrible . . . Terrible. What we actually lost was part of our lives . . . There was so much more, culturally, intellectually. We loved travelling and often went to West Berlin – to the theatre, concerts, exhibitions, everything. We particpated. The only consolation the whole time was that we did not know how long this division was to last. If we had suspected then that it would be there for almost 30 years, we would have gone crazy.'

Despite the Berlin Wall and their antipathy towards the communist regime, the Hildebrandts made a go of things in the East. Regine Hildebrandt completed her biology studies at Humboldt University and became a scientific researcher. Jörg Hildebrandt worked as a lecturer for 25 years. Between 1969 and 1974, they had three children: Frauke, Jan and Elske.

'We got on with our lives, but there was never one day in all those years when the Wall was not present for me,' said Mr Hildebrandt. 'Having experienced Berlin as one, I could never accept its division. We tried to bring up our children to think the Wall would not last. It was difficult. As far as they were concerned, West Berlin was a foreign country like America. We showed them Bernauer Strasse from a distance. It was important to remind them of the past: where we used to live, the church we used to attend. We never wanted them to think that the world ended at the Wall.'

The end of the Wall, when it came, caught the Hildebrands – as, indeed, it caught the world – completely by surprise. 'The ninth of November 1989 happened to be Jan's eighteenth birthday. We had invited a few people down. I remember we were discussing politics. A lot had already changed. But none of us had heard the latest, astonishing news. At about 10 pm a friend rang up and asked if we were going to West Berlin. I could barely believe what I was hearing.

'We soon realised that it must be true. Normally, the streets would have been dead – instead, they were packed. We drove to Bornholmer Strasse. It was pandemonium. We parked and joined the throng, taking photos of everything: the cars, the people flooding over the border, the popping Sekt corks. On the other side, the reception was incredible. West Berliners greeted us cheering and smiling, offering flowers and money. We lost our children in the chaos. Jörg and I went down to the Brandenberg Gate and saw the dancing on the Wall. We phoned our relatives and got them out of bed. The ninth of November – what a brilliant night. It was something I always hoped we would see. I was convinced our children would see it. But the way it came – suddenly – nobody expected that. . . . Ah, it was crazy.'

Adrian Bridge in 'The Independent'

Reflections

* 'We though the barriers would only last a few days.'
  'The human suffering caused by the Wall was indescribable.'

'It was something I always hoped we would see. I was convinced our children would see it.'

These three sentences capture both the despair and the hope which the Hildebrandt family – in common with thousands of others – experienced for three decades. The story of the Berlin Wall is a story of tragedy – but also of hope. We must admire the patience and faith of so many families who endured its divisions but remained optimistic that one day the barrier *would* be demolished. That day came in November 1989.

5 Personal faith: 'St. Joan'

Introduction

There are some people in our communities who show great personal faith – that is, a belief in their 'cause' or what they are doing. Some people are prepared to die for their religious or political beliefs. There are also examples of individuals in history whose personal beliefs have led to the destruction of others – such as Hitler.

Joan of Arc was an ordinary French girl from a farming background. Joan believed she heard voices from heaven telling her what to do. So strong was her faith that she persuaded French army leaders to let her lead their forces in wars against the English in the early 15th century. Joan led the army to victory, but other people did not share her belief that her voices came from heaven. She was pronounced a witch and burned at the stake because she would not renounce her beliefs.

The two passages here come from George Bernard Shaw's play *St. Joan*. In the first passage, Joan is speaking to her friend Jack about the importance of the voices that call her to do God's work. The second extract comes from near the end of Shaw's play. Here Joan tells those around her that she would rather be burnt at the stake than desert her faith.

Reading

St. Joan

(i) JOAN. Jack: the world is too wicked for me. If the goddams and the Burgundians do not make an end of me, the French will. Only for my voices I should lose all heart. That is why I had to steal away to pray here alone after the coronation. I'll tell you something, Jack. It is in the bells I hear my voices. Not today, when they all rang: that was nothing but jangling. But here in this corner, where the bells come down from heaven, and the echoes linger, or in the fields, where they come from a distance through the quiet of the countryside, my voices are in them. [*The cathedral clock chimes the quarter*] Hark! [*She becomes rapt*] Do you hear? 'Dear-child-of-God': just what you said. At the half-hour they will say 'Be-brave-go-on.' At the three-quarters they will say 'I-am-thy-Help.' But it is at the hour, when the great bell goes after 'God-will-save-France': it is then that St. Margaret and St. Catherine and sometimes even the blessed Michael will say things that I cannot tell before hand.

(ii) JOAN. There is no help, no counsel, in any of you. Yes: I am alone on earth: I have always been alone. My father told my brothers to drown me if I would not stay to mind his sheep while France was bleeding to death: France might perish if only our lambs were safe. I thought France would have friends at the court of the king of France; and I find only wolves fighting for pieces of her poor torn body. I thought God would have friends everywhere, because He is the friend of everyone; and in my innocence I believed that you who now cast me out would be like strong towers to keep harm from me. But I am wiser now; and nobody is any the worse for being wiser. Do not think you can frighten me by telling me that I am alone. France is alone; and God is alone; and what is my loneliness before the loneliness of my country and my God? I see now that the loneliness of God is His strength: what would He be if He listened to your jealous little counsels? Well, my loneliness shall be my strength too; it is better to be alone with God: His friendship will not fail me, nor His counsel, nor His love. In His strength I will dare, and dare, and dare, until I die. I will go out now to the common people, and let the love in their eyes comfort me for the hate in yours. You will all be glad to see me burnt; but if I go through the fire I shall go through it to their hearts for ever and ever. And so, God be with me!

From 'Saint Joan' by George Bernard Shaw

Reflections

* What shines through these speeches in the play is Joan of Arc's great personal faith. We do not know much about what the real Joan thought and felt. But we do know that as a young girl she claimed she heard God's calling. And she was prepared to die for this belief – she was burned at the stake in the French city of Rouen in 1431. Interestingly, the Catholic Church later decided to make Joan a Saint.

* We may find it hard to understand how a person could hold so strongly to their beliefs that they would undergo death by fire. But throughout history – and even today – there have been people who possess an unshakeable belief in themselves and their inner faith. We may question this self-belief, or we may admire it.
  We should try to respect another person's convictions, even when we do not agree with them. Sometimes, in extreme cases, we may actively seek to challenge where a person's self-belief may lead – for that individual and those around them.

6 Life after death

Introduction

There are few subjects in the arena of faith and religion which divide people more than the question: 'Is there life after death?' Most religions hold that there is some kind of life after death; some people believe in reincarnation; others that the soul or spirit lives on in some way, separate from or reunited with its mortal being.

The following passage tries to identify what it means to be a person, to be alive. The writer has some interesting things to say abut the role of *memory* in our lives. He then goes on to argue that the belief we survive death has no scientific basis.

The words are those of one of our greatest 20th century philosophers, Bertrand Russell.

Reading

Do men survive death?

The most essential thing in the continuity of a person is memory. Whatever I remember, happened to me; and what you remember, happened to you. It might be objected that there are public events which many people remember; but, in fact, there are always differences between one man's experience of a public event and another man's. We may, therefore, take memory as what defines the continuity of a person.

The question whether we survive death thus becomes the question: Are there, after a man dies, memories of what happened to him while he lived on earth? If there are such memories, we may say that he has survived death; but if not, not.

When this question is viewed scientifically, and not through a fog of emotion, it is very difficult to see any reason for expecting survival. It is fairly certain that memories are connected with the brain, and quite certain that the brain suffers dissolution after death. It is, perhaps, not logically impossible that a new brain, with the same organisation as the old one, should arise with the resurrection of the body; but, except as a miracle revealed by Faith, this seems an extraordinarily improbable hypothesis. One might just as well expect that, when a building has been ruined by an earthquake, a new eruption will build it up again.

When I mention the brain in this connection, I shall expect to be accused of materialism. This accusation, however, would be unjust. I believe a living brain to be composed of thoughts and feelings, those very thoughts and feelings which we observe in ourselves. But thoughts and feelings are evanescent and, if it is they that constitute a living brain, it is natural to suppose that they cease or become greatly changed when the brain ceases to live.

*   *   *

The belief that we survive death seems to me on such grounds to have no scientific basis. I do not think it would ever have arisen except as an emotional reaction to the fear of death. Many people speak of death as a mystery, and they believe, also, that there is something mysterious about the relation of mind and body. For my part, I think this is a mistake.

The word 'mystery' is used only when there is something people do not want to admit. Otherwise, they are content to say that something is unknown. A great many things are unknown. Some may, in time, be discovered; others, we can hardly hope to know either now or later. But when the word 'mystery' is used, it is used to put a stop to inquiry and to sanctify obstinate ignorance. Moreover – what is even worse – those who use the word always go on to speak as though they know all about what they have declared to be unknowable.

I may be told that the view I am setting forth is bleak and cheerless. Undoubtedly, when those we love die, it is an immense comfort to believe that we shall meet them again in heaven. But I see no reason whatever to suppose that the universe takes any interest in our hopes and desires. Whatever of good is to exist in the life of mankind must be put into it by mankind.

Apart from life on this planet, we do not know of anything either good or bad.

There may be happier worlds on other planets, and there may be worlds even worse than our own, but as to this our ignorance is complete. We have no right to expect the universe to adapt itself to our emotions, and I cannot think it right or wise to cherish beliefs for which there is no good evidence, merely on the ground that fairy tales are pleasant.

> *'Do Men Survive Death' by Bertrand Russell, from*
> *'The Great Mystery of Life Hereafter'*

Reflections

* Bertrand Russell sets forth his argument in four main parts:

• first, that memory defines the continuity of a person;
• second, that memory and thoughts cannot survive death;
• third, that 'mystery' is a misused word in this field of debate;
• fourth, that we have no right to expect that the scientific universe should offer us a convenient after-life.

This is an interesting piece of writing, characteristic of an atheist (someone who does not believe in a god or gods).
Clearly, Bertrand Russell's views challenge those of many world religions.
It is important to respect different viewpoints and in the end be true to your own, whatever that might be. But Bertrand Russell's words are worth thinking about: 'Whatever of good is to exist in the life of mankind must be put into it by mankind'.

7 Heaven and hell

Introduction

The atheist believes that there is no life after death (see Bertrand Russell, page 69). For the Buddhist there is nirvana. For the Muslim there is purgatory and paradise. For the Christian there is the belief in 'heaven' and 'hell'.

The following piece by Dorothy Sayers, a famous author of detective fiction, offers a committed *Christian* view of what happens after death.

Reading

Christian belief about heaven and hell

If we are to understand the Christian doctrine about what happens at death, we must first rid our minds of every concept of time and space as we know them. Our time and space have no independent reality: they belong to the universe and were created with it. Take down any novel you like from the shelf. The story it tells may cover the events of a few hours or of many years; it may range over a few acres or the whole globe. But all that space-time is contained within the covers of the book, and has no contact at any point with the space-time in which you are living. It, and the whole universe of action which goes on inside the book, are made things, deriving their existence from the mind of their maker.

Christians believe that our universe of space and time is, similarly, a made thing. It is quite 'real' so far as it goes, but its reality is dependent on that of its Maker, who is alone real in His own right. They also believe that the soul of Man has been so made that it is capable of entering into the true Reality which we call 'Heaven' or 'the presence of God.' so that when we die, it is not as though the characters and action of the book were 'continued in our next' like a serial; it is as though they came out from the book to partake of the real existence of their author.

If this real existence involves anything at all corresponding to 'time' and 'space,' these do not coincide with ours in any way, and we can have no conception of them. We call them 'eternity' and 'infinity' simply to mark their total unlikeness to anything that we experience; and when we speak of God's 'time' as an 'eternal present' we mean to exclude every idea of duration in *our* time.

*　　　*　　　*

God *sends* nobody to Hell; only a wicked ignorance can suggest that He would do to us the very thing He died to save us from. But He has so made us that what in the end we choose, that in the end we shall have. If we enter the state called Hell, it is because we have willed to do so.

*　　　*　　　*

Christians believe that 'in the end of the world' God will make 'a new heaven and a new earth,' and that the body will then be raised from the dead and be united to the soul, so that the whole man will be restored in his completeness. About this we know very little. The only resurrection-body of which we have any knowledge is that of the risen Christ, and it is clear from the Gospel narrative that, although it could manifest itself in our time and space, its relation to them was of a very special kind, and that it did not belong to our universe at all. St. Paul calls the resurrection body 'a spiritual body,' and stresses its *difference*: 'It is sown in corruption, it is raised in incorruption: it is sown in weakness, it is raised in power.'

In any case, we need not puzzle our wits to find a time and place for it within the universe, because, in the end of time, that universe 'shall be rolled together as a scroll' (that is, as a reader shuts up a volume when he has finished with it), and God will write a new book.

From 'The Great Mystery' by Dorothy Sayers

Reflections

* Dorothy Sayers organises her argument about the Christian heaven and hell in four parts:

- first, that the concepts of 'time' and 'space' are created by humans;
- second, that God's 'time' and 'space' are very different: they go beyond human understanding;
- third, that hell exists only for those who will it to exist;
- fourth, that there is a great gulf between what humans understand by the word 'universe' and what the Christian God's view of it must be.

Such arguments, of course, are pinned upon her faith as a Christian. Her faith is important to her. It helps her come to terms with the ever-present question in our lives: 'Is there life after death'?

Muslims, Buddhists and members of other faiths – as well as atheists – see the answer to this question in different ways. What is interesting for us to reflect on is how important and fundamental a question it appears to be for all humankind. For many scientists and philosophers it remains *the* great unanswered question.

8 Is there a God?

Introduction

One of the fundamental questions throughout human history has been: 'Is there a God'?

Different religions of the world interpret this question differently. Many will answer that there *is* one God – theirs.

Many people believe that there is no God – they are called *atheists*. *Agnostics* do not believe in a particular god, but neither do they deny that there might be one.

There are many others who are not sure or who have not made up their minds. You may be someone who believes strongly in a particular God, or you may be an atheist or agnostic.

One famous twentieth century playwright called Samuel Beckett wrote a play titled *Waiting for Godot*. It tells the story of two men who spend the whole play – nearly two hours – standing on a stage, not doing much, but waiting for God to arrive. He doesn't.

The first of the readings that follow comes from the opening of the play. The second comes from its closing lines.

Reading

Waiting for Godot (preferably, two readers)

Act 1

> *Estragon, sitting on a low mound, is trying to take off his boot. He pulls at it with both hands, panting. He gives up, exhausted, rests, tries again. As before.*
> *Enter Vladimir.*

ESTRAGON: (*giving up again*). Nothing to be done.

VLADIMIR: (*advancing with short, stiff strides, legs wide apart*). I'm beginning to come round to that opinion. All my life I've tried to put it from me, saying, Vladimir, be reasonable, you haven't yet tried everything. And I resumed the struggle. (*He broods, musing on the struggle. Turning to Estragon.*) So there you are again.

ESTRAGON: Am I?

VLADIMIR: I'm glad to see you back. I thought you were gone for ever.

ESTRAGON: Me too.

VLADIMIR: Together again at last! We'll have to celebrate this. But how? (*He reflects.*) Get up till I embrace you.

ESTRAGON: (*irritably*). Not now, not now.

VLADIMIR: (*hurt, coldly*). May one enquire where His Highness spent the night?

ESTRAGON: In a ditch.

VLADIMIR: (*admiringly*). A ditch! Where?

ESTRAGON: (*without gesture*). Over there.

VLADIMIR: And they didn't beat you?

ESTRAGON: Beat me? Certainly they beat me.

VLADIMIR: The same lot as usual?

ESTRAGON: The same? I don't know.

VLADIMIR: When I think of it . . . all these years . . . but for me . . . where would you be . . .? (*Decisively.*) You'd be nothing more than a little heap of bones at the present minute, no doubt about it.

ESTRAGON: And what of it?

VLADIMIR: (*gloomily*). It's too much for one man. (*Pause. Cheerfully.*) On the other hand what's the good of losing heart now, that's what I say. We should have thought of it a million years ago, in the nineties.

ESTRAGON: Ah stop blathering and help me off with this bloody thing.

VLADIMIR: Hand in hand from the top of the Eiffel Tower, among the first. We were presentable in those days. Now it's too late. They wouldn't even let us up. (*Estragon tears at his boot.*) What are you doing?

ESTRAGON: Taking off my boot. Did that never happen to you?

VLADIMIR: Boots must be taken off every day, I'm tired telling you that. Why don't you listen to me?

ESTRAGON: (*feebly*). Help me!

Act II

ESTRAGON: What's wrong with you?

VLADIMIR: Nothing.

ESTRAGON: I'm going.

VLADIMIR: So am I.

ESTRAGON: Was I long asleep?

VLADIMIR: I don't know.
Silence.

ESTRAGON: Where shall we go?

VLADIMIR: Not far.

ESTRAGON: Oh yes, let's go far away from here.

VLADIMIR: We can't.

ESTRAGON: Why not?

VLADIMIR: We have to come back tomorrow.

ESTRAGON: What for?

VLADIMIR: To wait for Godot.

ESTRAGON: Ah! (*Silence.*) He didn't come?

VLADIMIR: No.

ESTRAGON: And now it's too late.

VLADIMIR: Yes, now it's night.

ESTRAGON: And if we dropped him? (*Pause.*) If we dropped him?

VLADIMIR: He'd punish us. (*Silence. He looks at the tree.*) Everything's dead but the tree.

ESTRAGON: (*looking at the tree*). What is it?

VLADIMIR: It's the tree.

ESTRAGON: Yes, but what kind?

VLADIMIR: I don't know. A willow.
Estragon draws Vladimir towards the tree. They stand motionless before it. Silence.

ESTRAGON: Why don't we hang ourselves?

VLADIMIR: With what?

ESTRAGON: You haven't got a bit of rope?

VLADIMIR: No.

ESTRAGON: Then we can't.
            Silence.

VLADIMIR: Let's go.

ESTRAGON: Wait, there's my belt.

VLADIMIR: It's too short.

ESTRAGON: You could hang on to my legs.

VLADIMIR: And who'd hang on to mine?

ESTRAGON: True.

VLADIMIR: Show all the same. (*Estragon loosens the cord that holds up his trousers which, much too big for him, fall about his ankles. They look at the cord.*) It might do at a pinch. But is it strong enough?

ESTRAGON: We'll soon see. Here.
            They each take an end of the cord and pull. It breaks. They almost fall.

VLADIMIR: Not worth a curse.
            Silence.

ESTRAGON: You say we have to come back tomorrow?

VLADIMIR: Yes.

ESTRAGON: Then we can bring a good bit of rope.

VLADIMIR: Yes.
            Silence.

ESTRAGON: Didi.

VLADIMIR: Yes.

ESTRAGON: I can't go on like this.

VLADIMIR: That's what you think.

ESTRAGON: If we parted? That might be better for us.

VLADIMIR: We'll hang ourselves tomorrow. (*Pause.*) Unless Godot comes.

ESTRAGON: And if he comes?

VLADIMIR: We'll be saved.
            Vladimir takes off his hat (Lucky's), peers inside it, feels about inside it, shakes it, knocks on the crown, puts it on again.

ESTRAGON: Well? Shall we go?

VLADIMIR: Pull on your trousers.

ESTRAGON: What?

VLADIMIR: Pull on your trousers.

ESTRAGON: You want me to pull off my trousers?

VLADIMIR: Pull on your trousers.

ESTRAGON: (*realizing his trousers are down*). True. *He pulls up his trousers.*

VLADIMIR: Well? Shall we go?

ESTRAGON: Yes, let's go.
            They do not move.

CURTAIN

From 'Waiting for Godot' by Samuel Beckett

Reflections

* Samuel Beckett wrote the play as a dramatic exploration of the question 'Is there a God?'

The play is concerned with the nature of faith and belief. It also focuses on the absurdity of human existence. Nothing ever happens!

It is a play which makes us think about the 'big' questions in our world, about such matters as life after death and the reason why we are on this earth.

What are your reflections on this subject?

* *Hebrews 11: 1–6*

Now faith is being sure of what we hope for and certain of what we do not see. This is what the ancients were commended for.

By faith we understand that the universe was formed at God's command, so that what is seen was not made out of what was visible.

By faith Abel offered God a better sacrifice than Cain did. By faith he was commended as a righteous man, when God spoke well of his offerings. And by faith he still speaks, even though he is dead.

By faith Enoch was taken from this life, so that he did not experience death; he could not be found, because God had taken him away. For before he was taken, he was commended as one who pleased God. And without faith it is impossible to please God, because anyone who comes to him must believe that he exists and that he rewards those who earnestly seek him.

9 Blasphemy

Introduction

The Satanic Verses, a novel by Salman Rushdie, was published in 1988. Shortly afterward, he was attacked as someone who had committed blasphemy against the Muslim faith. The Muslim community in Iran went as far as issuing a death threat, and the author was forced into hiding.

Publishers of the book received hate mail and threatening phone calls, death threats and bomb scares. Bookshops selling the book were threatened and actually fire-bombed.

Rarely has a book caused such a reaction.

The author himself has said it's all a question of free speech and faith.

In the following newspaper article he sets out his views on the furore caused by *The Satanic Verses*.

Reading

In good faith

The Satanic Verses is, I profoundly hope, work of radical dissent and questioning and re-imagining. It is not, however, the book it has been made out to be, that book containing 'nothing but filth and insults and abuse' that has brought people out on to the streets across the world.

That book simply does not exist.

This is what I want to say to the great mass of ordinary, decent, fair-minded

Muslims, of the sort I have known all my life, and who have provided much of the inspiration for my work: to be rejected and reviled by, so to speak, one's own characters is a shocking and painful experience for any writer. I recognise that many Muslims have felt shocked and pained, too. Perhaps a way forward might be found through the mutual recognition of that mutual pain. Let us attempt to believe in each other's good faith.

I am aware that this is asking a good deal. There has been too much name-calling. Muslims have been called savages and barbarians and worse. I, too, have received my share of invective. Yet I still believe – perhaps I must – that under-standing remains possible, and can be achieved without the suppression of the principle of free speech.

What it requires is a moment of good will; a moment in which we may all accept that the other parties are acting, have acted, in good faith.

You see, it's my opinion that if we could only dispose of the 'insults and abuse' accusation, which prevents those who believe it from accepting that *The Satanic Verses* is a work of any serious intent or merit whatsoever, then we might be able, at the very least, to agree to differ about the book's real themes, about the relative value of the sacred and the profane, about the merits of purity and those of hotch-potch, and about how human beings really become whole: through the love of God or through the love of their fellow men and women.

In the meantime, I am asked, how do I feel? I feel grateful to the British government for defending me. I hope that such a defence would be made available to any citizen so threatened, but that doesn't lessen my gratitude. I needed it, and it was provided.

I feel grateful, too, to my protectors, who have done such a magnificent job, and who have become my friends.

I feel grateful to everyone who has offered me support. The one real gain for me in this bad time has been the discovery of being cared for by so many people. the only antidote to hatred is love.

Above all, I feel gratitude towards, solidarity with and pride in all the publishing people and bookstore workers around the world who have held the line against intimidation, and who will, I am sure, continue to do so as long as it remains necessary.

I feel as if I have been plunged, like Alice, into the world beyond the looking-glass, where nonsense is the only available sense. And I wonder if I'll ever be able to climb back through the mirror.

Do I feel regret? Of course I do: regret that such offence has been taken against my work when it was not intended – when dispute was intended, and dissent, and even, at times, satire, and criticism of intolerance, and the like, but not the thing of which I'm most often accused, not 'filth', not 'insult', not 'abuse'. I regret that so many people who might have taken pleasure in finding their reality given pride of place in a novel will now not read it because of what they believe it to be, or will come to it with their minds already made up.

And I feel sad to be so grievously separated from my community, from India, from everyday life, from the world.

Please understand, however: I make no complaint. I am a writer. I do not accept my condition; I will strive to change it; but I inhabit it, I am trying to learn from it.

Our lives teach us who we are.

Salman Rushdie

Reflections

* The whole case illustrates the power of religion and faith in society. Rushdie writes: 'Let us attempt to believe in each other's good faith'. He clearly feels that he has been misrepresented.

It also illustrates intolerance on a large scale, together with the fact that in British Law, blasphemy only applies to Christianity, although we live in a society with many, many faiths.

It is important that we uphold freedom of speech. It is equally important that we respect one another's cultures and faiths.

The case presented by *The Satanic Verses* shows that some cases just do not have simple right and wrong answers. As Rushdie writes at the end of his piece: 'Our lives teach us who we are.'

* *Mark 4: 35–41*

That day when evening came, he said to his disciples, 'Let us go over to the other side'. Leaving the crowd behind, they took him along, just as he was, in the boat. There were also other boats with him. A furious squall came up, and the waves broke over the boat, so that it was nearly swamped. Jesus was in the stern, sleeping on a cushion. The disciples woke him and said to him, 'Teacher, don't you care if we drown?'

He got up, rebuked the wind and said to the waves, 'Quiet! Be still!' Then the wind died down and it was completely calm.

He said to his disciples, 'Why are you so afraid? Do you still have no faith?' They were terrified and asked each other, 'Who is this? Even the wind and the waves obey him!'

10 Having a vision

Introduction

Throughout history there have always been individuals who have had a particular vision, either for themselves or for those around them. For example, the vision of the ancient Egyptian King Menes around 3000 BC led to the growth of the magnificent early civilisations of the Nile. The vision of the Ming dynasty enabled China to develop an advanced way of life in the 14th and 15th centuries. In the 20th century the vision of the Japanese people immediately after the second world war ended in 1945 has led to their amazing industrial and commerical success as the 21st century approaches.

In England, in the late 18th century, a poet and artist by the name of William Blake saw around him poverty and deprivation which he believed should be removed from England, and London in particular.

The following two poems set down both the poverty he saw and his vision of a better land. You may recognise the second one as a popular hymns.

Reading

London

I wander thro' each charter'd street,
Near where the charter'd Thames does flow
And mark in every face I meet
Marks of weakness, marks of woe.

In every cry of every Man,
In every Infants cry of fear,
In every voice; in every ban,
The mind-forg'd manacles I hear

How the Chimney-sweepers cry
Every blackning Church appalls,
And the hapless Soldiers sigh
Runs in blood down Palace walls

But most thro' midnight streets I hear
How the youthful Harlots curse
Blasts the new-born Infants tear
And blights with plagues the Marriage hearse

William Blake

Jerusalem

And did those feet in ancient time
  Walk upon England's mountains green?
And was the holy Lamb of God
  On England's pleasant pasture seen?

And did the countenance divine
  Shine forth upon our clouded hills?
And was Jerusalem builded here
  Among these dark Satanic mills?

Bring me my bow of burning gold,
  Bring me my arrows of desire,
Bring me my spear, O clouds, unfold!
  Bring me my chariot of fire!

I will not cease from mental fight,
  Nor shall my sword sleep in my hand,
Till we have built Jerusalem
  In England's green and pleasant land.

William Blake

Reflections

* Both these poems offer challenging ideas. 'Jerusalem' sets forth a vision of
  improvement for 18th century England as the poet knew it, in language which
  stirs everyone who has read or sung it.

It is important, occasionally, to put out of mind the trivial aspects of our lives and think about the future and what it might have in store for us, or what we might plan to do. For many people, personal or religious faith guides them in that planning. For others, having a vision *and* seeking to achieve it is important. In society at large we are often dependent on those individuals who have a vision for their community, whether that is the scientist, the inventor, the religious leader, the politician or the poet.

Schools, of course, contain tomorrow's vision-makers. Our own thoughts should sometimes be with them – and with our own personal visions.

11 Acting in good faith

Introduction

What do we mean when we say that we are 'acting in good faith'? Do we mean that we are being true to ourselves, to our conscience, to our principles? Do we mean simply that we are doing our best, given a certain situation?

A dictionary definition of the word 'faith' offers: 'strong or unshakeable belief in something, especially without proof or evidence'. The following reading focuses on issues of faith, belief, proof and evidence.

It is taken from a very moving play entitled *Whose Life Is It Anyway?*. Ken, a man paralysed from the neck down, seeks to persuade those who are nursing him 24 hours a day that he should be allowed to die. He repeatedly requests that the doctors and nurses should not care for him, but should discharge him from hospital.

At this point, near the end of the play, an independent judge has been called in to decide whether Ken should be granted his request for 'mercy killing'.

Reading

Whose Life Is It Anyway?

KEN: Of course I want to live but as far as I am concerned, I'm dead already. I merely require the doctors to recognise the fact. I cannot accept this condition constitutes life in any real sense at all.

JUDGE: Certainly, you're alive legally.

KEN: I think I could challenge even that.

JUDGE: How?

KEN: Any reasonable definition of life must include the idea of its being self-supporting. I seem to remember something in the papers – when all the heart transplant controversy was on – about it being alright to take someone's heart if they require constant attention from respirators and so on to keep them alive.

JUDGE: There also has to be absolutely no brain activity at all. Yours is certainly working.

KEN: It is and sanely.

JUDGE: That is the question to be decided.

KEN: My Lord, I am not asking anyone to kill me. I am only asking to be discharged from this hospital.

JUDGE: It comes to the same thing.

KEN: Then that proves my point; not just the fact that I will spend the rest of my life in hospital, but that whilst I am here, everything is geared just to keeping my brain active, with no real possibility of it ever being able to direct anything. As far as I can see, that is an act of deliberate cruelty.

JUDGE: Surely, it would be more cruel if society let people die, when it could, with some effort, keep them alive.

KEN: No, not *more* cruel, *just* as cruel.

JUDGE: Then why should the hospital let you die – if it is just as cruel?

KEN: The cruelty doesn't reside in saving someone or allowing them to die. It resides in the fact that the choice is removed from the man concerned.

JUDGE: But a man who is very desperately depressed is not capable of making a reasonable choice.

KEN: As you said, my Lord, that is the question to be decided.

JUDGE: Alright. You tell me why it is a reasonable choice that you decide to die.

KEN: It is a question of dignity. Look at me here. I can do nothing, not even the basic primitive functions. I cannot even urinate, I have a permanent catheter attached to me. Every few days my bowels are washed out. Every few hours two nurses have to turn me over or I would rot away from bedsores. Only my brain functions unimpaired but even that is futile because I can't act on any conclusions it comes to. This hearing proves that. Will you please listen.

JUDGE: I am listening.

KEN: I choose to acknowledge the fact that I am in fact dead and I find the hospital's persistent effort to maintain this shadow of life an indignity and it's inhumane.

JUDGE: But wouldn't you agree that many people with appalling physical handicaps have overcome them and lived essentially creative, dignified lives?

KEN: Yes, I would, but the dignity starts with their choice. If I choose to live, it would be appalling if society killed me. If I choose to die, it is equally appalling if society keeps me alive.

JUDGE: I cannot accept that it is undignified for society to devote resources to keeping someone alive. Surely it enhances that society.

KEN: It is not undignified if the man wants to stay alive, but I must restate that the dignity starts with his choice. Without it, it is degrading because technology has taken over from human will. My Lord, if I cannot be a man, I do not wish to be a medical achievement.

From 'Whose Life is it Anyway?' by Brian Clark

Reflections

* Where do your sympathies lie?
  Both Ken and the doctors are acting in what they believe to be good faith; the Judge will wish to do the same, weighing up the evidence on both sides. What will he decide?
  In the end he adjudicates as follows:
  'I am satisfied that Mr Ken Harrison is a brave and cool man who is in complete control of his faculties and I shall therefore make an order for him to be set free.'
  Such a decision offers a challenge to those whose faith would say that 'mercy

killing' goes against the laws of Nature. They would argue that this is a verdict, not in good faith, but in *bad* faith.

Others might argue that if Ken wishes to follow his personal faith and let himself die, that is for him to decide.

What do *you* think?

* *Matthew 7: 7–12*

'Ask and it will be given to you; seek and you will find; knock and the door will be opened to you. For everyone who asks receives; he who seeks finds; and to him who knocks, the door will be opened.

Which of you, if his son asks for bread, will give him a stone? Or if he asks for a fish, will give him a snake? If you, then, though you are evil, know how to give good gifts to your children, how much more will your Father in heaven give good gifts to those who ask him! So in everything, do to others what you would have them do to you, for this sums up the Law and the Prophets.'

12 Six religions of the world

Note

The purpose of this section is to offer background information on six of the world's major religions. Those leading the assembly will want to select from the material and design their own Reflections, as appropriate.

For example, the Readings may be linked with particular festival days in the course of the school year.

Introduction

We live in a predominantly Christian country and culture. The symbols of Christianity are everywhere – in the art, architecture, literature and music of Britain.

Yet the history of these islands is one of many comings and goings. Many hundreds of years ago, waves of invaders (Romans, Anglo-Saxons, Vikings, Normans . . .) imposed their language and belief systems on the people of Britain.

In the 20th century people have come to Britain from Ireland, Germany, the West Indies, India, Pakistan and many other countries. These people have brought with them their religions, languages and traditions to enrich British culture.

Britain is a multi-cultural society. It is important, therefore, that we all study and try to understand the religions which are practised by our neighbours and millions of people throughout the world.

Each of the following passages introduces us to a major world religion through descriptions of its:

- origins
- places of worship
- scriptures
- festivals

Readings
(With acknowledgements to Helen Blythe)

Buddhism

- Buddhism began in North India in the sixth century BC. Although it is usually said that Siddhartha Gautama is the founder of Buddhism in fact Buddhists would say that the Buddha discovered the truth about the way things are – the DHARMA. Thus DHARMA (truth), is the foundation of Buddhism. There are a number of different ways of following Buddhism. The Buddhism of Sri Lanka, Burma and Thailand keeps to the original teaching of the Buddha – this way is called THERAVADA. China, Japan and North India follow the MAHAYANA. This claims that there is more than one path which has grown from the original teaching of the Buddha. The Zen school is within the MAHAYANA. Tibetan Buddhists belong to the VAJRAYANA.
- It is not obligatory for a Buddhist to worship as part of a community so there is often a shrine or meditation room in the home. In traditional Buddhist countries, however, people might visit the temple daily. In Britain they often go to the VIHARA weekly. Most Buddhists would try to go to the VIHARA for special festivals.
- The VIHARA contains a shrine room which has an image (or several) of the Buddha. The image is usually raised so that it can easily be seen by everyone. There is often a raised platform for members of the SAN-GHA (the monastic community). The shrines are very colourful, with flowers to honour the Buddha, candles, incense, water and music. A bell sometimes replaces the music. Some VIHARAS also contain a meditation room which is simpler and has space for both walking and sitting meditation.
- Buddhists regard the study of the Scriptures as important but recommend that they should be explained by living teachers. Texts are put in shrine rooms and meditation rooms below the images of the Buddha. The THERAVADAN scriptures are called the PALI CANON (or TRIPITAKA). The MAHAYANA and VAJRAYANA scriptures include the PALI CANON but have additional material.
- Buddhists will usually have a place in the home where they keep an image of the Buddha or a picture – but it is regarded as sacred, never as an ornament. Preferably it is placed in the highest room in the house, or kept on a top shelf. Prayers can be said anywhere but the best time is early in the morning. Prayer beads and prayer wheels are used. Meditation is an important part of the Buddhist's life. There are two main kinds of meditation – the VIPASSANA (insight) develops the concentrated mind to see things as they really are, and SAMATHA (calm) is the stability and concentration of a peaceful mind.

Christianity

- Christianity began as a movement within Judaism. The first Christians were Jews who worshipped in the Temple at Jerusalem and in the synagogues. Jesus was a good Jew who worshipped in the temple and the synagogue and kept the festivals. Much of his teaching could be accepted by the Jews but his refusal to disclaim that he was the Messiah and would establish the Kingdom of God, could not be tolerated by them. Jesus was arrested, tried and crucified. The Gospel stories include details of these events and of his disciples' accounts of how he rose from the dead after three days and was seen by them, and that they were present when he ascended into heaven from the Mount of Olives. Christians believe that through Jesus, God showed his love for all people and reestablished his covenant, not only with the Jews but with all humanity.

- The buildings where Christians worship are called churches (sometimes chapels). The principal church of a diocese is called a cathedral. There is tremendous variety of worship even between churches of the same denomination. The main meeting for worship takes place on a Sunday. While there is great diversity of forms of worship with in the churches there are two main kinds of service – one is sacramental (based on the Last Supper or the Eucharist), the other is non-sacramental (based on the reading of the Bible).
- The Scriptures include the whole of the Jewish Bible, and the New Testament, which is a collection of books written by early Christians. The Christian Bible is almost always used in worship, except for the meetings of the Society of Friends (the Quakers). The Friends believe that the Spirit of God is in everyone and although they will refer to the Bible and sometimes read from it, they prefer to listen to the word of God from within a person.
- The three most important festivals in the Christian church are Christmas, Easter and Pentecost (Whitsun). Christmas celebrates the birth of Christ, Easter celebrates the death and resurrection, and Pentecost the coming of the Holy Spirit. Most Christians observe Lent – a period of forty days before Easter – in some form or other. Traditionally it is a time of fasting and penance.
- The Christian church recognises membership through baptism (christening) which in the beginning was received by those old enough to profess the Christian faith. For centuries it has been widely administered in infancy. Confirmation is a way of remembering baptism and in most churches is necessary before taking part in the Eucharist.

Islam

- Islam originated in the Middle East in the seventh century CE. The founder of Islam is the prophet Mohammed who was born in Mecca in Saudi Arabia in 570 CE. Mohammed rejected the worship of the moon and many gods made of stone and wood. Whilst travelling he met many Christians who believed in one God, and one day he had a vision of the angel Gabriel which led him to later begin preaching (about 610 CE). His message was that there was one God and that people should live as brothers and be compassionate towards one another. Islam has ten basic principles which every Muslim must follow – the Pillars of faith:

  1 Belief in one God.
  2 Belief in the Angels.
  3 Belief in many prophets but one message.
  4 Belief in the Day of Judgement.
  5 Belief in the QADAR (the timeless knowledge of God).
  6 The Creed (ASH-SHAHADAH).
  7 Prayer five times daily (SALAT).
  8 Payment of ZAKAT (an obligation to give away a portion of your wealth).

9 SIYAM (fasting during RAMADAN).

10 HAJJ (pilgrimage to Mecca – every Muslim hopes to go to Mecca once for HAJJ).

- Muslims meet for worship in the mosque. The mosque is primarily a place for worship, in particular Friday prayers, and it is built to face Mecca. When entering a mosque you should remove your shoes and cover your head. Outside the room used for worship there are facilities for washing the hands and feet. The mosque is also a school – children will often go there daily during the evening. It is also a meeting place for the community. The religious leader is called an IMAM, and he teaches and leads prayers. Men and boys will attend the mosque whenever they can for prayers, but they will make a special effort on a Friday for the midday prayers. Women usually pray at home.
- The QUR'AN is the name given to the Muslim scriptures. It is treated with great reverence both in the mosque and in the home. Most Muslim children learn to read the QUR'AN in Arabic and some learn it by heart. The QUR'AN contains many references to the Jewish Prophets of the Old Testament and to Jesus and his mother Mary. There are no statues or pictures in the mosque, but there are often geometrical designs and beautiful calligraphy on the walls.
- The Month of RAMADAN – a time of fasting for Muslims – is followed by the festival of EID-UL-FITR. The festival begins after the sighting of the new moon. Men and boys will worship in the mosque and then there will be parties and the exchange of presents. Giving to the poor is an important part of EID-UL-FITR.

Hinduism

- The word 'Hindu' comes from 'Sindhu' which means river. The river Indus gets its name from the word. The Persians called India 'the land beyond the Sindhu', and pronounced the word Hindu. The name was first used to describe people who lived in India and then gradually came to describe the faith of the people as well.
- A notable feature of Hinduism is that it does not originate from one prophet or teacher. The earliest record of Hindu teaching is found in the VEDAS (c 3000 BC) but many authorities believe Hinduism is as old as the universe, being based upon the eternal truths which have no mental source. Hinduism is not a religion as such, but DHARMA – i.e. the code of life. For Hindus, ultimately there is only one God, the creator and father of all beings, who is known by different names.
- The different denominations of Hinduism fall within three main groups:-

VAISHNAVISM – the worship of KRISHNA and his incarnations
SHAIVISM   – worship of SHIVA
SHAKTAS   – those who worship KALI.

The all embracing nature of Hinduism often appears confusing, but despite external variety, much philosophy is common for all Hindus – 'For the soul, there is never birth nor death. Nor having once been, does it ever cease to be. It is unborn ever-existing, undying and primeval. It is not slain when the body is slain.' (BHAGAVAD – GITA).

- For Hindus worship (PUJA) is an integral part of their daily life. The home is an important place for worship and there will be a place set apart for this. This area will have pictures and images of one or more Gods and it will be decorated with flowers, lights and tinsel. The mother is usually the member of the family who performs PUJA – early in the morning and evening. At the small shrine or altar a ghee lamp is lit and a small chanting ceremony is performed. The worship may take a variety of forms – giving incense, light or flowers to the statue, washing or decorating it, or offering food and praying. The statue is looked upon as a representation of God and is not worshipped for itself. Food which is offered to God is called PRASAD and Hindus believe that God has provided the food, therefore it should be offered to him first. In keeping with the principle of non-violence and the offering of food, all Hindus are usually vegetarian or even vegan.

Prayers are often said on the way to work, particularly the GAYATRI MANTRA – 'Let us meditate on the most excellent light of the Creator. May he guide our minds and inspire us with the understanding'. (From the Rigveda 3, 62, 10.)

- In India, Temples (MANDIR) vary from the large and ornate to the small and simple. The shrine (GARBAGRIHA) is at one end of the room. On it there are fruit and flowers which have been offered, ghee, incense sticks, KUMKUM (the red paste which is put on the forehead), a five-fold lamp, bells and somewhere to put monetary offering. Shoes are left outside the shrine room. In England, the temple is usually a converted building and will serve as a meeting place for Hindus as well as a place for worship. Hindus visit a temple as often as possible – preferably daily, but in England this is not always possible. Apart from daily ceremonies, many rituals are performed in the temple – e.g. marriage; the giving of first solid food to a baby; the first hair-cutting of a male child, etc. Before leaving the temple it is customary for people to receive PRASAD – the blessed food.

Judaism

- The synagogue is the name given to the building where Jews worship. Originally it meant a congregation of worshippers. Together with the home it is a focal point of spiritual training. The synagogue became an important institution after the destruction of the Temple in Jerusalem in 70 CE.

  The main feature of the synagogue is the Ark of the Covenant (ARON HAKODESH) which is an alcove or cupboard concealed by a curtain. The scrolls of the TORA are kept in the ARK, and it faces towards Jerusalem. In many synagogues the Ten Commandments are written above the Ark. In front of the Ark a perpetual light shines (NER TAMID). This is a reminder of the seven-branched candlestick (MENORAH) which burned continuously in the Temple in Jerusalem. There is a raised platform (BIMAH), usually in the centre of the synagogue. Readings from the Bible take place on this. There are no images or pictures. At Orthodox services men sit separately from women and cover their heads.

- The Rabbi is the chief official of the Jewish congregation, though not all synagogues have a Rabbi. Where there is a Rabbi he usually acts as preacher, teacher and lawyer.

- The main services of the week are the Sabbath morning service and Friday evening. The Jewish Sabbath begins traditionally at sundown on Friday though this is not always possible to observe in Britain. The Sabbath is a day of rest but it is also a day when families do things together. The Sabbath begins with the lighting of candles in the home and it ends with a ceremony of candles, wine and

spices (HAVDALH), which emphasises the distinction between the sacred Sabbath and the secular weekdays.
- The majority of Jews in Britain belong to an Orthodox synagogue, although they may not be Orthodox themselves. The orthodox Jew accepts the views of God as developed in the bible and the Rabbinic writings of the Talmud and Midrash. He does not believe that any law or ceremony can be changed or abolished. There are other Jews who believe that change and development within Judaism is necessary from time to time and they accept reform of ideas and practices. Non-Orthodox Jews are known as Reform, Liberal or Progressive Jews.
- The main festivals which Jews celebrate are ROSH HASHANAH or New Year – which is in September or October. YOM KIPPUR – the Day of Atonement – is the holiest day of the Jewish year and it is a day of fasting. This is followed a few days later by SUCCOT – Tabernacles – which is a joyful festival. CHANUKAH is a festival of light and is held in December. PURIM is a spring festival and celebrates deliverance as does the best known of Jewish festivals PESACH (passover).

Sikhism

- Sikhism began in the Punjab area of North India in the fifteenth century, CE. It has more in common with Hinduism than with the other faiths since it originated and developed within it. Hindus and Sikhs will still share each other's festivals. Belief in one God is basic to Sikhism. Family life is central to the faith and there is a strong commitment to working hard and sharing with the poor.
- There are five symbols of the Sikh faith known as the five Ks. These are the:

  - KESH, the uncut hair and beard,
  - KANGA, the comb,
  - KARA, the steel wrist band,
  - KACCHA, the short trousers,
  - KIRPAN, the sword.

  These five symbols are worn after the initiation ceremony, which often takes place at the festival of BAISAKHI – a festival which could be regarded as the birthday of Sikhism. Sikh men take the name SINGH and women take the name KAUR.
- The Sikh place of worship is called a GURDWARA – the house of the Guru. It is where the Holy Scriptures of the Sikhs – the GURU GRANTH SAHIB is kept. The GURDWARA may be in a house or it may be a purpose built building or an adapted one.
  Visitors are always welcome to a GURDWARA but they should take off their shoes and cover their heads before they go into the hall or room where worship is taking place. They should not carry cigarettes or tobacco. Men and women sit separately, cross-legged on the floor and they should not point their feet in the direction of the GURU GRANTH SAHIB. There is a raised platform at one end of the room and the GURU GRANTH SAHIB is placed on this, under a canopy. During worship a reader (GRANTHI) sits behind the GURU GRANTH SAHIB with a CHAURI in his hand – a symbol of royalty. The CHAURI is made of peacock feathers tied together or of nylon or yak hairs embedded in wood or metal. The GRANTHI waves the CHAURI from time to time over the GURU GRANTH SAHIB.

- The GURDWARA always has a LANGAR attached to it. This is a free kitchen where everyone is welcome to sit and share a meal, irrespective of their creed or their status. Everyone is equal and people sit at long tables down the room. The meal is provided by members of the Sikh community who take turns to cook and serve it.
- Private meditation is very important for Sikhs and this should begin early in the morning, preferably after a bath or shower. If it is not possible to pray early in the morning then another time should be found. Both private prayer and public worship are an obligation. Sikhism is a community of followers and whole families worship together on a Sunday.

Our Global Village

1 Commonwealth

Introduction

The British Commonwealth of Nations was first declared in 1931. The Commonwealth family now includes some 50 member states, representing over one billion people, and one quarter of the land surface of the globe.

The Commonwealth has faced some testing moments in its history, particularly when the leaders of its member states have not been able to agree over an international matter.

The leader of the Commonwealth is the British monarch. We live in an era where people are questioning the role of the British monarchy more and more frequently. Many people feel that Britain no longer needs a King or Queen.

In the following passages the Queen gives her Commonwealth Day message for 1990.

Reading

Commonwealth Day Message 1990

Every year, when we celebrate Commonwealth Day, it reminds me that we are celebrating something which is quite unique. Nothing quite like the Commonwealth has ever been created or evolved before. Its comparative lack of rules, its human richness and its geographical diversity, make the Commonwealth as hard to define as it is easy to criticise.

The members of any family, and that is what the Commonwealth most nearly resembles, will vary widely in age, appearance, tastes, talents and temperament. From time to time they will hold some very different opinions. Yet members of a family have no difficulty in recognising each other as relations, and in putting a value upon their kinship. They are able to sum one another up with both realism *and* affection. They appreciate each other's special qualities. Above all, they have learned to feel at home with each other. So have we in the Commonwealth.

It is a feature of our association that we learn from each other and influence each other, but do not expect to agree on everything all the time. In the last resort, there is no compulsion to conform. If we are sometimes critical of each other, or disappointed, it is because we expect more of members of our family than we do of others. Now and then a member may even feel constrained to go off on his own. Some years ago this happened to Pakistan for example. Yet today we have the joy of having Pakistan back in the family. This illustrates perfectly the nature of the underlying bond which distinguishes the Commonwealth from all other international organisations.

The Commonwealth has other strengths too. One of them is that it appeals to the young as much as to the old, to peoples and nations at all phases of political, economic, cultural and social development, to reformers and lovers of tradition alike.

Another strength of the Commonwealth is the multiplicity of strands that bind us together. We should remember that the Commonwealth relationship is not limited to the contacts between political leaders. Each and every national organisation and profession seems to have its Commonwealth counterpart. They give it life and diversity and map out the paths of its future achievements.

On Commonwealth Day especially we greet each other as members of the biggest and most unusual family on earth.

ELIZABETH R.

Reflections

* This speech clearly reflects the fact that the Commonwealth nations had that year been experiencing some differences in opinion. The Queen says firmly that she believes there is a place, always for 'uniting all differences intact'. The Commonwealth represents many, many countries. All communities – schools, hospitals, prisons, countries – depend on being able to sort out differences within a framework of rules and regulations. We should always try to find solutions to difficulties when they present themselves within a community.

  We may not always agree with one another *today* – but *tomorrow* and the next day we have to live and work together.

* *Romans 12: 9–18*

  Love must be sincere. Hate what is evil; cling to what is good. Be devoted to one another in brotherly love. Honour one another above yourselves. Never be lacking in zeal, but keep your spiritual fervour, serving the Lord. Be joyful in hope, patient in affliction, faithful in prayer. Share with God's people who are in need. Practise hospitality.

  Bless those who persecute you; bless and do not curse. Rejoice with those who rejoice; mourn with those who mourn. Live in harmony with one another. Do not be proud, but be willing to associate with people of low position. Do not be conceited. Do not repay anyone evil for evil. Be careful to do what is right in the eyes of everybody. If it is possible, as far as it depends on you, live at peace with everyone.

2 Poverty

Introduction

We live in a society which manages to feed, house and clothe almost all of its citizens – at least in a basic way. Of course some people have great wealth, others live comfortably, while others still live on or below the poverty line. But our society is very rich in comparison with others around the world. There are beggars in our society – we can see them in city doorways, or sleeping rough in parks and alleys. But in some countries there are thousands – even millions – of beggars. And, sadly, many of them are children.

Reading

Helping the wealthy to find a way to heaven

NEW DELHI – What do you do about India's beggars? 'Run them over,' one of my more intemperate friends suggested. He spoke more from weariness than spite. Though the throng of melancholy mendicants is a great Indian tragedy, it is hard, if you live here, to maintain a convincing pose of concern.

The trouble is that there are simply too many beggars, and dealing with them becomes the sickest of jokes. 'We were walking in Calcutta,' another friend told me. 'All of a sudden we saw in front of us this hideous stump, a legless torso and misshapen head. It was riding a skateboard down the pavement, beaming wildly, its arms out-stretched.' Suddenly seized by shame and revulsion, my friend sought the only possible escape from a legless beggar riding a skateboard. He ran up some stairs.

Everyone has their favourite beggar's story. An Indian journalist I know claims to have been approached by a man who thrust a piece of paper in his hand. It announced the bearer as mute, with the words: 'I am deaf and dumb and can get no work.' The journalist pocketed the paper and went on his way. 'Give me my paper back,' the dumb beggar shrieked.

My own worst experience occurred in New Delhi. I was reading a newspaper in the back of a taxi waiting at traffic lights. I heard a faint sound. I looked up to see a leper wiping the bandaged stump of his arm across my window. The bandage was soaked in blood and pus. It left a repulsive stain across the glass. My second thought (the first was 'Ugh') was that this leper seriously needed a change in tactics if he expected people like me to wind the window down.

I feel sad and ashamed that I have become so cruel. But like any other misery that you have to deal with daily, emotional responses are blunted by routine. The truth is that every time I stop at the traffic lights less than a quarter of a mile from my home, I know that my car will be approached by any one of a dozen beggars.

What do you do about India's beggars? I am indebted to Giriraj Agarwal, a journalist who lent me a copy of an-as-yet unpublished study he recently completed. According to statistics quoted in Mr Agarwal's research, there are at least 1.5 million Indians who beg for a living. Almost a third of them are crippled or handicapped in some way. Children beg because the alternative is often forced factory labour where they earn less than 15p for a 10-hour day. Despite continuing campaigns to eradicate child labour, the Indian Planning Commission estimates there are still 17.5 million children who are working.

Women beg because they are widows or abandoned wives, and are spurned not only by their husband's families, but their own. There are professional begging rings where children are deliberately disfigured to heighten the chances of gain. There are criminal begging rings, employing Dickensian child pick-pockets, prostitutes and drug-addicts. Mr Agarwal reports that a tenth of all beggars masquerade as *sadhus* – holy men collecting for some spuriously religious cause.

There are government schemes aimed at reducing the problem. In Delhi there are 12 homes where 3,000 beggars are provided with clothes and two meals a day. But what the city authorities advertise as vocational training sometimes turns into forced labour instead.

None of the government schemes has had much of an effect. Forced repatriation to rural areas has not worked. There are laws against begging, but they are rarely enforced. Mr Agarwal blames state agencies for allowing the problem to drift. He also blames those who make begging worthwhile. He concluded his study: 'As long as the people feel that the doors of heaven can be opened by giving alms or feeding beggars, this social evil will not stop'.

So what do you do about India's beggars? I only have one rule, and that is not to give anything to children. Why encourage them to get started on such a depressing way of life?

But I don't know what you do with India's beggars. I don't know of anybody who does.

Tony Allen-Mills

Reflections

* 'So what *do* you do about India's beggars?'
  This writer contrasts some of the funny accounts with some of the deeply disturbing stories of New Delhi's beggar army. You may find some of the humour here cruel. But it's there to make a point – a point of contrast.
  If you are a person with money in such a society the very presence of so many beggars must call you to question your own wealth.
  In our own community, whenever we see people without the basics for human life, it must make us reflect carefully on the nature of our society. For this observer, the plight of children is particularly distressing:
  'I only have one rule, and that is not to give anything to children. Why encourage them to get started on such a depressing way of life?'
  He is saying here that children and their attitudes are the key to the future of any society. But the situation in New Delhi remains – as he says at the end – one without a solution in sight:
  'I don't know what you do with India's beggars. I don't know of anybody who does.'

  It is a pessimistic conclusion – and one which must cause us to reflect upon our own national well-being, by way of contrast. What can countries like Britain do within the Global Village to relieve poverty elsewhere, poverty which we can, via satellite television, see in our living rooms as it happens?

* *Corinthians 1: 26–31*
  Brothers, think of what you were when you were called. Not many of you were wise by human standards; not many were influential; not many were of noble birth. But God chose the foolish things of the world to shame the wise; God chose the weak things of the world to shame the strong. He chose the lowly things of this world and the despised things – and the things that are not – to nullify the things that are, so that no-one may boast before him. It is because of him that you are in Christ Jesus, who has become for us wisdom from God – that is, our righteousness, holiness and redemption. Therefore, as it is written: 'Let him who boasts boast in the Lord'.

3 War (1)

Introduction

It is a sad fact of human life that, if you look back through the pages of history, war appears on just about every one, in one form or another.

If you look around the world today, many countries are locked in conflict. Why do countries fight each other? Why do groups within a country engage in civil war? Is it for territory? For human rights? For ideals? For religious differences?

In this century there have been two world wars. Both of them have had a significant impact on people living in Britain. And in part of Britain – Northern Ireland – a bitter conflict is still going on today.

The following passages and readings look at these three conflicts.

The First World War

Britain declared war on Germany on 4 August 1914. Many people thought the war would be over by Christmas, but it lasted until 1918. Troops from Britain, France, Italy, Russia and later the USA fought troops from Germany, Austro-Hungary and Turkey. There was fighting on land and sea, but the war is especially remembered for the trench warfare in western Europe. Ten million soldiers were killed and 21 million wounded in the war. On the first day of the Battle of the Somme (1 July 1916), 19,000 British troops were killed and 57,000 were wounded.

Some of the artists and writers involved in this war created images which still have the power to move and disturb us today. One of them was the poet Wilfred Owen, himself killed in the trenches in the closing days of the war in 1918. This poem tells of a gas attack:

Dulce et Decorum Est

Bent double, like old beggars under sacks,
Knock-kneed, coughing like hags, we cursed through sludge,
Till on the haunting flares we turned our backs
And towards our distant rest began to trudge.
Men marched asleep. Many had lost their boots
But limped on, blood-shod. All went lame; all blind;
Drunk with fatigue; deaf even to the hoots
Of gas shells dropping softly behind.

Gas! GAS! Quick, boys! – An ecstasy of fumbling,
Fitting the clumsy helmets just in time;
But someone still was yelling out and stumbling,
And flound'ring like a man in fire or lime ...
Dim, through the misty panes and thick green light,
As under a green sea, I saw him drowning.

In all my dreams, before my helpless sight,
He plunges at me, guttering, choking, drowning.

If in some smothering dreams you too could pace
Behind the wagon that we flung him in,
And watch the white eyes writhing in his face,

His hanging face, like a devil's sick of sin;
If you could hear, at every jolt, the blood
Come gargling from the froth-corrupted lungs,
Obscene as cancer, bitter as the cud
Of vile, incurable sores on innocent tongues, –
My friend, you would not tell with such high zest
To children ardent for some desperate glory,
The old Lie: Dulce et decorum est
Pro patria mori.*
(* It is sweet and fitting to die for your country.)

Wilfred Owen

The Second World War

The 1939–45 war was a global war, with fighting occurring across the world, on land, at sea and in the air. Tanks, aeroplanes and submarines were the machines of war. British troops were mostly involved in fighting in Europe, North Africa and the Far East. At home, cities were bombed, in what was called the Blitz. City children were evacuated – sent off to live in the country, away from the danger of bombs. The worst civilian casualties occurred in Europe, where an estimated ten million people were systematically killed in Nazi concentration camps. Many of them were Jews.

The war in Europe ended in May 1945. In the Far East, it did not end until August, after US planes dropped atomic bombs on the Japanese cities of Hiroshima and Nagasaki.

45 million people lost their lives in the Second World War, including 20 million Russians, seven million Germans and 400,000 Britons. The majority of deaths were civilian; this tells us something of the kind of war it was. The statistics are terrible, but they can never convey the true horrors of the fighting.

The following poem reminds us that even the survivors of war cannot forget what they have experienced.

Casualty – Mental Ward

Something has gone wrong inside my head.
The sappers have left mines and wire behind;
I hold long conversations with the dead.

I do not always know what has been said;
The rhythms, not the words, stay in my mind;
Something has gone wrong inside my head.

Not just the sky but grass and trees are red,
The flares and tracers – or I'm colour-blind;
I hold long conversations with the dead.

Their presence comforts and sustains like bread;
When they don't come it's hard to be resigned;
Something has gone wrong inside my head.

They know about the snipers that I dread
And how the world is booby-trapped and mined;
I hold long conversations with the dead;

As all eyes close, they gather round my bed
And whisper consolation. When I find
Something has gone wrong inside my head
I hold long conversations with the dead.

Vernon Scannell

Ireland

Conflict in Ireland has a long history, but the current 'troubles' started in the late 1960s. The British army was sent to protect the Catholic minority in Northern Ireland from the majority Protestant community. Since then, sectarian conflict between the two communities has escalated. Fighting between the Irish Republican Army, Loyalist forces and the British Army has continued, alongside the horrors of internment, hunger strikes, bombings and many civilian deaths.

Loyalists seek to retain the link with Britain; Republicans want to join up with Eire to form a united Ireland. Neither side will compromise. Over 3,000 people have so far been killed in the 'troubles'.

The following poem brings home the *personal* tragedy of war.

The Identification

So you think it's Stephen?
Then I'd best make sure
Be on the safe side as it were.
Ah, there's been a mistake. The hair
you see, it's black, now Stephen's fair . . .
What's that? The explosion?
Of course, burnt black. Silly of me.
I should have known. Then let's get on.

The face, is that a face I ask?
That mask of charred wood
blistered, scarred could
that have been a child's face?
The sweater, where intact, looks
in fact all too familiar.
But one must be sure.

The scoutbelt. Yes that's his.
I recognize the studs he hammered in
not a week age. At the age
when boys get clothes-conscious
now you know. Its almost
certainly Stephen. But one must
be sure. Remove all trace of doubt.
Pull out every splinter of hope.

Pockets. Empty the pockets.
Handkerchief? Could be any schoolboy's.
Dirty enough. Cigarettes?
Oh this can't be Stephen.
I don't allow him to smoke you see.
He wouldn't disobey me. Not his father.

But that's his penknife. That's his alright.
And that's his key on the keyring
Gran gave him just the other night.
So this must be him.

I think I know what happened
...... about the cigarettes
No doubt he was minding them
for one of the older boys.
Yes that's it.
That's him.
That's our Stephen.

Roger McGough

Reflections

* There are no easy answers to the 'rights' and 'wrongs' of war. There will always
be people who passionately oppose any kind of war because they feel that nothing
can justify the destruction and waste of human life.
Equally, there will always be people who believe so strongly in a particular cause
that they are ready to kill – or be killed – for that cause. If war is the only way
to achieve their aim and defeat the enemy, then the ends justify the means.
When we read or hear about any conflict, we need to think carefully about its
origins and make up our own minds about the rights and wrongs. This is particularly important in today's world, where conflicts all over the world are brought to
us via television and newspaper reports, as they happen. And it's important, too,
to remember that we are not always told the whole truth about any situation.

* *Psalm 91*
He who dwells in the shelter of the Most High will rest in the shadow of the
Almighty.
I will say of the LORD, 'He is my refuge and my fortress. My God, in whom I
trust.'

Surely he will save you from the fowler's snare
and from the deadly pestilence.
He will cover you with his feathers,
and under his wings you will find refuge;
his faithfulness will be your shield and rampart.
You will not fear the terror of night,
nor the arrow that flies by day,
nor the pestilence that stalks in the darkness,
nor the plague that destroys at midday.
A thousand may fall at your side,
ten thousand at your right hand,
but it will not come near you.
You will only observe with your eyes
and see the punishment of the wicked.

If you make the Most High your dwelling –
even the LORD, who is my refuge –
then no harm will befall you,
no disaster will come near your tent.

For he will command his angels concerning you
to guard you in all your ways;
they will lift you up in their hands,
so that you will not strike your foot
against a stone.
You will tread upon the lion and the cobra;
you will trample the great lion and the serpent.

'Because he loves me,' says the LORD,
'I will rescue him:
I will protect him, for he acknowledges my name.
He will call upon me, and I will answer him;
I will be with him in trouble,
I will deliver him and honour him.
With long life will I satisfy him
and show him my salvation.'

4 War (2)

Introduction

One of the common features of war is that it produces *anti*-war protest.

Protest sometimes takes the form of words between politicians, or letters in the press, or even letters from serving soldiers to those in command.

Some wars prove so unpopular with the people at home that protest movements start to grow. In the 1960s hundreds of thousands of people protested against America's involvement in the war in Vietnam.

One of the most powerful sources of anti-war protest has come through the words and music of folk and rock songs.

Reading

Masters of War

Come you masters of war
You that build all the guns
You that build the death planes
You that build the big bombs
You that hide behind walls
You that hide behind desks
I just want you to know
I can see through your masks

You that never done nothin'
But build to destroy
You play with my world
Like it's your little toy
You put a gun in my hand
And you hide from my eyes

And you turn and run farther
When the fast bullets fly

Like Judas of old
You lie and deceive
A world war can be won
You want me to believe
But I see through your eyes
I see through your brain
Like I see through the water
That runs down my drain

You fasten the triggers
For the others to fire
Then you sit back and watch
When the death count gets higher
You hide in your mansion
As young people's blood
Flows out of their bodies
And is buried in the mud

You've thrown the worst fear
That can ever be hurled
Fear to bring children
Into the world
For threatenin' my baby   .
Unborn and unnamed
You ain't worth the blood
That runs in your veins

How much do I know
To talk out of turn
You might say that I'm young
You might say I'm unlearned
But there's one thing I know
Though I'm younger than you
Even Jesus would never
Forgive what you do

Let me ask you one question
Is your money that good
Will it buy you forgiveness
Do you think that it could
I think you will find
When your death takes its toll
All the money you made
Will never buy back your soul

And I hope that you die
And your death'll come soon
I will follow your casket
In the pale afternoon
And I'll watch while you're lowered

Down to your death bed
And I'll stand o'er you're grave
'Till I'm sure that you're dead

Bob Dylan

Russians

In Europe and America, there's a growing feeling of hysteria
Conditioned to respond to all the threats
In the rhetorical speeches of the Soviets
Mr Krushchev said we will bury you
I don't subscribe to that point of view
It would be such an ignorant thing to do
If the Russians love their children too

How can I save my little boy from Oppenheimer's deadly toy
There is no monopoly of common sense
On either side of the political fence
We share the same biology
Regardless of ideology
Believe me when I say to you
I hope the Russians love their children too

There is no historical precedent
To put words in the mouth of the president
There's no such thing as a winable war
It's a lie we don't believe anymore
Mr Reagan says we will protect you
I don't subscribe to this point of view
Believe me when I say to you
I hope the Russians love their children too

We share the same biology
Regardless of ideology
What might save us me and you
Is that the Russians love their children too.

Sting

Reflections

* What is clear in the song by Bob Dylan is the anger the writer feels towards
  those who plan war but never have to experience the battlefront themselves.
  Wars usually highlight *differences* between people. The so-called Cold War between Russian and America was a backcloth for world politics during the 1960–
  1990 period, before the move away from Communism. The song by Sting suggests
  that as *people*, all of us have more in common than politicians would have us
  believe:

  'We share the same biology
  Regardless of ideology'

* Discussions about war leave us with the question:

Do the ends justify the means? Never? Sometimes? Always?
The answer to that will be a personal one – and the question is one which will always create heated debate.

* *Matthew 5: 43–48*
You have heard that it was said, 'Love your neighbour and hate your enemy'. But I tell you: Love your enemies, bless those who curse you, do good to those who hate you, and pray for those who persecute you, that you may be sons of your Father in heaven. He causes his sun to rise on the evil and the good, and sends rain on the righteous and the unrighteous. If you love those who love you, what reward will you get? Are not even the tax collectors doing that? And if you greet only your brothers, what are you doing more than others? Do not even pagans do that? Be perfect, therefore, as your heavenly Father is perfect.'

5 Famine

Introduction

One of the results of living in a television age is that when something happens in one part of the world, the rest of the world's population can witness it almost first-hand on television sets in their homes.

Sitting in your living-room watching fellow human beings struggling for their lives as a result of an air disaster or earthquake can have the effect of making life and death seem rather unimportant.

Watching such scenes happen 'live', but many thousands of miles away, can also lead you to feel a sense of complete helplessness. The following extract comes from Bob Geldof's autobiography *Is That It*? He writes here of his own first re-actions to seeing famine victims on the television.

Reading

Is that it?

It was coming to the end of 1984 and I could see no prospect for the release of an album the Boomtown Rats and I had sweated over and were proud of. All day I had been on the phone trying to promote a single from the album. I went home in a state of blank resignation and switched on the television. But there I saw something that placed my worries in a ghastly new perspective.

The news report was of famine in Ethiopia. From the first seconds it was clear that this was a horror on a monumental scale. The pictures were of people who were so shrunken by starvation that they looked like beings from another planet. Their arms and legs were as thin sticks, their bodies spindly. Swollen veins and huge, blankly staring eyes protruded from their shrivelled heads. The camera wandered amid them like a mesmerised observer, occasionally dwelling on one person so that he looked directly at me, sitting in my comfortable living room. And there were children, their bodies fragile and vulnerable as premature babies but with the consciousness of what is happening to them gleaming dully from their eyes. All around was the murmur of death like a hoarse whisper, or the buzzing of flies.

From the first few seconds it was clear that this was a tragedy which the world had somehow contrived not to notice until it had reached a scale which constituted an international scandal. You could hear that in the tones of BBC reporter Michael Buerk. It was the voice of a man who was registering despair, grief and disgust at what he was seeing. At the end the newscasters remained silent. Paula burst into tears, and then rushed upstairs to check on our baby, Fifi, who was sleeping peacefully in her cot.

The images played and replayed in my mind. What could I do? Did not the sheer scale of the thing call for something more? Michael Buerk had used the word biblical: a famine of biblical proportions. A horror like this could not occur today without our consent. We had allowed this to happen. I would send money. But that was not enough. I was stood against the wall. I had to withdraw my consent. What else could I do? I was only a pop singer – and by now not a very successful pop singer. All I could do was make records that no one bought. But I would do that, I would give the profits of the next Rats record to Oxfam. What good would that do? It would be a pitiful amount. But it would be more than I could raise by simply dipping into my shrunken bank account. Maybe some people would buy it just because the profits were going to Oxfam. And I would withdraw my consent. Yet that was not enough.

Bob Geldof

Reflections

* Bob Geldof here clearly felt powerless in the face of a terrible human tragedy. His wife Paula's reaction was, quite naturally, to check the safety of her own baby.
  Faced with the thought of not being able to do anything for the people in Ethiopia, Bob Geldof went on to launch *Live Aid* – a concert which brought together popular musicians to raise funds to relieve famine in Africa.
  Bob Geldof's story perhaps makes us feel both helpless and powerful.
  We may not be able to launch another Live Aid, but perhaps in small ways – through prayer, fund-raising, making others more aware of the problems – we can help each other right across the world.
  Watching others' disasters serves always to remind us that there is a great international community which lies beyond our own village, town and country.

* *Matthew 16: 24–28*
  'Then Jesus said to his disciples, 'If anyone would come after me, he must deny himself and take up his cross and follow me. For whoever wants to save his life will lose it, but whoever loses his life for me will find it. What good will it be for a man if he gains the whole world, yet forfeits his soul? Or what can a man give in exchange for his soul? For the Son of Man is going to come in his Father's glory with his angels, and then he will reward each person according to what he has done. I tell you the truth, some who are standing here will not taste death before they see the Son of Man coming in his kingdom'.

6 The scourge of malnutrition

Introduction

For many peoples of the world, daily routine is one of survival: the struggle to seek out just enough water and basic food to live. As one definition has it: two-thirds of the world's population live on a bowl of rice a day.

For us, such a daily quest for food is unthinkable. But we cannot shut our eyes to the pictures of starving children, disease and poverty that are brought to us by television, newspapers, magazines ... We cannot ignore the plight of millions of people around the world.

The following passage is entitled *The scourge of malnutrition*. It describes – with painful detail – what hunger really means to those who suffer it.

Reading

The Scourge of Malnutrition

There are many kinds of hunger and a variety of consequences. At one extreme there is acute starvation. This has the effect of turning its victims into scarecrows, and killing them fairly quickly. At the other end of the famine spectrum is the type of prolonged malnutrition which has no obvious appearance on the surface but which produces chronic illness.

Like all machines, the human body depends for its survival on fuel. This is converted to energy to enable the machine to perform its functions. In the case of living machines, the fuel required is food. Where living organisms differ from other machines is in their ability to grow, repair and replace worn parts, and monitor their health and well-being. Such highly complicated tasks are accomplished through the intake and conversion of food.

Complete absence of food will, in a short while, lead to deterioration of the body, and death. But there are several kinds of food deprivation that can cause damage without immediately leading to death. These can be grouped into two sections: general starvation and hidden starvation. In the past, most victims of famine simply succumbed to the chronic effects of general starvation and died. Today, hidden hunger (a lack of specific vital types of food) is the most common type.

Hidden hunger exists in three forms: protein, vitamin or mineral deficiency. They are usually present together.

Proteins are the body-building elements which we get from meat, milk, eggs and vegetables, although only animal products contain all the essential proteins we need. A baby that is given too little milk will suffer physical and mental damage that will scar it for life. It will be weak physically and even, perhaps, mentally retarded. Its growth will be slower than other children's, so that it may reach adulthood with a stunted stature. A diet containing insufficient protein will cause the victim much suffering: his body will be less resistant to disease, particularly infectious illnesses like tuberculosis and typhoid.

Diets lacking in certain essential minerals can lead to rickets, severe tooth decay, softening of the bones, and various mental and physical deformities. Iron deficiency induces anaemia – a severe blood condition which reduces a victim's ability to resist attacks from parasites, such as worms. About 300 million people suffer from goitre or cretinism, a severe mental illness caused by a lack of iodine. This can also lead to dwarfism and feeblemindedness.

Vitamin deficiency causes a vast range of illnesses and, in extreme cases, premature death. Blindness, stunted growth, beri-beri, scurvy, pellagra and rickets are all symptoms of diets which lack one or more essential vitamins.

Almost 1,300 million people are seriously malnourished. Besides early death, which strikes an unknown but high number of victims, the results of severe under and bad feeding are chronic illness and the misery that comes from never being free from the pains of hunger. In Latin America, every second death of a child is caused by diet deficiency. Every year, 100,000 Asian children go blind because they lack vitamin A.

The absurd thing is that overeating is one of the leading causes of death in the developed world. If the wealthy nations could be persuaded of this, they might be induced to cut down on overconsumption, and redirect resources to where they are urgently needed.

Martin Schultz

Reflections

* A sobering piece! As well as describing the details and statistics associated with malnutrition, the final paragraph draws attention to the absurd and ironic situation in places like Britain and America where *overeating* (leading to heart disease) is one of the major causes of death.

  One of the lessons, then, of the late 20th century is the inter-dependence of the developing and developed world. We need to think carefully as individuals, as a nation, and as part of the European Community . . . What steps can we take to even out something as basic as levels of food consumption?

* Can we call ourselves an advanced and civilised society when we know millions in other countries are starving?

  When we eat our meals today, let's pause to reflect on what some of the children of Latin America have eaten in the past 24 hours.

  Is the problem so enormous and chronic that we feel powerless to help?

7 Mother Teresa

Introduction

In 1948 a solitary nun left behind her the relative security of the Loreto School in Calcutta, India and stepped out into that city's streets to live as one of the poorest of the poor, and to found a new Congregation committed to their service.

Today, Mother Teresa's mission, which began unpretentiously in some of India's most disease-ridden slums, is a global one. Mother Teresa herself has become the reluctant holder of a string of honours including the Nobel Peace Prize which she accepted 'unworthily but gratefully in the name of the poor, the hungry, the sick and the lonely'. She sees herself as 'the little pencil in God's hand'. Her story follows.

Reading

Mother Teresa: A woman for others

1910 – 26th August: Mother Teresa was born Agnes Bojaxhiu in Skopje, Yugoslavia, and decided at the age of 12 that she wanted to become a missionary.

1928 – She went to the Loreto Sisters at Rathfarnham Abbey, Dublin, Eire, and from there to Darjeeling in India to begin her noviciate. She took her first vows in 1931 and her final vows in 1937.

1929–1948: She taught geography and history at St. Mary's High School in Calcutta. For some years she was Principal of the school and was also in charge of the Daughters of St. Anne, the Indian religious order attached to the Loreto Sisters.

1946, 10th September: 'Inspiration Day'

Believing God had called her to work among the 'poorest of the poor', Mother Teresa requested permission from her Superiors to live alone outside the cloister and to work in the Calcutta slums.

1948 – On 8th August Mother Teresa received permission from the Church authorities to lay aside the habit of the Sisters of Loreto and to put on the sari of poor Bengali women. It was made of cheap white cotton and had a blue border. Her first step was to travel to Patna, Bihar, where the American Medical Missionaries gave her a short intensive nursing course. In December 1948 she returned to Calcutta and began her new work for Jesus. Around her, refugees from East Pakistan filled the pavements bringing their agony to a city already overwhelmed with human need.

Her first work for the poor was a free school. She set up benches under a tree in the Motijhil Slum and gathered a few children around her. Lacking equipment, she used the dusty earth for a blackboard, marking the letters with a stick. In February 1949 she was given the attic in the home of some friends, where a former pupil joined her as the first volunteer.

As other former students and young Indian girls volunteered for work with the poor, a new community came into being. On October 7th 1950, the congregation of the Missionaries of Charity (carriers of God's love) was started in Calcutta with the permission of the Holy See. As well as the usual promises of poverty, chastity and obedience, the new community pledged itself to 'wholehearted free service to the poorest of the poor'.

The little community moved to the present Mother House in Lower Circular Road, Calcutta, in February 1953, and the Sisters started schools and ran clinics in the neediest slums.

In 1965 the Congregation became a Society of Pontifical Right, which permitted Mother Teresa and her Sisters to extend their Mission to the poor in other countries.

Invitations soon came to Calcutta from overseas and there are now Missionaries of Charity working in most countries of the world.

Co-Workers of Mother Teresa

Reflections

* Although Mother Teresa saw the poor in the slums every day from her window and longed to be able to help them, she did not simply make a decision to help

the poor. She believes that she received a call from God to be His love and compassion to the poorest of the poor.

Over the years Mother Teresa's own perception of poverty and suffering has grown. Work in more affluent countries has brought her to the recognition that spiritual poverty, loneliness and lack of love are far more difficult problems to solve than physical deprivation. Within our global village she has repeatedly called upon those caught up in the materialism of the West to reflect on 'the anguish of plenty'. Her story is an arresting one.

* The Co-Workers' Prayer

Make us worthy, Lord, to serve our fellow men
throughout the world who live and die in poverty
and hunger.

Give them, through our hands, this day their
daily bread; and by our understanding love, give
peace and joy.

Lord, make me a channel of Thy peace that where
there is hatred, I may bring love; that where there is
wrong, I may bring the spirit of forgiveness; that
where there is discord, I may bring harmony; that
where there is error, I may bring truth; that where
there is doubt, I may bring faith; that where there is
despair, I may bring hope; that where there are
shadows, I may bring light; that where there is
sadness, I may bring joy.

Lord, grant that I may seek rather to comfort than
to be comforted; to understand than to be
understood; to love than to be loved; for it is by
forgetting self that one finds; it is by forgiving
that one is forgiven; it is by dying that one awakens
to eternal life.

Amen

8 First World versus Third World: The Myth of Overpopulation*

Introduction
Western politicians and economists tend to divide the world's countries into four groups, according to economic strength. These groups are referred to as 'worlds'.

The First World consists of wealthy, heavily-industrialised countries such as those in Europe and North America.

The Second World refers to countries of Eastern Europe which are industrialised but not as wealthy as the West.

The Third World consists of semi-industrialised countries in the Middle East, Latin America and Asia.

The Fourth World countries are the poorest – they have almost no industry and are unable to support themselves.

Using these categories tends to emphasise differences rather than similarities between countries. Not everyone agrees with these divisions. Listen to the following argument by writer Germain Greer which challenges Western assumptions about the so-called 'Third World'.

She starts by attacking the words of the successful American author Paul Ehrlich, who has written much about overpopulation in countries such as India.

Reading

The Myth of Overpopulation

Is the world overpopulated? If I must adopt some position on this point, it will be a highly compromised one. I have been to old Delhi, as Paul Ehrlich has, but somehow, as usual, I saw the wrong thing. Here follows the apocalyptic vision of Paul Ehrlich, set out on page one of his bestseller, under the heading 'The Problem.'

I have understood the population problem intellectually for a long time. I came to understand it emotionally one stinking hot night in Delhi a few years ago. My wife and daughter and I were returning to our hotel in an ancient taxi. The seats were hopping with fleas. The only functional gear was third. As we crawled through the city, we entered a crowded slum area. The temperature was well over 100° F; the air was a haze of dust and smoke. The streets seemed alive with people. People eating, people washing, people sleeping. People visiting, arguing and screaming. People thrusting their hands through the taxi window begging. People defecating and urinating. People clinging to buses. People herding animals. People, people, people, people. As we moved slowly through the mob, hand horn squawking, the dust, noise, heat and cooking fires gave the scene a hellish aspect. Would we ever get to our hotel? All three of us were, frankly, frightened. It seemed that anything could happen – but, of course, nothing did. Old India hands will laugh at our reaction. We were just some over-privileged tourists, unaccustomed to the sights and sounds of India. Perhaps, but since that night I've known the feel of over-population.

This then is the problem that Ehrlich and his paymasters and the gullible public are setting out to solve. It is composed first of heat, apparently. Some parts of the world are hot and not less likely to be so when they are more sparsely populated. The only remedy that can be suggested for this aspect of the problem is that people like Dr Ehrlich who waste emotional energy in resenting other people's weather had better stay out of it. Even more alarming than the weather however, was the taxi. The fact that virtually every car ever put on the roads in India is still in service is probably intolerable to a citizen of an automobile-producing nation; some of us are delighted with the ingenuity of Indians in this regard. The taxi may have been driven in third because there was no other gear, but is more likely to be driven without recourse to the lower gears in order to save petrol. India has only very small reserves of oil and must buy at the market price. The taxi-driver will only realise his minute profit if he husbands every millilitre of petrol. It is a little hard on the passengers, especially if the taxi – which is usually as clean as human hands and little else can make it, because the driver spends so much time waiting for a fare – is full of fleas, something which I have never encountered in India. It is amusing to speculate just how someone as savvy as Ehrlich got himself into this jam; if for example he made the driver empty out a load of goats so he could commandeer the taxi, he was probably driven into the slum as a punishment. As you can hire an immaculate car with a uniformed driver for twenty dollars a day in Delhi, it seems that somebody who should have been looking after Ehrlich threw him to the pi-dogs. If Dr Ehrlich and his fellow-Americans, by the way, were more tolerant of small changes in temperature, and did not instantly squander fuel in raising it or lowering it, their driver might have been able to afford enough petrol and oil to drive his taxi in a more seemly manner, and to maintain it a little better.

If we exclude the carping about the taxi and the temperature, we are left with people, people, people, people. This slum is rather odd in that there are buses and people herding animals in it, so we might guess that Ehrlich did not get himself inside a real slum, where there is no room for buses, taxis or herds, just huts. What he seems to have seen were settlements. The area was certainly not more crowded than Manhattan at three o'clock on a weekday afternoon: the difference is that in Delhi the people were all at pavement level. If they had been nicely shut up in high-rises Ehrlich would not have troubled his head about them, even if he had heard that most of them were drugging themselves with heroin or alcohol or doctors' substitutes. He saw no drunks, no crazy people, no obese people, either, I'll be bound. If he did, he does not say. He does not say that he saw anyone laughing, or men and women playing with their babies. Some of the smells around those tiny fires, made by burning the tips of scrap wood, were spicy and good. Those people had not come there as a couple, years ago, and multiplied until they filled up the area. If he had been less of a ninny and got out of the taxi to talk to the people (who are better at speaking his language than he is at speaking theirs) he might have found out how they got there.

But no. Intellectual understanding precludes investigation. If he had gone into the shanties, he would have been surprised to find that the earthen floors were swept smooth, that the family possessions, most of them the wife's dowry, were neatly hung on poles or standing on a narrow shelf, the brass bowls polished till they shine in the darkness, reflecting every sliver of available light, polished with earth. He did not notice that the people doing their washing-up were not using detergents. Cow-dung smoke and dust are hard on the sinuses but they are less deadly than industrial effluent and exhaust fumes, which Dr Ehrlich seems to prefer. He did not notice the complete absence of the United States' principal product, trash. The greatest insult about all these people living shoulder to shoulder, the visible counterpart of the population planner's nightmare, is that they make do with so little. Such low purchasing power is anathema to men of Ehrlich's kidney. He does not tell us how he treated the beggars, whose presence seems to indicate that he did not get very far off the beaten track. If he had gone to some parts of Delhi in 1970 he would have found American teenagers begging to support their drug habit, much as they do in America.

In order to feel in his bowels the reality of overpopulation Ehrlich had to go to India; others feel it more strongly when they come across discarded aluminium beer cans in the wilderness. If we agree that the world is overpopulated we have still to decide what we mean by the term and what the phenomenon consists in. An Indian Paul Ehrlich might see the sudden exponential increase in the global human population as the result of an ecological disaster which happened about five hundred years age, namely the explosion of Europe.

From 'The Myth of Overpopulation' in 'Sex and Destiny'
by Germaine Greer

Reflections

* Under her title 'The Myth of Overpopulation' Germaine Greer is heavily critical of those – like the author Dr Paul Ehrlich – who blame many of the world's problems on Third World countries whose population growth, he claims, is too great.
  She rather turns the tables and asks us to judge India and its people by *their* values and standards; and *not* through the lens of an American or European telescope. Indeed, Greer is quick to point out the social problems of drugs, crime and trash associated with the equally crowded city, New York.

* There is no doubt, statistically, that countries in Latin America and Asia are now growing in population more quickly than the USA and Europe. Germaine Greer's plea is that, as people living on the same planet, we do not judge and condemn one another's countries: the challenge is to find solutions to problems *together*. Change and development will be a constant feature of our lives into the 21st century. Countries will need to work *with* each other, not against one another's interests.

9 Contrasting cultures

Introduction

Our world comprises very different civilisations, at varying stages of development. Attitudes and values vary from country to country. What might be seen as modern or advanced in one culture may be considered old-fashioned by another.

All communities value 'education' – the original Latin means 'developing' or 'leading out'. But what we think of as a good education might be seen rather differently in another culture. Our knowledge and learning may not equip us for survival in another environment.

The following reading comes from the novel *Walkabout* by James Vance Marshall, set in the Australian desert. Eight-year-old Peter and sister Mary, 13, are children from a comfortable suburban background who suddenly find themselves alone in the desert following a plane crash. They are the only survivors. In this extract they come upon an Aborigine boy who is in the middle of his 'walkabout', a trial all 14-year-olds in the boy's tribe have to undergo as part of their education and to prove their manhood. It is the Aborigine's knowledge of the desert which finally leads Mary and Peter to safety, but as events turn out, only with tragic consequences for the Aborigine.

Reading

Walkabout

The girl's first impulse was to grab Peter and run; but as her eyes swept over the stranger, her fear died slowly away. The boy was young – certainly no older than she was; he was unarmed, and his attitude was more inquisitive than threatening: more puzzled than hostile.

He wasn't the least bit like an African Negro. His skin was certainly black, but beneath it was a curious hint of undersurface bronze, and it was fine-grained: glossy, satiny, almost silk-like. His hair wasn't crinkly but nearly straight; and his eyes were blue-black: big, soft and inquiring. In his hand was a baby rock wallaby, its eyes, unclosed in death, staring vacantly above a tiny pointed snout.

All this Mary noted and accepted. The thing that she couldn't accept, the thing that seemed to her shockingly and indecently wrong, was the fact that the boy was naked.

The three children stood looking at each other in the middle of the Australian desert. Motionless as the outcrops of granite they stared, and stared, and stared. Between them the distance was less than the spread of an outstretched arm, but more than a hundred thousand years.

Brother and sister were products of the highest strata of humanity's evolution. In them the primitive had long ago been swept aside, been submerged by mechanization, been swamped by scientific development, been nullified by the standardized pattern of the white man's way of life. They had climbed a long way up the ladder of progress; they had climbed so far, in fact, that they had forgotten how their climb had started. Coddled in babyhood, psycho-analysed in childhood, nourished on predigested patent foods, provided with continuous push-button entertainment, the basic realities of life were something they'd never had to face.

It was very different with the Aboriginal. He knew what reality was. He led a way of life that was already old when Tut-ankh-amen started to build his tomb; a way of life that had been tried and proved before the white man's continents were even lifted out of the sea. Among the secret water-holes of the Australian desert his people had lived and died, unchanged and unchanging, for twenty thousand years. Their lives were unbelievably simple. They had no homes, no crops, no clothes, no possessions. The few things they had, they shared: food and wives; children and laughter; tears and hunger and thirst. They walked from one water-hole to the next; they exhausted one supply of food, then moved on to another. Their lives were utterly uncomplicated because they were devoted to one purpose, dedicated in their entirety to the waging of one battle: the battle with death. Death was their ever-present enemy. He sought them out from every dried-up salt pan, from the flames of every bush fire. He was never far away. Keeping him at bay was the Aboriginals' full-time job: the job they'd been doing for twenty thousand years: the job they were good at.

The desert sun streamed down. The children stared and stared.

Mary had decided not to move. To move would be a sign of weakness. She remembered being told about the man who'd come face to face with a lion, and had stared it out, had caused it to slink discomfited away. That was what she'd do to the black boy; she'd stare at him until he felt the shame of his nakedness and slunk away. She thrust out her chin, and glared.

Peter had decided to take his cue from his sister. Clutching her hand he stood waiting: waiting for something to happen.

The Aboriginal was in no hurry. Time had little value to him. His next meal – the rock wallaby – was assured. Water was near. Tomorrow was also a day. For the moment he was content to examine these strange creatures at his leisure. Their clumsy, lumbering movements intrigued him; their lack of weapons indicated their harmlessness. His eyes moved slowly, methodically from one to another: examining them from head to foot. They were the first white people a member of his tribe had ever seen.

Mary, beginning to resent this scrutiny, intensified her glare. But the bush boy seemed in no way perturbed; his appraisal went methodically on.

After a while Peter started to fidget. The delay was fraying his nerves. He wished someone would do something: wished something would happen. Then, quite involuntarily, he himself started a new train of events. His head began to waggle; his nose tilted skywards; he spluttered and choked; he tried to hold his breath; but all in vain. It had to come. He sneezed.

It was a mighty sneeze for such a little fellow: the release of a series of concatenated explosions, all the more violent for having been dammed back.

To his sister the sneeze was a calamity. She had just intensified her stare to the point – she felt sure – of irresistibility, when the spell was shattered. The bush boy's attention shifted from her to Peter.

Frustration warped her sense of justice. She condemned her brother out of court; was turning on him angrily, when a second sneeze, even mightier than the first, shattered the silence of the bush.

Mary raised her eyes to heaven: invoking the gods as witnesses to her despair. But the vehemence of the second sneeze was still tumbling leaves from the humble-bushes, when a new sound made her whirl around. A gust of laughter: melodious laughter; low at first, then becoming louder: unrestrained: disproportionate: uncontrolled.

She looked at the bush boy in amazement. He was doubled up with belly-shaking spasms of mirth.

Peter's incongruous, out-of-proportion sneeze had touched off one of his people's most highly developed traits: a sense of the ridiculous; a sense so keenly felt as to be almost beyond control. The bush boy laughed with complete abandon. He flung himself to the ground. He rolled head-over-heels in unrestrained delight.

His mirth was infectious. It woke in Peter an instant response: a like appreciation of the ludicrous. The guilt that the little boy had started to feel, melted away. At first apologetically, then whole-heartedly, he too started to laugh.

The barrier of twenty thousand years vanished in the twinkling of an eye.

From 'Walkabout' by James Vance Marshall

Reflections

* Two sentences in that passage stand out when we think about education and values in different cultures:
'Between them the distance was less than the spread of an outstretched arm, but more than a hundred thousand years.'
'The barrier of twenty thousand years vanished in the twinkling of an eye.'
Too often we see cultural differences as problems, when in fact we should properly see differences as something to be valued and celebrated. In the desert, Peter's and Mary's education is useless to them, whereas the so-called 'primitive' education of the Aborigine boy is what eventually leads them to safety: because it is he – not they – who is able to find food and water in the desert environment. And though on the surface the children seem very far apart, it is the basic human quality of humour which causes the barriers to fall. At the end of the passage, in the flash of an eye, they are united as human beings.
It is increasingly important in our global village that children and adults alike recognise and affirm what *unites* us as human beings, rather than what might divide us.

10 Racial differences

Introduction

When we read a newspaper or watch television news we could be forgiven for often thinking that our world is a place of differences and divisions, rather than a place within which humankind lives in harmony.

Anyone travelling around the world, is certain to come upon different lifestyles; and this of course leads them to think about how their own country is organised in comparison with others. Imagine yourself a traveller in the solar system, being able to contrast one *planet* with another. What conclusions might you draw about planet Earth?

The following science-fiction story by Arthur C Clarke offers us such a glimpse – with a rather dramatic ending.

Reading

Reunion

People of Earth, do not be afraid. We come in peace – and why not? For we are your cousins; we have been here before.

You will recognize us when we meet, a few hours from now. We are approaching the solar system almost as swiftly as this radio message. Already, your sun dominates the sky ahead of us. It is the sun our ancestors and yours shared ten million years ago. We are men and women as you are; but you have forgotten your history, while we have remembered ours.

We colonized Earth, in the reign of the great reptiles, who were dying when we came and whom we could not save. Your world was a tropical planet then, and we felt that it would make a fair home for our people. We were wrong. Though we were masters of space, we knew so little about climate, about evolution, about genetics...

For millions of summers – there were no winters in those ancient days – the colony flourished. Isolated though it had to be, in a universe where the journey from one star to the next takes years, it kept in touch with its parent civilization. Three or four times in every century, starships would call and bring news of the galaxy.

But two million years ago, Earth began to change. For ages it had been a tropical paradise; then the temperature fell, and the ice began to creep down from the poles. As the climate altered, so did the colonists. We realize now that it was a natural adaptation to the end of the long summer, but those who had made Earth their home for so many generations believed that they had been attacked by a strange and repulsive disease. A disease that did not kill, that did no physical harm – but merely disfigured.

Yet some were immune; the change spared them and their children. And so, within a few thousand years, the colony had split into two separate groups – almost two separate species – suspicious and jealous of each other.

The division brought envy, discord, and, ultimately, conflict. As the colony disintegrated and the climate steadily worsened, those who could do so withdrew from Earth. The rest sank into barbarism.

We could have kept in touch, but there is so much to do in a universe of a hundred trillion stars. Until a few years ago, we did not know that any of you had survived. Then we picked up your first radio signals, learned your simple languages, and discovered that you had made the long climb back from savagery. We come to greet you, our long-lost relative – and to help you.

We have discovered much in the eons since we abandoned Earth. If you wish us to bring back the eternal summer that ruled before the Ice Ages, we can do so. Above all, we have a simple remedy for the offensive yet harmless genetic plague that afflicted so many of the colonists.

Perhaps it has run its course – but if not, we have good news for you. People of Earth, you can rejoin the society of the universe without shame, without embarrassment.

If any of you are still white, we can cure you.

From 'Reunion' by Arthur C Clarke

Reflections

* The story has a challenging final line!
  This splendidly–crafted tale has two key points it is worth reflecting upon:

  – first, it is always worth putting situations in context: this fictional example suggests that Earth's own problems are parallelled elsewhere in the solar system.
  – second, one of the underlying social challenges in our world today is that of ethnic and racial differences.

* 'Differences' do not mean 'problems'; schools are places where young people from a wide range of backgrounds come together for the purpose of learning. One of the most important aspects of education is learning to live in harmony with others, irrespective of their sex, race, religion or heritage tongue.
  The values of such harmony – or indeed, what happens when they are lost – are highlighted in *Reunion*.

11 Third World driving hints and tips

Introduction

The fact that international communications and travel are so easy in today's world means that we are increasingly in a position to observe and comment on the customs and habits of other countries. In particular, the dominance of American culture and its spread throughout much of the world by way of film, advertising and music is something which not everyone welcomes as desirable.

The following passage (taken from a book called 'Holidays In Hell') is written by an American journalist who has some witty but unfavourable things to say when he compares driving a car in the USA with what it's like to drive in what he calls 'The Third World'. What he writes therefore is very much the personal view of an *outsider* in foreign lands.

Reading

Third World Driving Hints and Tips

During the past couple of years I've had to do my share of driving in the Third World – in Mexico, Lebanon, the Philippines, Cyprus, El Salvador, Africa and Italy. (Italy is not technically part of the Third World, but no one has told the Italians.) I don't pretend to be an expert, but I have been making notes.

Road hazards
What would be a road hazard anywhere else, in the Third World is probably the road. There are two techniques for coping with this. One is to drive very fast so your wheels 'get on top' of the ruts and your car sails over the ditches and gullies. Predictably, this will result in disaster. The other technique is to drive very slowly. This will also result in disaster. No matter how slowly you drive into a ten-foot hole, you're still going to get hurt. You'll find the locals themselves can't make up their minds. Either they drive at 2 m.p.h. – which they do every time there's absolutely no way to get around them. Or else they drive at 100 m.p.h. – which they do coming right at you when you finally get a chance to pass the guy going 2 m.p.h.

Basic information
It's important to have your facts straight before you begin piloting a car around an underdeveloped country. For instance, which side of the road do they drive on? This is easy. They drive on your side. That is, you can depend on it, any oncoming traffic will be on your side of the road. Also, how do you translate kilometres into miles? Most people don't know this, but one kilometre = ten miles, exactly. True, a kilometre is only 62 per cent of a mile, but if something is one hundred kilometres away, read that as one thousand miles because the roads are 620 per cent worse than anything you've ever seen. And when you see a 50-k.p.h. speed limit, you might as well figure that means 500 *m.p.h.* because nobody cares. The Third World does not have the Highway Patrol. Outside the cities, it doesn't have many police at all. Law enforcement is in the hands of the army. And soldiers, if they feel like it, will shoot you no matter what speed you're going.

Traffic signs and signals
Most developing nations use international traffic symbols. Americans may find themselves perplexed by road signs that look like Boy Scout merit badges and by such things as an iguana silhouette with a red diagonal bar across it. Don't worry, the natives don't know what they mean, either. The natives do, however, have an elaborate set of signals used to convey information to the traffic around them. For example, if you're trying to pass someone and he blinks his left turn signal, it means go ahead. Either that or it means a large truck is coming around the bend, and you'll get killed if you try. You'll find out in a moment.

Signalling is further complicated by festive decorations found on many vehicles. It can be hard to tell a hazard flasher from a string of Christmas-tree lights wrapped around the bumper, and brake lights can easily be confused with the dozen red Jesus statuettes and the ten stuffed animals with blinking eyes on the package shelf.

Dangerous curves
Dangerous curves are marked, at least in Christian lands, by white wooden crosses positioned to make the curves even more dangerous. These crosses are memorials

to people who've died in traffic accidents, and they give a rough statistical indication of how much trouble you're likely to have at that spot in the road. Thus, when you come through a curve in a full-power slide and are suddenly confronted with a veritable forest of crucifixes, you know you're dead.

Learning to drive like a native
It's important to understand that in the Third World most driving is done with the horn, or 'Egyptian Brake Pedal', as it is known. There is a precise and complicated etiquette of horn use. Honk your horn only under the following circumstances:

1 When anything blocks the road.
2 When anything doesn't.
3 When anything might.
4 At red lights.
5 At green lights.
6 At all other times.

Road-blocks
One thing you can count on in Third World countries is trouble. There's always some uprising, coup or Marxist insurrection going on, and this means military road-blocks. There are two kinds of military road-block, the kind where you slow down so they can look you over, and the kind where you come to a full stop so they can steal your luggage. The important thing is that you must *never* stop at the slow-down kind of road-block. If you stop, they'll think you're a terrorist about to attack them, and they'll shoot you. And you must *always* stop at the full-stop kind of road-block. If you just slow down, they'll think you're a terrorist about to attack them, and they'll shoot you. How do you tell the difference between the two kinds of road-block? Here's the fun part: you can't!

(The terrorists, of course, have road-blocks of their own. They always make you stop. Sometimes with land mines.)

Animals in the right of way
As a rule of thumb, you should slow down for donkeys, speed up for goats and stop for cows. Donkeys will get out of your way eventually, and so will pedestrians. But never actually stop for either of them or they'll take advantage, especially the pedestrians. If you stop in the middle of a crowd of Third World pedestrians, you'll be there buying Chiclets and bogus antiquities for days.

Drive like hell through the goats. It's almost impossible to hit a goat. On the other hand, it's almost impossible *not* to hit a cow. Cows are immune to horn-honking, shouting, swats with sticks and taps on the hind quarters with the bumper. The only thing you can do to make a cow move is swerve to avoid it, which will make the cow move in front of you with lightning speed.

Actually, the most dangerous animals are the chickens. In the United States, when you see a ball roll into the street, you hit your brakes because you know the next thing you'll see is a kid chasing it. In the Third World, it's not balls the kids are chasing, but chickens. Are they practising punt returns with a leghorn? Dribbling it? Playing stick-hen? I don't know. But Third Worlders are remarkably fond of their chickens and, also, their children. If you hit one or both, they may survive. But you will not.

Accidents
Never look where you're going – you'll only scare yourself. Nonetheless, try to avoid collisions. There are bound to be more people in that bus, truck or even on

that moped than there are in your car. At best you'll be screamed deaf. And if the police do happen to be around, standard procedure is to throw everyone in jail regardless of fault. This is done to forestall blood feuds, which are a popular hobby in many of these places.

If you do have an accident, the only thing to do is go on the offensive. Throw big wads of American money at everyone, and hope for the best.

Safety tips
One nice thing about the Third World, you don't have to fasten your safety belt. It takes a lot off your mind when average life expectancy is forty-five minutes.

From 'Third World Driving Hints and Tips' in Holidays in Hell
by P J O'Rourke

Reflections

* The passage certainly has some funny lines. Yet much of its humour depends on stereotyping the habits of others – that is, exaggerating something to make a particular point. Humour is frequently based on caricature or stereotype, and by laughing at and with something we can often understand it a little better. Equally, P J O'Rourke's essay here is a caution to us that within our global village we must seek to understand and appreciate differences between countries rather than wish everyone else to be 'just like us'.

  The phrase 'The Third World' is interesting in itself; it suggests a rank order of merit and civilisation. It is more helpful to think of countries like Bangladesh and Ethiopia as *Developing* countries, not Third World countries.

  Writers like P J O'Rourke should remind us that cultural differences exist and must continue to exist. We should not attempt to impose the values and customs of one country upon another.

12 Nuclear weapons

Introduction
Few subjects promote such strong feelings 'for' and 'against' as nuclear weapons. It is a frightening but true fact that human beings now possess the ability to destroy the entire planet with nuclear bombs.

The following passage is taken from a book by Martin Amis called, provocatively, *Einstein's Monsters*. Of course there is always more than one side to an argument, but here the author puts forward the *anti*-nuclear point of view. What are your thoughts?

Reading

Nuclear Weapons

I was born on 25 August 1949: four days later, the Russians successfully tested their first atom bomb and *deterrence* was in place. So I had those four carefree days, which is more than my juniors ever had. I didn't really make the most of them. I spent half the time under a bubble. Even as things stood, I was born in a state of acute shock. By the fourth day I had recovered, but the world had taken a turn for the worse. It was a nuclear world. To tell you the truth, I didn't feel very well at all. I was terribly sleepy and feverish. I kept throwing up. I was given to fits of uncontrollable weeping . . . When I was eleven or twelve the television started showing target-maps of South East England: the outer bands of the home counties, the bull's-eye of London. I used to leave the room as quickly as I could. I didn't know why nuclear weapons were in my life or who had put them there. I didn't know what to do about them. I didn't want to think about them. They made me feel sick.

Now, in 1987, thirty-eight years later, I still don't know what to do about nuclear weapons. And neither does anybody else. If there are people who know, then I have not read them. The extreme alternatives are nuclear war and nuclear disarmament. Nuclear war is hard to imagine; but so is nuclear disarmament.

Nuclear war is seven minutes away, and might be over in an afternoon. How far away is nuclear disarmament? We are waiting. And the weapons are waiting.

What is the only provocation that could bring about the use of nuclear weapons? Nuclear weapons. What is the priority target for nuclear weapons? Nuclear weapons. What is the only established defence against nuclear weapons? Nuclear weapons. How do we prevent the use of nuclear weapons? By threatening to use nuclear weapons. And we can't get rid of nuclear weapons, because of nuclear weapons. The intransigence, it seems, is a function of the weapons themselves. Nuclear weapons can kill a human being a dozen times over in a dozen different ways; and, before death – like certain spiders, like the headlights of cars – they seem to paralyse.

Indeed they are remarkable artefacts. They derive their power from an equation: when a pound of uranium-235 is fissioned, the 'liberated mass' within its (1,132,000,000,000,000,000,000,000) atoms is multiplied by the speed of light squared – with the explosive force, that is to say, of 186,000 miles per second times 186,000 miles per second. Their size, their power, has no theoretical limit. They are biblical in their anger. They are clearly the worst thing that has ever happened to the planet, and they are mass-produced, and inexpensive. In a way, their most extraordinary single characteristic is that they are man-made. They distort all life and subvert all freedoms. Somehow, they give us no choice. Not a soul on earth wants them, but here they all are.

I am sick of them – I am sick of nuclear weapons. And so is everybody else. When, in my dealings with this strange subject, I have read too much or thought too long – I experience nausea, clinical nausea. In every conceivable sense nuclear weapons make you sick. What toxicity, what power, what range. They are there and I am here – they are inert, I am alive – yet still they make me want to throw up, they make me feel sick to my stomach; they make me feel as if a child of mine has been out too long, much too long, and already it is getting dark. This is appropriate, and good practice. Because I will be doing a lot of that, I will be doing a lot of throwing up, if the weapons fall and I live.

Every morning, six days a week, I leave the house and drive a mile to the flat where I work. For seven or eight hours I am alone. Each time I hear a sudden whinning in the air or one of the more atrocious impacts of city life, or play host to a certain kind of unwelcome thought, I can't help wondering how it might be. Suppose I survive. Suppose my eyes aren't pouring down my face, suppose I am untouched by the hurricane of secondary missiles that all mortar, metal and glass have abruptly become: suppose all this. I shall be obliged (and it's the last thing I'll feel like doing) to retrace that long mile home, through the firestorm, the remains of the thousand-mile-an-hour winds, the warped atoms, the grovelling dead. Then – God willing, if I still have the strength, and, of course, if they are still alive – I must find my wife and children and I must kill them.

What am I to do with thoughts like these? What is anyone to do with thoughts like these?

From 'Nuclear weapons' in 'Einstein's Monsters' by Martin Amis

Reflections

* There is no mistaking this writer's viewpoint, is there? Two of his sentences are worth pausing over:

1 'In a way, their most extraordinary single characteristic is that they are man-made.'

It is a terrifying and sobering thought that these weapons of mass destruction exist only because *we* have invented them. What a strange people we are, Amis seems to be saying, to want to destroy ourselves.

2 'They distort all life and subvert all freedoms'

Here he appears to suggest that *all* that human beings stand for – 'life, liberty and the pursuit of happiness,' as the American constitution phrases it – is distorted and made meaningless by the very existence of these weapons.

The reading ends with the question: 'What is anyone to do with thoughts like these?' Perhaps having heard the words of someone who is against the bomb, a useful next step would be to read and listen to arguments of those who believe that the *deterrent* effect of nuclear war actually keeps the peace in our world. There are no easy answers to the nuclear question. The important point is to be aware of the issues, the debate, the facts as they are presented – and to come to your own conclusions. They may or may not be similar to those of Martin Amis.

Shakespeare's Universal Themes

General Introduction

William Shakespeare is generally recognised as the greatest playwright to have written in the English language. He was born in 1564 and died in 1616. His writing career was at its height during the reigns of Queen Elizabeth I and King James I. Not much is known about Shakespeare's life but it is clear that he was both a writer and an actor, writing plays for the company of actors of which he was a leading member. His company made famous the Globe Theatre, the great playhouse of Elizabethan London.

Shakespeare's literary life is broadly divided into four main creative periods. In each period he moulded his work to suit the tastes of his contemporary audience and of the particular section of society that he happened to be entertaining.

When we pick up a volume of Shakespeare's plays we can see that they are divided into:

– Tragedies
– Histories
– Comedies

We should always remember that his work is meant to be *seen* on stage as well as read from the page.

What makes Shakespeare one of the greatest writers in our history is his ability to create great moments of drama on the stage and to draw memorable and colourful characters. He wrote, too, about ideas and human emotions that were relevant to his own Elizabethan audiences and which remain equally relevant in today's world.

The fact that Shakespeare's writings are studied all over the world is further evidence that the content of his plays appeals to women and men of all cultures. The great plays like *Romeo and Juliet*, *Macbeth*, *Othello*, *Hamlet*, and *King Lear*, contain beautifully crafted speeches that have a 'universal appeal'.

The BBC radio programme *Desert Island Discs* offers its weekly castaway eight records and an item of luxury to take to the desert island – *plus* a copy of the Bible and Shakespeare's plays. That perhaps is another tribute to the power and constant relevance of his plays, his characters and his ideas.

Note

The themes which follow are: 1 Seven Ages of Man
2 Life and Death
3 Sleep
4 Patriotism
5 Good character

6 Conscience
7 Honour, Loyalty, Ambition
8 Betrayal, Murder
9 Mercy
10 Kingship
11 Love
12 Time

Each of the 'themes' is illustrated by one or two speeches from the plays. For an assembly, a tried and tested format is as follows:

(a) introduce the theme and put it in context
(b) read the speech
(c) pick out certain key phrases for reflection/values
(d) re-read the speech
(e) recommend to students that they look up the speech and play in a 'Collected Works of Shakespeare'.

Seven Ages of Man

JAQUES.
              All the world's a stage,
And all the men and women merely players:
They have their exits and their entrances;
And one man in his time plays many parts,
His acts being seven ages. As, first the infant,
Mewling and puking in the nurse's arms.
And then the whining schoolboy, with his satchel
And shining morning face, creeping like snail
Unwillingly to school. And then the lover,
Sighing like furnace, with a woeful ballad
Made to his mistress' eyebrow. Then the soldier,
Full of strange oaths, and bearded like the pard,
Jealous in honour, sudden and quick in quarrel,
Seeking the bubble reputation
Even in the cannon's mouth. And then the justice
In fair round belly with good capon lined,
With eyes severe and beard of formal cut,
Full of wise saws and modern instances;
And so he plays his part. The sixth age shifts
Into the lean and slipper'd pantaloon,
With spectacles on nose and pouch on side;
His youthful hose, well saved, a world too wide
For his shrunk shank; and his big manly voice,
Turning again toward childish treble, pipes
And whistles in his sound. Last scene of all,
That ends this strange eventful history,
Is second childishness and mere oblivion,
Sans teeth, sans eyes, sans taste, sans every thing.

As You Like It Act II. scene vii.

Life and Death

HAMLET.

To be, or not to be, – that is the question: –
Whether 'tis nobler in the mind to suffer
The slings and arrows of outrageous fortune,
Or to take arms against a sea of troubles,
And by opposing end them? – To die, – to sleep, –
No more; and by a sleep to say we end
The heart-ache, and the thousand natural shocks
That flesh is heir to, 'tis a consummation
Devoutly to be wisht. To die, – to sleep; –
To sleep! perchance to dream: ay, there's the rub;
For in that sleep of death what dreams may come,
When we have shuffled off this mortal coil,
Must give us pause: there's the respect
That makes calamity of so long life;
For who would bear the whips and scorns of time,
The oppressor's wrong, the proud man's contumely,
The pangs of despised love, the law's delay,
The insolence of office, and the spurns
That patient merit of the unworthy takes,
When he himself might his quietus make
With a bare bodkin? who would fardels bear,
To grunt and sweat under a weary life,
But that the dread of something after death, –
The undiscover'd country, from whose bourn
No traveller returns, – puzzles the will,
And makes us rather bear those ills we have
Than fly to others that we know not of?
Thus conscience does make cowards of us all;
And thus the native hue of resolution
Is sicklied o'er with the pale cast of thought;
And enterprises of great pith and moment,
With this regard, their currents turn awry,
And lose the name of action.

'Hamlet' Act III. scene i.

*   *   *

SEYTON.

The queen, my lord, is dead.

MACBETH.

She should have died hereafter;
There would have been a time for such a word. –
To-morrow, and to-morrow, and to-morrow,
Creeps in this petty pace from day to day,
To the last syllable of recorded time;
And all our yesterdays have lighted fools

The way to dusty death. Out, out, brief candle!
Life's but a walking shadow; a poor player,
That struts and frets his hour upon the stage,
And then is heard no more: it is a tale
Told by an idiot, full of sound and fury,
Signifying nothing.

Macbeth Act V. scene v.

*   *   *

CLAUDIO.

Ay, but to die, and go we know not where;
To lie in cold obstruction, and to rot;
This sensible warm motion to become
A kneaded clod; and the delighted spirit
To bathe in fiery floods, or to reside
In thrilling region of thick-ribbed ice;
To be imprison'd in the viewless winds,
And blown with restless violence round about
The pendent world; or to be worse than worst
Of those that lawless and incertain thought
Imagine howling! – 'tis too horrible!
The weariest and most loathed worldly life
That age, ache, penury, and imprisonment
Can lay on nature, is a paradise
To what we fear of death.

Measure For Measure Act III. i.

Sleep

KING HENRY.

How many thousand of my poorest subjects
Are at this hour asleep! – O sleep, O gentle sleep,
Nature's soft nurse, how have I frighted thee,
That thou no more wilt weigh my eyelids down,
And steep my senses in forgetfulness?
Why rather, sleep, liest thou in smoky cribs,
Upon uneasy pallets stretching thee,
And husht with buzzing night-flies to thy slumber,
Than in the perfumed chambers of the great,
Under the canopies of costly state,
And lull'd with sound of sweetest melody?
O thou dull god, why liest thou with the vile
In loathsome beds, and leavest the kingly couch
A watch-case or a common 'larum-bell?
Wilt thou upon the high and giddy mast
Seal up the ship-boy's eyes, and rock his brains
In cradle of the rude imperious surge,

And in the visitation of the winds,
Who take the ruffian billows by the top,
Curling their monstrous heads, and hanging them
With deafening clamour in the slippery shrouds,
That, with the hurly, death itself awakes? –
Canst thou, O partial sleep, give thy repose
To the wet sea-boy in an hour so rude;
And in the calmest and most stillest night,
With all appliances and means to boot,
Deny it to a king? Then, happy low, lie down!
Uneasy lies the head that wears a crown.

King Henry The Fourth Part Two Act III. scene i.

Patriotism

JOHN OF GAUNT.
This royal throne of kings, this scepter'd isle,
This earth of majesty, this seat of Mars,
This other Eden, demi-Paradise;
This fortress built by Nature for herself
Against infection and the hand of war;
This happy breed of men, this little world;
This precious stone set in the silver sea,
Which serves it in the office of a wall,
Or as a moat defensive to a house,
Against the envy of less happier lands;
This blessed plot, this earth, this realm, this England,
This nurse, this teeming womb of royal kings,
Fear'd by their breed, and famous by their birth,
Renowned for their deeds as far from home, –
For Christian service and true chivalry, –
As is the sepulchre, in stubborn Jewry,
Of the world's ransom, blessed Mary's Son; –
This land of such dear souls, this dear dear land,
Dear for her reputation through the world,
Is now leased out – I die pronouncing it –
Like to a tenement or pelting farm:
England, bound in with the triumphant sea,
Whose rocky shore beats back the envious siege
Of watery Neptune, is now bound in with shame,
With inky blots, and rotten parchment bonds:
That England, that was wont to conquer others,
Hath made a shameful conquest of itself.
Ah, would the scandal vanish with my life,
How happy then were my ensuing death!

King Richard The Second Act II. scene i.

KING HENRY:

This day is call'd the feast of Crispian:
He that outlives this day, and comes safe home,
Will stand a tip-toe when this day is named,
And rouse him at the name of Crispian.
He that shall live this day, and see old age,
Will yearly on the vigil feast his neighbours,
And say, 'To-morrow is Saint Crispian:'
Then will he strip his sleeve and show his scars,
And say, 'These wounds I had on Crispin's day.'
Old men forget; yet all shall be forgot,
But he'll remember with advantages
What feats he did that day: then shall our names,
Familiar in their mouths as household words, –
Harry the king, Bedford and Exeter,
Warwick and Talbot, Salisbury and Gloster, –
Be in their flowing cups freshly remember'd.
This story shall the good man teach his son;
And Crispin Crispian shall ne'er go by,
From this day to the ending of the world,
But we in it shall be remembered, –
We few, we happy few, we band of brothers;
For he to-day that sheds his blood with me
Shall be my brother; be he ne'er so vile,
This day shall gentle his condition:
And gentlemen in England now a-bed
Shall think themselves accurst they were not here;
And hold their manhoods cheap whiles any speaks
That fought with us upon Saint Crispin's day.

King Henry The Fifth Act IV. scene iii.

Good character

POLONIUS.

There, my blessing with thee!
[*Laying his hand on Laertes' head.*]
And these few precepts in thy memory
See thou character. Give thy thoughts no tongue,
Nor any unproportion'd thought his act.
Be thou familiar, but by no means vulgar.
The friends thou hast, and their adoption tried,
Grapple them to thy soul with hoops of steel;
But do not dull thy palm with entertainment
Of each new-hatch'd, unfledged comrade. Beware
Of entrance to a quarrel; but being in,
Bear't, that the opposed may beware of thee.

Give every man thine ear, but few thy voice:
Take each man's censure, but reserve thy judgment.
Costly thy habit as thy purse can buy,
But not express'd in fancy; rich, not gaudy:
For the apparel oft proclaims the man;
And they in France of the best rank and station
Are most select and generous, chief in that.
Neither a borrower nor a lender be:
For loan oft loses both itself and friend,
And borrowing dulls the edge of husbandry.
This above all: to thine own self be true,
And it must follow, as the night the day,
Thou canst not then be false to any man.
Farewell: my blessing season this in thee!

Hamlet Act I, scene iii.

Conscience

Macbeth.   Methought I heard a voice cry 'Sleep no more!
Macbeth does murder sleep' – the innocent sleep,
Sleep that knits up the ravelled sleave of care,
The death of each day's life, sore labour's bath,
Balm of hurt minds, great Nature's second course,
Chief nourisher in life's feast, –
Lady M.   What do you mean?
Macbeth. Still it cried 'Sleep no more!' to all the house:
'Glamis hath murdered sleep, and therefore Cawdor
Shall sleep no more: Macbeth shall sleep no more!'
Lady M.   Who was it that thus cried? Why, worthy thane,
You do unbend your noble strength, to think
So brainsickly of things. Go get some water,
And wash this filthy witness from your hand.
Why did you bring these daggers from the place?
They must lie there: go carry them, and smear
The sleepy grooms with blood.
Macbeth.   I'll go no more:
I am afraid to think what I have done;
Look on't again I dare not.
Lady M.   Infirm of purpose!
Give me the daggers: the sleeping and the dead
Are but as pictures: 'tis the eye of childhood
That fears a painted devil. If he do bleed,
I'll gild the faces of the grooms withal,
For it must seem their guilt.

[*she goes up. A knocking heard*

Macbeth.   Whence is that knocking?
How is't with me, when every noise appals me?
What hands are here? ha! they pluck out mine eyes!
Will all great Neptune's ocean wash this blood
Clean from my hand? No; this my hand will rather
The multitudinous seas incarnadine,
Making the green – one red.
            Lady Macbeth returns, closing the inner door
Lady M.   My hands are of your colour; but I shame
To wear a heart so white. [*knocking*] I hear a knocking
At the south entry: retire we to our chamber:
A little water clears us of this deed:
How easy is it then! Your constancy
Hath left you unattended. [*knocking*] Hark! more knocking.
Get on your nightgown, lest occasion call us
And show us to be watchers: be not lost
So poorly in your thoughts.
Macbeth.   To know my deed, 'twere best not know myself.
                                              [*knocking*
Wake Duncan with thy knocking! I would thou coldst!
                                      [*they go in*
                                      Macbeth. Act II, scene ii.

Honour, Loyalty, Ambition

MARCUS ANTONIUS.

Friends, Romans, countrymen, lend me your ears;
I come to bury Caesar, not to praise him.
The evil that men do lives after them;
The good is oft interred with their bones;
So let it be with Cœsar. The noble Brutus
Hath told you Cœsar was ambitious:
It it were so, it was a grievous fault;
And grievously hath Cœsar answer'd it.
Here, under leave of Brutus and the rest, –
For Brutus is an honourable man;
So are they all, all honourable men, –
Come I to speak in Cœsar's funeral.
He was my friend, faithful and just to me:
But Brutus says he was ambitious;
And Brutus is an honourable man.
He hath brought many captives home to Rome,
Whese ransoms did the general coffers fill:
Did this in Cœsar seem ambitious?
When that the poor have cried, Cœsar hath wept:
Ambition should be made of sterner stuff:

Yet Brutus says he was ambitious;
And Brutus is an honourable man.
You all did see that on the Lupercal
I thrice presented him a kingly crown,
Which he did thrice refuse: was this ambition?
Yet Brutus says he was ambitious;
And, sure, he is an honourable man.
I speak not to disprove what Brutus spoke,
But here I am to speak what I do know.
You all did love him once, – not without cause:
What cause withholds you, then, to mourn for him?
O judgement, thou art fled to brutish beasts,
And men have lost their reason! – Bear with me;
My heart is in the coffin there with Cœsar,
And I must pause till it come back to me.

Julius Cœsar Act III. scene ii.

*   *   *

MACBETH.
If it were done – when 'tis done – then 'twere well
It were done quickly: if th'assassination
Could trammel up the consequence, and catch,
With his surcease, success; that but this blow
Might be the be-all and the end-all here,
But here, upon this bank and shoal of time,
We'ld jump the life to come. But in these cases
We still have judgement here; that we but teach
Bloody instructions, which, being taught, return
To plague th'inventor: this even-handed justice
Commends th'ingredients of our poison'd chalice
To our own lips. He's here in double trust:
First, as I am his kinsman and his subject,
Strong both against the deed; then, as his host,
Who should against his murderer shut the door,
Not bear the knife myself. Besides, this Duncan
Hath borne his faculties so meek, hath been
So clear in his great office, that his virtues
Will plead like angels, trumpet-tongued, against
The deep damnation of his taking-off;
And pity, like a naked new-born babe,
Striding the blast, or heaven's cherubin, horsed
Upon the sightless couriers of the air,
Shall blow the horrid deed in every eye,
That tears shall drown the wind, – I have no spur
To prick the sides of my intent, but only
Vaulting ambition, which o'erleaps itself,
And falls on th'other.

Macbeth. Act I. scene vii.

Betrayal, Murder

MACBETH.

Is this a dagger which I see before me,
The handle toward my hand? Come, let me clutch thee: –
I have thee not, and yet I see thee still.
Art thou not, fatal vision, sensible
To feeling as to sight? or art thou but
A dagger of the mind, a false creation,
Proceeding from the heat-oppressed brain?
I see thee yet, in form as palpable
As this which now I draw.
Thou marshall'st me the way that I was going;
And such an instrument I was to use.
Mine eyes are made the fools o'th'other senses,
Or else worth all the rest: I see thee still;
And on thy blade and dudgeon gouts of blood,
Which was not so before. – There's no such thing:
It is the bloody business which informs
Thus to mine eyes. – Now o'er the one half-world
Nature seems dead, and wicked dreams abuse
The curtain'd sleep; now witchcraft celebrates
Pale Hecate's offerings; and wither'd murder,
Alarum'd by his sentinel, the wolf,
Whose howl's his watch, thus with his stealthy pace,
With Tarquin's ravishing strides, towards his design
Moves like a ghost. – Thou sure and firm-set earth,
Hear not my steps, which way they walk, for fear
Thy very stones prate of my whereabout,
And take the present horror from the time,
Which now suits with it. – Whiles I threat, he lives:
Words to the heat of deeds too cold breath gives.

[*A bell rings.*

I go, and it is done; the bell invites me.
Hear it not, Duncan; for it is a knell
That summons thee to heaven or to hell.

Macbeth Act II. scene i.

Mercy

PORTIA.

The quality of mercy is not strain'd. –
It droppeth as the gentle rain from heaven
Upon the place beneath: it is twice blest, –
It blesseth him that gives, and him that takes:

'Tis mightiest in the mightiest: it becomes
The throned monarch better than his crown;
His sceptre shows the force of temporal power,
The attribute to awe and majesty,
Wherein doth sit the dread and fear of kings;
But mercy is above this sceptred sway, –
It is enthroned in the hearts of kings,
It is an attribute to God himself;
And earthly power doth then show likest God's
When mercy seasons justice. Therefore, Jew,
Though justice be thy plea, consider this, –
That, in the course of justice, none of us
Should see salvation: we do pray for mercy;
And that same prayer doth teach us all to render
The deeds of mercy. I have spoke thus much
To mitigate the justice of thy plea;
Which if thou follow, this strict court of Venice
Must needs give sentence 'gainst the merchant there.

Merchant of Venice Act IV. scene i.

Kingship

KING RICHARD.

Let's talk of graves, of worms, and epitaphs;
Make dust our paper, and with rainy eyes
Write sorrow on the bosom of the earth.
Let's choose executors, and talk of wills:
And yet not so, – for what can we bequeath,
Save our deposed bodies to the ground?
Our lands, our lives, and all are Bolingbroke's,
And nothing can we call our own but death,
And that small model of the barren earth
Which serves as paste and cover to our bones.
For God's sake, let us sit upon the ground,
And tell sad stories of the death of kings: –
How some have been deposed: some slain in war;
Some haunted by the ghosts they have deposed;
Some poison'd by their wives; some sleeping kill'd;
All murder'd: – for within the hollow crown
That rounds the mortal temples of a king
Keeps Death his court; and there the antick sits,
Scoffing his state, and grinning at his pomp;
Allowing him a breath, a little scene,
To monarchize, be fear'd, and kill with looks;
Infusing him with self and vain conceit, –
As if this flesh, which walls about our life,

Were brass impregnable: an humour'd thus,
Comes at the last, and with a little pin
Bores through his castle-wall, and – farewell king!
Cover your heads, and mock not flesh and blood
With solemn reverence; throw away respect,
Tradition, form, and ceremonious duty;
For you have but mistook me all this while:
I live with bread like you, feel want,
Taste grief, need friends: – subjected thus,
How can you say to me, I am a king?

King Richard The Second Act III. scene ii.

Love

SONNET 2.

When forty winters shall besiege thy brow,
And dig deep trenches in thy beauty's field,
Thy youth's proud livery, so gazed on now,
Will be a totter'd weed, of small worth held:
Then being askt where all thy beauty lies,
Where all the treasure of thy lusty days;
To say, within thine own deep-sunken eyes,
Were an all-eating shame and thriftless praise.
How much more praise deserved thy beauty's use,
If thou couldst answer, 'This fair child of mine
Shall sum my count, and make my old excuse,'
Proving his beauty by succession thine!
    This were to be new made when thou art old,
    And see thy blood warm when thou feel'st it cold.

SONNET 18.

Shall I compare thee to a summer's day?
Thou art more lovely and more temperate:
Rough winds do shake the darling buds of May,
And summer's lease hath all to short a date:
Sometime too hot the eye of heaven shines,
And often is his gold complexion dimm'd;
And every fair from fair sometime declines,
By chance, or nature's changing course, untrimm'd;
But thy eternal summer shall not fade,
Nor lose possession of that fair thou ow'st;
Nor shall Death brag thou wander'st in his shade,
When in eternal lines to time thou grow'st:
    So long as men can breathe, or eyes can see,
    So long lives this, and this gives life to thee.

Time

SONNET 60.

Like as the waves make towards the pebbled shore,
So do our minutes hasten to their end;
Each changing place with that which goes before,
In sequent toil all forwards do contend.
Nativity, once in the main of light,
Crawls to maturity, wherewith being crown'd,
Crooked eclipses 'gainst his glory fight,
And Time that gave doth now his gift confound.
Time doth transfix the flourish set on youth,
And delves the parallels in beauty's brow;
Feeds on the rarities of nature's truth,
And nothing stands but for his scythe to mow:
And yet, to times in hope my verse shall stand,
Praising thy worth, despite his cruel hand.

SONNET 65.

Since brass, nor stone, nor boundless sea,
But sad mortality o'ersways their power,
How with this rage shall beauty hold a plea,
Whose action is no stronger than a flower?
O, how shall summer's honey breath hold out
Against the wrackful siege of battering days,
When rocks impregnable are not so stout,
Nor gates of steel so strong, but Time decays?
O fearful meditation! where, alack,
Shall Time's best jewel from Time's chest lie hid?
Or what strong hand can hold his swift foot back?
Or who his spoil of beauty can forbid?
O, none, unless this miracle have might,
That in black ink my love may still shine bright.

Equal Opportunities

1 Discrimination at work

Introduction

If you look at many advertisements for jobs these days you will see the words 'Equal Opportunity Employer'.

This heading will often be followed by:

'We are an equal opportunities employer and welcome all applications irrespective of sex, ethnic origin, disability or marital status.'

Such phrases are only a relatively recent occurrence with many employers – and for some they would still seem a little alien. Take, for example, the following short story by Bernard Ashley, a well-known writer for young people.

Reading

Equal rights

'Can't you read?'

The man was looking at me and reaching under the counter as if he was going for his gun. He came up with another one of his signs to spread over the front of a paper.

'"Only two children at a time allowed in this shop"', he read out, loudly.

I looked across at the two kids in the corner. They were pretending to pick Penny Chews while they gawped at the girls on the magazines. O.K., I made three, but I wasn't there for the same reason as them. Couldn't he recognise business when he saw it?

'I'm not buying,' I said, 'I've come about the job.'

He frowned at me, in between watching the boys in the corner. 'What job?' he said. He was all on edge with three of us in the shop.

'"Reliable paper boy wanted"', I told him. '"Enquire within." It's in the window. I'm enquiring within.'

'Hurry up, you two!' he shouted. And then he frowned at me again as if I was something from outer space.

'But you're not a boy,' he said. '"Reliable paper *boy* required", that says. If I'd meant "boy *or girl*" I'd have put it on, wouldn't I? Or "paper *person*"!' He did this false laugh for the benefit of a man with a briefcase standing at the counter.

'Oh,' I said, disappointed. 'Only I'm *reliable*, that's all. I get up early with my dad, I'm never off school, and I can tell the difference between the *Sun* and the *Beano*.'

'I'm glad someone can,' the man with the briefcase said.

But the paper man didn't laugh. He was looking at me, hard.

'Where d'you live?' he asked.

'Round the corner.'

'Could you start at seven?'

'Six, if you like.'

'Rain or shine, winter and summer?'

'No problem.' I stared at him, and he stared at me. He looked as if he was deciding whether or not to give women the vote.

'All right,' he said, 'I'll give you a chance. Start Monday. Seven o'clock, do your own marking-up. Four pounds a week, plus Christmas tips. Two weeks' holiday without pay ...'

Now that he'd made up his mind he smiled at me over-doing the big favour.

'Is that what the boys get?' I asked. 'Four pounds a week?'

He started unwrapping a packet of fags. 'I don't see how that concerns you. The money suits or it doesn't. Four pounds is what I said, and four pounds is what I meant. Take it or leave it.' He looked at Briefcase again, shaking his head at the cheek of the girl.

I walked back to the door. 'I'll leave it, then,' I said, 'seeing the boys get five pounds, *and* a week's holiday with pay.' I knew all this because Jason used to do it. 'Thanks anyway, I'll tell my dad what you said ...'

'Please yourself.'

I slammed out of the shop. I was mad, I can tell you. Cheap labour, he was after: thought he was on to a good thing for a minute, you could tell that.

The trouble was, I really needed a bit of money coming in, saving for those shoes and things I wanted. There was no way I'd get them otherwise. But I wasn't going to be treated any different from the boys. I wouldn't have a shorter round or lighter papers, would I? Everything'd be the same, except the money.

I walked the long way home, thinking. It was nowhere near Guy Fawkes, and Carol Singing was even further away. So that really only left car washing – and they leave the rain to wash the cars round our way.

Hearing this baby cry gave me the idea. Without thinking about it I knocked at the door where the bawling was coming from.

The lady opened it and stared at me like you stare at double-glazing salesmen, when you're cross for being brought to the door.

'"Baby-play calling"', I said – making up the name from somewhere.

The lady said, 'Eh?' and she looked behind me to see who was pulling my strings.

'"Baby-play"', I said. 'We come and play with your baby in your own home. Keep it happy. Or walk it out – not going across main roads.'

She opened the door a bit wider. The baby crying got louder.

'How much?' she asked.

That really surprised me. I'd felt sorry about calling from the first lift of the knocker, and here she was taking me seriously.

'I don't know,' I said. 'Whatever you think ...'

'Well ...' She looked at me to see if she'd seen me before; to see if I was local enough to be trusted. Then I was glad I had the school jumper on, so she knew I could be traced. 'You push Bobby down the shops and get Mr Dawson's magazines, and I'll give you twenty pence. Take your time, mind ...'

'All right,' I said. 'Thank you very much.'

She got this little push-chair out, and the baby came as good as gold – put its foot in the wheel a couple of times and nearly twisted its head off trying to see who I was, but I kept up the talking, and I stopped while it stared out a cat, so there wasn't any fuss.

When I got to the paper shop I took Bobby in with me.

'Afternoon,' I said, trying not to make too much of coming back. 'We've come down for Mr Dawson's papers, haven't we, Bobby?'

You should have seen the man's face.

'Mr Dawson's?' he asked, burning his finger on a match. 'Number twenty-nine?'

'Yes, please.'

'Are you . . .?' He nodded at Bobby and then at me as if he was making some link between us.

'That's right,' I said.

He fumbled at a pile behind him and lifted out the magazines. He laid them on the counter.

'Dawson', it said on the top. I looked at the titles to see what Mr Dawson enjoyed reading.

Workers' Rights was one of them. And *Trade Union Times* was the other. They had pictures on their fronts. On had two men pulling together on a rope. The other had a woman bus-driver waving out of her little window. They told you the sort of man Mr Dawson was – one of those trade union people you get on television kicking up a fuss over wages, or getting cross when women are treated different to men. Just the sort of bloke I could do with on my side, I thought.

The man was still fiddling about with his pile of magazines.

'Oh, look,' he said, with a green grin. 'I've got last month's *Pop Today* left over. You can have it if you like, with my compliments . . .'

'Thanks a lot,' I said. Now I saw the link in his mind. He thought I was Mr Dawson's daughter. He thought there'd be all sorts of trouble now, over me being offered lower wages than the boys.

'And about that job. Stupid of me, I'd got it wrong. What did I say – *four* pounds a week?'

'I think so,' I said. 'It sounded like a four.'

'How daft can you get? It was those kids in the corner. Took my attention off. Of course it's *five*, you realise that. Have you spoken to your dad yet?'

'No, not yet.'

He stopped leaning so hard on the counter. 'Are you still interested?'

'Yes. Thank you very much.'

He came round the front and shook hands with me. 'Monday at seven,' he said. 'Don't be late . . .' But you could tell he was only saying it, pretending to be the big boss.

'Right.' I turned the push-chair round. 'Say ta-ta to the man, Bobby,' I said.

Bobby just stared, like at the cat.

The paper man leaned over. 'Dear little chap,' he said.

'Yeah, smashing. But Bobby's a girl, not a chap, aren't you, Bobby? At least, that's what Mrs Dawson just told me.'

I went out of the shop, while my new boss made this funny gurgling sound, and knocked a pile of papers on the floor.

He'd made show-up of himself, found out too late that I wasn't Mr Dawson's daughter.

I ran and laughed and zig-zagged Bobby along the pavement. 'Good for us! Equal rights, eh, Bobby? Equal rights!'

But Bobby's mind was all on the ride. She couldn't care less what I was shouting.

All she wanted was someone to push her fast, to feel the wind on her face. Boy or girl, it was al the same to her.

'*Equal Rights' by Bernard Ashley*

Reflections

* Have you had experiences of this kind?
  Is it true that there is still discrimination in employing people, and particularly in the employment of young people? What might your reaction have been in similar circumstances to those faced by the girl in this story?

  It is important that we all strive for equality of opportunity. Sometimes – as in this story – a few well chosen words can achieve as much as being aggressive towards someone about their out-of-date practices.

  It is important, however, to challenge unjust practices whenever we come across them. One unjust employer brings a bad name to all good employers, in the same way that one person in any community who 'breaks the rules' lets everyone else down.

2 Equal Rights*

Introduction

British society has developed considerably since the early years of the twentieth century when Emily Pankhurst and others fought for the vote for women. As young people enter the worlds of higher education and careers in the 1990s, the debate continues about the relative roles of women and men in the workplace and in the home.

The following poem/song uses some fairly direct language on this subject – seen from a female standpoint. Its title is *Maintenance Engineer*.

Reading

Maintenance Engineer

One Friday night it happened, soon after we were wed,
When my old man came in from work as usual I said:
'Your tea is on the table, clean clothes are on the rack,
Your bath will soon be ready, I'll come up and scrub your back.'
He kissed me very tenderly and said, 'I'll tell you flat
The service I give my machine ain't half as good as that.'

I said . . .

Chorus

I'm not your little woman, your sweetheart or your dear
I'm a wage slave without wages, I'm a maintenance engineer.

Well then we got to talking. I told him how I felt,
How I keep him running just as smooth as some conveyor belt!

Well after all, it's I'm the one provides the power supply
He goes just like the clappers on me steak'n kidney pie.
His fittings are all shining 'cos I keep 'em nice and clean
And he tells me his machine tool is the best I've ever seen.

But . . .

Chorus

The terms of my employment would make your hair turn grey,
I have to be on call you see for 24 hours a day.
I quite enjoy the perks though while I'm working through the night
For we get job satisfaction. Well he does, and then I might.
If I keep up full production, I should have a kid or two,
So some future boss will have a brand new labour force to screw.

So . . .

Chorus

The truth began to dawn then, how I keep him fit and trim
So the boss can make a nice fat profit out of me and him.
And, as a solid union man, he got in quite a rage
To think that we're both working hard and getting one man's wage.
I said 'And what about the part-time packing job I do?
That's three men that I work for love, my boss, your boss and you.'

So . . .

Chorus

He looked a little sheepish and he said, 'As from today
The lads and me will see what we can do on equal pay.
Would you like a housewives' union? Do you think you should get paid?
As a cook and as a cleaner, as a nurse and as a maid?'
I said, 'Don't jump the gun love, if you did your share at home,
Perhaps I'd have some time to fight some battles of my own.'

For . . .

Chorus

I've often heard you tell me how you'll pull the bosses down.
You'll never do it brother while you're bossing me around.
'Til women join the struggle, married, single, white and black
You're fighting with a blindfold and one arm behind your back.'
The message has got over now for he's realised at last
That power to the sisters must mean power to the class.

And . . .

Chorus

Repeat: *I'm not your little woman, your sweetheart or your dear*
          I'm a wage-slave without wages
          I'm a maintenance engineer.

Sandra Kerr

Reflections

* 'Maintenance Engineer' has some powerful points to make about women 'serving' men in contemporary society. The song serves as a kind of rallying call to women and, by extension, other groups who are repressed in society.

  Many people – perhaps men, especially – would argue with Sandra Kerr's message. But she throws down the gauntlet very powerfully.

  If we look around our own community, what messages are given to females and males about future roles? This is a question that schools and all organisations need to ask themselves regularly.

3 Expectations

Introduction

Expectations play a key part in our lives: our own expectations of ourselves and what others expect of us. This is true whether we are talking about how we learn, behave or treat our family and friends.

But does society have different expectations of girls and of boys? If so, how early in our lives does this begin?

The following extract comes from a short story called *Baby X*.

Reading

Baby X

Once upon a time a baby named X was born. This baby was named X so that nobody could tell whether it was a boy or a girl. Its parents could tell of course but they couldn't tell anybody else. They couldn't even tell Baby X at first.

You see, it was all part of a very important, secret scientific Xperiment known officially as Project Baby X.

Long before Baby X was born a lot of scientists had to be paid to work out the details of the Xperiment and to write the Official Instructions Manual for baby X's parents and most important of all to find the right set of parents to bring up Baby X.

But finally the scientists found the Joneses, who really wanted to raise an X more than any other kind of baby, no matter how much trouble it would be. Ms and Mr Jones had to promise that they would take equal turns caring for X and feeding it and singing it lullabies.

The day the Joneses brought their baby home lots of friends and relatives came over to see it. None of them knew about the secret Xperiment though. When the Joneses smiled and said, 'It's an X,' nobody knew what to say. They couldn't say 'Look at her cute little dimples' and they couldn't say 'Look how strong his muscles are' and they couldn't say just plain 'kitchy coo'. In fact they all thought the Joneses were playing some kind of rude joke.

But of course, the Joneses were not joking. 'It's an X' was absolutely all they would say, and that made the friends and relatives very angry. The relatives all felt very embarrassed about having an X in the family. 'People will think there's something wrong with it' some of them whispered. 'There is something wrong with it,' others whispered back.

'Nonsense' the Joneses told them cheerfully. 'What could possibly be wrong with this perfectly adorable X? Nobody could answer that except Baby X who had just finished its bottle. Baby X's answer was a loud satisfied burp!

Clearly, nothing at all was wrong. Nevertheless none of the relatives felt comfortable about buying a present for a Baby X. The cousins who sent the baby a tiny pair of boxing gloves would not come and visit anymore, and the neighbours who sent a pink flowered romper suit drew their curtains when the Joneses passed their house.

Ms and Mr Jones had to be Xtra careful about how they played with little X. They knew that if they kept bouncing it in the air and saying how strong and active it was they'd be treating it more like a boy than an X. But if all they did was cuddle and kiss it and tell it how sweet and dainty it was, they'd be treating it more like a girl than an X. On page 1,654 of the Official Instructions Manual the scientists prescribed 'plenty of bouncing and plenty of cuddling both'. X ought to be strong and sweet and active – forget about the dainty altogether.

Meanwhile the Joneses were worrying about other problems. Toys, for instance. And clothes. Mr Jones wandered helplessly up and down the aisles finding out what X needed. But everything in the store was piled up in sections marked 'Boys' or 'Girls'. There were 'Boys' pyjamas' and 'Girls' underwear' and 'Boys' fire engines' and 'Girls' housekeeping sets.' Mr Jones went home without buying anything for X. That night, he and Ms Jones consulted page 2,326 of the Official Instructions Manual. 'Buy plenty of everything' it said firmly. So they bought plenty of sturdy blue pyjamas in the Boys department and cheerful flowered underwear in the Girls department and they bought all kinds of toys. A boy doll that made pee-pee and cried Papa, and a girl doll that talked in three languages and said 'I am the president of General Motors'. They also bought a story book about a brave princess who rescued a handsome prince from his ivory tower and another one about a sister and brother who grew up to be a baseball star and a ballet star and you had to guess which was which.

By the time X grew big enough to play with other children the Joneses' trouble had grown bigger too. Once a little girl grabbed X's shovel in the sandbox and zonked X on the head with it. 'Now Tracy,' the little girl's mother scolded. 'Little girls mustn't hit little . . .' and she turned to ask X, 'Are you a boy or a girl dear?' Mr Jones who was sitting near held his breath. X smiled and even though its head had never been zonked so hard before, replied 'I'm an X', 'You're a what?' exclaimed the lady. 'You're a little brat, you mean.' 'But little girls mustn't hit little X's either,' said X retrieving the shovel and smiling again. 'What good does hitting do anyway?' X's father grinned at X. At their next secret Project X meeting the scientists grinned and said Baby X was doing fine.

But it was then time for X to start school. The Joneses were really worried about this because school was even more full of rules for boys and girls, and there were no rules for Xs. The teacher would tell boys to form one line and girls to form another. There would be boys' games and girls' games and boys' secrets and girls' secrets. The school library would have a list of recommended books for boys and another for girls. Pretty soon boys and girls would hardly talk to each other. What would happen to poor little X?

The Joneses had asked X's teacher if the class could line up alphabetically instead of boys and girls, and if X could use the principal's bathroom as it wasn't marked Boy or Girl. X's teacher promised to take care of all these problems; but no one could help with X's biggest problem, 'Other Children'.

After school X wanted to play with Other Children. 'How about football?' it asked the girls. They giggled. 'How about weaving baskets?' it asked the boys. They giggled too and made faces. That night Ms and Mr Jones asked how things had gone at school. X said sadly the lessons were OK but otherwise school was a terrible place for an X – it seemed as if Other Children never wanted an X for a friend.

Once more, the Joneses read the Official Instructions Manual. Under 'Other Children' they found the message 'What do you expect? Other Children have to obey all the silly boy and girl rules because their parents taught them to. Lucky X, you don't have to stick to rules at all. All you do is be yourself. PS We're not saying it will be easy.'

X liked being itself. But X cried a lot that night partly because it felt afraid. So X's father held X tight and cuddled it and couldn't help crying too. And X's mother cheered them both up by reading an Xciting story about an enchanted prince called Sleeping Handsome who woke up when Princess Charming kissed him. The next morning they all felt much better and little X went back to school with a brave smile.

There was a relay race in the gym, and a baking contest and X won the relay race and almost won the baking contest Xcept it forgot to light the oven, which only proves that nobody is perfect.

One of the Other Children noticed something else. 'Winning or losing doesn't seem to matter to X. X seems to have fun at boy and girl skills.'

'Come to think of it' said another child, 'Maybe X is having twice the fun we are.' So after school that day, the girl who won the baking contest gave X a big slice of cake and the boy who nearly won the race asked X to race him home. From then on some funny things happened. Susie, who sat next to X, refused to wear pink dresses to school anymore. She wanted to wear red and white check overalls like X's, they were better for climbing monkey bars. Then Jim, the class football nut, started wheeling his sister's doll's pram round the football field. He'd put on his football uniform except the helmet. Then he put the helmet in the pram lovingly tucked under a set of shoulder pads. Then he'd push it round the football field singing 'Rockabye baby' to his helmet. He told his family X did the same thing so it must be OK, after all, X was now the team's quarterback.

Susie's parents were horrified by her behaviour and Jim's were worried sick about him. But the worst came when the twins Joe and Peggy decided to share everything with each other. Peggy used Joe's hockey skates and his microscope and shared his newspaper round. Joe used Peggy's needlework kit and cookbooks and took three of her baby-sitting jobs. Peggy used the lawnmower and Joe the vacuum cleaner.

Their parents weren't one bit pleased with Peggy's wonderful chemistry experiments or with Joe's embroidered pillows. They didn't care that Peggy mowed the lawn better and that Joe vacuumed the carpet better. In fact they were furious. 'It's all that little X's fault' they agreed. 'Just because X doesn't know what it is, or what it's supposed to be, it wants to get everyone mixed up too.' Peggy and Joe were forbidden to play with X. So was Susie and then Jim and then all the Other Children. But it was too late. The Other Children stayed mixed up and happy and free and refused to go back to the way they had been before.

Reflections

* Does the tale ring true?
  Do parents behave like those in the story?
  Do children behave in this way?
  Do relatives respond to girls and boys differently?
  And what about the way *schools* are organised?

* Such a story makes us aware of gender expectations in a light-hearted and amusing way. The more serious message is something we might reflect upon further in our school community.

4 It's a man's job being a mother

Introduction

Our society is still very much organised around mothers looking after babies, with fathers out at work. Depending on your point of view, this may or may not be a good thing. But will change come? Will 'male motherhood' become more common? And what are the pros and cons of this for mothers and fathers alike? Listen to the following newspaper article, *It's a Man's job being a Mother*.

Reading

It's a man's job being a mother

Thursday afternoon, there we all sit amid the shrieks, wails and rebukes, infants on every knee, at the shrine of Babyrama. I must say there's a certain satisfaction at being the only man at the Welfare Clinic. Male mothers, being thin on the ground in our small town, enjoy a mild and entirely spurious celebrityhood, but much more interesting is to penetrate the secret society of female mothers. So *this* is what they get up to.

When my wife's pregnancy was confirmed, we didn't have much of a decision to take. We are both journalists but her job meant a lot to her – and a monthly cheque, too. As a freelance, I earned much less, and was happy not to be bound to regular hours; so I prepared to face the frightening prospect of five-day motherhood. Then, luckily, my wife managed to arrange a basic three-day office week, making up the rest while at home.

Susie, our daughter, is now 16 months old. Since she was four months and moved on to a bottle – she has had more or less equal time from us. It's a three-and-a-half day shift. My wife may be exhausted most of the time, but she's not your traditional housebound mum, always there and fussing, and I'm not the traditional glamorous stranger of a father who briefly comes home to dig the garden and refuel for the great mysterious bacon-hunt out there in the wider world.

My first day alone with Susie was a trial, but we got through it. I didn't poison her or skewer her with a safetypin. I gratefully learned that babies are brave, utterly sincere, and really want to live. Looking after her seemed possible, if gruelling, and indeed it has become more enjoyable by the day. So far.

Any fool can tell when a nappy needs changing, when to administer fuel, and to keep razor blades off the floor. Beyond the obvious physical differences – there have been times when I'd have liked a good pair of baby-perching hips – we haven't found that parental excellence has a great deal to do with sex.

Not that it's the same for both of us. Given the choice, Susie tends to go to her mother for comfort and to me for games. *Mamama* usually means I am not happy and *Dadada* means I want some action, and so either of us can be mam or dad to her. Perhaps the seeds of confusion are being sown, but Susie seems to be doing well enough. She doesn't compare with one three-year-old we knew who called men in the street daddy and her father Uncle Tony. But she seemed to do all right, too.

I never did overcome my prejudices enough to take Susie down the High Street in her pram; with me, she's always travelled by baby buggy or shoulder. In the early days, I used to check whether Susie had puked down her front when tight-faced women passed us, and once a minibus full of homebound workmen started howling and jeering as we trundled by.

But I'm a lot less sheepish now I realise it's often sour grapes. 'All right for some,' moans my neighbour, a husky carpenter; he says he'd love to give his job to his wife and do what I'm doing. I would have thought more women would have been offended at a man staying at home with the baby, but most, even a great-grannie over the road, seem delighted to see a man getting a taste of their timeless lot. And I don't feel particularly emasculated.

It wasn't always easy, however, to convince other mothers that I could cope. Just as baby manuals tend to patronise mothers, so they patronised me from time to time, and once I had a yelling Susie literally ripped from my arms by a well-meaning soul. I was flabbergasted, but happily the crone's gurglings only made her cry the more. Even at six months she knew which side her bread was buttered.

She's always been a good companion, too. Far from the inert blank sheet I'd been expecting, I soon found myself thinking of Susie as a fully-developed character from another planet, struggling to adapt to earthling ways. It's treat to see through her fresh new eyes, to see how she takes things, and even to catch on to one-year-old jokes, which are frequently hysterical.

One temptation is simply to spend all day messing about the house with her. But as the advert says, Painful Piles can spoil the Joy of Motherhood, so most days we set off on long exploring expeditions. She loves it, while for me she's been a passport to all sorts of forgotten pleasures; just standing and looking, for example.

Not that male motherhood is a free cruise; but I suspect that hurled food and broken heirlooms are easier to take when you don't feel that looking after the baby is an inevitable burden bequeathed by sex and history.

At any rate, more and more men seem to be doing it. If only the Inland Revenue would accept that some of us aren't bread-winners and transfer allowances accordingly. For four years we've been trying to get mortgage relief off my freelance account – which is always in arrears – and on to my wife's PAYE. This is quite legit, but the inspectors can't seem to believe that my wife intends to continue to work.

More encouraging, however, is the news from the Department of Health and Social Security. Equal contributions and equal benefits are on the way. About time we sent our wives out to get the ulcers, said the man.

'It's a man's job being a mother' by Rick Sanders

Reflections

* 'Looking after the baby is an inevitable burden bequeathed by sex and history' is a striking phrase to reflect on.

  Different patterns of child-care are found in different parts of the world; some cultures tend to be matriarchal, some patriarchal. This passage certainly challenges the stereotype of women and babies in the home, men out at work. Clearly these parents had the advantage of paid employment outside the home which could be organised flexibly. For many women and men in today's society, if your employment doesn't lend itself to a job-share then shared baby-care is almost impossible.

  But society changes and evolves. What will the picture be like in ten, 20 or 50 years time? For the present generation in schools, with greater equal opportunities for all, perhaps more questions will be asked of employers in future years. 'Male motherhood' and 'Female fatherhood' are interesting phrases to conjure with.

5 Education of girls: going to University*

Introduction

Students today who are taking A and A/S levels have a good chance of obtaining a University or Polytechnic place to pursue academic study at a higher level. There has been a long-standing debate about whether everyone has full opportunity to go on to higher education. To take one example, the question of 'who pays?' continues to be argued out between politicians and educationists around the world.

There have long been battles about access to higher education – as is revealed in this extract from Carol Adams's history book, *Ordinary Lives*.

Reading

Education of girls: going to University

GOING TO UNIVERSITY

One reason parents may have felt it wasn't worth sending their daughters to school in the mid-nineteenth century was that they could not go to university. While boys' schools entered their pupils for the equivalent of today's O-levels, girls could not take these before the 1860s. In 1863 Emily Davies persuaded the Oxford and Cambridge local examination boards to allow girls to sit the exams. This started a national debate. Here are some of the arguments used at the time:

'"There is no question that in the highest departments of original and creative power, the mind of woman is or ever can be equal to that of men." Dr Hodgson, educationalist.

"The examiners will favour pretty candidates." [difficult since they never saw them] – *Saturday Review*

"Higher education will produce flat-chested women unable to suckle their babies." Dr Spencer, medical doctor

"Giving them a boy's education will damage their reproductive organs." *The Lancet* (a medical journal)

"The creation of a new race of puny, sedentary and unfeminine students would destroy the grace and charm of social life." *Contemporary Review Magazine*

"There is a strong and ineradicable male instinct that a learned or even over-accomplished woman is one of the most intolerable monsters in creation." Dr Hodgson, educationalist'

By 1870, once the battle for girls to take school-leaving exams had been won, they were allowed to attend some university lectures. The first women's college, Girton College, Cambridge was established in 1874.

The college buildings were not in fact in Cambridge, but 26 miles away at Hitchen – a 'safe' distance from the men. A chaperone – an older married woman to keep an eye on the girls – was required to attend lectures with women students until 1893. They sat in the corner knitting:

'It is curious to look back now and see how necessary the chaperone was. In 1890 girls had hardly begun to walk about Oxford alone . . . and Oxford was particularly ready to remark on any advanced behaviour on the part of a woman student.'

Vera Brittain, *Women at Oxford*

The behaviour of girls at university was more restricted than that of boys, as Dora Russell remembers:

'You could not receive a young man in your room; you might be permitted to have him to tea in one of the public reception rooms, but you could accept no invitation from young men to tea or other entertainment without a chaperone from the college.'

Dora Russell, *The Tamarisk Tree*

Among the middle classes, university education for a girl was considered odd, while for a boy it was expected, as Vera Brittain found:

'In spite of his limited qualities of scholarship and his fitful interest in all non-musical subjects, the idea of refusing Edward a university education never so much as crossed my father's mind.

The most flattering of my school reports had never, I knew, been regarded more seriously than my inconvenient thirst for knowledge and opportunities; in our family, to adapt a famous present-day phrase, what mattered was not the quality of the work, but the sex of the worker.'

Vera Brittain, *Testament of Youth*

After she had applied to university, Vera Brittain's mother was asked by her friends: 'How can you send your daughter to college, Mrs Brittain? Don't you want her ever to get married?'

Although by the end of the century women were allowed to take all the exams for degrees and could graduate at London and other new universities, they were not awarded degrees at Oxford until 1920: at Cambridge it was not until 1948.

A similar struggle was fought to open medical training to women. The first woman doctor, Elizabeth Garrett Anderson, only got on to the Medical Register in 1865 by taking the exam for Apothecaries after private study; she could not study at an all-male medical school. At Edinburgh, where women were first allowed to attend some classes, they were jeered and ridiculed by male students, and when they were finally allowed to take the exam, in 1870, the men pushed a live sheep into the examination room. Sophia Jex Blake, who led the women's campaign at Edinburgh, started the London School of Medicine for Women and, in 1878, London University finally accepted women for degrees in medicine. By 1890 there were 110 registered women doctors.

Although a small minority, the women who went into higher education a hundred years ago made a great impact on society. Many became suffragettes and campaigned for women's rights; many became teachers and greatly improved the quality of girls' education; others who did not have outstanding careers, made their mark as educated, intelligent women, not prepared to go along with the old Victorian ideal of the accomplished but idle lady.

From 'Ordinary Lives' by Carol Adams

Reflections

* This selection of quotations reveals some extraordinary prejudices. Happily, we can paint a different picture today in relation to courses on offer to women and men. But attitudes have been slow to change right through the education system, as the following quotations from Government reports on schools highlight. Note the dates of the reports and how attitudes have (or have not) changed.

1874: 'A girl is not necessarily a better woman because she knows the height of all the mountains of Europe, and can work a fraction in her head; but she is decidedly better fitted for the duties she will be called upon to perform in life if she knows how to wash and tend a child, cook simple food well, and thoroughly clean a house.'

Board School Report

1904: 'The course should provide ... Geography, History, Mathematics, Science and Drawing, with due provision for Manual Work and Physical Exercises, and, in a girls' school for Housewifery.'

Government Regulations for Secondary Schools

1943: 'Domestic science is a necessary equipment for all girls as potential makers of homes.'

The Norwood Report on curriculum and examinations

1959: 'With the less able girls, however, we think schools can and should make adjustments to the fact that marriage now looms much larger and nearer in the pupils' eyes than ever before.'

The Crowther Report on education from 15–18

1963: 'For all girls, too, there is a group of interests relating to what many, perhaps most of them, regard as their most important vocational concern – marriage.'

The Newsom Report on pupils of less than average ability

* The challenge for today's 18-year-olds is to ensure that equality of opportunity, having been fought for, remains secure for future generations of students.

6 The 1990s: Decade of women in leadership

Introduction

If you look closely at the majority of organisations that employ women and men in equal numbers, you will tend to find that the higher up the organisation's hierarchy and management structure you go, the fewer women you will find.

Our own House of Commons – the place where laws are made for this country – offers a very poor example: out of 650 Members of Parliament only around 50 are women. In fact, a society exists called the 300 Club which aims to achieve 300 women MPs.

But perhaps times are changing. In fact, according to the following American writer, by the end of the 1990s women will be sharing equal leadership roles with men.

Reading

The 1990s: decade of Women in Leadership

THE DECADE OF WOMEN IN BUSINESS

Corporations as we have known them were created by men for men. After World War II America's veterans exchanged their military uniforms for factory overalls and gray flannel suits. But the bureaucratic, authoritarian military model from the 19th century remained the organizational system by which they governed themselves. Yet since World War II the number of working women has increased 200 per cent.

For the last two decades US women have taken two thirds of the millions of new jobs created in the information era and will continue to do so well into the millennium.

The days of women as some sort of minority in the work force are over. Women without children are *more* likely to work than men. Today about 74 per cent of men work. But 79 per cent of women with no children under eighteen work. So do 67 per cent of women with children, almost as high a percentage as men. Half of women with small children work, too.

In business and many professions women have increased from a minority as low as 10 per cent in 1970 to a critical mass ranging from 30 to 50 per cent in much of the business world, including banking, accounting, and computer science.

An important symbol is the history of *Working Woman* magazine, whose circulation grew from 450,000 in 1981 to 900,000 in 1988, surpassing *Fortune, Forbes*, and finally, at 850,000, *Business Week*. The only business periodical with a larger circulation is the *Wall Street Journal*.

Women are starting new businesses twice as fast as men. In Canada one third of small businesses are owned by women. In France it is one fifth. In Britain since 1980 the number of self-employed women has increased three times as fast as the number of self-employed men. As workers, professionals, and entrepreneurs women dominate the information society.

To be a leader in business today, it is no longer an advantage to have been socialized as a male.

Although we do not fully realize it as yet, men and women are on an equal playing field in corporate America. Women may even hold a slight advantage since they need not 'unlearn' old authoritarian behaviour to run their departments or companies.

Like their male colleagues (who probably did not serve in the military either), they must learn to coach, inspire, and gain people's commitment. They must set personal examples of excellence.

After two decades of quietly preparing, gaining experience, and being frustrated with the male establishment, women in business are on the verge of revolutionary change. Older, wiser, more numerous, and well represented in cutting-edge industries like computers, finance, and advertising, women are ready to break through the 'glass ceiling,' the invisible barrier that has kept them from the top. As the nineties progress, conventional wisdom will concede that women and men function equally well as business leaders, and women will achieve leadership positions denied them in years past.

From 'The 1990s: Decade of women in leadership' in 'Megatrends 2000' by
Naisbitt and Aburdene

Reflections

Two key points emerge from this American commentary:

First, 'corporations as we have them were created by men for men'.

Second, 'to be a leader in business today, it is no longer an advantage to have been socialized as a male.'

If you examine British society today, to what extent is the first statement true? We would probably say that it is.

But what are implications of the second point? This presumably suggests that the culture of business is changing in favour of women. Time will no doubt tell. In the meantime we need to examine within the school community how we educate all young people in a climate of equal opportunity – and, crucially, in a climate of equal *access* to that opportunity.

Only in that way will women 'achieve leadership positions denied them in years past'.

7 Sexism in language

Introduction

Language comes naturally to most of us. We learn it from our parents and develop it with relatives and friends, then in school. If the language around us at an early age is English, Urdu, Swahili or Japanese, that will become our heritage tongue. Many observers say that English is man-made language and that through our words we convey powerful images about males, and less favourable ones about females. These observers go on to claim that this process begins at a very early age. Listen to the following piece about an American author who has attempted to rewrite some traditional nursery rhymes.

Reading

The man who made the gander blander

We all know what Mother Goose is like: mature, stout and matronly, fond of a joke. She has seen it all in her day – fallen cradles, cats down wells, beatings, pig-rustling, and sexual harassment by Georgie Porgie. Still, she is of a good family and we know her well. We grew up with her.

But who is Father Gander? I will tell you. His name is Dr Doug Larche and he is author of *Father Gander Nursery Rhymes*. He is a 37-year-old professor and chairperson of the Speech and Theatre Department of Grand View College, Iowa, USA. He is into 'Arts, ecology, human communication, energy, and a liberal, renaissance-person approach'. Unlike Mother Goose, he believes that we can all live together in harmony. Even his version of *Humpty Dumpty* ends on an inspiring note of sex equality, achievement and republicanism (no King's horses): 'All of the horses, the women and men/Put Humpty Dumpty together again!'

Doug Larche first became interested in nursery rhymes 10 years ago when his own children were aged three and one. It was sexism that first got him going: 'My son Jason was able to glory in the rhymes, be a king and an adventurer. My daughter Elisa could rarely be the star. She had to play around with strawberries and sewing and cushions.'

So he began to add balancing verses, about Joe Peep joining Bo, and Little Girl Green who works with Boy Blue and, of course, Sally Shaftoe (although Sally doesn't go to sea with silver buckles on her knee; she has merely 'gone away/To a job for equal pay').

But it didn't stop there. 'My unease about sexism led me on to unease about the other negative aspects of the nursery rhyme. I found really difficult violence: kids beaten till they run crying down the street, little animals drowned in wells, attacks on disabled mice.'

Now the red-blooded British response to all this is either to become incensed, or to take the Little Dog's part and merely laugh to see such fun as the Professor runs off with the (wooden) spoon. But what is really wrong with adding a new second verse to *Jack and Jill*, omitting the obsolete remedy of vinegar and brown paper, and relating that the next time they went up, 'They climbed with care, got safely there/And finished the job they began'? Why should there not be an ecologically caring denouement to the new *Ms Muffet* in which the spider helps her 'to frighten the insects away'?

Certainly the book is being warmly welcomed in some quarters, particularly for its non-sexism. Letterbox Library, the feminist children's book collective, have adopted it for their new catalogue: 'We do believe that small children have sexist messages beamed at them from all over the place. There are 3,000 children's books published every year and it's difficult to find 80 which are non-sexist and give positive pictures of girls, the disabled, black people, and unconventional family structures. But people get very upset about nursery rhymes being changed.'

Oh, they do, they do. I rang Iona Opie who has devoted her life to researching nursery rhymes and children's games. 'This man sounds ghastly. Oh, poor nursery rhymes, they were only ever meant for fun. Can't he see that?'

Down at the local primary school a group listened attentively to Father Gander, rejected most of it, but quite liked the lack of parental beatings. They poured united scorn on the new *Georgie Porgie* in which the girls 'sigh' and Georgie is a regular guy who 'asks the boys to stay and play' instead of running away.

'Nah', said Simon, aged seven, 'I prefer ones where the girls cry and eggs get smashed to pieces.'

Libby Purves

Reflections

* Having listened to what Doug Larche has to say, and indeed what some primary children replied, do you feel language is sexist? If it is, what should we try to do about it? There is no doubt that our use of language, our choice of words, *is* important in showing our values and attitudes.

    Critics of Doug Larche would argue that worrying about so-called sexist nursery rhymes is just silly. Language *is* how it is and we can't change it. What about the following, for example?

Proverbs and Sayings

A man is as old as he feels and a woman is as old as she looks.
Every man for himself.
Manners maketh man.
The way to a man's heart is through his stomach.
A woman a dog and a walnut tree: the more you beat them the better they be.
A woman and a ship ever want mending.
A woman's place is in the home.
A woman's work is never done.
Silence is a woman's best garment.
Never choose your women or your linen by candlelight.
Woman and a crowing hen are neither fit for God nor men.
Man to man.
May the best man win.
You can't keep a good man down.
Be a man.
The wife.

From The Bible

And God said: let us make man in our own image.
It is not good that the man should be alone; I will make an help meet for him.
Therefore shall a man leave his father and his mother and shall cleave unto his wife; and they shall be one flesh.
Doth not even nature itself teach you that, if a man have long hair it is a shame unto him? But if a woman have long hair, it is a glory to her.
Let a woman learn in silence with all subjection. But I suffer not a woman to teach, nor to usurp authority over the man, but to be in silence.

* You can see that the use of 'man' rules strongly in our language, and there are some fairly sexist proverbs and words in the Bible about women's and men's roles. Does it matter? A question for you to reflect on.

    But it is surely important to remember that words can offend.
    Words *are* powerful. Used unthinkingly, or maliciously, a word can cause real embarrassment or deep hurt. In the school community we must remember at all

times not to use words that would offend someone's character, sex, race, religion or creed.

8 Changing cultures

Introduction

What is it like moving to live in another country, particularly when that country has a way of life rather different from the one you're used to?

Sour Sweet, a novel by Timothy Mo, is a witty and eventful story of one Chinese family's arrival in the tightly-knit Chinese community in London. Through Chen, the central character, and through his wife Lily's involvement in business and their son's education into British society and its schools, the author presents a fascinating picture of a family caught between two contrasting cultures. In the following extract the Chens have recently arrived in London. Chen himself is getting used to his place of work and forming first impressions of London street and restaurant life.

Reading

Sour sweet

The Chens had been living in the UK for four years, which was long enough to have lost their place in the society from which they had emigrated but not long enough to feel comfortable in the new. They were no longer missed; Lily had no living relatives anyway, apart from her sister Mui, and Chen had lost his claim to clan land in his ancestral village. He was remembered there in the shape of the money order he remitted to his father every month, and would truly have been remembered only if that order had failed to arrive.

But in the UK, land of promise, Chen was still an interloper. He regarded himself as such. True, he paid reasonable rent to Brent Council for warm and comfortable accommodation, quarters which were positively palatial compared to those which his wife Lily had known in Hong Kong. That English people had competed for the flat which he now occupied made Chen feel more rather than less of a foreigner; it made him feel like a gatecrasher who had stayed too long and been identified. He had no tangible reason to feel like this. No one had yet assaulted, insulted, so much as looked twice at him. But Chen knew, felt it in his bones, could sense it between his shoulder-blades as he walked past emptying public houses on his day off; in the shrinking of his scalp as he heard bottles rolling in the gutter; in a descending silence at a dark bus stop and its subsequent lifting; in an unspoken complicity between himself and others like him, not necessarily of his race. A huge West Indian bus conductor regularly undercharged him on his morning journey to work. He knew because the English one charged him three-pence more. Chen was sure the black man's mistake was deliberate. He put the threepences for luck in an outgrown sock of his little son, Man Kee. Chen was not an especially superstitious man but there were times, he felt, when you needed all the luck you could lay your hands on.

Chen's week had a certain stark simplicity about it. He had once worked out the fractions on the back of his order-pad, dividing the hours of the week like a cake. He worked seventy-two hours at his restaurant, slept fifty-six, spent forty hours with his wife and child (more like thirty-two minus travelling time, and, of course, Man Kee was often asleep when he was awake). This was on a rotation of six days a week at the restaurant with one off (Thursday). That day was spent in recuperation on his back on the sofa, generally with open eyes, for his feet ached after the hours of standing. It was hard and the money came at a cost but he wasn't complaining: the wages were spectacularly good, even forgetting the tips.

Chen's restaurant was in Soho, just off Gerrard Street and its complex of travel agencies, supermarkets, fortune tellers, quack acupuncturists and Chinese cinema clubs, in a quiet lane whose only establishments were restaurants. At the end of the row was a passage with a double bend, so that what seemed to strangers like a blind alley was in reality a concealed entrance, constructed on the same principle as a crude lobster trap. A sharp right turn after passing an iron bollard took the knowledgeable or intrepid into a gloomy canyon formed by the blind backs of two forty-feet high Georgian terraces. Rubbish filled the alley. At night rats scrabbled in the piles of rotting vegetable leaves and soggy cardboard boxes. There was a muffled silence in the enclosure. At the other end another series of baffles led, quite suddenly, into the brightness and sound of Leicester Square. This was Chen's habitual short-cut to the Underground station.

From Sour Sweet by Timothy Mo

Reflections

* The reading describes a family moving from one culture to another in search of new opportunities. The phrase which helps us on the subject of equal opportunities came at the beginning of the reading: 'Four years . . . long enough to have lost their place in the society from which they had emigrated but not long enough to feel comfortable in the new.'

  Within our school community there will always be new arrivals – pupils and teachers. Some will come from other parts of the country, some may come from another country or culture. It is our individual and collective responsibility to give everyone a feeling of equal opportunity, and to try and minimise for the new-comer the sense that Chen feels in this story of being an interloper, an outsider.

9 Conflicting generations

Introduction

Depending on your age and background culture, what may appear as a good opportunity for one person may appear quite the reverse to someone else. And this is so often the case when parents try to map out for their children the path they would like to see them follow.

The following reading is taken from a semi-autobiographical book called *Sumitra's Story* by Rukshana Smith. Expelled from Uganda in the 1970s by President Amin,

Sumitra and her family arrive to start a new life in Britain. For the four young daughters their formative years become ones of questioning and confusion. In particular, Sumitra finds herself increasingly torn between her parents' strict Hindu values and the more liberal attitudes she encounters at school and among friends. As Rukshana Smith observes: 'Her parents assume that she will continue their traditions, while Sumitra has ambitions and wishes of her own'.

Reading

Sumitra's Story

'Belt up, Sumitra,' shouted Sandya from the next room, banging crossly on the wall. 'I'm trying to do my homework!' Mai was calling up the stairs, 'Come and help me, stop playing that guitar. I wish Martin had never given it to you!' Sumitra closed her eyes as the anger spluttered like a fire-cracker inside her. The vision of headlines reading: 'Sue Patel Takes New York by Storm! Beautiful Girl Singer from London, England, an Overnight Success!' faded, and she strummed three angry chords before throwing the guitar on her bed. She went downstairs to exchange the sweet smell of success for the acrid fumes of boiling *ghee*.

As she fried the rounds her mother rolled out, a huge wave of misery engulfed her. Hilary and Lynne had gone to a local college dance, while Cinderella Patel remained at home, reeking of oil and dry flour. She turned suddenly and looked at Mai. 'Do you like cooking?' she asked, wondering how her mother could bear this life, day after day. Mai was bewildered. 'What questions you ask!' she replied. 'I don't know. Women cook for their families. You must help me and learn to cook for your own family. You are sixteen. Soon we must start thinking about looking for a husband. It is good you have passed your exams. You will marry well!'

Sumitra's tongue stuck to her mouth like an uncooked lump of dough. She turned the *poori* deftly as her mind screamed, 'Never, never, never!' in the kitchen of her brain.

Mai patted her arm, leaving a floury impression like a palm print decorating a temple. 'It's all right,' she said with unusual gentleness. 'It is the custom. You'll get used to the idea, there's no need to be shy. We all get used to it.'

It had never occurred to Mai that her daughters might be questioning their way of life. Despite their smart clothes and the fact that at the weekends they wore sweaters and jeans like any other teenager, she was sure that their attitudes and conventions were Indian. She had never sat down and thought about it; she never thought about her children as separate entities. When she told Bap, her husband, that she was worried about them, she meant that she was concerned that they would take suitable jobs, choose the right friends, marry decent partners. The criterion in each case was whether or not she would approve of their choice. So Mai was part of the Banquo line, carefully bequeathing to her children the ideas and philosophies that had been bequeathed to her. The fact that these conventions had evolved in different ages and in different countries was immaterial.

Mai never doubted that the girls would lead their lives in the same way as she lived hers, marrying someone carefully chosen by the parents, bearing children who would, of course, speak Gujarati and Hindi. She had no reason to doubt it when all around her she saw other cultures passing on their various truths to their own children and carefully isolating them from the British tradition in which they lived. She had seen synagogues, mosques, Greek and Russian orthodox churches, and behind each of these institutions was a sub-culture energetically devoted to keeping a particular tradition alive.

Mai, like thousands of other mothers of minority groups, had many ways of perpetuating tradition. There was emotional, social and financial pressure. Thus the little dictatorships of family life flourished in the British democracy. Children were unhappy, rejected their parents' demands temporarily, made their heroic gestures, but were usually defeated by the sanctions imposed. Mothers wept, fathers talked of sacrifices, grand-parents disapproved, and the son or daughter conceded and was sucked back into the family group.

Life continued as it had always done. The shrine was cleaned and polished, sandalwood paste prepared. Offerings were left for the gods and roses decorated the ceremonial place. The girls plaited Gopal and Jayant braids at Rakshabandan in order to ensure their health and happiness. They all went to the temple and, occasionally, to Indian films and dances.

As long as the outside culture remained beyond her house, Mai was content. The letters and notes from the alien society were ignored as if they had no right to be there. Requests to attend school functions or parents' evenings were left unanswered. What could she or Bap do at school? She trusted the teachers to do their job and, besides, she couldn't speak English. So she lived in her comfortable cocoon, only venturing out to go to work and surrounding herself with the friends she had known in Uganda.

Sumitra and some of her Indian friends, however, were beginning to resent the tight community laws. They objected to being relegated to the Bottom Division at the back of the temple. As sexual objects women distracted the men from their prayers, so the men prayed while the women sat behind the barrier and gossiped. Then the women went to the communal kitchen to prepare food for the men. This division of labour annoyed the girls, who at school were encouraged to be independent, thoughtful, integrated, and at home to be docile, submissive and dutiful. Sumitra had to listen to the adults decrying the British way of life, while being educated into it herself.

Sumitra and her parents lived under the same roof without speaking to each other. Of course they talked; they spoke about the things that did not matter, but about the serious business of the meaning of life they were silent. There was no point of contact, and any questioning was called disobedience and would cause a scene. So Sumitra acted one part at home and another at school, and was never sure which role was really hers.

Sometimes events on the news reached out and touched them. Incidents of growing racial tension in Notting Hill, Birmingham, Southall. The places were different but the causes were the same: a lack of Government awareness and initiative and an unfriendly host population causing the immigrants to turn in on themselves. One side felt threatened, the other rebuffed.

Sumitra felt all these pressures. One part of her wanted to live as an Indian girl, carrying on the great traditions and culture, while another part of her wanted to participate in Western freedom. On the one hand they read of incidents in Southall, of young Asians being attacked and even murdered. This made them fearful, retreating into the group. These racial incidents defined certain boundaries between the minority groups and host society, and caused Bap to give his weekly lecture on the superiority of their own way of life.

On the other hand there were occasionally reports in the paper about young Asian girls killing themselves because they had not wanted to go through with an arranged marriage, or because the strain of living two lives was overwhelming. As she watched yet another *poori* puff up and turn brown, Sumitra wondered if that was the only way out. She had often wished lately that she was dead.

From 'Sumitra's Story' by Rukshana Smith

Reflections

* Here is a teenage girl torn between what her family traditions expect of her, and what she increasingly wants for herself. The passage ends on a note of depression, though the rest of the book describes how Sumitra gradually manages to resolve her problems of identity.

  Her story helps us to understand the situation of those among us who might, even at this moment, be wrestling with conflict between future opportunities and parental expectations.

* It is important to remember that talking through a problem with someone will usually help. If it can't be a parent or teacher, an older sister/brother or friend whom you trust is usually on hand. Sharing such a problem also reminds us that we are not alone in experiencing conflict between generations.

10 Racism (1)

Introduction

In some parts of the world, equal opportunities are denied to certain groups of people because of the colour of their skin. This has been true in South Africa for many years, though the situation is beginning to change and many aspects of the historically apartheid (racially segregated) society are improving for the black population.

The following extract is taken from the novel *Muriel at Metropolitan* by Miriam Tlali. The author was born in Johannesburg and her own experiences there inspired this first novel, published in 1979.

Reading

Muriel at Metropolitan

Just then the tea-boy passed and Mrs Stein called him.

'Jonas, go and buy me the newspapers. Get me the *Transvaler* and the *Star*.'

Mrs Singham looked up. 'Did you read last night's paper? The heart transplant was a success.'

The other two said they had seen it.

Mrs Singham asked, 'But they put a Coloured's heart into a white man. How can they do that when they believe in apartheid?'

That sparked off one of the most heated arguments I have ever heard. I keep quiet and listened.

Mrs Stein immediately look up the remark as if it were a personal challenge. 'Well, you see, Mrs Singham, the heart is merely a muscle. It merely pumps the blood.'

I could not resist asking, 'Surely the Coloured's heart was cleaned out or steri-lised first to make sure that none of his blood would be introduced in the white man's veins?'

Mrs Singham said, 'It couldn't have been altogether drained of the Coloured's blood. And possibly the Coloured's blood was of the same group as that of the white man so that his system would not reject it.'

'In any case,' I said more firmly, 'blood is blood and the four main human blood groups are found in every racial group. There is no such thing as white blood or non-white blood.'

Mrs Singham agreed. 'The whole thing is ridiculous.'

'Mind you, we've also had whites as donors for Bantus and Coloureds,' Mrs Stein said, looking first at Mrs Singham and then at me. 'What about that kidney transplant we were reading about the other day, Mrs Kuhn?'

'Yes, Mrs Stein, but that's for a kidney and not the heart. I can understand about the kidney, but the heart!'

'To me your heart is your soul,' Mrs Singham said, emphasising the last word.

'How South Africa's enemies will howl,' Mrs Kuhn said, shaking her head sadly.

'Yes, they'll say these whites here are hypocrites,' I added, 'that when they are faced with death and are in fear, they shed all their pride.'

'It just goes to show that all people are the same,' said Mrs Singham.

Mrs Stein was not disposed to agree. 'The critics overseas are ill-informed about the true situation. They only receive false information. South Africa is a most peaceful country. People are free to go where they like, and say what they feel, I mean . . .'

She went on to insist that all racial groups were happy and living with each other in harmony, how for nearly a decade now there had not been any uprisings or strikes unlike other countries such as America where there were killings and riots. I listened, trying very hard to be patient. I could not understand how anyone in full control of his or her faculties could claim that South Africa was a peaceful country, that all its peoples were happy.

From 'Muriel at Metropolitan' by Miriam Tlali

Reflections

* This extract highlights the horrid absurdity of dividing people by skin colour. Apartheid on racial grounds has long existed and does still exist in our world today. In our own community we must each do all in our power to reject atti-tudes which seek to deny opportunities to someone because of their race, creed or colour, or indeed because of *any* prejudice that might lie within ourselves.

* What prejudice is and does to the individual who is prejudiced is skilfully summed up in this poem, written by a 16-year-old.

The racist
Sweats to build a cage
For the black
Eagerly and urgently hammering in
Every bolt for every bar
While the cancer of fear and hate
Eats away at his heart

At last he looks round at his work
And gives a start
For the mighty cage is complete
And he, too, is inside.

'The Cage' by Savitri Hensman

11 Racism (2)

Introduction

Have you ever experienced prejudice of any kind – that is, being pre-judged? Have you ever been denied the opportunity to do something

- because of where you live?
- because of your religion or language?
- because of your appearance?
- because of your interests?
- because of your ability, or achievements?

In order to witness first-hand the experience of colour in 1950s America, writer John Griffin disguised himself as a black man. He wrote up his findings in *Black Like Me*. The following reading comes from this book.

Reading

Black Like Me

I developed a technique of zigzagging back and forth. In my bag I kept a damp sponge, dyes, cleansing cream and Kleenex. It was hazardous, but it was the only way to traverse an area both as Negro and white. As I travelled, I would find an isolated spot, perhaps an alley at night or the brush beside a highway, and quickly apply the dye to my face, hands and legs, then rub off and reapply until it was firmly anchored in my pores. I would go through the area as a Negro and then, usually at night, remove the dyes with cleansing cream and tissues and pass through the same area as a white man.

I was the same man, whether white or black. Yet when I was white, I received the brotherly-love smiles and the privileges from whites and the hate stares or obsequiousness from the Negroes. And when I was a Negro, the whites judged me fit for the junk heap, while the Negroes treated me with great warmth.'

Three days in Mobile. I spent them walking through the town, searching jobs, and then every night I met my host on the corner opposite the bus station and we went to his house to sleep.

Again, an important part of my daily life was spent searching for the basic things that all whites take for granted: a place to eat, or somewhere to find a drink of water, a rest room, somewhere to wash my hands. More than once I walked into drugstores where a Negro can buy cigarettes or anything else except soda fountain service. I asked politely where I might find a glass of water. Though they had water not three yards away, they carefully directed me to the nearest Negro café. Had I asked outright for a drink they would perhaps have given it. But I never asked. The Negro dreads rejection, and I waited for them to offer the drink. Not one ever did. No matter where you are, the nearest Negro café is always far away, it seems. I learned to eat a great deal when it was available and convenient, because it might not be available or convenient when the belly next indicated its hunger. I have been told that many distinguished Negroes whose careers have brought them South encounter similar difficulties. All the honours in the world cannot buy them a cup of coffee in the lowest greasy-spoon joint. It is not that they crave service in the white man's café over their own – it is simply that in many sparsely settled areas Negro cafés do not exist; and even in densely settled areas, one must sometimes cross town for a glass of water. It is rankling, too, to be encouraged to buy all of one's goods in white stores and then be refused soda fountain or rest-room service.

No, it makes no sense, but in so far as the Negro is concerned, nothing makes much sense. This was brought home to me in another realm many times when I sought jobs.

The foreman of one plant in Mobile, a large brute, allowed me to tell him what I could do. Then he looked me in the face and spoke to me in these words:

'No, you couldn't get anything like that here.'

His voice was not unkind. It was the dead voice one often hears. Determined to see if I could not break in somehow, I said: 'But if I could do you a better job, and you paid me less than a white man . . .'

'I'll tell you . . . we don't want you people. Don't you understand that?'

'I know,' I said with real sadness. 'You can't blame a man for trying at least.'

'No use trying down here,' he said. 'We're gradually getting you people weeded out from the better jobs at this plant. We're taking it slow, but we're doing it. Pretty soon we'll have it so the only jobs you can get here are the ones no white man would have.'

'How can we live?' I asked hopelessly, careful not to give the impression I was arguing.

'That's the whole point,' he said, looking at me square in the eyes, but with some faint sympathy, as though he regretted the need to say what followed: 'We're going to do our damndest to drive every one of you out of the state.'

Despite his frankness and the harshness of his intentions, I nevertheless had the impression he was telling me: 'I'm sorry. I've got nothing against you personally, but you're coloured, and with all this noise about equality, we just don't want you people around. The only way we can keep you out of our schools and cafés is to make life so hard for you that you'll get the hell out before equality comes.'

This attitude cropped up often. Many otherwise decent men and women could find no other solution. They are willing to degrade themselves to their basest levels to prevent the traditional labourer from rising in status or, to put it bluntly, from 'winning', even though what he wins has been rightfully his from the moment he was born into the human race.

I walked through the streets of Mobile throughout the afternoon. I had known the city before, in my youth, when I sailed from there once to France. I knew it then as a privileged white. It had impressed me as a beautiful Southern port town, gracious and calm. I had seen the Negro dock workers stripped to the waist, their bodies glistening with sweat under their loads. The sight had chilled me, touched me to pity for men who so resembled beasts of burden. But I had dismissed it as belonging to the natural order of things. The Southern whites I knew were kind and wise. If they allowed this, then surely it must be right.

Now, walking the same streets as a Negro, I found no trace of the Mobile I formerly knew, nothing familiar. The labourers still dragged out their ox-like lives, but the gracious Southerner, the wise Southerner, the kind Southerner, was nowhere visible. I knew that if I were white, I would find him easily, for his other face is there for whites to see. It is not a false face; it is simply different from the one the Negro sees. The Negro sees him as a man with muscular emotions who wants to drive out all of his race except the beasts of burden.

I concluded that, as in everything else, the atmosphere of a place is entirely different for Negro and white. The Negro sees and reacts differently not because he is Negro, but because he is suppressed. Fear dims even the sunlight.

From 'Black Like Me' by John Griffin

Reflections

* 'Fear dims even the sunlight' is a phrase which echoes in the mind at the end of this account. It is taken from 1950s USA, but its message rings true to this day in any situation where we encounter prejudice. For prejudice is all about pre-judging someone for some reason, before you really know them.

 Schools must stand up against prejudice in all forms, so that no-one in a school community ever feels that they have been denied an opportunity to do something simply because, as the saying goes, 'their face doesn't fit'.

 'Fear', as John Griffin describes it, should never dim anyone's aspirations – whether that is answering a question in class, attending a sports or music trial, or taking part in a school production or school journey.

12 'To thine own self be true'

Introduction

We often read stories of the 'rags to riches' kind, either as fact or fiction. One famous example in American history is that of Conrad Hilton. He began life with little money but went on to create the Hilton Hotel chain, one of the biggest international organisations today. Looking back on his life he wrote in his autobiography that opportunity is there for everyone, no matter what their background. The difficult part of life is to grasp that opportunity and develop it.

Hilton died a very wealthy man, though he begins the following passage from his autobiography with some challenging comments about 'wealth'. He then goes on to identify *ten* ingredients for a successful life.

Reading

To thine own self be true

What is this thing – success?

It cannot be measured by the accumulation of money. Too many rich men are failures and too many poor men masters at the art of living to make this the criterion.

The workman is worthy of his hire, yes, but you cannot reckon his achievements by his bank account. Mahatma Gandhi, one of the most successful statesmen of our time, left upon his death as his entire worldy estate: two rice bowls, one spoon, two pairs of sandals, his copy of the Bhagavad-Gita, his spectacles and an old-fashioned turnip watch. Helen Keller, another outstanding success, overcame tremendous handicaps to prove that the blind deaf-mute was not mentally retarded, unteachable, thus setting free hundreds of her fellow sufferers. She has succeeded in raising many, many thousands of dollars to benefit her fellows. Yet Miss Keller herself has had only the most ordinary personal comforts. Saint Francis of Assisi during his lifetime affected his entire world, rulers and princes, prelates, artists, businessmen, farmers and housewives. Seven hundred years after his death he continues to affect people in all walks of life in many countries. Yet his very influence was based on maintaining absolute poverty. He was, perhaps, the most successful poor man who ever lived.

The yardstick for measuring success would seem to be not how much a man gets as how much he has to give away.

The true fruits of successful living are not material. They are contentment, the joy of usefulness, growth through the fulfillment of our particular talent. Viewed this way God is always on the side of success for the objective is fulfilling a talent He gave, and which he will support and maintain.

To me there are ten ingredients which must be blended in each and every one of us if we are to live successfully.

Find Your Own Particular Talent: As surely as none of us was given the same thumb print, so surely none of us possesses the exact same talent. This does not mean there will not be two housewives, two carpenters, two artists or two hotel men. We each have two thumbs. But the individual print is uniquely our own.

Emerson says, 'Each man has his own vocation. The talent is the call ... He inclines to do something which is easy for him, and good when it is done, but which no other man can do ... His ambition is exactly proportioned to his powers. The height of the pinnacle is determined by the breadth of the base.'

Finding this particular talent or vocation is the first step in the art of successful living. Great frustration and the feel of failure can be present in the face of material success if we follow someone else's footsteps rather than our own.

Be Big: Think Big. Act Big. Dream Big: Your value is determined by the mould you yourself make. It doesn't take any more energy to expect to be the best housewife, the finest cook, the most capable carpenter.

It has been my experience that the way most people court failure is by misjudging their abilities, belittling their worth and value. Did you every think what can happen to a plain bit of iron, worth about $5.00? The same iron when made into horseshoes is worth $10.50. If made into needles, it is worth $3,250.85, and if turned into balance springs for watches its value jumps to $250,000.

The same is true of another kind of material – You!

Be Honest: What I have in mind is something more than the negative virtues of not cheating, not lying, not stealing. It is a bold, direct, open stand for the truth as we know it, both to ourselves and others. My mother had two old-fashioned quotations she dished out with our oatmeal. The first was Shakespeare: 'To thine own self be true, and it must follow as the night the day, Thou canst not then be false to any man.' The second was Sir Walter Scott: 'Oh, what a tangled web we weave, when first we practice to deceive!'

Live with Enthusiasm: It has been my experience that there is nothing worth doing that can be done without it. Ability you must have, but ability sparked with enthusiasm. Enthusiasm is an inexhaustible force, so mighty that you must ever tame and temper it with wisdom. Use it and you will find yourself constantly moving forward to new forms of expression.

Don't Let Your Possessions Possess You: I have in my lifetime had everything – and nothing. In my Bible it doesn't say that money is the root of all evil, but the 'love of' money. I believe that to be true and I believe the exact same to be true about possessions.

They are very nice to have, to enjoy, to share. But if you find even one that you can't live without – hasten to give it away. Your very freedom depends on it.

Don't Worry about Your Problems: The successful life is a balanced life and includes thought, action, rest, recreation. The artist in living will neither work himself to death nor play until he reaches satiety. Now the chronic worrier is all out of balance. He is like a dog with a bone. Problems, and we all have them, are puzzles offered us for solution and we solve them by keeping in balance, alert mentally and well physically, or we handicap ourselves. To worry your difficulties after the sun is set and you have done all you can for the day is useless – and an act of distrust.

Don't Cling to the Past: Not through regret. Not through longing. To do so is to tie yourself to a memory, for yesterday is gone. It is wisdom to profit by yesterday's mistakes. It is fatal to hang on to yesterday's victories. You limit yourself. The future should be expanding. Yesterday's experiences are the foundation on which you build today.

Look Up to People When You Can – Down to No One: Who and what is your neighbor? Do you know him?

The solitary Robinson Crusoe, in order to know the benighted savage who inhabited his island, Friday, had to adventure in trust, confidence, reliance, and growing insight until loyalty and faith, friendship in fact, welded the unlikely two together.

As we strive to know more about people, to understand rather than to be understood, we are in a better position to fulfill the commandment to 'love our neighbour as ourselves.'

Assume Your Full Share of Responsibility for the World in Which You Live: develop your own policy, domestic and foreign. Give it thought. And then effort. Stand on it! Stand for it! Live it!

The whole purpose of democracy is for the participation of the individual. The will of the people. You cannot have 'government of the people, by the people, for the people' without the active participation of those people.

Nor can your life be a personal success unless, as a citizen, tourist, voter, you share in shaping your own world.

Pray Consistently and Confidently: What I like about prayer is that it is a means of communication with God. You can speak to Him any time, night or day, and you can know with certainty that He is listening to you.

For me, in personal living, in fulfilling our place in the world, in faithful use of our talents, each of these is a spoke in the circle of successful living. Prayer is the hub that holds the wheel together. Without our contact with God we are nothing. With it we are 'a little lower than the angels, crowned with glory and honour.'

From 'Be my guest' by Conrad Hilton

Reflections

* This is an interesting list to reflect on. Perhaps it is only possible to look *back* on your life – as Conrad Hilton does here – and identify successful ingredients. Looking *ahead* is much more difficult!

Science and Technology

1 The beginnings of science

Introduction

If we read in our history books about how the ancient Egyptians, the Romans and Greeks – for all their advanced civilisation – explained the world, we see their strong belief in the work of the Gods. For these civilisations, science as we know it *today* had little meaning or place in their lives.

It was during the Renaissance period of the 15th and 16th centuries that humans saw a flowering of scientific endeavour that was to shape the future quite significantly.

The following reading is taken from Bertholt Brecht's play *Life of Galileo*; the play is a retelling of Galileo's life and his first realisation that the certainties of past centuries were being challenged by inventors, astronomers and thinkers such as himself in the 16th century.

Reading

Life of Galileo

GALILEO: for two thousand years people have believed that the sun and all the stars of heaven rotate around mankind. Pope, cardinals, princes, professors, captains, merchants, fishwives and schoolkids thought they were sitting motionless inside this crystal sphere. But now we are breaking out of it, Andrea, at full speed. Because the old days are over and this is a new time. For the last hundred years mankind has seemed to be expecting something.

Our cities are cramped, and so are men's minds. Superstition and the plague. But now the word is 'that's how things are, but they won't stay like that'. Because everything is in motion, my friend.

I like to think that it began with the ships. As far as men could remember they had always hugged the coast, then suddenly they abandoned the coast line and ventured out across the seas. On our old continent a rumour sprang up: there might be new ones. And since our ships began sailing to them the laughing continents have got the message: the great ocean they feared, is a little puddle. And a vast desire has sprung up to know the reasons for everything: why a stone falls when you let it go and why it rises when you toss it up. Each day something fresh is discovered. Men of a hundred, even, are getting the young people to bawl the latest example into their ear. There have been a lot of discoveries, but there is still plenty to be found out. So future generations should have enough to do.

As a young man in Siena I watched a group of building workers argue for five minutes, then abandon a thousand-year old method of shifting granite blocks in favour of a new and more efficient arrangement of the ropes. Then and there I knew, the old days are over and this is a new time. Soon humanity is going to understand its abode, the heavenly body on which it dwells. What is written in the old books is no longer good enough. For where faith has been enthroned for a thousand years doubt now sits. Everyone says: right, that's what it says in the books, but let's have a look for ourselves. That most solemn truths are being familiarly nudged; what was never doubted before is doubted now.

This has created a draught which is blowing up the gold-embroidered skirts of the prelates and princes, revealing the fat and skinny legs underneath, legs like our own. The heavens, it turns out, are empty. Cheerful laughter is our response. But the waters of the earth drive the new spinning machines, while in the ship-yards, the ropewalks and sail-lofts five hundred hands are moving together in a new system.

It is my prophecy that our own lifetime will see astronomy being discussed in the marketplaces. Even the fishwives' sons will hasten off to school. For these novelty-seeking people in our cities will be delighted with a new astronomy that sets the earth moving too. The old idea was always that the stars were fixed to a crystal vault to stop them falling down. Today we have found the courage to let them soar through space without support; and they are travelling at full speed just like our ships, at full speed and without support.

And the earth is rolling cheerfully around the sun, and the fishwives, merchants, princes, cardinals and even the Pope are rolling with it.

The universe has lost its centre overnight, and woken up to find it has countless centres. So that each one can now be seen as the centre, or none at all. Suddenly there is a lot of room.

Our ships sail far overseas, our planets move far out into space, in chess too the rooks have begun sweeping far across the board.

What does the poet say? O early morning of beginnings . . .

O early morning of beginnings
O breath of wind that
Cometh from new shores!

From 'Life of Galileo' by Bertholt Brecht

Reflections

* Galileo has some interesting lines here:

'What is written in the old books is no longer good enough.'
'For where faith has been enthroned for a thousand years doubt now sits.'
'What was never doubted before is doubted now.'
'The universe has lost its centre overnight, and woken up to find it has countless centres.'

What he is drawing attention to here of course is the emergence of new scientific ideas challenging the old religious beliefs about the way the world was designed. Four centuries after Galileo, even more of the old certainties have been challenged. But interestingly, the more humans have discovered about their scientific world, the more they have discovered that they *don't* know.

* That remains one of the great challenges for scientists operating in the late 20th century. They will go on discovering new things in our world which, in turn, will lead to even more questions. The *social* aspect of science runs ever parallel with its physical development.

2 Science: for good or ill (1)

Introduction

With scientific progress, as we climb one hill another has a way of coming into view. For example, agricultural and industrial science has enabled us to produce more food, but the processes are using up more and more of the world's limited natural resources.

The following two extracts from a biography of Marie Curie – the celebrated French physicist – highlight the dilemma of progress. Marie and her husband Pierre shared a Nobel prize for Physics in 1903; and in 1911 Marie gained one for Chemistry.

Reading

Marie Curie

It would not be unreasonable to date the atomic age from November 8th, 1895. On that day an observation had been made in a Bavarian laboratory which ever after altered physicists' views of their subject. Wilhelm Röntgen had taken a pear-shaped cathode ray tube from its rack, part-connected it in a circuit, surrounded it with black cardboard and, having completely darkened the room, passed a high tension discharge across it. All he was concerned with was whether the cardboard was completely shielding the tube. Having satisfied himself that this was so, he was in the act of moving towards the apparatus to continue the experiment when, about a yard from the tube, he saw a glimmer of light. He lit a match to see where it was coming from. He found it to be a small card coated with barium platinocyanide, which was luminescing, in spite of the fact that it was completely shielded from the cathode ray tube by a thick sheet of cardboard. He switched off the tube: the barium-coated card stopped glowing. He switched it on, and it glowed again. Röntgen has discovered X-rays.

He gave the rays the name X because this was a physicist's usual symbol for an unknown (and in this case a not understood) factor. But by December 28th, when he made his first report, Röntgen had carried out a systematic and thorough examination of the rays and was able to give an accurate description of most of their basic properties. Four weeks later he gave the first public lecture on his discovery to a crowded auditorium. At one point he asked permission from the distinguished 78-year-old anatomist Albert von Kölliker to photograph his hand. Von Kölliker agreed; when Röntgen later held up the developed plate showing the old man's bone structure, the audience burst into loud cheers.

Pierre Curie's speech at the Nobel prize-giving ceremony, June 1905.

'It might even be thought that radium could become very dangerous in criminal hands, and here the question can be raised whether mankind benefits from knowing

the secrets of Nature, whether it is ready to profit from it or whether this knowledge will not be harmful for it. The example of the discoveries of Nobel is characteristic, as powerful explosives have enabled man to do wonderful work. They
are also a terrible means of destruction in the hands of great criminals who lead
the people towards war. I am one of those who believe with Nobel that mankind
will derive more good than harm from the new discoveries.'

It was an arguable eulogy of Nobel, the armaments manufacturer, but it had a
strange prescience. It showed that Pierre and Marie Curie were beginning to see
applications for radium beyond that of adding to physics' store of knowledge of the
atom. The purity of discovery was their responsibility, but who would answer for
the applications? Radium-therapy, or Curie-therapy as it became known in France,
was already being employed by French doctors using radium loaned by the Curies.
This was the optimistic face of the applications. But his pessimism had seen
something foreboding ahead. Could radium and the knowledge derived from it
have terrible applications, even in warfare?

From 'Marie Curie' by Robert Reid

Reflections

* The great advances in science made by the Curie team doubtless benefited hospital
  patients then, and millions upon millions ever since. But the curies could not
  have anticipated the later development of the nuclear bomb, a weapon of mass
  destruction. We can only pray that, as the boundaries of science go on being
  pushed ever further, humans learn to harness new discoveries in the long-term
  interests of planet Earth, rather than using them to destroy it.

* Her Majesty Queen Elizabeth wrote in her Commonwealth Day Message in
  1991:
  'Science poses a serious dilemma. In itself, it is neither good nor bad; the problems
  are only created by the way it is used. The challenge to scientists today is to
  bring benefits of science to the less prosperous communities whilst at the same
  time safeguarding the natural world. To do this successfully our scientists will
  need the understanding and encouragement of the population as a whole.'

3 Science: for good or ill (2)*

Introduction

Medical science has made it possible for more children to survive and for more
adults to live healthier and longer lives. This is a positive achievement, but it has
also resulted in an alarming growth in the world's human population.

Now we have the scientific knowledge to 'tinker' or 'tamper' with nature. Listen
to the following newspaper article, published as long ago now as 1978, when test-
tube babies were first newsworthy.

Reading

The brave new world of test tube babies

Baby Brown of Oldham, the world's first child from an egg fertilized outside the
womb, created reverberations throughout the Western world yesterday. 'All hell

will break loose,' was the prediction seven years ago of Dr James Watson, of DNA fame, but he was thinking of the moral and ethical outrage which some thought might accompany the proof of successful scientific tampering with the process of procreation. There are no signs of outrage.

In the United States gynacologists are already seeing this as a great boon to the tiny percentage of infertile women to whom it may be of value, and you can almost hear the cash registers ringing with joy. For, after all, if you can pop an undamaged blastocyst – fertilized and nurtured through its first cell divisions in the laboratory – back into its mum's womb and bring it happily to full term, you can probably bring it to full term in somebody else's womb. The surrogate mum, if that is the appropriate term, could make quite a decent living for a decade or so. That would worry our administrators.

The fact that it is 13 years since the first human oocyte was (probably) fertilized in the laboratory (since the egg did not go through multiple divisions the fertilization was observed but not proven), and the work of Dr Robert Edwards on the biochemical complexities of the reproductive cycle began a decade before that, indicates that we are not dealing with a 'breakthrough' as everyone seems to think, but rather the steady advance of knowledge and techniques. Mice were having 'test tube babies' in 1966, and the Steptoe–Edwards collaboration on the human development has been a long haul.

The great difficulties lie in providing the right environments in the laboratory for the various maturation and division phases of the sperm, the oocyte and the fertilized egg, and manipulation and surgical procedures which preclude – or at least minimize – the possibility of damage to the germ cells and to the growing blastocyst. This, in conjunction with techniques for monitoring the growing foetus, reduces the risk of bringing a laboratory-deformed infant into the world. The enormous care and great caution and patience which have characterized the Edwards–Steptoe collaboration is itself a demonstration of the scientific integrity of their purpose.

But what happens after the full publication of their techniques, when a full spectrum of the medical and biochemical professions can practise on mice and then have a go? How do you control that, worldwide? And since natural biological processes lead to a vast wastage of human oocytes and sperm, a loss which nobody worries about, why should not some of this loss be turned to genuine scientific use? Chick embryos are a crucial component of many research and pharmaceutical operations, but there is a vast range of research areas in which human embryos would be preferable. Many disease organisms, for example, will not grow satisfactorily in culture – but they would grow in an embryo. And if you want to test a substance for its effect on a growing foetus, why not do it in batches in the laboratory?

The revulsion that we feel about such a possibility, which would open up an enormous range of research into genetic and developmental effects which at the moment are barred, cannot rest on logic. Women are endowed with about half a million oocytes at birth and discharge most of them into the sewers, a fate which we accept. And the annual volume of sperm which never gets within a wiggle of an oocyte would probably sink the *Ark Royal*.

Surely, given the technique which blessed us with Baby Brown, we can put this enormous wastage to important use? In the clinical and anonymous isolation of the laboratory any sense of personal attachment is lost: and since no 'life' is created (the life resides in the oocytes and spermatozoa) and no additional humans result (experimental animals are disposed of at the end of an experiment) there appear to be great advantages.

This unsavoury prospect is real. Then add the existing technology of sperm banks, extend it to oocyte banks, and we can have surrogate mums carrying the offspring of famous, highly gifted, or merely deceased persons, as a matter of highly paid routine. You do not need the still distant possibility of human cloning to begin to get worried. Today's cheers and congratulations, however warm and appropriate, have little to do with implications. As Dr James Watson said, all hell will break loose, politically and morally. In a world already grossly overcrowded, it is not easy to understand the joy. Perhaps that is because knowledge and wisdom are far from synonymous.

From 'The Brave New World of Test Tube Babies' by Anthony Tucker in the 'Guardian' 27 July 1978.

Reflections

* Scientific tampering with nature clearly raises moral and ethical questions to which there are few straightforward answers. This reading ends with the thought-provoking words that perhaps 'knowledge and wisdom are far from synonymous'. Since that article was written, in 1978, scientists have made great advances in the area of procreation. Newspapers and television have reported the issues and controversies surrounding surrogate mothers and invitro fertilisation.

It is certain that this scientific 'progress' in increasing fertility rates and 'manufacturing' human life will continue in the future. Pupils studying in our schools today are the future scientists of the 21st century. As a society we need to ensure that there are sensitive and sensible laws and guidelines to help scientists work within an acceptable moral and ethnical framework. We should not forget the valuable saying, 'wisdom *follows* knowledge'.

4 Misuse of medicine*

Introduction

In terms of improving the basic quality of human life, advances in medicine during the past 200 years have been of vital importance. You only have to think about dentistry in the Middle Ages or medical practices in the Elizabethan age to realise how our lives today have been transformed for the better by medical science.

Sadly, as with so many human endeavours, we have the power with medical science to act for good or for evil. During the Second World War the Nazis established a concentration camp at a place called Dachau, in which they carried out shocking medical experiments on fellow humans. Seven of the doctors from Dachau were later sentenced to death for war crimes. What follows is the testimony of someone who witnessed the experiments.

Reading

Dachau: the medical experiments, 1941–5

I was sent as a prisoner to the Dachau Concentration Camp in April 1941, and remained there until the liberation of the camp in April 1945. Until July 1941, I worked in a Punishment Company. After that I was sent to the hospital and subjected to the experiments in typhoid being conducted by Dr Mürmelstadt. After that I was to be made the subject of an experimental operation, and only succeeded in avoiding this by admitting that I was a physician. If this had been known before I would have suffered, because intellectuals were treated very harshly in the Punishment Company. In October 1941, I was sent to work in the herb plantation, and later in the laboratory for processing herbs, In June 1942, I was taken into the hospital as a surgeon. Shortly afterwards I was directed to conduct a stomach operation on twenty healthy prisoners. Because I would not do this I was put in the autopsy room, where I stayed until April 1945. While there I performed approximately 7,000 autopsies. In all, 12,000 autopsies were performed under my direction.

From mid-1941 to the end of 1942 some 500 operations on healthy prisoners were performed. These were for the instruction of the SS medical students and doctors and included operations on the stomach, gall bladder, spleen and throat. These were performed by students and doctors of only two years' training, although they were very dangerous and difficult. Ordinarily they would not have been done except by surgeons with at least four years' surgical practice. Many prisoners died on the operating table and many others from later complications. I performed autopsies on all of these bodies.

During my time at Dachau I was familiar with many kinds of medical experiments carried on there with human victims. These persons were never volunteers but were forced to submit to such acts. Malaria experiments on about 1,200 people were conducted by Dr Klaus Schilling between 1941 and 1945. The victims were either bitten by mosquitoes or given injections of malaria sporozoites taken from mosquitoes. Different kinds of treatment were applied, including quinine, pyrifer, neosalvarsan, antipyrin, pyramidon and a drug called 2,516 Behring. I performed autopsies on bodies of people who died from these malaria experiments. Thirty to forty died from the malaria itself. Three hundred to four hundred died later from diseases which proved fatal because of the physical condition resulting from the malaria attacks. In addition there were deaths resulting from poisoning due to overdoses of neosalvarsan and pyramidon. Dr Schilling was present at the time of my autopsies on the bodies of his patients.

In 1942 and 1943 experiments on human beings were conducted by Dr Sigismund Rascher to determine the effects of changing air pressure. As many as twenty-five persons were put at one time into a specially constructed van in which pressure could be increased or decreased as required. The purpose was to find out the effects of high altitude and of rapid parachute descents on human beings. Through a window in the van I have seen the people lying on the floor of the van. Most of the prisoners who were made use of died as a result of these experiments, from internal haemorrhages of the lungs or brain. The rest coughed blood when taken out. It was my job to take the bodies out and to send the internal organs to Munich for study as soon as they were found to be dead. About 400 to 500 prisoners were experimented on. Those not dead were sent to invalid blocks and liquidated shortly afterwards. Only a few escaped.

Rascher also conducted experiments on the effect of cold water on human beings. This was done to find a way for reviving aviators who had fallen into the ocean. The subject was placed in ice-cold water and kept there until he was unconscious. Blood was taken from his neck and tested each time his body temperature dropped one degree. This drop was determined by a rectal thermometer. Urine was also periodically tested. Some men lasted as long as 24 to 36 hours. The lowest body temperature reached was 19 degrees C., but most men died at 25 degrees C., or 26 degrees C. When the men were removed from the ice water attempts were made to revive them by artificial warmth from the sun, from hot water, from electrotherapy or by animal warmth. For this last experiment prostitutes were used and the body of the unconscious man was placed between the bodies of two women. Himmler was present at one such experiment. I could see him from one of the windows in the street between the blocks. I have personally been present at some of these cold-water experiments when Rascher was absent, and I have seen notes and diagrams on them in Rascher's laboratory. About 300 persons were used in these experiments. The majority died. Of those who lived many became mentally deranged. Those not killed were sent to invalid blocks and were killed, just as were the victims of the air-pressure experiments. I only know two who survived – a Yugoslav and a Pole, both of whom have become mental cases ...

From 'Dachau: the medical experiments, 1941–5' Dr Franz Blaha

Reflections

* This man's evidence to the Nuremberg War Crimes trials goes on to describe even more horrible experimentation on prisoners of war. The lessons for succeeding generations must surely be that as human beings we must ensure such medical knowledge and power is never again abused in the way it was in Nazi Germany.
  As fellow human beings our prayers and thoughts must go out to those who died and who witnessed such scenes as described by Dr Blaha. And, indeed, to any victims of such unthinkable treatment anywhere in our world today.

5 Humans in the air

Introduction

'One small step for man. One giant leap for mankind.'

These were the celebrated words of Neil Armstrong, the first man on the moon in 1969. But, as in all scientific and technological endeavour, these words would not have been possible had it not been for the forerunners of Armstrong and his colleagues. The following two readings, taken together, show just how far humans have travelled up the technological ladder in the course of the 20th century.

Reading

The First Channel Flight, 25 July 1909

Blériot's 28-h.p. monoplane averaged 46 mph, making the crossing in 40 minutes.

In the early morning of Sunday, 25 July 1909, I left my hotel at Calais and drove out to the field where my aeroplane was garaged. On the way I noted that the weather was favourable to my endeavour. I therefore ordered the destroyer *Escopette*, placed at my disposal by the French Government, to go to sea. I examined my aeroplane. I started the engine, and found it worked well. At half-past four we could see all round. Daylight had come. My thoughts were only upon the flight, and my determination to accomplish it this morning.

Four thirty-five. *Tout est prêt*! In an instant I am in the air, my engine making 1,200 revolutions – almost its highest speed – in order that I may get quickly over the telegraph wires along the edge of the cliff. As soon as I am over the cliff I reduce my speed. There is now no need to force my engine. I begin my flight, steady and sure, towards the coast of England. I have no apprehensions, no sensations, *pas du tout*. The *Escopette* has seen me. She is driving ahead across the Channel at full speed. She makes perhaps 26 miles per hour. What matters? I am making over 40 mph. Rapidly I overtake her, travelling at a height of 250 feet. The moment is supreme, yet I surprised myself by feeling no exultation. Below me is the sea; the motion of the waves is not pleasant. I drive on. Ten minutes go. I turn my head to see whether I am proceeding in the right direction. I am amazed. There is nothing to be seen – neither the destroyer, nor France, nor England. I am alone. I am lost.

Then I saw the cliffs of Dover! Away to the west was the spot where I had intended to land. The wind had taken me out of my course. I turned and now I was in difficulties, for the wind here by the cliffs was much stronger, and my speed was reduced as I fought against it. My beautiful aeroplane responded. I saw an opening and I found myself over dry land. I attempted a landing, but the wind caught me and whirled me round two or three times. At once I stopped my motor, and instantly my machine fell straight on the ground. I was safe on your shore. Soldiers in khaki ran up, and also a policeman. Two of my compatriots were on the spot. They kissed my cheeks. I was overwhelmed.

Louis Blériot

The First Men on the Moon, 21 July 1969

Apollo II, carrying Neil Armstrong, Lieutenant-Colonel Michael Collins, and Colonel Edwin Aldrin, was launched on 15 July. At 03.56 BST on 21 July Armstrong stepped off the ladder of lunar landing vehicle Eagle on to the Moon.

NEIL ARMSTRONG: The most dramatic recollections I had were the sights themselves. Of all the spectacular views we had, the most impressive to me was on the way to the Moon, when we flew through its shadow. We were still thousands of miles away, but close enough, so that the Moon almost filled our circular window. It was eclipsing the Sun, from our position, and the corona of the Sun was visible around the limb of the Moon as a gigantic lens-shaped or saucer-shaped light, stretching out to several lunar diameters. It was magnificent, but the Moon was even more so. We were in its shadow, so there was no part of it illuminated by the Sun. It was illuminated only by earthshine. It made the Moon appear blue-grey, and the entire scene looked decidedly three-dimensional.

I was really aware, visually aware, that the Moon was in fact a sphere not a disc. It seemed almost as if it were showing us its roundness, its similarity in shape to our Earth, in a sort of welcome. I was sure that it would be a hospitable host. It had been awaiting its first visitors for a long time . . .

[*After touchdown*] The sky is black, you know. It's a very dark sky. But it still seemed more like daylight than darkness as we looked out the window. It's a peculiar thing, but the surface looked very warm and inviting. It was the sort of situation in which you felt like going out there in nothing but a swimming suit to get a little sun. From the cockpit, the surface seemed to be tan. It's hard to account for that, because later when I held this material in may hand, it wasn't tan at all. It was black, grey and so on. It's some kind of lighting effect, but out the window the surface looks much more like light desert sand than black sand . . .

EDWIN E. ALDRIN [*on the moon*]: The blue colour of my boot has completely disappeared now into this – still don't know exactly what colour to describe this other than greyish-cocoa colour. It appears to be covering most of the lighter part of my boot . . . very fine particles . . .

[*Later*] The Moon was a very natural and pleasant environment in which to work. It had many of the advantages of zero gravity, but it was in a sense less lonesome than Zero G, where you always have to pay attention to securing attachment points to give you some means of leverage. In one-sixth gravity, on the Moon, you had a distinct feeling of being somewhere . . . As we deployed our experiments on the surface we had to jettison things like lanyards, retaining fasteners, etc., and some of these we tossed away. The objects would go away with a slow, lazy motion. If anyone tried to throw a baseball back and forth in that atmosphere he would have difficulty, at first, acclimatizing himself to that slow, lazy trajectory; but I believe he could adapt to it quite readily . . .

Odour is very subjective, but to me there was a distinct smell to the lunar material – pungent, like gunpowder or spent cap-pistol caps.

Neil Armstrong and Edwin E Aldrin

Reflections

* These two accounts: the first by an aviator, the second by an astronaut (notice the changing words), help us to reflect on the speed of technological change in the 20th century. We can only guess where the next half-century of space exploration will take human beings. Wherever that may be, the sheer enormity of our solar system will be a constant reminder that humans and planet Earth are a relatively tiny dot in the great scheme of things.

* For those who hold to strong religious beliefs, their God remains supreme. This poem of reflection was written by a pilot serving with the Royal Canadian Air Force in the Second World War. He was killed at the age of 19.

High Flight

Oh! I have slipped the surly bonds of earth
And danced the skies on laughter-silvered wings;
Sunward I've climbed, and joined the tumbling mirth
Of sun-split clouds – and done a hundred things
You have not dreamed of – wheeled and soared and swung
High in the sunlit silence. Hovering there,
I've chased the shouting wind along, and flung
My eager craft through footless halls of air.
Up, up the long, delirious, burning blue
I've topped the wind-swept heights with easy grace
Where never lark, nor even eagle flew.
And, while with silent, lifting mind I've trod
The high untrespassed sanctity of space,
Put out my hand, and touched the face of God.

John Magee

6 Space exploration

Introduction

Most of the great statesmen and women in the world have their major speeches written for them.

Each of you could write a speech on one of several topics which interest you – the state of the local environment or why shops don't open on Sundays, or whatever. But to write a speech to order to cater for millions of listeners requires a special ability – particularly when it might have to be done very quickly.

Peggy Noonan was one of the leading speech writers for American President Ronald Reagan (1980–88). Much of her success she attributes to being well versed in poetry.

The occasion of the Challenger disaster (1982), when seven astronauts were lost in space, called for a very special speech.

Millions of Americans watched the disaster live, as the space shuttle blew up on their television screens. This is what Peggy Noonan wrote.

Reading

Challenger

'Ladies and gentlemen, I had planned to speak to you tonight to report on the State of the Union, but the events of earlier today have led me to change those plans. Today is a day for mourning and remembering.

We know we share this pain with all of the people of our country. This is truly a national loss.

'Nineteen years ago almost to the day, we lost three astronauts in a terrible accident on the ground. But we have never lost an astronaut in flight. We have never had a tragedy like this. And perhaps we have forgotten the courage it took for the crew of the shuttle. But they, the *Challenger* Seven, were aware of the dangers – and overcame them, and did their jobs brilliantly.

'We mourn seven heroes – Michael Smith, Dick Scobee, Judith Resnik, Ronald McNair, Ellison Onizuka, Gregory Jarvis, and Christa McAuliffe. We mourn their loss as a nation, together.

'To the families of the Seven: We cannot bear, as you do, the full impact of this tragedy – but we feel the loss, and we are thinking about you so very much. Your loved ones were daring and brave and they had that special grace, that special spirit that says Give me a challenge and I'll meet it with joy. They had a hunger to explore the universe and discover its truths. They wished to serve and they did – they served us all.

'And I want to say something to the schoolchildren of America who were watching the live coverage of the shuttle's takeoff. I know it's hard to understand, but sometimes painful things like this happen – it's all part of the process of exploration and discovery – it's all part of taking a chance and expanding man's horizons. The future doesn't belong to the fainthearted, it belongs to the brave. The *Challenger* crew was pulling us into the future – and we'll continue to follow them.

'I've always had great faith in and respect for our space program – and what happened today does nothing to diminish it. We don't hide our space program, we don't keep secrets and cover things up, we do it all up front and in public. That's the way freedom is, and we wouldn't change it for a minute.

'We'll continue our quest in space. There will be more shuttle flights and more shuttle crews and, yes, more volunteers, more civilians, more teachers in space. Nothing ends here – our hopes and our journeys continue.

'I want to add that I wish I could talk to every man and woman who works for NASA or who worked on this mission and tell them: Your dedication and professionalism have moved and impressed us for decades, and we know of your anguish. We share it.

'There's a coincidence today. On this day 390 years ago the great explorer Sir Francis Drake died aboard ship off the coast of Panama. In his lifetime the great frontiers were the oceans. and a historian later said, 'He lived by the sea, died on it, and was buried in it.' Today we can say of the *Challenger* Crew: Their dedication was, like Drake's, complete.

'The crew of the space shuttle *Challenger* honored us by the manner in which they lived their lives. We will never forget them, nor the last time we saw them – this morning, as they prepared for their journey, and waved good-bye, and 'slipped the surly bonds of earth' to 'touch the face of God.'

From 'What I saw at the Revolution' by Peggy Noonan

Reflections

* The speech captures a sense of national mourning.

  It also makes the point very clearly that exploration and discovery involve risk. Modern-day scientific and technological advance are not always won easily.

  In this case the American space exploration programme led to the death of seven human beings. The speech – with all its patriotic overtones – tells the American people that 'the future belongs to the brave'. New scientific developments are always going to present humans with difficult decisions and problems. Space exploration, of course, continues today, certainly not halted by this one tragedy.

* *Corinthians 15: 51–58*

  Listen, I tell you a mystery: We will not all sleep, but we will all be changed – in a flash, in the twinkling of an eye, at the last trumpet. For the trumpet will sound, the dead will be raised imperishable, and we will be changed. For the perishable must clothe itself with the imperishable, and the mortal with immortality. When the perishable has been clothed with the imperishable, and the mortal with immortality, then the saying that is written will come true: 'Death has been swallowed up in victory'.

  'Where, O death, is your victory?

  Where, O death, is your sting?'

  The sting of death is sin, and the power of sin is the law. But thanks be to God! He gives us the victory through our Lord Jesus Christ.

7 Life in the Siberian cold

Introduction

All around us we see new developments in science and technology. Many of the advances are welcome. Others we might see as threatening the environment or changing our life-style in a way we don't want.

In some parts of the world conditions of climate are so extreme that even modern technology is defeated. The following article is by a visitor to one of the coldest areas on Earth – a place called Yakutsk in Siberia, Russia.

Reading

Life struggles with the permafrost in Siberia's cold war

YAKUTSK, Siberia – For a town whose abiding interest is its weather, the inhabitants of Yakutsk are pretty vague on the details. What is the all-time record in the city? I enquired. Sixty-one degrees under, 64 degrees, 67 degrees, came the different answers. In the end though it didn't matter. Yakutsk is cold: the coldest city, they say, on the planet.

It is a quite preposterous place. Why, one may ask, do 220,000 people choose to live there at all? Admittedly there are compensations. In mid-winter it may be too cold even to ski on snow as fine as sand, but you can make a breathtaking drive along a temporary motorway on the frozen Lena amid flat vistas of jagged pack-ice. True to the Russian love of diminutives, the locals refer to it simply as the '*rechka*', or little river, although it is several miles wide.

Or you can travel a few miles into the wilderness and experience the deafening dusk silence of the Siberian taiga, as tiny particles of frost dance in the air and a milky-yellow northern sun sinks from an endless sky.

But in a place where winter lasts eight months, such pleasures must wear thin. Set atop the permafrost, Yakutsk is, as someone remarked, 'the end of the line, except there is no line'. I was lucky – the temperature only once brushed minus 40 during my visit. Much lower, and a thick fog can descend, to make isolation complete. The last snow falls in early May, the first in mid-September. In between is a short, sharp summer when temperatures can reach 33 degrees – enough to thaw two or three metres of topsoil, the so-called 'active layer', upon which Siberia's fragile environment depends.

But as the ice melts, a million lakes and rivers spawn the most ferocious mosquitos on the face of the Earth. And even in summer agriculture cannot relax. A few years ago, I was told, a frost of minus 6 centigrade one mid-July night wiped out that year's crops of hardy wheat, potatoes and cabbage.

Everything is conditioned by the cold. In Moscow buildings have double doors and double windows. Here they are triple-layered. Car windows are double glazed, otherwise they frost over in 30 seconds. In a bad winter their engines run all day and all night, belching white plumes of exhaust. If they are turned off, they will never restart.

Building is so difficult that a square metre of living space costs three times more than in Moscow. In the old quarters of Yakutsk, you see traditional one-storey wooden houses sagging at weird angles, or half sunken into an earth softened by the heat they emit.

The city is dotted with abandoned, more modern, buildings. The rents and fissures in their walls testify to an architect's misjudgement – or the gradual growth of a '*kryopeg*', a sort of permafrost cancer of soft spots where natural or man-made salts have filtered through the 'active layer' to melt the ice which should hold the undersoil rock solid.

Today's technique is to build new blocks of flats on concrete stilts. But sinking them the required 10 metres is an engineering feat in itself. One morning, with the temperature hovering at a balmy minus 25, the city's chief architect, Fyodor Shishigyn, took me to a building site to see how it was done.

Basically there are two ways. One is to direct a thin tube into the earth, and blast steam into the permafrost. As the earth briefly softens, the concrete pile is manoeuvred into position and then hammered down into the temporarily yielding earth. Within days, it is locked fast for ever as the permafrost refreezes.

I witnessed the other way – a clanking 40-foot drill with a three-foot bore, chewing and tearing out of the ground great lumps of frozen earth. When the required depth is reached, the concrete unit is picked up and lowered into position. A few yards away though, they had hit a '*kryopeg*'. At the bottom of a 15ft pit, men wrapped in furs and greatcoats were trying to clear a bog of browny-grey mud from which the stilts protruded at odd angles. As they attacked this semi-frozen swamp, their breath billowed in white clouds. It was the filthiest work I have ever seen.

At minus 51, however, even in Yakutsk everything comes to a halt. Construction stops because metal becomes as brittle as glass. At that temperature camera film snaps, rubber soles on shoes break like china plates. Schools close, and classes are transmitted by television. A few, however, relish this. 'We need the cold,' someone insisted to me, lamenting the clemency of this winter. 'People are suffering now it's so warm. Minus 30 is not enough. Only minus 60 will get rid of all the germs.' I was not sympathetic.

'Out of the USSR' by Rupert Cornwell

Reflections

* Life in Siberia obviously contrasts with how we live in our own environment. What is interesting is how humans adapt to whatever climate they find themselves in. Why do they go on living there? you might ask. Well, for them it is their home – their families have lived there for generations. Their way of life and culture is adapted to the extremes of cold.

  Modern technology has made life in Sibera a little more tolerable, but nature proves that in some ways it can never be tamed. Perhaps one day future generations of scientists will conquer extremes of heat and cold – we can only guess. For all our technological know-how, some of Earth's challenges still lie ahead for humankind. In the meantime, we can only marvel at people's stamina and determination in such conditions.

8 Word processors and language*

Introduction

Throughout human history inventions have come along which have changed attitudes and life-styles.

When the wheel, the car engine, the television and the jet engine were invented they each had an impact on the way people lived. In the 15th and 16th centuries, the development of printing had a major effect on communication and attitudes towards reading and learning.

In the past ten years, the introduction of the word processor into the workplace, homes and schools has had a similar impact.

How exactly is it changing human thought?

The following essay reflects on this subject.

Reading

Infomania

What is the state of the language? No state at all. It is in process. Our language is being word-processed. If languages have states of health, get sick or well, then ours is manic.

We face a tidal wave of written words. The wave of future shock swelled on the horizon. First came speed reading – a twentieth-century version of literacy. Next Xerox duplication, the word processor, and the fax machine. Now we drive a technology that drives our verbal life faster and faster. The word processor is computerising our language.

Word-processed submissions have doubled the workload of editors at commercial and academic presses. Writers grow prolix, with manuscripts bloated to twice normal size. The prose is profuse, garbled, disorganized – as if the difference between writing and revising were passé. Pages are becoming more difficult to read. Reams of paper pour out unedited streams of consciousness. The only writer who admits he is no faster than he was before computers is Isaac Asimov, who published 141 books in 138 months.

During the 1980s a new vocabulary established the computerisation of English. To be initiated, you had to repeat buzzwords like *access*, *input*, and *output*. You learned to speak of files having no apparent physical dimensions, *menus* offering a selection of nonedibles, and *monitors* providing vigilance over your own words. You learned to navigate with *wraparound* and with a *cursor* – sometimes dubbed *cursee* as it became the recipient of your profanities. You may have even explored *mouse compatibility*, the ASCII *code*, and the difference between RAM and ROM memory. At the very least, you addressed yourself to *floppies* and *windows*, to *function keys* and program *documentation* (read: instruction manual). You had to take into account *block moves*, *hyphenation zones*, and *soft spaces* versus *hard*. The editorial *cut-and-paste* became yours electronically. You learned not only to *delete* but also to *unerase*, then to *search-and-replace*, and onward to *globally search-and-replace*. *Automatic formatting* and *reformatting* entered your writing routine.

Once initiated into the basics of word processing you sigh, this is bliss! No more cutting paper and pasting, no more anxiety about revisions. Now you can get to work without the nuisance of typing and retyping. Words dance on the screen. Sentences slide smoothly into place, making way for one another, while paragraphs ripple rhythmically. Words become highlighted, vanish and then reappear instantly at the push of a button. Digital writing is nearly frictionless. You formulate thoughts directly on screen. You don't have to consider whether you are writing the beginning, middle, or end of your text. You can snap any passage into any place with the push of a key. The flow of ideas flashes directly on screen. No need to ponder or sit on an idea – capture it on the fly!

But the honeymoon fades, and the dark side of computing descends upon you. The romance with computers shows its pathological aspects: mindless productivity and increased stress.

Your prose now reads, well, differently. You no longer formulate thoughts carefully before beginning to write. You think on screen. You edit more aggressively as you write, making changes without penalty of retyping. Possible changes occur to you rapidly and frequently, so that a leaning tower of printouts stretches from the waste-basket to the heights of perfection – almost. The power at your fingertips tempts you to believe that faster is better, that ease means instant quality.

Word processing makes us information virtuosos, as the computer automatically transforms all we write into information code. But human we remain. For us, significant language always depends on the felt context of our own limited experience. We are biologically finite in what we can attend to meaningfully. When we pay attention to the significance of something, we cannot proceed at the computer's breakneck pace. We have to ponder, reflect, contemplate.

Infomania erodes our capacity for significance. With a mindset fixed on information, the attention span shortens. We collect fragments. We become mentally poorer in overall meaning. We get into the habit of clinging to knowledge bits and lose our feel for the wisdom behind knowledge. In the Information Age some people even believe that literacy or culture is a matter of having the right facts at our fingertips.

We expect access to everything now, instantly and simultaneously. We suffer from a logic of total management where everything must be at our disposal. Eventually our madness will cost us. There is a law of diminishing returns: the more information accessed, the less significance is possible. We must not lose our appreciation for the expressive possibilities of our language in the service of thinking.

From 'Infomania' by Michael Heim

Reflections

* A developed language system is the one thing that distinguishes humans from other living animals. This writer is suggesting that the word processor might be changing the way we think and write.

  There is no doubt that the word processor, as part of a much bigger change in communication systems, has changed lifestyles. People can work at home rather than go into offices. Is it changing our attitudes in schools towards examinations and spelling?

  Where will this end? Already some people – for reasons of faith – will not touch computers and word processors because they see them as 'inhuman' and the hand of the Devil.

  Human invention will always offer us 'progress' – but we need to be cautious about whether progress always means moving forward.

  As this writer observes: 'Eventually our madness will cost us'.

* *Psalm 32*

  I will instruct you and teach you in the way you should go;
  I will counsel you and watch over you.
  Do not be like the horse or the mule, which have no understanding but must be controlled by bit and bridle or they will not come to you.
  Many are the woes of the wicked, but the Lord's unfailing love surrounds the man who trusts in him.

9 Certainties of science and technology

Introduction

We are all fallible. It is a feature of being human that nothing is certain. Sometimes we may forget this. We rely heavily on science and technology working for us, confident that it will never let us down. But accidents do happen – although sometimes it is scarcely possible to believe.

One such accident happened in April 1912, when the supposedly 'unsinkable' passenger liner, the Titanic, sank.

The following are accounts from survivors of this great maritime disaster.

Reading

The *Titanic*: A Fireman's Story, 15 April 1912

I was in my bunk when I felt a bump. One man said, 'Hello. She has been struck.' I went on deck and saw a great pile of ice on the well deck before the forecastle, but we all thought the ship would last some time, and we went back to our bunks. Then one of the firemen came running down and yelled, 'All muster for the lifeboats.' I ran on deck, and the Captain said, 'All firemen keep down on the well deck. If a man comes up I'll shoot him.'

Then I saw the first lifeboat lowered. Thirteen people were on board, eleven men and two women. Three were millionaires, and one was Ismay [J Bruce Ismay, Managing Director of the White Star Line; a survivor].

Then I ran up on to the hurricane deck and helped to throw one of the collapsible boats on to the lower deck. I saw an Italian woman holding two babies. I took one of them, and made the woman jump overboard with the baby, while I did the same with the other. When I came to the surface the baby in my arms was dead. I saw the woman strike out in good style, but a boiler burst on the Titanic and started a big wave. When the woman saw that wave, she gave up. Then, as the child was dead, I let it sink too.

I swam around for about half an hour, and was swimming on my back when the Titanic went down. I tried to get aboard a boat, but some chap hit me over the head with an oar. There were too many in her. I got around to the other side of the boat and climbed in.

Harry Senior

The *Titanic*: The Wireless Operator's Story, 15 April 1912

From aft came the tunes of the band. It was a ragtime tune. I don't know what. Then there was 'Autumn' . . . I went to the place I had seen the collapsible boat on the boat deck, and to my surprise I saw the boat, and the men still trying to push it off. I guess there wasn't a sailor in the crowd. They couldn't do it. I went up to them and was just lending a hand when a large wave came awash of the deck. The big wave carried the boat off. I had hold of an oarlock and I went with it. The next I knew I was in the boat. But that was not all. I was in the boat, and the boat was upside-down, and I was under it. And I remember realizing I was wet through and that whatever happened I must not breathe, for I was under water. I knew I had to fight for it, and I did. How I got out from under the boat I do not know but I felt a breath of air at last. There were men all around me – hundreds of them. The sea was dotted with them, all depending on their lifebelts. I felt I simply had to get away from the ship. She was a beautiful sight then. Smoke and sparks were rushing out of her funnel. There must have been an explosion, but we heard none. We only saw the big stream of sparks. The ship was turning gradually on her nose – just like a duck that goes for a dive. I had only one thing on my mind – to get away from the suction. The band was still playing. I guess all of them went down. They were playing 'Autumn' then. I swam with all my might. I suppose I was 150 feet away when the Titanic, on her nose, with her after-quarter sticking straight up in the air, began to settle – slowly.

When at last the waves washed over her rudder there wasn't the least bit of suction I could feel. She must have kept going just so slowly as she had been . . . I felt after a little while like sinking. I was very cold. I saw a boat of some kind near me, and put all my strength into an effort to swim to it. It was hard work. I was all done when a hand reached out from the boat and pulled me aboard. It was our same collapsible. The same crowd was on it. There was just room for me to roll on the edge. I lay there not caring what happened. Somebody sat on my legs. They were wedged in between slats and were being wrenched. I had not the heart left to ask the man to move. It was a terrible sight all around – men swimming and sinking.

Harold Bride

The *Titanic*: From a Lifeboat, 15 April 1912

We did not begin to understand the situation till we were perhaps a mile or more away from the Titanic. Then we could see the rows of lights along the decks begin to slant gradually upward from the bow. Very slowly the lines of light began to point downward at a greater and greater angle. The sinking was so slow that you could not perceive the lights of the deck changing their position. The slant seemed to be greater about every quarter of an hour. That was the only difference.

In a couple of hours, though, she began to go down more rapidly. Then the fearful sight began. The people in the ship were just beginning to realize how great their danger was. When the forward part of the ship dropped suddenly at a faster rate, so that the upward slope became marked, there was a sudden rush of passengers on all the decks towards the stern. It was like a wave. We could see the great black mass of people in the steerage sweeping to the rear part of the boat and breaking through into the upper decks. At the distance of about a mile we could distinguish everything through the night, which was perfectly clear. We could make out the increasing excitement on board the boat as the people, rushing to and fro, caused the deck lights to disappear and reappear as they passed in front of them.

This panic went on, it seemed, for an hour. Then suddenly the ship seemed to shoot up out of the water and stand there perpendicularly. It seemed to us that it stood upright in the water for four full minutes.

Then it began to slide gently downwards. Its speed increased as it went down head first, so that the stern shot down with a rush.

The lights continued to burn till it sank. We could see the people packed densely in the stern till it was gone . . .

As the ship sank we could hear the screaming a mile away. Gradually it became fainter and fainter and died away. Some of the lifeboats that had room for more might have gone to their rescue, but it would have meant that those who were in the water would have swarmed aboard and sunk her.

Mrs D H Bishop

Reflections

* When the Titanic sank, 1,513 lives were lost. In fact the ship had only 1,178 lifeboat spaces for the 2,224 people aboard, and this was its maiden voyage. The ship had set sail from London to New York with great ceremony and great acclaim for its engineering excellence; it was considered to be truly unsinkable. Yet certainties do not exist – or at least the one true certainty is that there is *uncertainty*. We should not let the wonders of modern science blind us to this basic fact of life. And when tragedy does occur we need to avoid blaming a failed machine – it is we, as humans, who create and operate our technology.

10 Fears of technological progress

Introduction

In a celebrated song lyric by American folk singer Bob Dylan these words appear:
    'You've thrown the worst fear that can ever be hurled, Fear to bring children into the world.'
    This song 'Masters of War' was written at a time of campaign against the development of nuclear weapons in the 1960s. As the 21st century approaches, rapid advances are being made in science and technology. Some people fear where such advances may take humankind.
    Listen to the following thought-provoking poem.
    It is titled 'Prayer Before Birth'.

Reading

Prayer before Birth

I am not yet born; O hear me.
Let not the bloodsucking bat or the rat or the stoat or the club-footed ghoul come
    near me.
I am not yet born; console me
I fear that the human race may with tall walls wall me, with strong drugs dope me,
    with wise lies lure me,
        on black racks rack me, in blood-baths roll me.

I am not yet born, provide me
With water to dandle me, grass to grow for me, trees to talk to me, sky to sing to
    me, birds and a white light
        in the back of my mind to guide me.

I am not yet born; forgive me
For the sins that in me the world shall commit, my words
    when they speak me, my thoughts when they think me,

my treason engendered by traitors beyond me,
  my life when they murder by means of my
    hands, my death when they live me.

I am not yet born; rehearse me
In the parts I must play and the cues I must take when
  old men lecture me, bureaucrats hector me, mountains
    frown at me, lovers laugh at me, the white
      waves call me to folly and the desert calls
        me to doom and the beggar refuses
          my gift and my children curse me.

I am not yet born; O hear me,
Let not the man who is beast or who thinks he is God come near me.

I am not yet born; O fill me
With strength against those who would freeze my
  humanity, would dragoon me into a lethal automaton,
    would make me a cog in a machine, a thing with
      one face, a thing, and against all those who
        would dissipate my entirety, would
          blow me like thistledown hither
            like water held in the
              hands would spill me.

Let them not make me a stone and let them not spill me.
Otherwise kill me.

Louis MacNeice

Reflections

* Here the poet is clearly voicing his worries for future generations. Certain phrases
linger in our minds:
  'I fear that the human race may with tall walls wall me'
  'O fill me/With strength against those who would freeze my humanity, would
  dragoon me into a lethal automaton'
  Science and technology can be used both to improve the quality of life and to
  endanger it.
  It is the challenge for each generation to pass on to the next one a spirit that wants
  to improve society and harness the enormous technological knowledge now at
  our command, to the benefit of local, national and international communities.

11 Technology and the world of work*

Introduction

With the development of sophisticated information technology in the 1970s, futu-
rologists predicted that there would be great social changes, particularly in relation

to work habits. This article – written in the 1970s – reminds us that while patterns of work have changed over the centuries, this change has been relatively gradual in the 20th century. Perhaps it offers us a glimpse into the problems and opportunities the 21st century may hold.

Reading

The abolition of work

The group is called the Futures Network, and is itself a mini-work-revolution. It joins people from different institutions who share the same interests, cuts across job-boundaries and hierarchies, and is devoted to the most fashionable of the new 'soft' sciences, futurology.

.... We have to face the fact that from now on there isn't going to be much work of the sort that we now know.

The futurists see it as no catastrophe, but the way to a merrier world. By strenuous effort and job-sharing, they point out that what bodes to be a mass redundancy problem can be avoided.

It is the dawn of the era when worklessness becomes a positive good: when people would be paid to do nothing, for the sake of the economy. It is the beginning of a world in which a small educated élite (or a collection of boring technologists, depending on your side of the fence) would keep the automated factories rolling, while we redundant drones are told to go away and play quietly: or rather, to lead lives of immense civilised and creative idleness supported by the State.

The futurists aren't quite suggesting a society in which we all lie around orgiastically consuming free bread and circuses, with the noise of giant automated factories in the background. They compromise with the idea of one where automated factories provide all the essential needs and a basic social wage, but where an informal economy provides the quality part of life, both in products and in work.

Picture it in a form which makes full use of the most humanly helpful technological tools: sophisticated electronic communications and storage systems, which could free a huge number of people, particularly the office based, from having to go to their soulless anonymous organisations to do their work.

Picture the decision-making ranks of industry in their thirties: managers, researchers, financiers, marketers, communicators and secretariats, all plugged into computer terminals, viewdata banks, open-line conference telephone lines, telexes and private-circuit television systems. Not in offices already separated from one another and from the workplace, but separated just a little farther still – in other words, at home.

Picture skilled workers like toolmakers, toolsetters and maintenance men freed likewise, but in visual and aural contact at any moment of the day, able to monitor gauges and machinery, visiting frequently and always on call. Actual on-the-spot tending of machinery could be done by the semi-skilled and supervised by the second ranks of management.

Because of what is seen as the frowning monotony and lightness of this sort of work, it should not be done by people in the prime of life, but by the young and the old. The young, because to compensate for the monotony they have a sense of newness, a lively personal life and the freedom to travel to leaven the boredom with new environments. Above all, in the course of this monotonous apprenticeship they can learn trades, skills and professions which they can apply more creatively and to their own ends later on.

The old should provide the supervision and teaching. They can tolerate monotony better, after a full and lively life; but like the young they need the identity and status of a real role; and they too are free to travel.

It would be up to the mid-age groups in the top and skilled jobs, already professionally established with clear social identities, to bear the first brunt of freedom, and to pioneer new ways of work. Based at home, many of them will already have saved half a day in travelling time and breaks, and much in transport energy. They will have time to observe local and home needs and immediate realities, as well as their work world, and as well as tending their formal employment, they can in their new time apply their skills to this.

They would scrutinise local housing, schools, roads, hospitals, government and environment with more vigour than an anonymous organisation can ever inspire.

The local building site and garage would have a crowd of heavily-involved, but incorrupt unofficial supervisors around it all day. In due course, these side-line spectators would be in there doing their bit according to their appropriate skills: converting houses, building custom-built cars, re-organising the local hospital, landscaping the neighbourhood.

And in all these activities, they would take their sons and daughters along – fulfilling, as they can't do now, their family role.

Soon they would amalgamate in loose confederations with others of varying skills and backgrounds in their neighbourhood, to work on local and individual projects. Their home-based contacts and experience would enrich their remoter work-world, and their work-world their home-based projects and businesses.

With luck, by the time they have passed through this strenuous active era, they will have generated massive work in the way of projects, co-operatives and small businesses to tend in leisurely fashion in their old age. Suddenly, there would be no problem of growth, let alone of unemployment and leisure.

Already this kind of economy is growing. In weekends, holidays, and days off work, and on the quiet: in conflict with formal employment. It could be dovetailed with it. But so far people have clung on desperately to the disappearing and dreary past, outlawing all these self-starting activities: while the young unemployed get more violent. The paradigm shift has yet to occur.

You and I my not see it, resting after a 50-hour week, but society, it seems, is on the brink of a paradigm shift towards the abolition of work. At least, work as we know it now.

A paradigm shift, for collectors of Newspeak, is what happened when people realised the earth was round, or when Darwin demonstrated men were descended from monkeys. It's a mental knock on the head, a complete change of focus, topsy-turvying all held ideas to produce a changed world. This kind of cerebral gymnastic is about to take place any moment now in the way we view the daily traipse to the office and the boring things we do there. So say a gathering of academics, economists psychologists, managers, writers and mathematicians, who met recently in Wales to debate the revolution in work.

From 'The abolition of work' in The Observer 13/8/78

Reflections

* Time will tell whether or not 'the paradigm shift' occurs. As with all change brought about by technological development, it is worth reflecting on the social and moral implications:

Could you imagine a society like the one envisaged here?
What would be the implications for family life?
What would be the reactions of young and old alike?
Are we a human race that *needs* to be employed?
And what do we mean by *employment*, paid or unpaid?

* *Ecclesiasticus 38*

The wisdom of a learned man cometh by opportunity of leisure;
And he that hath little business shall become wise.
How can he get wisdom that holdeth the plough,
And that glorieth in the goad,
That driveth oxen, and is occupied in their labours,
And whose talk is of bullocks?
He giveth his mind to make furrows;
And is diligent to give the kine fodder.

So every carpenter and workmaster,
That laboureth night and day:
And they that cut and grave seals,
And are diligent to make great variety,
And give themselves to counterfeit imagery,
And watch to finish work;
The smith also sitting by the anvil,
And considering the iron work,
The vapour of the fire wasteth his flesh,
And he fighteth with the heat of the furnace:
The noise of the hammer and the anvil is ever in his ears,
And his eyes look still upon the pattern of the thing that he maketh:
He setteth his mind to finish his work,
And watcheth to polish it perfectly,

So doth the potter sitting at his work,
And turning the wheel about with his feet,
Who is alway carefully set at his work,
And maketh all his work by number;
He fashioneth the clay with his arm,
And boweth down his strength before his feet;
He applieth himself to lead it over;
And he is diligent to make clean the furnace:
And every one is wise in his work.
Without these cannot a city be inhabited.

12 Transforming lifestyles

Introduction

Technological developments of recent years have made some things into a reality
which were, only a decade ago, almost unimaginable. In particular, the coming

together of information technology and biotechnology, and the economics linked to them, is set to make our world a different place in the 21st century. This is how one contemporary writer sees the future.

Reading

Transforming lifestyles

Information technology links the processing power of the computer with the micro-waves, the satellites, and the fibre optic cables of telecommunications. It is a technology which is leaping rather than creeping into the future. It is said that if the automobile industry had developed as rapidly as the processing capacity of the computer we would now be able to buy a 400 mile-per-gallon Rolls-Royce for £1.

   Biotechnology is the completely new industry that has grown out of the interpretation of DNA, the genetic code at the heart of life. It is only one generation old as a science and as an industry, and is only now becoming evident in everyday life with new types of crops, genetic fingerprinting and all the possibilities, good and bad, of what is called bio-engineering.

   These two technologies are developing so fast that their outputs are unpredictable, but some of the more likely developments in the next ten to twenty years could change parts of our lives, and other peoples' lives, in a dramatic fashion. A group of young executives who were asked by their companies to contemplate 2000 AD came up with the following possibilities and probabilities.

Cordless telephones Mark 2
The next generation of cordless telephones (already being tested in Britain) may give everyone their own portable personal telephone to be used anywhere at affordable prices. Link it to a lap-top computer and a portable fax and a car or train seat becomes an office.

The transgenic pig
The possibility of using animal organs in humans has been under investigation of some time. The pig is biologically similar to humans and experiments are under way to engineer embryos to produce the transgenic pig, an animal with organs more man-like than piglike. Pig farms may one day mean something quite different from what they do today and replacement organs could be available on demand.

Water fields
Crops can now be genetically engineered to grow on poor quality soil or even in water (without tasting like seaweed!). Under development is an idea to engineer crops which can take their nitrogen directly from the air instead of from the ground, reducing the need for fertilizer. Any country could one day grow all the food it needs.

The hearing computer
Voice-sensitive computers which can translate the spoken word into written words on a screen will be on every executive's desk one day, turning everyone into their own typist whether they can use a keyboard or not.

Irradiated food

Irradiation, once we are convinced that it is safe, will make it possible to buy 'fresh' food from all round the world at any time of the year. There will also be appetite-reducing drugs for those who find the new foods too tempting, and even health-increasing foods for those who want it both ways.

Telecatalogues

Teleshopping, already in existence in experimental situations, will one day be commonplace. Every store will display its wares and prices on your home television teletext, with local pick-up centres available for those unwilling to pay the extra delivery charge. Personal shopping in the High Street will become a leisure activity rather than a necessity, with all the frills and fancies that go with something done for pleasure not for duty.

Smart cards

These cards, already in use in France, replace cash, keys, credit, debit and cash cards. They will not only let you into your home or your car but will automatically update all your bank account balances for you.

Genetic fingerprints

Instead of Personal Identification Numbers (PINs) which are easy to discover and replicate, we shall each have a fingerprint on our personal cards which cannot be reproduced by others.

Genetic fingerprinting can be used to detect criminals from remains of tissue left behind at the scene of a crime, and also to diagnose hereditary and latent diseases. A national data-bank of genetic fingerprints seems possible one day.

Soon, everything we know about ourselves, and some things we do not know, will be available to anyone with the right number or fingerprint. What price privacy then, many will ask.

The technology we shall undoubtedly take in our stride. Hole-in-the-wall banking caused hardly a flutter of an eyelid when it appeared and video-recorders are now part of the furniture in nearly half of British homes. It is not the technology itself that is important but the impact which, without conscious thought, it has on our lives. Microwave ovens were a clever idea, but their inventor could hardly have realized that the effect, once they were everywhere, would be to take the preparation of food out of the home and into the, increasingly automated, factory; to make cooking as it used to be into an activity of choice, not of necessity; to alter the habits of our homes, making the dining table outmoded for many, as each member of the family individually heats up his or her own meal as and when they require it.

Whether these developments are for good or for ill must be our choice. Technology in itself is neutral. We can use it to enrich our lives or to let them lose all meaning. What we cannot do is to pretend that nothing has changed and live in a garden of remembrance as if time had stood still. It doesn't and we can't.

From 'The Age of Unreason' by Charles Handy

Reflections

* In addition to listing the ingenious inventions that lie ahead for us, writer Charles Handy concludes with some important thoughts:

  – first, technology in itself is neutral; what humans *choose* to do with it is what matters and what leads to often difficult ethical decisions (test-tube babies are one example).
  – second, human beings will go on inventing new gadgets and drugs that will doubtless raise questions as well as fulfil needs and desires.

  His concluding words are worth repeating:

  'What we cannot do is to pretend that nothing has changed and live in a garden of remembrance as if time had stood still. It doesn't and we can't.'

Rights and Responsibilities

1 Stand up for your rights

Introduction
There are many famous – and indeed infamous – examples in history of people standing up for their rights. But few cases can have been so personally violent as that of Suffragette Lady Constance Lytton. Disguised as a working-class woman, she was arrested while campaigning for her cause and sent to Walton Gaol, Liverpool. While in prison, Lady Constance went on hunger strike, and as a result she was forcibly fed.

Reading

Force feeding

Suffragette Lady Constance Lytton, Disguised as a
Lower-Class Woman, Jane Warton, is Forcibly Fed in
Walton Gaol, Liverpool, 18 January 1910

I was visited again by the Senior Medical Officer, who asked me how long I had been without food. I said I had eaten a buttered scone and a banana sent in by friends to the police station on Friday at about midnight. He said, 'Oh, then, this is the fourth day; that is too long, I shall feed you, I must feed you at once,' but he went out and nothing happened till about six o'clock in the evening, when he returned with, I think, five wardresses and the feeding apparatus. He urged me to take food voluntarily. I told him that was absolutely out of the question, that when our legislators ceased to resist enfranchising women then I should cease to resist taking food in prison. He did not examine my heart nor feel my pulse; he did not ask to do so, nor did I say anything which could possibly induce him to think I would refuse to be examined. I offered no resistance to being placed in position, but lay down voluntarily on the plank bed. Two of the wardresses took hold of my arms, one held my head and one my feet. One wardress helped to pour the food.

The doctor leant on my knees as he stooped over my chest to get at my mouth. I shut my mouth and clenched my teeth. I had looked forward to this moment with so much anxiety lest my identity should be discovered beforehand, that I felt positively glad when the time had come. The sense of being overpowered by more force than I could possibly resist was complete, but I resisted nothing except with my mouth. The doctor offered me the choice of a wooden or steel gag; he explained elaborately, as he did on most subsequent occasions, that the steel gag would hurt and the wooden one not, and he urged me not to force him to use the steel gag.

But I did not speak nor open my mouth, so that after playing about for a moment or two with a wooden one he finally had recourse to the steel. He seemed annoyed at my resistance and he broke into a temper as he plied my teeth with the steel implement. He found that on either side at the back I had false teeth mounted on a bridge which did not take out. The super-intending wardress asked if I had any false teeth, if so, that they must be taken out; I made no answer and the process went on. He dug his instrument down on to the sham tooth, it pressed fearfully on the gum. He said if I resisted so much with my teeth, he would have to feed me through the nose. The pain of it was intense and at last I must have given way for he got the gag between my teeth, when he proceeded to turn it much more than necessary until my jaws were fastened wide apart, far more than they could go naturally. Then he put down my throat a tube which seemed to me much too wide and was something like four feet in length. The irritation of the tube was excessive. I choked the moment it touched my throat until it had got down.

Then the food was poured in quickly; it made me sick a few seconds after it was down and the action of the sickness made my body and legs double up, but the wardresses instantly pressed back my head and the doctor leant on my knees. The horror of it was more than I can describe. I was sick over the doctor and wardresses, and it seemed a long time before they took the tube out. As the doctor left he gave me a slap on the cheek, not violently, but, as it were, to express his contemptuous disapproval, and he seemed to take for granted that my distress was assumed. At first it seemed such an utterly contemptible thing to have done that I could only laugh in my mind. Then suddenly I saw Jane Warton lying before me, and it seemed as if I were outside of her. She was the most despised, ignorant and helpless prisoner that I had seen. When she had served her time and was out of the prison, no one would believe anything she said, and the doctor when he had fed her by force and tortured her body, struck her on the cheek to show how he despised her! That was Jane Warton, and I had come to help her.

When the doctor had gone out of the cell, I lay quite helpless. The wardresses were kind and knelt round to comfort me, but there was nothing to be done, I could not move, and remained there in what, under different conditions, would have been an intolerable mess. I had been sick over my hair, which, though short, hung on either side of my face, all over the wall near my bed, and my clothes seemed saturated with it, but the wardresses told me they could not get me a change that night as it was too late, the office was shut. I lay quite motionless, it seemed paradise to be without the suffocating tube, without the liquid food going in and out of my body and without the gag between my teeth. Presently the wardresses all left me, they had orders to go, which were carried out with the usual promptness. Before long I heard the sounds of the forced feeding in the next cell to mine. It was almost more than I could bear, it was Elsie Howey, I was sure. When the ghastly process was over and all quiet, I tapped on the wall and called out at the top of my voice, which wasn't much just then, 'No surrender,' and there came the answer past any doubt in Elsie's voice, 'No surrender.'

Constance Lytton

Reflections

* Lady Constance Lytton was a Suffragette. 'Suffragettes' was the popular name given to the Women's Social and Political Union, an organisation formed in order to put pressure on the government to give all women the right to vote for

MPs. Many women were imprisoned for their acts of defiance and law-breaking in support of this cause. All men were given the vote in 1918, but women did not gain the same rights until ten years later.

This disturbing passage makes us reflect on two things:

– first, the extraordinary conviction and personal faith of the suffragettes themselves, women who were willing to undergo great suffering for their cause;
– second, the equally extraordinary barbarism of force-feeding – carried out in the name of the law.

Each of us needs to come to our own conclusions about how *personal* rights and *public* responsibilities can be weighed up in such situations. And these conclusions extend to our own daily lives in our own communities.

2 Standing up for what is right

Introduction

'Rights' sometimes need to be vigorously defended if they are to triumph over prejudice or ignorance. Of course, one person's view of what is right may not be the same as the next person's – a 'terrorist' may be percieved as a freedom fighter by those who believe in that particular cause.

The following two readings focus on redressing wrongs. They come from very different sources. The first is from the pen of folk singer Bob Dylan, writing about what he saw as the victimisation of a black boxer for a crime he didn't commit (the song was based on a real incident). The second piece is by Siegfried Sassoon, a soldier and poet of the First World War (1914–18), who decided to speak out against what he saw as the blind leadership of generals and politicians in that war.

Readings

Hurricane

Pistol shots ring out in the barroom night
Enter Patty Valentine from the upper hall.
She sees the bartender in a pool of blood,
Cries out, 'My God, they killed them all!'
Here comes the story of the Hurricane,
The man the authorities came to blame
For somethin' that he never done.
Put in a prison cell, but one time he could-a been
The champion of the world.

Three bodies lyin' there does Patty see
And another man named Bello, movin' around mysteriously.
'I didn't do it' he says, and he throws up his hands
'I was only robbin' the register, I hope you understand.
I saw them leavin',' he says, and he stops
'One of us had better call up the cops.'
And so Patty calls the cops

And they arrive on the scene with their red lights flashin'
In the hot New Jersey night.

Meanwhile, far away in another part of town
Rubin Carter and a couple of friends are drivin' around.
Number one contender for the middleweight crown
Had no idea what kinda shit was about to go down
When a cop pulled him over to the side of the road
Just like the time before and the time before that.
In Paterson that's just the way things go.
If you're black you might as well not show up on the street
'Less you wanna draw the heat.

Alfred Bello had a partner and he had a rap for the cops.
Him and Arthur Dexter Bradley were just out prowlin' around
He said, 'I saw two men runnin' out, they looked like middleweights
They jumped into a white car with out-of-state plates.'
And Miss Patty Valentine just nodded her head.
Cop said, 'Wait a minute, boys, this one's not dead'
So they took him to the infirmary
And though this man could hardly see
They told him that he could identify the guilty men.

Four in the mornin' and they haul Rubin in,
Take him to the hospital and they bring him upstairs.
The wounded man looks up through his one dyin' eye
Says, 'Wha'd you bring him in here for? He ain't the guy!'
Yes, here's the story of the Hurricane,
The man the authorities came to blame
For somethin' that he never done.
Put in a prison cell, but one time he could-a been
The champion of the world.

Rubin could take a man out with just one punch.
But he never did like to talk about it all that much.
It's my work, he'd say, and I do it for pay
And when it's over I'd just as soon go on my way
Up to some paradise
Where the trout streams flow and the air is nice
And ride a horse along a trail.
But then they took him to the jailhouse
Where they try to turn a man into a mouse.

All of Rubin's cards were marked in advance
The trial was a pig-circus, he never had a chance.
The judge made Rubin's witnesses drunkards from the slums
To the white folks who watched he was a revolutionary bum
And to the black folks he was just a crazy nigger.
No one doubted that he pulled the trigger.
And though they could not produce the gun,
The DA said he was the one who did the deed
And the all-white jury agreed.

Rubin Carter was falsely tried.
The crime was murder 'one,' guess who testified?
Bello and Bradley and they both baldly lied
And the newspapers, they all went along for the ride.
How can the life of such a man
Be in the palm of some fool's hand?
To see him obviously framed
Couldn't help but make me feel ashamed to live in a land
Where justice is a game.

Now all the criminals in their coats and their ties
Are free to drink martinis and watch the sun rise
While Rubin sits like Buddha in a ten-foot cell
An innocent man in a living hell.
That's the story of the Hurricane,
But it won't be over till they clear his name
And give him back the time he's done.
Put in a prison cell, but one time he could-a been
The champion of the world.

Bob Dylan

(*Note* Rubin Carter was later released and cleared of all charges.)

The final statement read . . .

'I am making this statement as an act of wilful defiance of military authority, because I believe that the War is being deliberately prolonged by those who have the power to end it. I am a soldier, convinced that I am acting on behalf of soldiers. I believe that this War, upon which I entered as a war of defence and liberation, has now become a war of aggression and conquest. I believe that the purposes for which I and my fellow soldiers entered upon this War should have been so clearly stated as to have made it impossible to change them, and that, had this been done, the objects which actuated us would now be attainable by negotiation. I have seen and endured the sufferings of the troops, and I can no longer be a party to prolong these sufferings for ends which I believe to be evil and unjust. I am not protesting against the conduct of the War, but against the political errors and insincerities for which the fighting men are being sacrificed. On behalf of those who are suffering now I make this protest against the deception which is being practised on them; also I believe that I may help to destroy the callous complacency with which the majority of those at home regard the continuance of agonies which they do not share, and which they have not sufficient imagination to realize.'

'Statement' by Siegfried Sassoon

Reflections

* Individuals have always fought for their rights:

  - the right to defend a country
  - the right to form a trade-union
  - the right to vote
  - the right to a free press
  - the right to preserve a language

- the right for equality between races
- the right to fair working conditions

Yet along with all these rights go responsibilities.

- the responsibility not to abuse a free press
- the responsibility not to abuse trade union power
- the responsibility not to misuse defensive weapons
- and so on.

Rights and responsibilities need always to be carefully balanced. This is as true in the school community as it is in the home or the workplace.

3 The price of freedoms

Introduction

What is 'freedom'? The Oxford dictionary says: 'the quality or state of being free, especially to enjoy political and civil liberties'. We can, of course, interpret this word in many different ways, depending on the context in which it is used. In the family home, at school, with friends, in a place of work, on a group holiday – in all these contexts we may find ourselves wanting to do one thing while everyone else wants to do the opposite. How do we then decide *whose* freedom should be honoured?

The following newspaper article may offer some ideas.

Reading

The price of freedoms

There is something rather noble in the idea of a man or woman deciding that a particular activity, though risky, is just too enjoyable to give up. A poker player, for instance, who will not renounce his ways. Or a hang-glider leaping off some scarp in the breathless dawn. All the same I am perfectly sure that smoking ought to be banned from public places. I myself smoke, but I am not a committed smoker. I do a lot of it, and think I should not.

Even so, I have some sympathy with the person who says: 'I want to smoke, and it's my choice. If you don't like it, all of you, fit air conditioning.' She or he has a point, since it would clearly be agreeable for the world to be so rich that all our different whims for expenditure could be indulged. And there is clearly a level of spending at which anyone who wanted to smoke in, say, an office, could be atmospherically insulated from everyone else who did not want to be afflicted.

In the meantime, there is a difficult point. By what means do people who are inconvenienced by others prove that those who are inconvenienced have a stronger set of rights than the Inconveniencers?

There is in the end the rather sound legal principle by which people are assumed to have a right to quiet enjoyment of their houses, streets, and so on. But the law is expensive to invoke. One could hardly weigh into every teenager on the bus whose stereo was 'leaking', nor into the manager of the local swimming baths, which pumps out tinny pop while I swim there on Sunday mornings, with a legal threat. No, what they need to be persuaded of is the importance of the idea of the *radical monopoly*.

It involves one person or organisation operating in such a way as automatically to impinge on other people's freedom to enjoy simple pleasures, or pleasures which are at any rate prior to and simpler than those which threaten them.

In the money world, a monopoly stops a would-be competitor from getting going; and customers from choosing. The radical monopoly is yet more powerful.

The noise-maker banishes the right to silence. In the case of Muzak, it piles on to the necessary noise of a supermarket or swimming bath the unnecessary noise of poorly reproduced, unchosen, music. This is not like the case of a pub juke-box, in which the drinker is presumed to have chosen the pub because of what it is like, and could have chosen one without a juke-box. In the case of the leaking stereo, the infuriation runs deeper: here is music which one must hear but from the pleasure of which one is excluded.

Take a city street congested by cars. The principle of radical monopoly reminds us that the person who rides on a bus or bike is a more important user than the car-driver. What the former does is more convenient to everyone, more socially harmonious, than the latter. Some people on buses or bikes have no choice, if they are to be road-users at all. Yet a few people in cars can monopolise a radically scarce resource: road-space.

This would not matter if there was so much road space that people on buses could be found alternative routes to those fouled up by people in cars. But because, like quiet, the peace of country lanes and the cleanliness of office air, road space is universally shared and crucially limited, that cannot be.

Radical monopolists mess up the lives of people whose pleasures or needs are the simpler, and should be accorded the profounder right. They threaten others, in the case of transport, with intrusion, pollution and delay. Some of their vehicles may be necessary: ambulances, for instance. Others, like a car in the city centre, seldom are.

The radical monopolist is always obstructing some elementary pleasure or right and closing the option on someone else enjoying it. The smoker pushes foul air into the place of clean; so does the car-driver.

There are various enchanting characteristics of the idea of radical monopoly. One of them is that very often the idea can be extended to institutions. Thus schools have imposed a radical monopoly on education by making impossible to give one's children a 'normal' education outside of them (because almost all kids are in school).

It is natural that everywhere and always people impose on one another. Architects do it more than most, by the public nature of their art.

However, in limiting our behaviour, and circumscribing it so as to be agreeable to our neighbours, we should hold to the principle of asking if we are imposing a radical monopoly. We *will* be if the answers to the following questions are both No:

■ Are any adverse effects of my action avoidable by those who don't like them?
■ Is what I am doing as near to natural as the activity it displaces?

I am sorry if this is a tough rule, since I don't like tough rules myself.

Richard North

Reflections

* The reading raises the central and difficult question: 'By what means do people who are inconvenienced by others prove that *they* have a stronger set of rights than the inconveniencers?'

  Having listened to the piece, do you agree with this idea of the 'radical monopoly' and the writer's conclusions?

  In life, at home or in school, where does one person's freedom end so that another's can begin? This is a profound question which we all need to reflect on in our daily lives.

4 Right and wrong: Who's responsible?

Introduction

Below are some statements made by pupils after committing various anti-social offences. They are all transcripts of real conversations. Note carefully the nature of each offence committed, and the attitude of each pupil towards what they have done.

Do any of them ring true for you?

Reading

Who's responsible?

PUPIL A

Well I admit I did swear, but I wasn't swearing at the teacher, I was telling my mate something, so why should she have a go at me? Anyway, lots of kids swear so why pick on me? I bet she swears on the quiet. I don't really care if you do tell my mum 'cos she knows I swear and I hear adults sounding off so what's good enough for them is good enough for me.

PUPIL B

Just because I was chewing he started having a go at me. Then he tells me to pick up some rubbish on the floor. Well I picked up the bit I threw on the floor but I wasn't going to pick up the rest, I mean I didn't put it there did I! So then he tells me to sit in another seat and after a while I got bored and scribbled my name on the desk. Then he had another go at me so I pointed to all the scribbling on the wall to show him that I wasn't the only one.

PUPIL C

He says that if we lose our books or can't hand one in we have to pay for it. Well when somebody pinched my book out of my desk I waited around after the rest had gone out and nicked somebody else's. Well it's only fair isn't it, everybody does it! Anyway when I opened this desk I saw some money and had that as well. I knew he wouldn't miss it 'cos he's always splashing his money around and I don't get much pocket money.

PUPIL D

I don't see why I should be involved, it was nothing to do with me. We were all in the classroom playing about a bit and the next thing was he'd kicked a window in. Well I admit we all cheered and the next thing was he was having a go at the tannoy. Inside two minutes he'd had it off the wall and had left the room. No I'm not going to give you his name, I don't believe in grassing on my mates.

Reflections

* What do you think of the attitudes of the pupils here?
  How would you deal with each of them, if you were the teacher?
  What general points might be made about 'right' and 'wrong' here?
  What conclusions might you come to about the nature of responsibility?

5 Parents and children (1)

Introduction

If you talk to adults who are parents, some will say that their children owe them nothing; some will say that children owe their parents everything.

Here are two very different poems on parent/child relationships, which help us focus on the responsibilities of each.

Reading

Parental Instruction

Children, I am training you now
To carry out the only favour
I will ever ask you. Children,
I am working for the day when
All the slaps and shouts are
Cancelled out. Children, obey me.

I don't know for sure when
I will expect you to perform
This service. Let's say I'll
Live for three score years and ten
And am exactly halfway there.

So this is, in fact, a semi-anniversary:
The point at which your lesson
Should begin. Andrea, say after me:
'In my teenage days I hated him,
But later saw a core of good intent.
At all events, I remember him:
His name was Edwin and he lived'.

Nicholas say: 'He was never
A perfect father: too authoritarian;

Liable to shout loudly and retire
To a quiet corner with a book.
I remember the look of him:
His name was Edwin and he lived'.

I am trusting you to repeat these
Things, daily, for the remainder
Of your lives. And, later, to
Teach your baby-sister
Something similar to say.
I do not expect my discipline
To extend to the training of
Your children. When you die
I will accept the end: will
Open my mouth and let the crawling
Kingdom enter, and give my face
Leave to crumble from my head.

Edwin Brock

Son of Mine
(To Denis)

My son, your troubled eyes search mine,
Puzzled and hurt by colour line.
Your black skin as soft as velvet shine;
What can I tell you, son of mine?

I could tell you of heart-break, hatred blind,
I could tell you of crimes that shame mankind.
Of brutal wrongs and deeds malign,
Of rape and murder, son of mine;

But I'll tell instead of brave and fine
When lives of black and white entwine.
And men in brotherhood combine –
This would I tell you, son of mine.

Kath Walker

Reflections

* Both poems are addressed by parents to children.
  Do you find them optimistic or pessimistic, happy or sad descriptions of being
  a parent?
  They certainly help us to reflect on the responsibilities children and parents may
  have to each other.
  Perhaps they are best summed up in the following words from *The Prophet*:

  You may give them your love but not your thoughts,
  For they have their own thoughts,
  You may house their bodies but not their souls
  For their souls dwell in the house of tomorrow,
  Which you cannot visit, not even in your dreams.

6 Parents and children (2)

Introduction
For every 'right' there is a linked 'responsibility'.

What rights do children have?
What rights do parents have?
Who determines what a 'right' is?

Listen to the following piece from author Keith Waterhouse. He offers some challenging answers to these questions.

Reading

Charter of Parents' Rights

A couple of kids stopped me in Oxford Street and sold me, for five pence, a smudgy copy of the Charter of Children's Rights.

They'd run it off on a duplicator in flagrant breach, I suspect, of the original copyright.

Anyway, full marks for initiative. And full marks, too, to the Children's Charter which – although this particular copy of it was practically indecipherable – I happen to know is full of good sense.

'Children have the right to privacy of person and thought ... to freedom of expression ... to freedom from political indoctrination ...

'A child's personal appearance is his own and his family's concern ... Children have the right to such knowledge as is necessary to understand the society in which they live ... They shall have the freedom to make complaints about teachers and parents without fear of reprisal ...'

Fine. Agreed. Accepted. Right on.

But, dear children, has it ever occurred to you that parents have their rights too? I would be very surprised if this revolutionary thought has ever entered your heads, and for that reason, I have drafted, for your consideration, a Charter of Parents' Rights.

Run it off on your duplicator by all means but don't try to sell it to me. Sell it to each other.

1 Parents have the right to their sleep. If you've promised to be in by 10.30 they have no wish to be counting the flowers on the wallpaper at one in the morning.
2 Parents have the right to freedom from unnecessary worry. If it takes you three hours to nip out and buy an iced lolly it will not occur to your parents that half-way down the road you decided to go to a pop concert instead. They will conclude that you have been raped, kidnapped or murdered, or a grisly combination of all three.
3 A parent's personal appearance is his own concern. He does not want to be told that his hair is too short or that turn-ups are out of fashion. Nor does he require a psychedelic kipper tie on Father's Day.
4 Parents have the right to be human beings. That is to say, they have the right to fall into irrational rages, to contradict themselves, to change their minds without reason, to be stubborn, dogmatic and bloodyminded, and in general to

behave occasionally like children, who as you well know are the salt of the earth.

5 No parent shall be scoffed at, sneered at or in any way discriminated against for his opinions. If a parent takes the view that the popular ballad, 'Leap up and down, wave your knickers in the air' is not the greatest song since 'Greensleeves', that is entirely his own affair.

6 Parents have the right to freedom from political indoctrination. It may well be the case that the world would be perfect if all money were distributed equally, the police force abolished, pot legalised, and the factories turned into communes, but your parents are not necessarily shambling morons if they prefer to go on voting Co-op-Labour.

7 Parents have the right to the enjoyment of their own home. They are unlikely to enjoy their own home if one of the bedrooms appears to have been converted, without planning permission, into an indoor piggery. You may argue that your room is nothing to do with them. A glance at the rentbook will prove otherwise.

8 Parents shall have the freedom to make complaints about their children without fear of reprisal. The expression 'reprisal' includes sulking, screaming, slamming doors, making a motion with the hand as if winding up a gramophone, and threatening to throw yourself in the river.

9 All parents shall have the right to expect a reasonable return for their labour. Having acted, over the years, as your unpaid nurse, teacher, cook, cleaner, nightwatchman, swimming instructor, banker, valet, hairdresser, boot-black, launderer, odd-job man and general dogsbody, they are surely entitled to ask you to fill the coal bucket once in a while.

10 Parents have the right to such knowledge as is necessary for them to understand the society in which they live. This means that they should be told exactly why you have painted the words 'Screw the Pigs' in four-foot letters across the garage doors, what this inscription means, and how you propose to erase it.

11 Parents shall not be humilated because of their own inadequacies. They shall not be addressed in O-level French, grilled on the subject of the principal rivers of Australia, or be required to make head or tail of the New Mathematics. At public dances, parents have the right to foxtrot without being mocked.

12 Parents shall have the inalienable freedom to nag, criticise, threaten, cajole, warn, scold, and offer gratuitous advice. They carry on in this boring way not because they enjoy it but because they have a duty to exercise their most precious right of all which is:

13 Parents have the right to be parents.

Keith Waterhouse

Reflections

* From time to time you doubtless have disagreements with your parents. Every child does, whether they're 4 or 44. What Keith Waterhouse perhaps helps us to think about here is that there are two sides to 'rights'. Responsibilities and rights always go together, and we should not forget this, especially in our dealings with our parents.

7 Universal Declaration of Human Rights

Introduction

The idea of having an organisation in which all countries would cooperate to solve world problems was first launched during the Second World War. When the war ended in 1945 the United Nations came into existence. Today the UN has over 150 member states. On 10 December 1948 the General Assembly of the UN adopted the Universal Declaration of Human Rights.

The following is an extract from its Articles of Governance. Think about the aims of each Article as they are being read. Which are being honoured or broken in our world today?

Reading

Universal Declaration of Human Rights

Article 1 All human beings are born free and equal in dignity and rights. They are endowed with reason and conscience and should act towards one another in a spirit of brotherhood.

Article 2 Everyone is entitled to all the rights and freedoms set forth in this Declaration, without distinction of any kind such as race, colour, sex, language, religion, political or other opinion, national or social origin, property, birth or other status.

Article 3 Everyone has the right to life, liberty and security of person.

Article 4 No one shall be held in slavery or servitude; slavery and the slave trade shall be prohibited in all their forms.

Article 5 No one shall be subjected to torture or to cruel, inhuman or degrading treatment or punishment.

Article 6 Everyone has the right to recognition everywhere as a person before the law.

Article 7 All are equal before the law and are entitled without any discrimination to equal protection of the law.

Article 8 Everyone has the right to an effective remedy by the competent national tribunals for acts violating the fundamental rights granted him by the constitution or by law.

Article 9 No one shall be subjected to arbitrary arrest, detention or exile.

Article 10 Everyone is entitled in full equality to a fair and public hearing by an independent and impartial tribunal, in the determination of his rights and obligations and of any criminal charge against him.

Article 11 Everyone charged with a penal offence has the right to be presumed innocent until proved guilty according to law in a public trial at which he has had all the guarantees necessary for his defence.

Article 12 No one shall be subjected to arbitrary interference with his privacy, family, home or correspondence, nor to attacks upon his honour and reputation.

Article 13 Everyone has the right to freedom of movement and residence within the borders of each state. Everyone has the right to leave any country including his own, and to return to his country.

Article 14 Everyone has the right to seek and enjoy in other countries asylum from persecution.

Article 15 Everyone has the right to a nationality. No one shall be arbitrarily deprived of his nationality nor denied the right to change his nationality.

Article 16 Men and women of full age, without any limitation due to race, nationality or religion, have the right to marry and to found a family. They are entitled to equal rights as to marriage, during marriage and at its dissolution. Marriage shall be entered into only with free and full consent of the intending spouses.

Article 17 Everyone has the right to own property alone as well as in association with others. No one shall be arbitrarily deprived of his property.

Article 18 Everyone has the right to freedom of thought, conscience and religion; this right includes freedom to change his religion or belief, and freedom, either alone or in community with others and in public or private, to manifest his religion or belief in teaching, practice, worship and observance.

Article 19 Everyone has the right to freedom of opinion and expression; this right includes freedom to hold opinions without interference and to seek, receive and impart information and ideas through any media and regardless of frontiers.

Article 20 Everyone has the right to freedom of peaceful assembly and association. No one may be compelled to belong to an association.

Reflections

* The Declaration is an ideal; reading through it we are at once reminded that not all is perfect in our multi-cultural world. Freedoms of many kinds are being denied people every day – some 'rights' as basic as access to clean water, privacy in your own home, the right to express an opinion, or to travel to another country.

As we watch television and read newspapers we should reflect hard on this Declaration of Human Rights. It should be our individual and collective aim to do everything we can to realise its aims for *all* people.

8 What is democracy?*

Introduction

In this country we often speak proudly about living in a democracy. The word democracy comes from the Greek meaning 'government by the people'. Or as the American constitution describes it: government *for* the people, *by* the people, *of* the people. Different countries have different kinds of *democracy*. [Also, some countries have a *monarchy* (hereditary King or Queen); some have an *oligarchy* (government by a small group of people); some have a dictatorship (rule by an unelected leader); while a country without government is described as being an *anarchy*.]

But what are the origins of democracy? And why is this form of government always held up as the best way of protecting the rights and responsibilities of its citizens?

This reading comes from a celebrated book written by the great Greek philosopher Plato, in the fourth century BC. It is entitled *The Republic*. Listen carefully to the argument, which is set down in the form of a dialogue.

Reading

The Republic

'When a person's unhealthy, it takes very little to upset him and make him ill; there may even be an internal cause for disorder. The same is true of an unhealthy society. It will fall into sickness and dissension at the slightest external provocation, when one party or the other calls in help from a neighbouring oligarchy or democracy; while sometimes faction fights will start without any external stimulus at all.'

'Very true.'

'Then democracy originates when the poor win, kill or exile their opponents, and give the rest equal rights and opportunities of office, appointment to office being as a rule by lot.'

'Yes,' he agreed, 'that is how a democracy is established, whether it's done by force of arms or by frightening its opponents into retreat.'

'What sort of society will it be?' I asked, 'and how will it be run? The answer, obviously, will show us the character of the democratic man.'

'Obviously.'

'Would you agree, first, that people will be free? There is liberty and freedom of speech in plenty, and every individual is free to do as he likes.'

'That's what they say.'

'That being so, won't everyone arrange his life as pleases him best?'

'Obviously.'

'And so there will be the greatest variety of individual character?'

'There's bound to be.'

'I dare say that a democracy is the most attractive of all societies,' I said. 'The diversity of its characters, like the different colours in a patterned dress, make it look very attractive. Indeed,' I added, 'perhaps most people would, for this reason, judge it to be the best form of society, like women and children who judge by appearances.'

'Very likely.'

'And, you know, it's just the place to go constitution-hunting. It contains every possible type, because of the wide freedom it allows, and anyone engaged in founding a state, as we are doing, should perhaps be made to pay a visit to a democracy and make his choice from the variety of models it displays, before he proceeds to make his own foundation.'

'It's a shop in which he'd find plenty of models on show.'

'Then in democracy,' I went on, 'there's no compulsion either to exercise authority if you are capable of it, or to submit to authority if you don't want to; you needn't fight if there's a war, or you can wage a private war in peacetime if you don't like peace; and if there's any law that debars you from political or judicial office, you will none the less take either if they come your way. It's a wonderfully pleasant way of carrying on in the short run, isn't it?'

'In the short run perhaps.'

'And isn't there something rather charming about the good-temper of those who've been sentenced in court? You must have noticed that in a democracy men sentenced to death or exile continue, none the less, to go about among their fellows, who take no more notice of them than if they were invisible spirits.'

'I've often seen that.'

'Then they're very considerate in applying the high principles we laid down when founding our state; so far from interpreting them strictly, they really look down on them. We said that no one who had no exceptional gifts could grow into a good man unless he were brought up from childhood in a good environment and given a good training; democracy with a grandiose gesture sweeps all this away and doesn't mind what the habits and background of its politicians are, provided they profess themselves the people's friends.'

'All very splendid.'

'These, then, and similar characteristics are those of democracy. It's an agreeable, anarchic form of society, with plenty of variety, which treats all men as equal, whether they are equal or not.'

'The picture is easy to recognize.'

From 'The Republic' by Plato

Reflections

* This reading comes from a chapter in *'The Republic'* titled 'Imperfect Societies'. This description of a democracy demonstrates that if you have only rights, and no responsibilities, then anarchy will rule.

   Plato's dialogue helps us to reflect on what makes for fair and unfair democracy: the balance of 'rights' and 'responsibilities' for all citizens is a key to effective governance.

   And so it is in our own communities: schools, colleges, factories, offices, etc. Despite all its imperfections, most organisations in our society support the ideal of democracy. We all need to go on working with and within that system if it is to flourish.

9 Territory

Introduction

There can be few rights more regularly disputed – whether locally, nationally, or internationally – than rights relating to territory. Throughout the animal kingdom the idea of owning territory, of having a patch of land that you can call your own, seems to be a basic instinct. And humans are no exception.

Listen to the following two readings. The first is an animal story; the second a human tale.

Reading

What's a territory?

The mouse child, as he walked backwards, found himself facing the drummer boy. 'Is it really a war?' he asked the little soldier.

'Of course it is,' replied the shrew. 'Our territory's all hunted out, so we'll have to fight the shrews down by the stream for theirs.'

'It's the other way around, the way I heard it,' said the fifer. 'I heard *their* territory's all hunted out, and they invaded ours.'

'What's a territory?' asked the mouse child.

'What do you mean, "what's a territory?"' said the drummer boy. 'A territory's a territory, that's all.'

'Rations don't have territories,' said the fifer.

'Not after we catch them,' said the drummer boy, 'but they do before. *Everybody* does.'

'We didn't,' said the mouse child.

'No wonder you're rations now,' said the little shrew, 'What chance has anybody got without a territory?'

'But what *is* a territory?' asked the mouse child again.

'A territory is your place,' said the drummer boy. 'It's where everything smells right. It's where you know the runways and the hideouts, night or day. It's what you fought for, or what your father fought for, and you feel all safe and strong there. It's the place where, when you fight, you win.'

'That's *your* territory,' said the fifer. 'Somebody else's territory is something else again. That's where you feel all sick and scared and want to run away, and that's where the other side mostly wins.'

From 'The Mouse and His Child' by Russel Hoban

A True Story

Postmaster Bradbury of Leeds had just finished smoothing the cement of his forecourt when Chip, a local dog, trotted across it.

Mr Bradbury warned Chip off, re-smoothed his cement, and was easing his back when Chip did it again.

Mr Bradbury hurled his shovel at Chip, following it up with a kick. The kick landed on Mrs Rowley, Chip's owner.

Mrs Bradbury, who had observed the incident, decided to call the police. A similar decision was taken by Mrs Rowley.

Mrs Bradbury reached the telephone first. She dialled the first three nines when Mrs Rowley pulled her out of the box by the hair.

While settling their differences both ladies fell into the cement.

It was at this point that Mr Bradbury's mother-in-law, Mrs Stevens, decided to intervene. Both she and Mr Bradbury were pulled into the cement by the infuriated wives.

Mrs Stevens is in her late eighties.

Outraged at the behaviour of his neighbours towards his wife, Mr Rowley charged across the road and carried Mr Bradbury and himself back into the cement.

All five voters then waded into the cement and each other.

The Magistrate, Mr Walter Smart said:
'You'd better forget the whole thing.'

> *'A true story' by Christopher Logue, in 'Private Eye'*

Reflections

* It is easy to see the funny side of animals and humans behaving territorially. Sadly, possession and defence of territory lie at the heart of so many disputes between human beings.

  On a local level it may be a trivial matter of the positioning of a garden fence, or which part of the playground one group of friends play football in.

  On a larger scale, disputes over territory can be the focus of terrorism and protracted and horrific wars, as we have seen in Northern Ireland, the Middle East, and Vietnam in the past decades.

  Yes, ownership of a piece of land you can call your own is an important aspect of being human; but in our own communities we must be sensible about rights *and* responsibilities of ownership. And sometimes one of the responsibilities of ownership extends to *sharing* that space with others.

10 Pressure groups

Introduction

Many of the rights we take for granted were hard won. Throughout history there have been groups of people who campaigned for their particular cause. Three of these movements form the content of the following reading. They are Chartism, the Anti-Corn Law League and the Abolitionists. Each is a prime example of a pressure group.

Reading

Pressure Groups

There was the famous movement for political reform known as Chartism (1838–48), which suggested ideas harmless enough today, but which seemed very daring, even dangerous, then. The Chartists (in a charter) demanded universal male suffrage (the vote for all males over a certain age), equal electoral districts, annual parliaments, the ending of a property qualification for MPs, payment for MPs and voting by ballot. Only the idea of annual parliaments was foolish, because it would have been inefficient, expensive and time wasting, but the rest we now take for granted. Yet in the late 1830s and the 'Hungry Forties', when conditions were so bad that revolution seemed a real possibility, the Chartists did seem dangerous. The movement's size can be judged by a petition which it assembled in 1842 containing over three million signatures.

However, conditions got better as the decade wore on. By 1848, the 'Year of Revolutions' in Europe and the year of a third great petition to Parliament, Chartism, which had seemed so dangerous, was a spent force. Not for seventy years would all its best aims be achieved.

Another nineteenth-century struggle was the fight against the Corn Laws. There had been corn laws in Britain since 1436 because of the importance of bread to the nation. Both farmers and consumers had to be protected. When the Napoleonic Wars ended in 1815, cheap corn entered the country from abroad. An act of Parliament to protect the home market resulted in an outcry that the landowners were getting richer while the poor could not afford bread. Meanwhile, the landowners denounced industrialists for wanting cheap bread so that they could keep factory wages down.

In 1839, an Anti-Corn Law League was formed. Two of its leaders, both to become champions of free trade, were Richard Cobden and a famous MP, John Bright, who was widely regarded as the finest public speaker in Britain. He was an ideal leader of a pressure group, a master of the mass meeting. Finally, in 1846, the Tory Prime Minister, Sir Robert Peel, bowed to pressure and repealed the Corn Laws.

Bright's greatest service to his country is little remembered now. The American Civil War (1861–65) was fought over the joint issue of slavery and states' rights. In the Southerners' case, these included the right to own slaves, though only a minority did so. The North under Abraham Lincoln wanted to save the Union, and the powerful pressure group, the Abolitionists, wanted to free the slaves.

The majority of the British upper classes sided with the South, not because they approved of slavery but because the southern plantation owners were 'gentlemen' liked themselves. In 1862, the South, under its great commander, Robert E Lee, seemed certain to win the war, and Britain might have joined in on the Southern side. Yet one thing held them back, a giant pressure group led by John Bright, a group whose livelihood had actually been threatened by the war. These were the Lancashire cotton workers. They were suffering great hardships because Southern plantations were gradually running down in the war and the cotton could not be got across the Atlantic to Liverpool because the North's navy was stronger than the South's. Yet the cotton workers and others made it quite clear that they sympathized with the North for religious and moral reasons. John Bright was their impassioned leader. He used to correspond regularly with Lincoln, who was greatly moved by the cotton workers' stand against their own interests. Today, a statue of Lincoln stands in Platt Fields, Manchester, to recall those stirring times.

From 'Pressure Groups' by Robin May

Reflections

* These groups, along with all other pressure groups before and since, had one thing in common: none of them was 'government'. Pressure groups set out to influence and affect the way the country is governed; they do not aim to take over the government, even though some of their members may be in Parliament – as trade unionists, lawyers or farmers, for example. They try to influence public opinion in the hope that the public will in turn, exert pressure on those who rule or wish to rule the nation.

It is important to understand and appreciate the role of pressure groups in a democratic society. Some people believe that you can judge an effective democracy by the number of pressure groups it throws up. Even within schools, the workplace and other close-knit communities, the importance of informal pressure groups should not be underestimated. They can offer a channel of communication which might otherwise not exist, and can be a source for ensuring that everyone's rights and responsibilities are taken into account.

11 Terrorists and freedom fighters

Introduction

We would probably all support the view that it is important to stand up for what we believe in. But how far should we take this view? Some members of society believe that 'the ends justify the means' – and that therefore any kind of action is permissible if it means defending or promoting your beliefs. In many parts of the world today we see the activities of such people, often known as 'freedom fighters', or 'terrorists', depending on your point of view. The following account offers a contemporary analysis. It is titled 'Terrorists and Freedom Fighters'.

Reading

Terrorists and Freedom Fighters

The terms 'terrorism' and 'terrorist' arose from the events of the French Revolution of 1789. Following the overthrow of the monarchy, a group called the Jacobins took power and conducted a 'reign of terror' in France. The philosopher, Edmund Burke, wrote of 'thousands of hellhounds called terrorists' being 'let loose upon the people'.

The Jacobins inspired terror among the citizens by wielding state power. In the nineteenth century, however, the description of states and governments as 'terrorist' became less common. Instead the word came to denote revolutionaries who used violent methods against the state.

Terrorism is organized violence by small groups against the state for political purposes. There are four aspects to this definition.

First, terrorist activities are organized, and involve conscious planning and direction. A kidnap or hijack attempt, for example, requires co-operation within an organized group.

Secondly, terrorist projects are undertaken by small, usually secret bodies of armed men and women. Terrorist violence is not often undertaken by large groups of people, but by small groups excluded from power.

Thirdly, terrorism – even when its victims are ordinary citizens – is directed against the state and its representatives.

Fourthly, terrorism is used to further political aims.

There is little evidence to suggest that terrorism will cease to be a problem in the future. Terrorism can be traced back to specific causes – national divisions, frustrated minority groups, racial and social tensions – and it seems likely that, far from decreasing, these tensions may well increase in the future.

Terrorism will continue to plague the world so long as it is an effective means of drawing public attention to a cause. The capacity to terrorize may well increase as more sophisticated weapons become available to terrorists. The provision of arms, money and shelter by pro-terrorist states will continue to be an invaluable support to terrorists. As news and pictures of terrorist attacks reach the mass of the population, the terrorist will become an increasingly powerful figure. However, the media does have an important role in ensuring that terrorism does not become an accepted fact of life. So long as the public is repulsed by the terrorists' callous indifference to loss of life, there is likely to be public support for government measures taken to combat terrorism.

The attitude of governments to terrorist attacks will be a determining factor in the continuing survival of terrorism. There is no easy solution to the dilemma of whether to give in to terrorists' demands in return for hostages, or whether individuals should be sacrificed in the hope that terrorism will cease to be an effective means of coercing governments. Leon Trotsky wrote that 'what distinguishes a revolutionary is not so much his capacity to kill as his willingness to die.' The terrorists' readiness to die is perhaps their greatest strength.

Abu Yusuf, the Chief of Intelligence of Al Fatah killed by an Israeli bomb, said, 'We plant the seeds, and the others will reap the harvest. Most probably we'll all die ... But the youth will replace us.' The 'defiant hopelessness' of the terrorist guarantees their survival.

From 'Terrorists and Freedom fighters' by David Hayes

Reflections

* With terrorism, the first task is not just to condemn, but to understand it. In the late 20th century terrorist actions continue to have a dramatic impact. The number of people who have suffered from terrorist attacks is small in comparison with the victims of war, and the reaction evoked by the violence of terrorist groups may be out of proportion to the scale of their operations. But terrorism, like war, does not affect only its immediate victims: the terrorists' challenge to social peace and legal order is the concern of everyone.

* 'The tyrant dies and his rule ends; the martyr dies and his rule begins.'

Kierkegaard

12 The atomic bomb

Introduction

To what ends should humans go to defend their rights? Perhaps the greatest single test of this moral question occurred in September 1945, when the atomic bomb was dropped on Hiroshima in Japan.

Listen to the following eye-witness accounts of that momentous occasion.

Reading

Visiting Hiroshima, 9 September 1945

The bare cone of Fujiyama was just visible on the horizon as we flew over the 'inland sea' which lay beneath us like a lavender-blue carpet picked out in green and yellow with its numerous promontories and wooded islands...

Towards midday a huge white patch appeared on the ground below us. This chalky desert, looking almost like ivory in the sun, surrounded by a crumble of twisted ironwork and ash heaps, was all that remained of Hiroshima...

The journalist described the main official buildings of the town, which were built of reinforced concrete and dominated a sea of low-roofed Japanese houses extending over six miles to the wooded hills I could see in the distance.

'The town was not much damaged,' he explained. 'It had suffered very little from the bombing. There were only two minor raids, one on March 19th last by a squadron of American naval planes, and one on April 30th by a Flying Fortress.

'On August 6th there wasn't a cloud in the sky above Hiroshima, and a mild, hardly perceptible wind blew from the south. Visibility was almost perfect for ten or twelve miles.

'At nine minutes past seven in the morning an air-raid warning sounded and four American B-29 planes appeared. To the north of the town two of them turned and made off to the south and disappeared in the direction of the Shoho Sea. The other two, after having circled the neighbourhood of Shukai, flew off at high speed southwards in the direction of the Bingo Sea.

'At 7.31 the all-clear was given. Feeling themselves in safety people came out of their shelters and went about their affairs and the work of the day began.

'Suddenly a glaring whitish pinkish light appeared in the sky accompanied by an unnatural tremor which was followed almost immediately by a wave of suffocating heat and a wind which swept away everything in its path.

'Within a few seconds the thousands of people in the streets and the gardens in the centre of the town were scorched by a wave of searing heat. Many were killed instantly, others lay writhing on the ground screaming in agony from the intolerable pain of their burns. Everything standing upright in the way of the blast, walls, houses, factories and other buildings, was annihilated and the debris spun round in a whirlwind and was carried up into the air. Trams were picked up and tossed aside as though they had neither weight nor solidity. Trains were flung off the rails as though they were toys. Horses, dogs and cattle suffered the same fate as human beings. Every living thing was petrified in an attitude of indescribable suffering. Even the vegetation did not escape. Trees went up in flames, the rice plants lost their greenness, the grass burned on the ground like dry straw.

'Beyond the zone of utter death in which nothing remained alive houses collapsed in a whirl of beams, bricks and girders. Up to about three miles from the centre of the explosion lightly built houses were flattened as though they had been built of cardboard. Those who were inside were either killed or wounded. Those who managed to extricate themselves by some miracle found themselves surrounded by a ring of fire. And the few who succeeded in making their way to safety generally died twenty or thirty days later from the delayed effects of the deadly gamma rays. Some of the reinforced concrete or stone buildings remained standing but their interiors were completely gutted by the blast.

'About half an hour after the explosion whilst the sky all around Hiroshima was still cloudless a fine rain began to fall on the town and went on for about five minutes. It was caused by the sudden rise of over-heated air to a great height, where it condensed and fell back as rain. Then a violent wind rose and the fires extended with terrible rapidity, because most Japanese houses are built only of timber and straw.

'By the evening the fire began to die down and then it went out. There was nothing left to burn. Hiroshima had ceased to exist.'

The Japanese broke off and then pronounced one word with indescribable but restrained emotion: 'Look.'

We were then rather less than four miles away from the Aioi Bridge, which was immediately beneath the explosion, but already the roofs of the houses around us had lost their tiles and the grass was yellow along the road-side. At three miles from the centre of the devastation the houses were already destroyed, their roofs had fallen in and the beams jutted out from the wreckage of their walls. But so far it was only the usual spectacle presented by towns damaged by ordinary high explosives.

About two and a half miles from the centre of the town all the buildings had been burnt out and destroyed. Only traces of the foundations and piles of debris and rusty charred ironwork were left. This zone was like the devastated areas of Tokyo, Osaka and Kobé after the mass fall of incendiaries.

At three-quarters of a mile from the centre of the explosion nothing at all was left. Everything had disappeared. It was a stony waste littered with debris and twisted girders. The incandescent breath of the fire had swept away every obstacle and all that remained upright were one or two fragments of stone walls and a few stoves which had remained incongruously on their base.

We got out of the car and made our way slowly through the ruins into the centre of the dead city. Absolute silence reigned.

Marcel Junod

Reflections

* The atomic bomb on Hiroshima killed between 70,000 and 80,000 people, and injured more than 70,000 others. Nothing before or since has created such devastation in a single blow. The decision to drop the bomb was taken by the Americans and their allies in the hope that it would bring the Second World War to a sudden end. It did. The question that has always remained is 'Did these ends justify the means?'
  This is an unanswerable question in absolute terms. In the face of such a devastating loss of human life, it is difficult to come to a clear decision on whose rights were being safeguarded, whose responsibilities were being discharged.

* Such an incident, we all pray, will never be repeated. But it does lead us on to think hard about the question of just how far we are prepared to go in defence of what we believe to be right.
  On a day-to-day level, in our families and with our friends, we often have to weigh up rights and responsibilities. Through experience, through trial and error, we try to get the balance right, but we have to accept that we shall sometimes get things wrong.

* *Roman 5: 18–21*
  Just as the result of one trespass was condemnation for all men, so also the result of one act of righteousness was justification that brings life for all men. For just as through the disobedience of the one man the many were made sinners, so also through the obedience of the one man the many will be made righteous.
  The law was added so that the trespass might increase. But where sin increased, grace increased all the more, so that, just as sin reigned in death, so also grace might reign through righteousness to bring eternal life through Jesus Christ our Lord.

Health and Environment

1 Children in the workplace (1)

Introduction

Childhood today is taken for granted; for children in the first half of the 19th century things were very different. The Industrial Revolution had brought increasing mechanisation to industry. More and more people worked in factories – often 12 hours a day, or more, in appalling conditions. And this included young children!

As well as working in factories, small children worked down the mines, on the land and in many other trades – including chimney sweeping. Here is an account of the death of a chimney sweep, aged eight.

Reading

Death of a climbing boy, 29 March 1813

Evidence taken before the Parliamentary Committee on Climbing Boys, 1817

On Monday morning, 29 March 1813, a chimney sweeper of the name of Griggs attended to sweep a small chimney in the brewhouse of Messrs Calvert and Co. in Upper Thames Street; he was accompanied by one of his boys, a lad of about eight years of age, of the name of Thomas Pitt. The fire had been lighted as early as 2 o'clock the same morning, and was burning on the arrival of Griggs and his little boy at eight. The fireplace was small, and an iron pipe projected from the grate some little way into the flue. This the master was acquainted with (having swept the chimneys in the brewhouse for some years), and therefore had a tile or two broken from the roof, in order that the boy might descend the chimney. He had no sooner extinguished the fire than he suffered the lad to go down; and the consequence, as might be expected, was his almost immediate death, in a state, no doubt, of inexpressible agony. The flue was of the narrowest description, and must have retained heat sufficient to have prevented the child's return to the top, even supposing he had not approached the pipe belonging to the grate, which must have been nearly red hot; this however was not clearly ascertained on the inquest, though the appearance of the body would induce an opinion that he had been unavoidably pressed against the pipe. Soon after his descent, the master, who remained on the top, was apprehensive that something had happened, and therefore desired him to come up; the answer of the boy was, 'I cannot come up, master, I must die here.' An alarm was given in the brewhouse immediately that he had stuck in the chimney, and a bricklayer who was at work near the spot attended, and after knocking down part of the brickwork of the chimney, just above the fireplace, made a hole sufficiently large to draw him through. A surgeon attended, but all attempts to restore life were ineffectual. On inspecting the body, various burns appeared; the fleshy part of the legs and a great part of the feet more particularly were injured; those parts too by which climbing boys most effectually ascend or descend chimneys, viz. the elbows and knees, seemed burnt to the bone; from which it must be evident that the unhappy sufferer made some attempts to return as soon as the horrors of his situation became apparent.

Reflections

* Today we have laws and regulations governing the hours and conditions of work – especially for young people. The first Acts of Parliament designed to protect children at work were passed at the beginning of the 19th century – but reform was a long and slow process.
Listen to the following list of Acts:

 1802 Health and Morals of Apprentices Act (Textile Mills only). Hours of work limited to 12 hours daily between 6 am and 9 pm.
 Night shift forbidden and education to be provided in a suitable area of the building.
 1819 Factory Act (Textile Mills only).
 Employment of children under 9 years of age prohibited. Hours for those under 16 limited to 12 hours a day.
 (Both these Acts failed to provide for proper inspection, and were largely ignored by mill owners.)
 1833 Factory Act.
 No child under 9 to be employed. Children aged 9–13 could work a maximum of 9 hours a day and 48 hours a week. Some provision for 2 hours' education a day. Four inspectors were appointed to enforce the Act.
 1844 Factory Act.
 Children between the ages of 8 and 13 not to work for more than 6½ hours.
 Young persons and women limited to 12 hours a day.
 Dangerous machinery to be fenced, and accidents to be reported to a doctor.
 Certificates of age and school attendance made compulsory.

Despite the Acts, many young children continued to work – and sometimes die – in terrible circumstances. But the work of many of the great reformers of the 19th century did lead to the gradual abolition of young child labour.

* Our society is very conscious of health and safety in the workplace. But this reading does remind us how young people can be exploited as cheap labour if the law does not protect them. In this country the law does; in many parts of the world today, however, you will still see young children working in dangerous and unhealthy conditions for a meagre wage.
As we sit in our classrooms, our thoughts should go out to young children around the world who, because of poverty and exploitation, are being denied their childhood.

2 Children in the workplace (2)

Introduction

How many of you have some kind of part-time job?

How many of you, given the chance, would work more hours than you are allowed?

As you know, the law requires young people to stay at school until they are 16. During the 20th century the school-leaving age has been pushed upwards. The aim of this has been to improve educational opportunities for all young people and to prevent the exploitation of children in the workplace.

Listen to the following account of factory conditions in 1815. It is presented in the form of questions and answers.

Reading

Factory conditions

Evidence of a Female Millhand to the Parliamentary Commissioners

What age are you?
   Twenty-three.
Where do you live?
   At Leeds.
What time did you begin work at the factory?
   When I was six years old.
At whose factory did you work?
   Mr Burk's.
What kind of mill is it?
   Flax mill.
What was your business in that mill?
   I was a little doffer.
What were your hours of labour in that mill?
   From 5 in the morning till 9 at night, when they were thronged.
For how long a time together have you worked that excessive length of time?
   For about a year.
What were the usual hours of labour when you were not so thronged?
   From 6 in the morning till 7 at night.
What time was allowed for meals?
   Forty minutes at noon.
Had you any time to get your breakfast or drinking?
   No, we had to get it as we could.
Do you consider doffing a laborious employment?
   Yes.
Explain what you had to do?
   When the frames are full, they have to stop the frames, and take the flyers off, and take the full bobbins off, and carry them to the roller, and then put empty ones on, and set the frame going again.
Does that keep you constantly on your feet?
   Yes, there are so many frames and they run so quick.

Your labour is very excessive?
   Yes, you have not time for anything.
Suppose you flagged a little, or were late, what would they do?
   Strap us.
And they are in the habit of strapping those who are last in doffing?
   Yes.
Constantly?
   Yes.
Girls as well as boys?
   Yes.
Have you ever been strapped?
   Yes.
Severely?
   Yes.
Is the strap used so as to hurt you excessively?
   Yes it is . . . I have seen the overlooker go to the top end of the room, where the
   little girls hug the can to the backminders; he has taken a strap, and a whistle
   in his mouth, and sometimes he has got a chain and chained them, and strapped
   them all down the room.
What was his reason for that?
   He was very angry.
Did you live far from the mill?
   Yes, two miles.
Had you a clock?
   No, we had not.
Were you generally there in time?
   Yes, my mother has been up at 4 o'clock in the morning, and at 2 o'clock in the
   morning; the colliers used to go to their work at 3 or 4 o'clock, and when she heard
   them stirring she has got up out of her warm bed, and gone out and asked them the
   time; and I have sometimes been at Hunslet Car at 2 o'clock in the morning, when
   it was streaming down with rain, and we have had to stay till the mill was opened.
You are considerably deformed in person as a consequence of this labour?
   Yes I am.
And what time did it come on?
   I was about 13 years old when it began coming, and it has got worse since; it is
   five years since my mother died, and my mother was never able to get me a good
   pair of stays to hold me up, and when my mother died I had to do for myself,
   and got me a pair.
Were you perfectly straight and healthy before you worked at a mill?
   Yes, I was as straight a little girl as ever went up and down town.
Were you straight till you were 13?
   Yes, I was.
Did your deformity come upon you with much pain and weariness?
   Yes, I cannot express the pain all the time it was coming.
Do you know of anybody that has been similarly injured in their health?
   Yes, in their health, but not many deformed as I am.
It is very common to have weak ankles and crooked knees?
   Yes, very common indeed.
This is brought on by stopping the spindle?
   Yes.

Where are you now?
  In the poorhouse.
State what you think as to the circumstances in which you have been placed during all this time of labour, and what you have considered about it as to the hardship and cruelty of it.

The witness was too much affected to answer the question.

Elizabeth Bentley

Reflections

* The Parliamentary Commissioners heard a lot of evidence about children being exploited at work, and thus chronically damaging their health.
  This reminds us why it is important that employers follow strict guidelines when employing children, and how risky to health and well-being it is if young people work beyond the legal hours.
  As a young person you may find it frustrating not to be able to work those extra hours for extra cash. But reflect on this example, extreme though it must sound in today's society. The laws governing the employment of young people rightly exist to protect employer and employee alike.

3 Homelessness

Introduction

Most people would agree that possession of a decent home is the reasonable right of everyone in a fair and just society. Yet homelessness is a sad fact of life even in our so-called developed democracy of the late 20th century.

  The following reading comes from George Orwell's book *Down and Out in Paris and London*: it describes in some detail what it's like to be homeless. The hostel he stays in is called 'The Spike'.

Reading

The Spike

It was late afternoon. Forty-nine of us, forty-eight men and one woman, lay on the green waiting for the spike to open. We were too tired to talk much. We just sprawled about exhaustedly, with home-made cigarettes sticking out of our scrubby faces. Overhead the chestnut branches were covered with blossom, and beyond that great woolly clouds floated almost motionless in a clear sky. Littered on the grass, we seemed dingy, urban riff-raff. We defiled the scene, like sardine-tins and paper bags on the seashore.

  At six the gates swung open and we shuffled in. An official at the gate entered our names and other particulars in the register and took our bundles away from us. The woman was sent off to the workhouse, and we others into the spike. It was a gloomy, chilly, limewashed place, consisting only of a bathroom and dining-room and about a hundred narrow stone cells. The terrible Tramp Major met us at the door and herded us into the bathroom to be stripped and searched. He was a gruff, soldierly man of forty, who gave the tramps no more ceremony than sheep at the dipping-pond, shoving them this way and that and shouting oaths in their faces. But when he came to myself, he looked hard at me, and said:

'You are a gentleman?'

'I suppose so,' I said.

He gave me another long look. 'Well, that's bloody bad luck, guv'nor,' he said, 'that's bloody bad luck, that is.' And thereafter he took it into his head to treat me with compassion, even with a kind of respect.

It was a disgusting sight, that bathroom. All the indecent secrets of our under-wear were exposed; the grime, the rents and patches, the bits of string doing duty for buttons, the layers upon layers of fragmentary garments, some of them mere collections of holes, held together by dirt. The room became a press of steaming nudity, the sweaty odours of the tramps competing with the sickly, sub-faecal stench native to the spike. Some of the men refused the bath, and washed only their 'toe-rags', the horrid, greasy little clouts which tramps bind round their feet. Each of us had three minutes in which to bathe himself. Six greasy, slippery roller towels had to serve for the lot of us.

When we had bathed our own clothes were taken away from us, and we were dressed in the workhouse shirts, grey cotton things like nightshirts, reaching to the middle of the thigh. Then we were sent into the dining-room, where supper was set out on the deal tables. It was the invariable spike meal, always the same, whether breakfast, dinner or supper – half a pound of bread, a bit of margarine, and a pint of so-called tea. It took us five minutes to gulp down the cheap, noxious food. Then the Tramp Major served us with three cotton blankets each, and drove us off to our cells for the night. The doors were locked on the outside a little before seven in the evening, and would stay locked for the next twelve hours.

The cells measured eight feet by five, and had no lighting apparatus except a tiny, barred window high up in the wall, and a spyhole in the door. There were no bugs, and we had bedsteads and straw palliasses, rare luxuries both. In many spikes one sleeps on a wooden shelf, and in some on the bare floor, with a rolled-up coat for pillow. With a cell to myself, and a bed, I was hoping for a sound night's rest. But I did not get it, for there is always something wrong in the spike, and the peculiar shortcoming here, as I discovered immediately, was the cold. May had begun, and in honour of the season – a little sacrifice to the gods of spring, perhaps – the authorities had cut off the steam from the hot pipes. The cotton blankets were almost useless. One spent the night in turning from side to side, falling asleep for ten minutes and waking half frozen, and watching for dawn.

As always happens in the spike, I had at last managed to fall comfortably asleep when it was time to get up. The Tramp Major came marching down the passage with his heavy tread, unlocking the doors and yelling to us to show a leg. Promptly the passage was full of squalid shirt-clad figures rushing for the bathroom, for there was only one tub full of water between us all in the morning, and it was first come first served. When I arrived twenty tramps had already washed their faces. I gave one glance at the black scum on top of the water, and decided to go dirty for the day.

We hurried into our clothes, and then went to the dining-room to bolt our breakfast. The bread was much worse than usual, because the military-minded idiot of a Tramp Major had cut it into slices overnight, so that it was as hard as ship's biscuit. But we were glad of our tea after the cold, restless night. I do not know what tramps would do without tea, or rather the stuff they miscall tea. It is their food, their medicine, their panacea for all evils. Without the half gallon or so of it that they suck down a day, I truly believe they could not face their existence.

From 'The Spike' from 'Down and Out in Paris and London'
by George Orwell

Reflections

* This description comes from 1933. The writer George Orwell (famous for his novels *Animal Farm* and *1984*) decided to live the life of a homeless tramp, to see what it was really like, so that he could write about conditions for his readers to share. Sadly, the picture he describes remains as true today. In our cities and towns we have people – many in their teens – who have, for one reason or another, no home to call their own. Many live in shop doorways or the kind of hostels Orwell describes here.

  If we are reflecting on the health and well-being of our society as a whole, and the environment in particular, we need to think hard about ways of removing the blight of homelessness. Our thoughts and prayers should go to those who will not sleep in a home of their own tonight.

4 Euthanasia

Introduction

Many of us feel uncomfortable when we talk about death. In our culture it remains a taboo subject. But death is something all human beings must face.

For some people, in extreme suffering, death can come as a merciful release. But should society allow 'mercy killing' or euthanasia – terminating life at the request of the patient?

Advances in medical science have greatly increased life expectancy – death is thus postponed. But what about the quality of life experienced by someone who is kept alive into old age by drugs and machinery?

Listen to the following short essay written by a man who has campaigned for euthanasia.

Reading

Euthanasia

When my mother was eighty she went to live in a private nursing home where I visited her regularly. She was not terminally ill in the sense of having cancer or some other fell disease, but her whole system had run down. Chronic arthritis and moments of giddiness kept her mostly in bed, and failing eyesight meant that she could no longer read or watch the television with any degree of enjoyment. In short, life had become a burden to her. When she was 83, and I asked her on one of my visits how she was, her answer surprised me: 'Oh, how I long to be gathered!' – the Scottish euphemism for death. On my subsequent visits she repeated this wish, adding that she had had a wonderful life, but the time had now come for it to end. But there was no means of ending it, and she survived for another year in increasing discomfort before I received a telephone call in the middle of the night that her wish had at last been granted.

Whether my mother would have been ready to embrace voluntary euthanasia, had it been available, I cannot say. But what I learned from her was something I had not realised before, that while today's world supports plenty of sprightly 90-year-olds, there are many other old people whose wish to die is no less strong than the wish of young people to live. Robert Louis Stevenson had the words to express it:

'It is not so much that death approaches as life withdraws and withers up from round about him. He has outlived his own usefulness and almost his own enjoyment; and if there is to be no recovery, if never again will he be young and strong and passionate ... if in fact this be veritably nightfall, he will not wish for the continuance of a twilight that only strains and disappoints the eyes, but steadfastly await the perfect darkness.'

Yet every year there are an increasing number of increasingly old and sick people for whom the twilight continues unbearably and whose steadfastness in awaiting the perfect darkness often falls short of what they would wish; for the prolongation of living which has been brought about by advances in medical science has also meant the prolongation of dying. For millions of people whose span of life has been extended, its quality has been diminished. Some are in pain from cancer or have a wasting muscular disease: some are in acute discomfort from vomiting, diarrhoea, insomnia, bed sores, flatulence and general exhaustion, being fed by drips in the vein or tubes up the nose and into the stomach. The law at present does not allow doctors to grant them their pleas for merciful release. The compassion we show to sick animals by putting them out of their misery, we deny to our fellow human beings.

In the old days when most people died at home, the family doctor often felt no compunction in administering a lethal drug to help a dying patient on his or her way; but now that most people die in hospitals, doctors cannot do it without the knowledge of the nursing staff and thus, because it is a criminal offence, they endanger their professional careers. The most we can expect of doctors at present is the exercise of what is called passive euthanasia, that is the withholding of some life-sustaining drug or giving sufficient analgesics to alleviate pain yet which can also shorten life; but the effect of opiates such as morphine and heroin is by no means certain, and death can take a dismayingly long time. In the old days too pneumonia often came to give a terminally ill patient a quiet and comparatively speedy death; but today, when pneumonia sets in it is quelled with antibiotics which will keep the patient's heart beating for a few more miserable weeks or months.

Nor is it only the patient who suffers. In hospitals there are paid staff to look after the terminally ill. But at home the job often falls on the wife or daughter or husband, having to feed and wash and nurse, often for months on end, a loved one who no longer wishes to live and whose relentless deterioration they can only helplessly watch. 'Opponents of euthanasia,' 'are apt to take a cynical view of the desires of relatives ... but it cannot be denied that a wife who has to nurse her husband through the last stages of some terrible disease may herself be so deeply affected by the experience that her health is ruined, either mentally or physically.'

There is another factor to be considered. Prolonged and painful dying, the gradual transformation of a much-loved parent or spouse or sibling from a familiar upright figure to that of a semi corpse can mean, when death finally comes, that they are not mourned. 'I had an excellent relationship with both my parents,' a woman wrote to me, 'but after watching the deterioration of their personalities and minds, caused by years of painkilling and life saving drugs, watching their suffering and coping with their irrational behaviour, I was glad when they died.' Sorting through their letters, she remembered how close they had once been and felt guilty about not mourning them. 'Parents should go when they are remembered as their true selves. Parents *should* be mourned. That is the healthy, natural way.'

Ludovic Kennedy

Reflections

* Clearly this is a difficult subject with no simple solutions. The author expresses powerful convictions:

  'For millions of people whose span of life has been extended, its quality has been diminished.'
  'The compassion we show to sick animals by putting them out of their misery, we deny to our fellow human beings.'

  On the other hand, consider the following questions:

  Should society agree to doctors being able to 'put humans out of misery'?
  Under what circumstances should they be allowed to do this?
  What are the medical and ethical issues facing a doctor over this question?
  What moral and emotional problems does euthanasia present to relatives?
  What answer can be made to people who argue that human life is sacred and should never be taken?

  Our faith and value systems are certainly challenged by these questions. But they are questions which will become more and more urgent as we reflect on the subject of health in the late twentieth century.

5 Mental health: teenage suicide

Introduction

An increasing number of schoolchildren are attempting suicide. On average, nearly two young people try to kill themselves every day.
  This is a very disturbing reflection on the 'mental health' of our society.
  What is it about the times in which we live that causes such teenage despair?
  A recent study revealed that three key factors are:

* problems with parents
* problems with school
* problems over girl/boyfriends

The following two case-studies come from The Samaritans, an organisation that exists to offer a sympathetic ear to people in distress – before it is too late.

Reading

Teenage Suicides

It was a beautiful sunny day in May three years ago when Linda Jones took her five-year-old daughter for a country walk. She left her eldest daughter, Anne, at home revising her GCSES.

When they returned, the house, normally filled with heavy metal music, was unusually quiet. Linda called out for her daughter but there was silence. She went up to Anne's room but it was empty.

Puzzled, Jones searched the house, then opened the garage door. Anne was dangling from a rope.

'I sent my little girl next door,' recalls Linda, 'but I didn't cry. I just wanted to get hold of Anne and do something. I didn't know if she was alive or dead. She had been standing on a stool. I cut the rope and held her for a moment. Then I tried mouth-to-mouth resuscitation. But it was too late.'

Anne Jones left no suicide note. She was 16. Hours before, at lunch, she had been talking about the problems of the Third World. 'We will never know why she killed herself,' said her mother. 'She was worried about so many things in the world. She took on board a lot of the larger problems. Her bedroom was covered with photographs of underprivileged people.'

Because teenagers' moods are so mixed, her mother said she found it impossible to know if Anne was unhappy or not. 'One is so close to children when they are little but as they get older you suddenly realise you've lost contact with a huge part of their lives,' she said.

Her daughter was a punk who liked to shock people and make them think. Anne's strength of character may have led her to a decision she could not back out of. 'She was a determined and definite person who found it difficult to change her mind once she'd made it up.'

'On the day she died she said she wouldn't come with us for a walk because she had revision to do, but she seemed to lack motivation. She had no need to worry about her exams because she was an exceedingly bright child. We feel, knowing the way she worried about so many things, that her exams may have seemed totally irrelevant.'

Her mother has many regrets. 'I would have liked to have told her I was proud that she was such an individualist, instead of complaining about the time she took doing her hair or talking about her outrageous clothes. I think it takes an awful lot of courage to kill yourself.'

Nick Paul, another victim of Britain's 50 per cent increase in teenage suicides through the 1980s, was tall, blond and blue-eyed. He was good-looking, sensitive, kind, loving and outgoing. But on October 1, 1988, after an apparently happy evening with friends, he parked his car in a Welsh forest, connected a hose to the exhaust pipe and turned on the engine. His body was found by his mother the next morning. He was 18.

Margaret Paul, his mother, says she saw no signs of depression beforehand. 'His friends told me he was on top of the world that night when they were out at dinner.'

Nick left school at 16 and had his own business selling farm produce from market stalls. Within 18 months he achieved a £140,000 turnover. But he gave it up to go back to college to take a course in business studies. He had been there only six weeks when he killed himself.

His funeral was a celebration of his life. His mother asked her son's friends not to wear black. 'Many of the young girls came in pretty, summery dresses and carried flowers.'

Nick left her and his friends notes. In his note to his mother, he said he loved her but didn't say he was sorry for taking his life. The note ended: 'I am sure my energies will be around somewhere and someone can make use of them. With love.'

Reflections

* This is a difficult subject but one which can suddenly touch a school or local community. Like the subject of child abuse it is one that people prefer not to talk about – until perhaps it is too late and damage has been done.

Is Anyone There? is the title of a book published by The Samaritans. The title is their way of emphasising that there *is* always someone there to listen to problems, if a young person feels they can't speak to a teacher, parent or friend. In a school community it is worth being alert to the fact of teenage suicide.

What seems to be common amongst all suicide victims is that at the time of taking their own life they felt desperately *alone*. Be aware of anyone in your own community who just might be so alone that they feel life is not worth continuing. We know that there is so much in our lives to live for, even though we all experience moments of great sadness, fear and pain.

* Death be not proud, though some have called thee
Mighty and dreadful, for, thou art not so,
For, those, whom thou thinkst, thou dost overthrow,
Die not, poor death, nor yet canst thou kill me.
Thou art slave to Fate, Chance, kings, and desperate men,
And dost with poison, war, and sickness dwell,
And poppy, or charms can make us sleep as well,
And better than thy stroke.
One short sleep past, we wake eternally,
And death shall be no more; death, thou shalt die.

John Donne

6 Living with disease (1)

Introduction

For most of us, health is something we take for granted – until we lose it. For those who enjoy good health it is difficult to imagine how quality of life can suffer when a chronic illness takes over.

Listen to the following, very moving account of Stephen Pegg. He was a teacher for 14 years until motor neurone disease, a debilitating disease of the central nervous system, altered his life – irreversibly. As he says, it can pounce upon the lives of ordinary people, 'like me and you'.

Reading

Life in slow motion

Motor neurone disease is not an illness that strikes only at a brilliant Cambridge scientist, a man who used to manage the England football team or one of Hollywood's most famous names. It is not exclusive to the rich, the celebrated, the distant. Motor neurone disease leaps out of the pages of medical textbooks and springs from the mouths of consultant neurogods, pouncing upon the lives of ordinary people. Like me and you.

Motor neurone disease doesn't just happen to someone else; it happens to someone's father, daughter, neighbour, mother, son, lover, uncle, distant cousin, best friend, husband, wife. Motor neurone disease doesn't just devastate someone's life; it alters forever the lives of someone's friends and family as they helplessly watch a sufferer deteriorate.

In May 1986, I ran eight miles in an hour-and-a-quarter, helping to raise money in a charity fun run near Helston, Cornwall. In July 1986, I played in the annual staff versus pupils rounders match at the school where I taught. I hit two rounders and took a diving catch to dismiss a boy called Jason.

In August, my wife, Ros, and I walked 20 miles along the Cornwall coast near Portscatho. We had an ambition eventually to walk the whole length of the Cornish coastal footpath.

In December 1986, I stopped playing squash twice a week because an elbow injury was making it difficult for me to hit the ball with both accuracy and power.

In April 1987, I travelled to Skegness with the Avon Schools' FA party for the annual English schools' soccer festival. In five days I refereed four matches and was linesman in five others.

In May 1987, I refereed a Woodspring league football match between Milton Nomads and Clevedon Town – my 685th official appointment since September 1971. The next day I went into hospital for three days of tests and investigations. Later that month I was informed that what I'd thought was a niggling sports injury was motor neurone disease.

In July 1987, I sat on a chair and kept the score in the annual rounders match at school.

In August, my wife and I went on our last long walk, from Middleton-in-Teesdale to High Force, County Durham. I had organized a family holiday there, suspecting that it might be our last chance to enjoy one together. My parents, Ros's parents and her sister shared adjoining cottages.

In September 1987, I stopped working.

In October, my three-year-old daughter, Eleanor, saw me fall down the stairs at home. Nowadays she refers to this incident as the cause of my illness.

In November 1987, I took my daughter swimming for the last time. I was having increasing difficulty dressing myself, and felt that some people were giving me strange looks as I struggled with socks and shoes.

In December 1987, I went to lift my sleeping daughter, intending to carry her upstairs to bed. She was too heavy for me. My wife picked up Eleanor and joked about putting her on a diet.

On Christmas Day I drove my car for the last time, the fingers of my left hand having become too weak to turn the ignition key.

Ros had to cut up my Christmas meal although I fed myself. Eleanor and I pulled three crackers together; she insisted that I told old jokes and wore a blue paper hat.

In January 1988, after walking about 400 metres, I keeled over backwards on the front doorstep. Unable to stop myself, I crashed to the ground like a felled elm.

In February 1988, we all went to Cornwall to stay in a friend's cottage. On the way home I read Eleanor a story for the last time, my croaky voice running out of expression on a dual carriageway near Exeter.

One Sunday morning in March we drove into Bristol for egg and bacon rolls from Brunel's Buttery, not far from the SS Great Britain. Ros had to feed me, my left hand now as useless as the right.

In April 1988, Eleanor, Ros and I visited the Cotswold Wildlife Park. This was the occasion of my public wheelchair debut. By May it was impossible for me to climb the stairs safely, even with three helpers, so I spent all day upstairs in wretched isolation.

In July 1988, I officially retired. I was 40.

In August, having had the downstairs toilet converted into a disabled person's shower room, my bed and I were moved to the little room that looks out on to the back garden. From here I was able to watch Eleanor laugh and swing on her new climbing frame.

In September 1988, Eleanor started school. I sat in the car and surprised her as she ran up the path with her friends at the end of her first day.

By November, my speech had deteriorated so much that only Ros and Eleanor could understand me.

In December 1988, my daughter was an angel in her school nativity play. A friend videoed the spectacle so that I could watch it in comfort at home.

On Christmas Day I asked to be wheeled into the kitchen so that I could sit at the table. Ros fed me and Eleanor pulled my cracker.

Reflections

* This is a simple and thought-provoking description of what it means to have your life gradually overtaken by disease. It should serve to remind us all to value good health as the greatest human possession; it should serve also to help us all understand what living through and with any kind of illness does mean, and how, in severe cases, the quality of someone's life is significantly affected.

* Our thoughts and prayers should be with all who live with illness day by day, whether their own or that of family and friends.

7 Living with disease (2)

Introduction

Living with an incurable disease is a sad fact of life for many people in our society, whether they experience it themselves or watch a friend or relative suffer.

Because we have good standards of health care, and many diseases can be cured, we may prefer not to think about individual suffering. But we should take time to reflect on the condition of those who, in the words of the following writer, are 'at war with their bodies'.

In this article, which was linked to a television documentary on the subject, Ivan is the man with the incurable disease; Dr Jonathan Miller is the television programme director.

Reading

Portrait of a man at war with his body

Seven years ago, when Ivan was an energetic man with a successful career, vivacious wife, Jan, and two children, Justin, then 11, and nine-year-old Sophie, he noticed a slight involuntary movement in the little finger of his left hand.

A few months later, as he gradually lost control of his whole hand, the shattering and unexpected diagnosis was made. 'Don't worry', he told Jan. 'I'll fight and get over it.'

They live in Cambridge where Ivan still lectures for two terms out of three and spends the rest of the time 'researching' his illness. He had swallowed a tablet of the so-called 'miracle' drug L-dopa, half an hour before I arrived. 'It is a race against time. I have to relax in order to get it synthesized inside the brain', he said.

It seemed to be working. His movements were only moderately jerky, and his voice was strong, although high pitched. He spoke lucidly about what he was doing, but there was already the eerie feeling that he was a divided personality: one part of him was commenting rationally on the irrational effect the drug was having on other parts.

He sat back in his chair, closed his eyes and muttered some gibberish. 'Dum, dum, one, two three, dum, dum four five six . . .' Then he smiled and said: 'Stay for a few hours and you will see what happens as it begins to wear off. I will be helpless and out of control. No heroics, though.'

The transformation, both mentally and physically, was to be phenomenal.

Jan came into the room occasionally to see how he was. 'It was ironic when Ivan first became ill because he had always been concerned about fitness,' she said. 'We had to adjust totally to the implications which were enormous. At first it was an incredible shock and I was very frightened. The immediate, misplaced reaction is to imagine what will happen over a period of time and to think, 'I won't be able to cope'. It takes a long while to realize that you only have to cope from day to day.

'I found it particularly difficult because Ivan didn't want to tell anyone. Our friends began to get very concerned and some drew their own conclusions – the marriage was breaking up, he was on drugs, or drank too much. I had to keep telling them, "No, he's fine" – and that was very tough. Once everyone knew, the whole thing became much more manageable.'

For 18 months, Ivan refused medication. 'I got into a rock bottom state and it was a little unfair on Jan. I didn't mind if people thought I was a joke, so long as they didn't know I had Parkinson's disease.

'The illness gives all the symptoms of a person who has totally collapsed. We shake and tremble and signal to the world, 'Don't fight me any more. I give in. I am a nonentity. All my prowess is dissipated. I'm the opposite of a bouncing conversationalist. I am a person with shaking limbs whose voice is a boring monotone and who cannot talk in a coherent fashion. Just leave me alone to shake and wither away.'

'I felt a sense of shame. However much you know objectively and intellectually that you are almost certainly not responsible for the illness, there is a constant feeling that you went wrong somewhere and mismanaged your life.'

Ivan was born and brought up in Liverpool and was a founder member of the Swinging Sixties philosophy. He was at school with Paul McCartney, grew up with John Lennon, and the two met for the first time at his house. 'I've often wondered if I over-taxed the cells where dopamine is created', he says. 'I have a whole range of speculation about why this happened to me.

'Maybe it is a sort of flu virus; I used to drink, make love, play squash and be in a state of high fever. I went without sleep – all these things together could have an effect, but I have no bitterness. At first I didn't treat it as fate because I wanted to question and fight it and search out what the hell had gone on. I soon realized I could either hide away and pretend I wasn't ill or turn it into an interest and a hobby. It was an easy decision to make.'

He felt that patients were under too much pressure: they were encouraged to take L-dopa all the time either in order to keep a job or from relatives and hard-pressed doctors who thought it would solve all problems. So he contacted Jonathan Miller.

'I heard this thin, voice and assumed he was an old, seer sort of figure who was boring me with his insistence that he was interesting', says Miller.

'Finally I agreed to see him. It soon became apparent that his was something extraordinary – partly because he was so much younger than most people who get the disease and partly because he had actually turned himself into an object of study and had made his disease an occupation rather than an affliction.

'The image that kept occurring to me was Robinson Crusoe, marooned on his own island, eager to map it and master it in great detail and to show visitors around. The thing about disabling illnesses is that people do feel they are alone and it is very easy to go mad in isolation.'

He spent a week with Ivan making the film which illustrates the remarkable effects of L-dopa, but also the battle Ivan has to keep off the drug.

Ordinarily, Ivan takes the drug intermittently and tries to leave his first dose until as late as possible in the morning. On waking there is the tortuous business of dressing – putting on a sock is a mammoth task – followed by an extraordinary six mile run, which is shown in the film. Then he showers and has breakfast, usually porridge mixed with ice cream.

'The challenges I had in the past are no less than the ones I have now. Eating a bowl of porridge may be a great achievement today, but before that it was winning a game of squash.'

Reflections

* Here is someone, then, who developed an incurable disease. His normal, healthy life was dramatically overtaken by Parkinson's disease. Some of Ivan's thoughts are worth reflecting upon:

'I felt a sense of shame.'
'There is a constant feeling that you went wrong somewhere and mismanaged your life.'
'Eating a bowl of porridge may be a great achievement today.'

Hearing about someone in Ivan's situation helps us to understand the full impact of chronic illness upon an individual and her or his family and friends.

* Let us all reflect on our own attitudes to those who do not enjoy good health. Let us try to appreciate good health and not take it for granted. Let us understand and support those in society who suffer from incurable illnesses.

8 Immunisation: a public health revolution

Introduction

Anyone who has ever watched a baby or young child wake up, stretch, open its eyes – then suddenly be fully alert – knows how beautiful it is to see a child in good health.

In this society we believe that every child has a right to good health and health care. But for many children throughout the world the chances of surviving childhood and developing into a healthy adult are slim.

UNICEF – the United Nations Children's Fund – exists to improve living conditions for the world's underprivileged children.

An important aspect of health care is immunisation. Probably all of us have had a series of immunisations as babies and as we grew up. The World Health Organisation has campaigned to extend innoculations and immunisation to as many of the world's children as possible. The following reading gives us some interesting detail on this vital issue of life and death.

Reading

Immunization: a public health revolution

During the mid-1970s, nearly 5 million young children were dying every year of measles, tetanus, whooping cough, diptheria, tuberculosis, and polio. Millions more were permanently disabled by these six diseases, all of which can be prevented by immunization.

When the World Health Organization launched the Expanded Programme on Immunization (EPI) in 1974, fewer than 5 per cent of children in the developing world were immunized. Three years later, the World Health Assembly resolved to make immunization against the six main vaccine-preventable diseases available to every child in the world by the end of 1990.

At the time, the goal of Universal Childhood Immunization seemed utopian. Yet in this decade, around 80 countries have sharply accelerated their immunization programmes. And today, a majority of developing nations have a realistic chance of achieving the goal. China, with one sixth of the world's children, is expected to achieve the target two years ahead of schedule. Countries such as Botswana, Cuba, Egypt, the Gambia, Iraq, Jordan, Oman, Rwanda, Tanzania and Saudi Arabia have reached or almost reached the target already. Others – such as Algeria, Brazil, Kenya, Mexico. Morocco, Pakistan and Turkey – are poised to reach 80 per cent–90 per cent coverage within the next two years.

In sum, there is now every prospect that 70 per cent–80 per cent of babies born during the 1990s in the developing world will be immunized by the age of 12 months.

Already, almost 50 per cent of babies born each year are vaccinated against measles, and over 55 per cent are immunized against the other five EPI diseases. Immunization of women against tetanus (which confers immunity on the newborn baby) still lags behind at just under 25 per cent. In total, immunization prevented, in 1987, the deaths of approximately 1.5 million infants and children from the six EPI diseases.

'In a little over a decade a public health revolution has quietly taken place', says Dr Ralph Henderson, Director of WHO's Expanded Programme on Immunization.

In part, this remarkable progress is a result of improvements in vaccines and in the equipment used to transport and store them. But social breakthroughs have been just as important. A major boost has come from the strategy of social mobilization – the involvement of all available government institutions, teachers, religious leaders, community organizations, and the mass media to inform and support parents in using immunization services.

In addition, over 100,000 health workers have been trained to manage immunization programmes more effectively. No longer is an acute illness, for example, regarded as a valid reason for witholding vaccination. Drop-out rates have also been cut in many countries by vaccinating children brought to health clinics for the treatment of illnesses such as diarrhoea and respiratory infections.

The challenge for the 1990s is to complete the building of a permanent vaccination system which will immunize almost every child in every country before his or her first birthday (and every woman of childbearing age). Strengthened disease surveillance systems should then begin to record the elimination of diseases such as polio and neonatal tetanus, and at least a 95 per cent reduction in today's 1.8 million measles deaths each year.

As the world stands on the brink of a new era in immunization technology – with the promise of vaccines against malaria, diarrhoeal diseases, and perhaps against AIDS – the infrastructure of immunization now being built to deliver the present vaccines may come to be seen as one of the greatest human investments ever made.

Reflection

* Something, then, that we take for granted . . . But as the reading suggests, immunisation on a global scale may well come to be seen as 'one of the greatest human investments ever made' as we move into the 21st century.

* UNICEF – the United Nations Children's Fund – is an organisation which we should all be aware of: an international charity which believes that the world's children have the following rights:

Mankind owes to the child the best it has to give
These words open the 'Declaration of the Rights of the Child', unanimously adopted by the General Assembly of the United Nations on 20 November 1959. Ten principles establish the rights that all children are entitled to:

1 The right to equality, regardless of race, religion, nationality or sex.
2 The right to special protection for full physical, intellectual, moral, spiritual and social development in a healthy and normal manner.
3 The right to a name and nationality.
4 The right to adequate nutrition, housing, and medical services.
5 The right to special care, if handicapped.

6 The right to love, understanding and protection.
7 The right to free education, to play and recreation.
8 The right to be among the first to receive relief in times of disaster.
9 The right to protection against all forms of neglect, cruelty and exploitation.
10 The right to protection from any form of discrimination, and the right to be brought up in a spirit of universal brotherhood, peace and tolerance.

9 The Third Age

Introduction

Health is a state of complete physical, mental and social well-being. It is much more than merely a state of 'non-illness': health is directly linked to the individual's environment.

As a nation – in common with the countries of Europe and North America – we are staying healthier longer and living longer. But what are the future implications for so many people living well into 'The Third Age'? The following reading offers some ideas.

Reading

'The Third Age'

In 1988 the Social Affairs Ministers of Europe met to contemplate the time when one person in five will be a pensioner and one in ten aged over 75, when there will be only three people of working age to support each pensioner and when old-age pensions may account for one-fifth of national income. It will be even worse for Switzerland and West Germany where there will be only two people of working age for each old person.

It will be 2040 before this scenario fully becomes a reality, but the people who will be old then are alive now and unless they quickly change their breeding habits the numbers of their children are quite predictable. This world will happen and it will start to happen before the end of this century.

Once again, there have been old people before, but never before so many of them. I knew only one grandparent – the others had died before I was born. My children knew all four. Their children will almost certainly know a great-grandparent or two. People in their sixties and retired will still be someone's children. The infrequent has become the commonplace and the world as we know it will inevitably change in some way.

It is happening because, in the richer countries, it is becoming harder to die. Each major cause of death is either diminished, like smallpox or polio and, one day, cancer, or postponed for a few more years or decades, like heart disease. Of course, nature, or man's tampering with nature, may trigger another plague and some wonder whether AIDS may not be just that plague, but such disasters excepted there seems little reason why many of today's teenagers cannot expect to live to 100, provided they do not drink, smoke or drive themselves to death.

The question is, will they want to live that long? When death as an act of God seems to be indefinitely postponed will we want to make it increasingly an act of mankind? Euthanasia, already quasi-legal in the Netherlands, may become more acceptable to more societies.

More urgent are the questions 'What will they live on?' 'What will they do?' 'Who will care for them?' By the year 2020, if nothing changes, Italy will be spending over a quarter of her national income on pensions, while Britain's health service spends ten times as much on a patient over 75 as on one of working age.

Like all discontinuities, however, this one contains opportunities as well as problems if the changes are seen coming and if everyone concerned can indulge in a little upside-down thinking.

They will not all be poor, for instance. An increasing number of them, in Britain, will own their own homes, an asset which can be turned into an annual income provided that they do not intend to bequeath it to the next generation (who will by then be in mid or late career with their own homes bought and paid for). Most of them will be healthy and active. That is, of course, why they are still alive. They are capable of working. One British study found that 43 per cent of over-65s regularly helped other elderly people, 25 per cent helped the disabled, 11 per cent helped neighbours. If we change our view of work to include such unpaid activity then these people are only retired in a legal or technical sense. After all, in the last century no one had heard of retirement – they worked till they dropped, or, as a farmer said once when I asked him what was the difference between farming at 75 and farming at 50, 'The same only slower!' Experience and wisdom can often compensate for energy.

So many older people will not go unnoticed, particularly when many more of them will have experienced responsibility earlier in life and will not be used to keeping quiet. If we are sensible we will want to use their talents in our organizations, but not full-time or on full pay. We shall need, then, to re-think what jobs call for part-time wisdom and experience and what work can be done at a distance by responsible people. We shall need to revise the tax rules for pensions to make it economic for such work to be done. Many people, active and healthy, will devise their own activities, organizing around their enthusiasms; we must not let too many rules from the past stand in their way. We will need to change the way we talk about them, words like 'retirement' will become as redundant as 'servant' today. Words are so often the bridges of social change, the outward signs of a discontinuity at work triggering some upside-down thinking.

Already the linguistic signposts are going up. The Third Age, the age of living, as the French would have it, which follows the first age of learning and the second of working, is already becoming a common term. There is a University of the Third Age, a network of people exchanging their skills and their knowledge. There will soon be more talk of Third Age Careers. Soon, no doubt, there will be Third Age societies and, ultimately, Ministers for the Third Age in all countries! The wrinklies, as my children fondly term us, can be assets as well as liabilities, *if* we want them to be.

If words are indeed the heralds of change, then the Third Age language suggests that before too long we shall be referring to people's job-careers as we now do to their education. 'Where did you work?' for a 65-year-old with fifteen years, at least, of life ahead will sound much like 'Where did you go to school?' It would all sound strange indeed to my father who died two years after retiring, at the age of 74. For him there was no Third Age worth living and the second age, of job and career, had long been a burden before he could afford to leave it.

It will be different for us, his children, and for our children. It need not be change for the worse if we can see it coming and can prepare for it.

From 'The Age of Unreason' by Charles Handy

Reflections

* Some challenges ahead for our society!
  The passage ends with the words: 'It need not be change for the worse if we can see it coming and can prepare for it.' The 16-year-old today will be part of this enlarged Third Age in the years 2040–2050, so though the time may seem distant it *is* important to start thinking about it now. Society clearly needs to think carefully in the coming years about how it will organise its tax revenues, health care, social services, leisure and work patterns for a future when a significant percentage of the population will be post-60.
  The writer's strong advice here is that we should see the *opportunities* not the *problems* ahead, advice that is always worth reflecting on whenever we meet change.

10 Overpopulation: 'A Modest Proposal'

Introduction

There is much discussion about the problems of overpopulation and the resultant poverty in certain parts of the world. We tend to think, therefore, that this is a problem only ever encountered in the continents of Asia and Africa. But the following passage reminds us that in 17th and 18th century Britain the issue of overpopulation and poverty was a live one.

How to deal with it? Well the writer Jonathan Swift proposed – *tongue-in-cheek* – quite a radical solution! What follows is now a celebrated piece from Irish literature.

Reading

A Modest Proposal

A Modest Proposal for preventing the children of Poor People from being a Burthen to their Parents, or the Country, and for making them Beneficial to the Publick.

It is a melancholy Object to those, who walk through this great Town, or travel in the Country, when they see the *Streets*, the *Roads*, and *Cabbin-Doors*, crowded with *Beggars* of the female Sex, followed by three, four, or six Children, *all in Rags*, and importuning every Passenger for an Alms. These *Mothers* instead of being able to work for their honest livelihood, are forced to employ all their time in Stroling, to beg Sustenance for their *helpless Infants*, who, as they grow up, either turn *Thieves* for want of work, or leave their *dear native Country to fight for the Pretender in Spain*, or sell themselves to the *Barbadoes*.

I think it is agreed by all Parties, that this prodigious number of Children, in the Arms, or on the Backs, or at the *heels* of their *Mothers*, and frequently of their *Fathers*, is *in the present deplorable state of the Kingdom*, a very great additional grievance; and therefore whoever could find out a fair, cheap and easy method of making these Children sound and useful Members of the common-wealth would deserve so well of the publick, as to have his Statue set up for a preserver of the Nation.

But my Intention is very far from being confined to provide only for the Children of *professed Beggars*: It is of a much greater extent, and shall take in the whole number of Infants at a certain Age, who are born of Parents in effect as little able to support them, as those who demand our Charity in the Streets.

As to my own part, having turned my thoughts, for many Years, upon this important Subject, and maturely weighed the several *Schemes of other Projectors*, I have always found them grossly mistaken in their computation. It is true a Child, *just dropt from it's Dam*, may be supported by her Milk, for a Solar year with little other Nourishment, at most not above the Value of two Shillings, which the Mother may certainly get, or the Value in *Scraps*, by her lawful Occupation of begging, and it is exactly at one year Old that I propose to provide for them, in such a manner, as, instead of being a Charge upon their *Parents*, or the *Parish*, or *wanting Food and Raiment* for the rest of their Lives, they shall, on the Contrary, contribute to the Feeding and partly to the Cloathing of many Thousands.

I shall now therefore humbly propose my own thoughts, which I hope will not be lyable to the least Objection.

I have been assured by a very knowing *American* of my acquaintance in *London*, that a young healthy Child well Nursed is at a year Old a most delicious, nourishing, and wholesome Food, whether *Stewed*, *Roasted*, *Baked*, or *Boyled*, and I make no doubt that it will equally serve in a *Fricasie*, or a *Ragoust*.

I do therefore humbly offer it to *publick consideration*, that of the hundred and twenty thousand Children already computed, twenty thousand may be reserved for Breed, whereof only one fourth part to be Males, which is more than we allow to *Sheep*, *black Cattle*, or *Swine*, and my reason is that these Children are seldom the Fruits of Marriage, a *Circumstance not much regarded by our Savages*, therefore *one Male* will be sufficient to serve *four Females*. That the remaining hundred thousand may at a year Old be offered in Sale to the *persons of Quality*, and *Fortune*, through the Kingdom, always advising the Mother to let them Suck plentifully in the last Month, so as to render them Plump, and Fat for a good Table. A Child will make two Dishes at an Entertainment for Friends, and when the Family dines alone, the fore or hind Quarter will make a reasonable Dish, and seasoned with a little Pepper or Salt will be very good Boiled on the fourth Day, especialy in Winter.

I have reckoned upon a Medium, that a Child just born will weigh 12 pounds, and in a solar Year if tollerably nursed encreaseth to 28 Pound.

I granted this food will be somewhat dear, and therefore very *proper for Landlords*, who, as they have already devoured most of the Parents, seem to have the best Title to the Children.

Infant's flesh will be in Season throughout the Year, but more plentiful in *March*, and a little before and after, for we are told by a grave Author an eminent *French* Physitian, that *Fish being a prolifick Dyet*, there are more Children born in *Roman Catholick Countries* abnout nine Months after *Lent*, than at any other Season: Therefore reckoning a Year after *Lent*, the Markets will be more glutted than usual, because the number of *Popish Infants*, is at least three to one in this Kingdom, and therefore it will have one other Collateral advantage by lessening the Number of *Papists* among us.

I have already computed the Charge of nursing a Beggars Child (in which list I reckon all *Cottagers*, *Labourers*, and four fifths of the *Farmers*) to be about two Shillings *per Annum*, Rags included, and I believe no Gentleman would repine to give Ten Shillings for the *Carcass of a good fat Child*, which, as I have said will make four Dishes of excellent Nutritive Meat, when he hath only some particular friend, or his own Family to Dine with him. Thus the Squire will learn to be a good Landlord, and grow popular among his Tenants, the Mother will have Eight Shillings neat profit, and be fit for Work till she produces another Child.

As to our City of *Dublin*, Shambles may be appointed for this purpose, in the most convenient parts of it, and Butchers we may be assured will not be wanting, although I rather recommend buying the Children alive, and dressing them hot from the Knife, as we do *roasting Pigs*.

'A Modest Proposal' from 'Irish Tracts' by Jonathan Swift

Reflection

* As a famous satirist, Swift of course was writing in his characteristically strong vein to make a point: namely that here was a great social problem of poverty that needed tackling, but few were prepared to do anything about it. His 'modest proposal' was his way of trying to stir people into action.

* In our own world today health and illness are a global phenomenon which concerns us all, the healthy and the sick, those who live in both under- and over-populated countries.

In the poorest regions of the world where a well-balanced diet is seldom available, drinking water is rare, and medical services are all still in the early stages, the very notion of 'health' can hardly be compared with ours. The weakest and most disadvantaged are always the first victims, and most often this is the world's *children*.

Swift's cruel, satirical proposals served to stir the imaginations of people living in the 18th century. As the 21st century approaches, those of us who live in nations which enjoy good health need to reflect on what we can do to enable a better quality of healthcare throughout the globe.

11 Progress

Introduction

What is progress? Our dictionary will tell us: 'movement forwards'; 'satisfactory development'; 'advance towards completion, maturity, or perfection'.

Change is a fact of life – but is it always progress, a going forward? Do we as humans go backwards as often as forwards?

When we consider advances in health care we would probably conclude that the 20th century has seen great progress. But when we look at our wider environment, would we reach the same conclusion?

Here are three poems with a particular view on environmental progress.

Reading

They Are Tracking Down Everything Picturesque

gentlemen came with portfolios and measuring rods
they measured the ground spread out their papers
workers shooed away the pigeons
ripped up the fence tore down the house
mixed lime in the garden
brought cement raised scaffolding
they are going to build an enormous apartment house

they are wrecking the beautiful houses one by one
the houses which nourished us since we were small
with their wide windows their wooden stairs
with their high ceilings laps on the walls
trophies of folk architecture

they are tracking down everything picturesque
chasing it away persistently to the upper part of the town
it expires like a revolution betrayed
in a little while it will not even exist in postcards
nor in the memory or souls of our children.

Dinos Chistianópoulos

'It Must All Be Done Over...'

Wherever I look the houses are coming down,
the yards are deserted,
people have taken to tents and caravans,
like restless cattle breaking stride,
going off with their wagons
under a rumbling cloud.

I have begun to believe those rumours
of the world's wheat being eaten
by metallic grasshoppers,
and columns of brutal strangers
advancing on the soul of Asia.

I hope I shall be able to leave
without too much baggage
or bitterness. I must make my life
into an endless camp,
learn to build with air, water and smoke.

John Haines

The Planster's Vision

Cut down that timber! Bells, too many and strong,
Pouring their music through the branches bare,

From moon-white church-towers down the windy air
Have pealed the centuries out with Evensong.
Remove those cottages, a huddled throng!
Too many babies have been born in there,
Too many coffins, bumping down the stair,
Carried the old their garden paths along.

I have a Vision of The Future, chum,
The workers' flats in fields of soya beans
Tower up like silver pencils, score on score:
And Surging Millions hear the Challenge come
From microphones in communal canteens
'No Right! No Wrong! All's perfect, evermore.'

John Betjeman

Reflections

* These three poets share the view that as time goes by humans cause a lot of
damage to their natural environment, often in the name of 'progress'.
The first poet writes: 'they are tracking down everything picturesque'.
The second fears 'metallic grasshoppers'.
The third describes planners saying: 'Remove those cottages, a huddled throng!'
As human beings our mental, social and physical health are closely linked with
the quality of the environment in which we live. We should not necessarily resist change, but we should always question whether 'progress' really means
just that. Or can it mean destruction of what is recognised to be valuable and
has stood the test of time? In relation to the environment in particular, these
questions need to be asked by writers, politicians, workers and all members of
our communities.

12 Architecture: 'A Vision of Britain'

Introduction
An important part of our society is the buildings in which we live and work. How
these buildings are designed and constructed profoundly affects our health, lifestyle
and quality of living. For example, life for a family with young children will clearly
difffer according to whether they live on the tenth floor of a high-rise block, or a
house with its own garden.

So the people who design buildings – architects – have an important part to play
in a society's well-being.

HRH Prince Charles has spoken out against what he sees as the damage done
to our environment by modern architects with lots of new ideas. He feels they are
forgetting the lessons to be learned by looking at the styles of older buildings.

Some of his outspoken criticisms of public buildings erected in the last 20 years
include: 'a monstrous carbuncle' 'mildewed elephant droppings covered in drain-
pipes' 'a Lego building' ' a word processor' (of a housing estate) 'people condemned to live out their lives in a grubby launderette'

The Prince published a book of his ideas on British architecture, called *A Vision of Britain*. Here are its concluding paragraphs:

Reading

A Vision of Britain

For those readers who may happen to be professional architects I dare say my expressed views have merely confirmed the opinions of those critics who say that since I have no professional training in architecture I should not be voicing my views so publicly. I can almost guarantee I will also be told that my apparent preference for a more classical, some would say nostalgic, style in architecture is stifling 'modern creativity'. I will be accused yet again of living in the past; as if it were an abominable sin to respect, admire, cherish or seek inspiration from the richness of our heritage.

It was Edmund Burke who wrote that a healthy civilisation exists with three relationships intact. It has a relationship with the present, a relationship with the future and a relationship with the past. When the past feeds and sustains the present and the future you have a civilised society. It was only in this century that we broke that pact with the past and tried to obliterate its meanings and its messages.

Nowadays, with the virtual demise of classical education and of any attempt to provide school-children with a perspective on our shared heritage of European civilisation, I suppose it is little wonder that any reference in our buildings to that European heritage is considered old-fashioned and irrelevant to today's 'modern' conditions. What is worse, such reference is dismissed derisively as 'pastiche'. The very word suggests that an ability to learn from the past is uncreative and deadening. It is inevitably used as an insult, accompanied by wearisome references to 'Disneyland'.

In fact, a respect for the past both disciplines and liberates at the same time. It gives us a measure for our own achievements as well as an endlessly rich source of examples for us to use.

The skills, the crafts, the art that went into the architecture of the past are still there – just. But they need to be revived and put to work again, so that we can build cities, towns and villages which seem to have grown out of the historical fabric of Britain and which better reflect the true aspirations of its people. We must concentrate on creating environments in which people can prosper psychologically, as human beings, not merely as cogs in a mechanical process. We need design and layout which positively encourage neighbourliness, intimacy and, where possible, a sense of shared belonging to a recognisable community.

What is the point, for example, of being the most technologically advanced society if, at the same time, we lose our soul, and forfeit the right to be considered civilised? For this is what we have allowed to happen by deluding ourselves that we are somehow immortal; by losing our faith in eternity; by believing that this Earth was made for our dominion, and by losing that proper sense of humility which enables us to live in gentle harmony with our surroundings and with God's creation. Why else is it that we now find ourselves confronted by such complex and disturbing environmental problems threatening, as they do, the very survival of this planet and *all* its living inhabitants?

Everything cries out for a reappraisal of our values and attitudes. Don't be intimidated by those who deride such views. They have had their day. Look at the soulless mess in which they have left us all . . .! Look at what has been done to the developing countries in the name of progress and technology. We have managed, through our Western arrogance, to make at least two generations feel ashamed of their ancient, traditional customs, culture and spiritual values. Now, I suggest, is the time when we should, in all humility, learn from our Third World neighbours. Perhaps they can teach us, before it is too late, how to reacquire those eternal values which, if properly understood, and blended with our technological expertise, could provide us with the essential balance and sense of proportion that we need in order to sustain both the visible and invisible aspects of our world.

You may ask how all this is relevant to what some people derisively term my 'pet hobby horse' – architecture? The answer is that since I believe architecture has always been the outward expression of an inner inspiration, it is only too clear that it has become dangerously unbalanced and, unless it is examined in the light of a reappraisal of basic values and principles, we will all be the poorer.

Reflections

* Many architects of course do not agree with these views. They believe that the Prince is *too* fond of tradition – and that tradition gets in the way of progress. This debate about the values of the 'old' and the 'new' is an interesting one, especially in our rapidly-changing society, where new technology is developing all the time.
  Everyone would agree that we need to create a built environment within which, as the Prince puts it, 'people can prosper psychologically as human beings'.
  Our built environment is important to our sense of values as a community – a healthy and flourishing community, whether at home, at school or at work.

* *Revelation 21: 1–4*
  Then I saw a new heaven and a new earth, for the first heaven and the first earth had passed away, and there was no longer any sea. I saw the Holy City, the new Jerusalem, coming down out of heaven from God, prepared as a bride beautifully dressed for her husband. And I heard a loud voice from the throne saying, 'Now the dwelling of God is with men, and he will live with them.
  They will be his people, and God himself will be with them and be their God. He will wipe every tear from their eyes. There will be no more death or mourning or crying or pain, for the old order of things has passed away'.

Justice and Ideals

1 A sense of community

Introduction

What do we mean by the word 'community'?

What helps create a sense of community?

It might be helpful to think about the community of an orchestra, and the amount of team-work required for it to be successful. Or think how people need to work closely together when an aeroplane is landing at an airport to ensure the safety of passengers. Or a ferry coming into port?

In 19th century Paris a group of people formed what they called a commune, with the particular intention of trying to live and work together as a close community. Here is an extract from one historian's account of what they achieved.

Reading

The Paris Commune

The people of Paris made the Commune. The Commune gave a lot of ordinary citizens the confidence to do things together that they would never have dared to do before – or have been allowed to do. Other countries with less democratic governments found the Commune alarming and, not surprisingly, the Communards got a very bad press outside. For example the London *Times* reported on 7 April 1871, 'The men of the Commune do not intend to be disappointed. They have promised themselves to annihilate Paris, its fortunes, its commerce, its population – and they keep their word. Never was the work of destruction carried on with a more wicked and brutal perseverance.' Communards were branded as 'the mob, red insurgents, bandits, anarchists, convicts, scum, moral gangrene, socialists'. Socialist was a dirty word then.

As usually happens in times of political change, a lot of new newspapers were rushed into print. But not everyone knew how to read them. The most direct way of taking part in Commune affairs was by joining one of the many political clubs. These were a tradition of revolutionary Paris, and had been revived during the siege. Their activities were often held in churches as these were the largest and most convenient local meeting places. People would hurry there after work to discuss the issues of the day. As the Communal Club of 111 Arrondissement pointed out:

Follow our example; open Communal clubs in all the churches. The priests can conduct services in the daytime and you can provide the people with political education in the evenings.

Here is another wall poster, signed by a Jules Morelly:

Citizens... It is only at public meetings that we are able to enlighten ourselves regarding the stormy times through which we are passing. We thus request your presence and participation, in order that each citizen know fully what is occurring, how it is occurring and how it ought to occur...

All sorts of subjects were discussed in the clubs – the position of the wealthy, the priests, prostitution, the equality of women, the abolition of marriage, how to win the civil war and what social reforms were needed. People argued and shouted a lot at each other, and sometimes the ideas put forward were crazy, but most of the time the discussions were serious and practical. Women were particularly active in the clubs. They really enjoyed the freedom, and, for the first time, were not afraid to speak in public. Listen to this unknown woman speaker at a club meeting in the Trinity church:

... Yes, you women are oppressed. But have just a little more patience, for the day that will bring justice and satisfaction for our demands is rapidly approaching. Tomorrow you will belong to yourselves and not to exploiters. The factories in which you are crowded together will belong to you; the tools placed in your hands will belong to you; the profit that results from your labour, your care, and the loss of your health, will be shared among you...

Citizeness Valentin, speaking in the Club of the Proletarians, proposed that women should, 'Guard the gates of Paris while the men go to battle.'

There was not much time for private life. On top of people's daily work there were meetings to attend, ideas to put to Commune members, and the trades unions to be got going again or new ones formed. By the middle of May there were about 90 trades unions, including women's ones, active in Paris.

One of the new ideas to change the system of work was the concept of workers' co-operatives. These would give people more control over their working lives. Everyone who worked in a factory or machine shop would be in charge of running the business, making the goods and sharing out the profits once the expenses had been paid. This was felt to be a good way of getting rid of bosses, low wages and unfair differences between people. The problem was that ordinary workers had no money to invest in these co-operatives. But the Commune helped financially and soon there were 43 such co-operatives working in the city. This was quite an achievement for such a radical and new way of running industry.

The bakers, whose work was hard, asked that night work be abolished, and the Commune agreed. This was good for the bakers, but not always convenient for the rest of the population who missed the freshly-baked bread in the mornings. Working people were also consulted about other laws to improve working and living conditions, which gave them the confidence to insist that the rights of labour were equal to those of private property.

Inspired by the possibilities opened up by the Commune ordinary people in streets and neighbourhoods became involved in working for the community. People felt they were not wasted.

From 'The Paris Commune' by Mary Kennedy

Reflections

* 'The Commune gave a lot of ordinary citizens the confidence to do things together that they would never have dared to do before – or have been allowed to do.'

'People felt they were not wasted.'

Whenever we reflect on the question of what makes a successful community we might remember these words.

* In our own school community many individuals come together as a team to ensure a successful community: pupils, teachers, secretaries, kitchen staff, caretakers, bursars, gardeners, etc.

What lies at the heart of a flourishing community is the sense of mutual respect among all those within it. The ideal of 'community' is one worth striving for, even though at times we may feel it is hard to achieve.

2 'I Have a Dream'

Introduction

Certain individuals in history have had the ability to lead and inspire others in pursuit of an ideal about which they believed passionately. One such person was Dr Martin Luther King who felt that he would not rest until justice and equal rights for black people had been achieved in the United States of America.

In August 1963 he delivered a speech at a civil rights demonstration in Washington – a speech which stands as a compelling piece of oratory and as a testament to a civil rights leader whose commitment was to peaceful protest but who himself died by an assassin's bullet.

This is an extract from that speech – listen both to its content and its poetic style.

Reading

I have a dream

I am happy to join with you today in what will go down in history as the greatest demonstration for freedom in the history of our nation.

I am not unmindful that some of you have come here out of great trials and tribulations. Some of you have come fresh from narrow jail cells. Some of you have come from areas where your quest for freedom left you battered by the storms of persecution and staggered by the winds of police brutality. You have been the veterans of creative suffering. Continue to work with the faith that unearned suffering is redemptive.

Go back to Mississippi, go back to Alabama, go back to South Carolina, go back to Georgia, go back to Louisiana, go back to the slums and ghettos of our northern cities, knowing that somehow this situation can and will be changed. Let us not wallow in the valley of despair.

I say to you today, my friends, even though we face the difficulties of today and tomorrow, I still have a dream. It is a dream deeply rooted in the American dream.

I have a dream that one day this nation will rise up and live out the true meaning of its creed: 'We hold these truths to be self-evident: that all men are created equal.'

I have a dream that one day on the red hills of Georgia the sons of former slaves and the sons of former slaveowners will be able to sit down together at the table of brotherhood.

I have a dream that one day even the state of Mississippi, a state sweltering with the heat of injustice, sweltering with the heat of oppression, will be transformed into an oasis of freedom and justice.

I have a dream that my four little children will one day live in a nation where they will not be judged by the colour of their skin but by the content of their character.

I have a dream today.

I have a dream that one day down in Alabama with its vicious racists, with its governor having his lips dripping with the words of interposition and nullification, one day right there in Alabama little black boys and black girls will be able to join hands with little white boys and white girls as sisters and brothers.

I have a dream today.

I have a dream that one day every valley shall be exalted, every hill and mountain shall be made low, the rough places will be made plains, and the crooked places will be made straight, and the glory of the Lord shall be revealed, and all flesh shall see it together.

This is our hope. This is the faith that I go back to the South with. With this faith we will be able to hew out of the mountain of despair a stone of hope. With this faith we will be able to transform the jangling discords of our nation into a beautiful symphony of brotherhood. With this faith we will be able to work together, to pray together, to struggle together, to go to jail together, to stand up for freedom together, knowing that we will be free one day.

This will be the day when all of God's children will be able to sing with new meaning 'My country 'tis of thee, sweet land of liberty, of thee I sing. Land where my fathers died, land of the pilgrim's pride, from every mountainside, let freedom ring.'

And if America is to be a great nation this must become true. So let freedom ring from the prodigious hilltops of New Hampshire. Let freedom ring from the mighty mountains of New York. Let freedom ring from the heightening Alleghenies of Pennsylvania!

Let freedom ring from the snowcapped Rockies of Colorado! Let freedom ring from the curvaceous slopes of California! But not only that; let freedom ring from Stone Mountain of Georgia! Let freedom ring from Lookout Mountain of Tennessee. Let freedom ring from every hill and mole hill of Mississippi. From every mountainside, let freedom ring, and when this happens, when we allow freedom to ring, when we let it ring from every village and every hamlet, from every state and every city, we will be able to speed up that day when all of God's children, black men and white men, Jews and Gentiles, Protestants and Catholics, will be able to join hands and sing in the words of the old Negro spiritual, 'Free at last! Free at last! Thank God almighty, we are free at last!'

'I have a dream' Dr Martin Luther King

Reflections

* Speeches like these made Dr Martin Luther King one of the greatest leaders of the 20th century. His quest for justice – alongside the work of many other black leaders – led to changes in the law of the USA, to the point where segregation and discrimination on grounds of race or ethnic background were made illegal. He was later assassinated.

   Of course, just because something is made illegal doesn't mean it ends. And that's why ideals are important; they offer each generation something to aim for, even though it might not always be achieved.

In the USA and throughout the world today, groups of people go on seeking the ideal of justice in the way that Martin Luther King did so powerfully in the 1960s on behalf of black people.

3 Prison life

Introduction

'The mood and temper of the public in regard to the treatment of crime and criminals is one of the most unfailing tests of the civilisation of any country.'

These are the words of Winston Churchill, speaking in the House of Commons in 1910. In other words, he is saying that a test of how humane our society is rests with how we treat our criminals.

The subject of prisons and prisoners can be an emotive one.

There are many who believe that prison should be a harsh place because the people who are put there have done wrong against society. There are others who feel that prisons should be about reform and not just punishment.

There is no easy answer.

The following passage comes from a book on the subject of Prisons and Penal Reform. You will see that the author, Tessa Blackstone, is very critical of the conditions prisoners experience.

Reading

Conditions in prison

A visit to a closed prison for the first time is a deeply disturbing experience. It is an assault on the senses: the stench of stale cabbage; the banging of cell doors on the echoing landings; the sight of three men to a cell built for one; airlessness; clanking keys; flaking paint. The most pervasive impression of all derives not, however, from the deplorable physical conditions, but from the sense of hopeless inactivity. In no other human institution are people to be found in such large numbers doing nothing for such long stretches of time. Whether locked in their cells or out 'on association' there is an overwhelming sense of purposelessness and of enforced sloth amongst the inmates. These employed to guard them also appear to be victims of the system, giving the impression of spending much of their time standing around, with little sign of meaningful activity or communication with their charges.

There are two aspects of life in prison which will make future historians amazed that an otherwise tolerant and humane society could have shirked prison reform for so long. The first is the disgraceful squalor of the physical conditions; the second is the repressive nature of the regime. The buildings in which many prisons are housed are unfit to live in; they are dark, dismal, in a state of disrepair and, above all, insanitary. The practice of slopping out has been condemned as repulsive and degrading by every commentator and every authority from the Chief Inspector of Prisons to the Prison Officers' Association. It is remarkable that the government has concentrated so much investment in building 28 new prisons, with the result that slopping out will probably continue in the older ones into the next century. Slopping out in any form is indefensible; slopping out in the overcrowded conditions of three to a cell built for one is a denial of the most basic human privacy. The general lack of privacy, in which no man sharing a cell can ever be alone, is dehumanising. The restrictions on having baths or showers and the infrequent provision of changes of clothes, the lack of access to a lavatory, all contribute to the brutalising of prison inmates.

However, the daily regime to which prisoners are subjected is even more damaging than the physical conditions. Many prisoners are locked in their cells for hours at a stretch – in some cases for as much as 23 hours a day. Individuals who are a threat to society because of their violent and anti-social behaviour must expect to be denied their freedom. But locking them up in tiny cells is not the answer. Yet it happens – not just to this group, but to thousands of others who are no more than a nuisance to society. In local prisons and remand centres young men are cooped up with a couple of strangers, with grossly inadequate opportunities for exercise. It is hardly surprising that the atmosphere in overcrowded prisons can become explosive. Yet the Home Office has been singularly unsuccessful in redistributing prisoners from grossly overcrowded local prisons to other prisons where overcrowding is not a problem. Many prisons do not allow their inmates to eat in association. Instead they must take their food and eat it in their cells. It is shocking that this is happening even in young offenders' establishments. Boys of 17 and 18 already locked up for most of the day are shut up to eat, because this is easier to supervise.

Prisons ought to provide opportunities for education and training, which many offenders desperately need to help them obtain jobs when they are released. They ought to provide some challenge to prisoners to set themselves objectives, to master skills and to acquire new knowledge. Above all they should help prisoners become less dependent and more self-disciplined, and as a result acquire a more positive self-image. Most prisons fail hopelessly in this respect. Even young offenders sit idle in prisons where facilities have been provided. Feltham Young Offenders' Establishment, for example, is a new prison, with workshops and instructors. Its workshops have been empty for substantial periods whilst its instructors stand about waiting for 'clients'. Meanwhile under-educated and untrained youngsters are locked in their cells because of difficulties in deploying prison officers to oversee their periods in the workshop. It is a scandalous waste of human and physical resources.

Tessa Blackstone

Reflections

* This extract presents one point of view – what we might call a 'charter for reform'. But of course the prison service has to compete with other public services for government resources and our taxes. Schools, hospitals, prisons, roads, libraries – where would *you* spend more money?
This is not an easy question.
But Winston Churchill's words remain interesting ones to reflect on. Should a society be judged on the way it treats its criminals?
Certainly any community needs rules and regulations, guidelines and common expectations if it is to run smoothly in the interests of everyone. What *do* you do with the minority who 'break the rules'?

* *John 1: 5–10*
This is the message we have heard from him and declare to you: God is light; in him there is no darkness at all. If we claim to have fellowship with him yet walk in the darkness, we lie and do not live by the truth. But if we walk in the light, as he is in the light, we have fellowship with one another, and the blood of Jesus, his son, purifies us from all sin.

If we claim to be without sin, we deceive ourselves and the truth is not in us. If we confess our sins, he is faithful and just and will forgive us our sins and purify us from all unrighteousness. If we claim we have not sinned, we make him out to be a liar and his word has no place in our lives.

4 Individual versus society

Introduction

There is a difference in our society between *justice* and *law*. Laws are set down by Parliament. If you break them, then you are punished by the legal system and the courts.

But if you are wrongly accused of a crime then it seems as if natural justice is working against you.

What is the link between the law and justice?

Can society be more just with individuals who don't fit in to its normal rules and who fight against the system?

As the following reading suggests, we need to look at the problems presented by those people who fight against society's rules.

What follows is an interview between a man called Tony Parker – a researcher into prison life – and Ron, a prisoner in one of our psychiatric prisons, Grendon Underwood in Buckinghamshire.

Reading

The frying pan

– I'm going to ask you something which I don't want you to try and answer straight away; instead perhaps you'd think about it over the week-end on your own, preferably without discussing it with anyone else. Come back on Monday and tell me your answer. This is the question:

Imagine it's about a year after your present sentence, and you're in trouble again. You've been found guilty of yet another offence exactly similar in nature to those you've already committed in the past. Imagine also that I'm the Judge you're eventually brought in front of, and I then have the unavoidable duty of dealing with you. But when you appear in court I say 'I've no idea what to do with you at all: I can't see much point in sending you back to prison yet again, but on the other hand I can't think of any suitable alternative. So what I'm going to do is remand you in custody for forty-eight hours; in that time I'd like you to think about the situation, and then tell me yourself what you suggest I ought to do.'

In other words; if you do offend again, what sentence do you think should be passed on you?

Ron

I gave this a hell of a lot of thought. I felt I had to, that it was worth thinking about; if you like I felt it was the sort of thing I had to be made to think about. I'm afraid I haven't been able to come up with anything very bright in the way of a suggestion, except that you should send me back here to Grendon again for a further period of two years.

I don't see what else I could ask you to do in view of my condition of mind and my antecedents. If you let me off, I'd be straight back in trouble within a week, so you'd only be postponing the problem of dealing with me. Probation would be no good whatsoever: hell, I've already had five probations, I can't see that a sixth would stand much chance of changing me.

The thing is that I am going to be me until the day I die; and you simply can't tolerate me. By 'you' I mean society in general, not just you the Judge or you the person. Somehow or other as far as you're concerned. I've got to be taught to conform; and until you can find a way of doing it I'm going to go on making a bloody nuisance of myself.

How you could teach me. I don't know. One of the things I read in that definition of psychopaths was that they couldn't profit from experience, they couldn't be taught: the only hope for them was that one day they grew out of it. It was quite right as far as I'm concerned in another way too: when it said they always have done. I'd like to be able to say to you 'Please don't send me back to prison, put me in the care of someone who'll try and deal with me without taking me to court or punishing me or rejecting me.' But I couldn't honestly say if you did it would necessarily make any difference. It probably wouldn't because I'm lacking in something, I'm lacking in a feeling for other people just as a one-armed man is lacking a limb.

Why I should ask for Grendon rather than any other prison isn't just because it's more comfortable, but because I definitely do think they're on the right lines here. I wouldn't say it was anything like ideal, or that it couldn't be made ten times better. But at least in my opinion it's a place where you do get opportunities to give a bit of time to thinking about yourself and your problems and discussing them, instead of the insane wasting of time which goes on in other prisons, where the following of petty rules and regulations is the sole occupation of everyone concerned.

So that would be my answer. 'Give me some more of the same thing.'

Yet, as soon as I say that I realise the implication of what I'm saying. I'm asking you to keep me a prisoner, aren't I? Well I wish I could answer that. I think I must have a very deep sense of not really belonging outside in community at all. Imprisonment is a very dehumanising experience, it takes away your manhood and your sense of identity and everything; the more you have of it, the more dehumanised you become. I suppose that's why I'm now incapable of thinking properly about myself as a person, as an individual any more. Not that I'm saying I was much of one ever, so far as I can remember; I think there's always been something lacking, something that makes me think of other people in the same way as I think of myself: impersonally, not as individuals.

All this isn't much help to you, I'm afraid. But if you can ask me that question, as you can and did, perhaps I can ask you one too. In the same way I'll ask you to take it away and think about if after you've gone. You asked me what you should do with me: my answer boils down to 'I don't know. I think all you can do is give me the same treatment again until something changes.' But that something might not be in me after all: it might be I can't change ever. In that case I think I've a right to put the same question: are *you* going to change either, in your methods of trying to deal with me? Or are we both – me as an individual and you as society – approaching the whole thing in completely the wrong way?

From 'The Frying Pan' by Tony Parker

Reflections

* This passage offers us some interesting and difficult questions.
  What is justice?
  As a society, what should our response be to the prisoner Ron?
  'Are we both approaching the whole thing in completely the wrong way?' he asks.
  Very often in our daily lives we feel unhappy about the way we've been treated, especially if we believe we've been misjudged in some way.
  Natural justice as well as society's justice are vital aspects of our lives.
  As a society we need to think about justice as it affects all aspects of our home, school or workplace.
  Perhaps we should more often ask the question Tony Parker poses:
  'If you do offend again, what sentence do you think should be passed on you?'

* *Romans 2: 1–11*
  You therefore have no excuse, you who pass judgment on someone else, for at whatever point you judge the other, you are condemning yourself, because you who pass judgment do the same things. Now we know that God's judgment against those who do such things is based on truth. So when you, a mere man, pass judgment on them and yet do the same things, do you think you will escape God's judgment? Or do you show contempt for the riches of his kindness, tolerance and patience, not realising that God's kindness leads you towards repentance?
  But because of your stubbornness and your unrepentant heart, you are storing up wrath against yourself for the day of God's wrath, when his righteous judgment will be revealed. God 'will give to each person according to what he has done'. To those who by persistence in doing good seek glory, honour and immortality, he will give eternal life. But for those who are self-seeking and who reject the truth and follow evil, there will be wrath and anger. There will be trouble and distress for every human being who does evil, but glory, honour and peace for everyone who does good.

5 Leadership and vision

Introduction

'Where there is no vision, the people perish.' (*Proverbs*)

Throughout world history there have been leaders of people. Some have proved to be of very great good to those they've led and served. Others have been forces for terrible evil.

In January 1961 John Kennedy was sworn-in as President of the United States. At that time, the people of America had great hopes for his leadership and vision. The following comes from his speech to the nation in that January.

Reading

'My fellow Americans'

My fellow Americans. We observe today not a victory of party but a celebration of freedom, symbolizing an end as well as a beginning, signifying renewal as well as change. For I have sworn before you and Almighty God the same solemn oath our forebears prescribed nearly a century and three-quarters ago.

The world is very different now. For man holds in his mortal hands the power to abolish all forms of human poverty and all forms of human life. And yet the same revolutionary belief for which our forebears fought is still at issue around the globe, the belief that the rights of man come not from the generosity of the state but from the hand of God.

We dare not forget today that we are the heirs of that first revolution. Let the word go forth from this time and place, to friend and foe alike, that the torch has been passed to a new generation of Americans, born in this century, tempered by war, disciplined by a hard and bitter peace, proud of our ancient heritage, and unwilling to witness or permit the slow undoing of those human rights to which this nation has always been committed, and to which we are committed today at home and around the world.

Let every nation know, whether it wishes us well or ill, that we shall pay any price, bear any burden, meet any hardship, support any friend, oppose any foe to assure the survival and the success of liberty.

This much we pledge – and more.

To those old allies whose cultural and spiritual origins we share, we pledge the loyalty of faithful friends. United, there is little we cannot do in a host of cooperative ventures. Divided, there is little we can do, for we dare not meet a powerful challenge at odds and split asunder.

To those new states whom we welcome to the ranks of the free, we pledge our word that one form of colonial control shall not have passed away merely to be replaced by a far more iron tyranny. We shall not always expect to find them supporting our view. But we shall always hope to find them strongly supporting their own freedom, and to remember that, in the past, those who foolishly sought power by riding the back of the tiger ended up inside.

To those peoples in the huts and villages of half the globe struggling to break the bonds of mass misery, we pledge our best efforts to help them help themselves, for whatever period is required, not because the Communists may be doing it, not because we seek their votes, but because it is right. If a free society cannot help the many who are poor, it cannot save the few who are rich.

To our sister republics south of our border, we offer a special pledge: to convert our good words into good deeds, in a new alliance for progress, to assist free men and free governments in casting off the chains of poverty. But this peaceful revolution of hope cannot become the prey of hostile powers. Let all our neighbours know that we shall join with them to oppose aggression or subversion anywhere in the Americas. And let every other power know that this hemisphere intends to remain the master of its own house.

To that world assembly of sovereign states, the United Nations, our last best hope in an age where the instruments of war have far outpaced the instruments of peace, we renew our pledge of support: to prevent it from becoming merely a forum for invective, to strengthen its shield of the new and the weak, and to enlarge the area in which its writ may run.

Finally, to those nations who make themselves our adversary, we offer not a pledge but a request: that both sides begin anew the quest for peace, before the dark powers of destruction unleashed by science engulf all humanity in planned or accidental self-destruction.

All this will not be finished in the first one hundred days. Nor will it be finished in the first one thousand days, nor in the life of this Administration, nor even perhaps in our lifetime on this planet. But let it begin.

In your hands, my fellow citizens, more than mine, will rest the final success or failure of our course. Since this country was founded, each generation of Americans has been summoned to give testimony to its national loyalty. The graves of young Americans who answered the call to service surround the globe.

Now the trumpet summons us again – not as a call to bear arms, though arms we need; not as a call to battle, though embattled we are; but a call to bear the burden of a long twilight struggle, year in and year out, 'rejoicing in hope, patient in tribulation,' a struggle against the common enemies of man: tyranny, poverty, disease and war itself.

Can we forge against these enemies a grand and global alliance. North and South, East and West, that can assure a more fruitful life for all mankind? Will you join in that historic effort?

In the long history of the world, only a few generations have been granted the role of defending freedom in its hour of maximum danger. I do not shrink from this responsibility; I welcome it. I do not believe that any of us would exchange places with any other people or any other generation. The energy, the faith, the devotion which we bring to this endeavour will light our country and all who serve it, and the glow from that fire can truly light the world.

And so, my fellow Americans, ask not what your country can do for you; ask what you can do for your country.

My fellow citizens of the world, ask not what America will do for you, but what together we can do for the freedom of man.

Finally, whether you are citizens of America or citizens of the world, ask of us here the same high standards of strength and sacrifice which we ask of you. With a good conscience our only sure reward, with history the final judge of our deeds, let us go forth to lead the land we love, asking His blessing and His help, but knowing that here on earth God's work must truly be our own.

Reflections

* In this famous speech, President Kennedy was setting out his vision of America and its role in the world for the 1960s. Within three years he had been assassinated; the Americans had become involved in the Vietnam war, and there were serious tensions between Russia and America.

But although many of his ideals were not realised, President Kennedy is now thought of as a man of vision. In this speech, he was setting out ideals by which his fellow Americans could live.

In any community we need to have a vision, a common purpose and goals for people in their lives and work. In schools, we are quick to recognise and reward academic and sporting talent and achievements. But perhaps we don't recognise often enough those amongst us who can offer vision and leadership.

President Kennedy's words can be applied to any community:

'Ask not what your country can do for you; ask what you can do for your country.'

6 Political prisoners (1)

Introduction

What is a prisoner of conscience? A prisoner of conscience is a man, woman or child detained because of their beliefs, colour, sex, ethnic origin, language or religion – a person who has neither used nor advocated violence.

As a Russian political prisoner once wrote:

'The first and most important Right, or rather, obligation to ourselves, is to stand by one's convictions. I'm frightened of prison, of camps, of lunatic asylums . . . but I'm more frightened of lies, base behaviour and my own participation in either of these, than of any prison. I'm not ashamed to be called a prisoner.'

Around the world many thousands of people are imprisoned, not because they have committed a crime as we recognise crime, but because of their beliefs. The following case-studies come from Amnesty International, the organisation that exists to help prisoners of conscience.

Reading

'Prisoners of conscience'

Safia Hashi Madar
Somalia
Age: 28
Status: Divorced with 2 children
Profession: Biochemist
Sentence: Life
Prison: Mogadishu Central Prison
Health: Very bad

Safia Hashi Madar was 9 months pregnant when, in July 1985, police broke into her house and took her away to the headquarters of the infamous National Security Service. There she was interrogated about possible links with the Somali National Movement which leads the armed opposition to the government of President Barre and put into a cell. Arrests of this kind are frequent in Somalia.

Next day, she gave birth to a boy, who was taken away from her immediately. She has not seen him since. In the months that followed she was tortured and raped.

After 10 months she was brought before a National Security Court and given a life sentence – in Somalia this means until death – for belonging to a subversive organisation. Her husband has divorced her; one of her brothers has been killed and others are either in prison or abroad. She is now ill herself, with kidney disease, acute toothache, severe malnourishment and depression.

Soh Sung
South Korea
Age: 43
Status: Single
Profession: Student
Sentence: Life imprisonment
Prison: Taejon Prison
Health: Severely disfigured after a suicide attempt

Soh Sung, the son of a pedlar who emigrated to Japan when Korea was under Japanese colonial control, has been in a South Korean prison for the last 17 years. He was a student at Seoul University when, in 1971, at a time of widespread student demonstrations against the way the presidential elections were being conducted, he was arrested and charged with spying for North Korea, and organising student demonstrations.

At his trial, despite his claim that his 'confession' had obviously been extracted under torture, Soh Sung was sentenced to death. This was later commuted to life imprisonment. He has always denied all the charges against him.

Soh Sung is now 43. He does not believe that he will ever be freed. During a suicide attempt he set fire to himself and is now severely disfigured – so scarred in fact that he thinks that no South Korean Government would ever dare to release him.

Xu Wenli
China
Age: 43
Status: Married with one daughter
Profession: Electrician and editor
Sentence: 15 years imprisonment
Prison: Beijing Prison No. 1
Health: Not known

Xu Wenli, who is an electrician by trade, was the editor and founder of several unofficial journals when, in 1981, he was arrested and accused of carrying out 'counter-revolutionary incitement and propaganda.' After being held incommunicado, and continually interrogated for 15 months, he was tried and sentenced to 15 years in jail. The Chinese authorities deny the existence of any prisoner of conscience, but admit to holding people they call 'counter-revolutionary.'

During the months that followed his trial, Xu Wenli wrote a secret journal describing what had happened to him. He called it 'My self defence.' When, late in 1985, it began circulating outside China, the authorities punished Xu Wenli by putting him in an underground windowless cell, cutting his rations, and taking his books away from him.

Alaattin Sahin
Turkey
Age: 40
Status: Single
Profession: Journalist
Sentence: 36 years
Prison: Canakkale, on the Dardanelles
Health: Not known

During the 1970s a large number of left-wing political groups in Turkey started producing their own newspapers and journals. In the months leading up to the coup of 1980, and immediately following it, editors and journalists on these papers were arrested. Alaattin Sahin, who was working on one of them, was also a member of the Turkish Workers' and Peasants' Party, which strongly opposed the political violence of the time.

Arrested four months before the coup, he was charged with making communist propaganda, insulting the authorities and inciting others to commit crimes. The result was a total prison sentence of 130 years – reduced to 36 on appeal – which he is serving in a special prison for political detainees. Some of the longest sentences imposed since the coup have been on journalists and editors.

Reflections

* Our thoughts and prayers extend to prisoners of conscience – wherever they may be. The following words are a reminder to free people everywhere that prisoners of conscience should never be forgotten.

First they came for the Jews
and I did not speak out
because I was not a Jew.

Then they came for the communists
and I did not speak out
because I was not a communist.

Then they came for the trade unionists
and I did not speak out
because I was not a trade unionist.

Then they came for me –
and there was no one left
to speak out for me.

Pastor Martin Niemoller

* And these are the words of the political hostage Terry Waite in 1991. He had been imprisoned for 1,763 days with a group of other hostages.
'I'll tell you a small story which I told in Damascus. I was kept in total and complete isolation for four years. I saw no one and spoke to no one apart from a cursory word with my guards when they brought me food.
And one day out of the blue a guard came with a postcard. It was a postcard showing a stained glass window from Bedford showing John Bunyan in jail.
And I looked at that card and I thought, 'My word Bunyan you're a lucky fellow. You've got a window out of which you can look, see the sky and here am I in a dark room. You've got pen and ink, you can write but here am I, I've got nothing and you've got your own clothes and a table and a chair'.
And I turned the card over and there was a message from someone whom I didn't know simply saying, 'We remember, we shall not forget. We shall continue to pray for you and to work for all people who are detained around the world'.
I can tell you, that thought, that sent me back to the marvellous work of agencies like Amnesty International and their letter-writing campaigns and I would say never despise those simple actions.

Something, somewhere will get through to the people you are concerned about as it got through to my fellows eventually.'

7 Political prisoners (2)*

Introduction

The Universal Declaration of Human Rights was proclaimed by all members of the United Nations in 1948. The Declaration set out what were then agreed to be the basic human rights to which every human being should be entitled. These included the right to freedom of conscience, expression and association; freedom from arbitrary arrests and torture or ill treatment; and the right to a fair and early trial.

A half-century later we still have a long way to go before the Declaration is universally upheld. Listen to the following disturbing account of life in a South African jail, in which this author was held for seven years for having political views opposed to those of the State.

Reading

Bandiet

Hangings usually took place on Tuesdays and Thursdays. We lined up as we did every day in the sections after breakfast, four-by-four, waiting for the instruction to march off. On Tuesdays or Thursdays – sometimes both days – there would be a delay, some minutes extra for you to chew on a final piece of breakfast katkop, to try to catch an extra puff or two in cupped hands, hiding behind the back of the man in front and waving your hand to disperse the smoke so that no wandering boer would see. Then off, two-by-two, through the Hall in silence, out through the C group yard and along to the B group yard, the long sandy yard with the line of boere across the near end, waiting to search you. And after the search you line up at the far end of the yard, four-by-four again, in teams, a team for every workshop.

On your left, as you stand facing the end of the soccer yard, is a high wall. On your right is the tall length of A section, three storeys of sheer wall with its three rows of window after barred window. In front of you, as you stand waiting in the soccer yard, is a tall two-and-a-half-storey building: roof and fanlight atop two-and-a-half solid storeys of windowless wall. No windows looking out of the gallows. You stand in the soccer yard, each morning, facing the wall of the gallows, waiting to lead off through to the workshops.

You go from the soccer yard up some steps and through a gate in the wall at the side of the tall gallows building. Two boere stand counting as you go through the gate into the short passage, then left up some more steps and out through large double doors, out into the inner road which runs the length of the workshops. On your right as you go through the first gate is a flight of steps, steps leading down to a single door, one door at the bottom of the tall building but no windows at all in that building, where the gallows are. Opposite the steps, immediately on your left as you go through the first gate, is a small room with a door and windows. The door on the right, at the bottom of the steps, and the door and windows on the left, are usually shut as you go through to the workshops.

On Tuesdays and Thursdays, after the unusual delay in the section after breakfast, you come through into the soccer yard and stand waiting in teams. The gate
ahead – the gate next to the wall of the gallows building – is shut. You stand,
silently waiting. The workshop boere, in their overalls, stand waiting too, silently watching to see that you stay silent. You can hear knocking. From behind the
wall ahead, the wall beside the gallows, you can hear a distant knocking. You
stand in the soccer yard in the early morning and hear knocking. Sometimes a
prolonged knocking, sometimes not much knocking – as they put on the coffin
lids.

The small room on the left as you go through the gate is the laying-out room.
The bodies are brought through the door on the right, up the steps and across the
passage-way into the small room on the left, and into the coffins.

You don't see any of that, waiting in the soccer yard. All you see is the locked
door in the wall. And you hear the knocking of the coffin lids being put on. Then
there's a long silence, broken sometimes by the distant sound of a truck pulling off,
or by a boer ahead opening a gate and peering through, and coming back to wait
until it's all right for us to walk through to the shops. Until everything's been
cleared up and finished.

Then you're marched off, two-by-two, up through the door in the wall and along
the short passage on the other side, past the steps going down on the right and the
small room on the left, and through the large double gates leading to the workshops.

Once – it was early in May, I remember – we were kept waiting a particularly
long time, and there had been considerable knocking. I glanced into the small
room on the left as we went past. The windows that were usually shut were open.
Inside was a table, like an operating table, flat and hard. On it lay a pair of khaki
shorts, the short khaki shorts worn by African bandiete. That day, said one of
young boere in the shop, they hanged six of them at the same time. That was why
we had waited so long in the yard. Six at once, he said. The man who does it, he
said, is very good with them: he puts the blindfolds on quickly and easily and talks
to them all the time and pulls the lever without the guy even really knowing it's
going to happen when it does happen. They go all right like that, he said. Sometimes
– not every week – there's sawdust scattered on the pathway between the door on
the right and the room on the left. Sometimes there was not enough sawdust to
cover the dark marks on the ground. Why sawdust, I asked. For the blood, explained one of the young workshop boere. There's often lots of blood at a hanging,
he said. It comes from all over the place. When they hang women, he said, they
have to strap them up between the legs beforehand. They scatter sawdust on the
ground so that on your way to the shops you don't step in the blood from the
bodies on their way to the coffins.

One day at the shops – on a morning in the week when we had waited in the
soccer yard – another of the young shop boere came in looking grim. He was
normally a sunny sort of person and spent quite a while every day chatting to
Jackie and me in our welding bay. This day he looked bad, green about the gills.
We laughed at him, joked, and made some remark about people who came to
work with hang-overs. He had been to his first hanging. Every warder is required,
at least once, to attend a hanging. This was Henning's first. He said he didn't want
to see another. There was this guy, this kaffir, who was hanged and the rope sort
of came up and pulled his face off. His whole face sort of came off. All the skin
from his chin upwards was up over his nose. All the blood around and everything.

They leave them hanging for twenty minutes to see that they're dead. It's all a hell of a mess, said Henning. He didn't want to see another one like that.

From 'Bandiet' by Hugh Lewin

Reflections

* Despite the promises that governments made in signing the Declaration of Human Rights, in perhaps half the countries of the world people are locked away for speaking their minds, often after trials that are no more than a sham; and in many of the world's nations, men, women and children are tortured or ill-treated.

* Our prayers and thoughts are with them.

Our Father in heaven,
hallowed be your name,
your kingdom come,
your will be done
on earth as it is in heaven.
Give us today our daily bread.
Forgive us our debts,
as we also have forgiven our debtors.
And lead us not into temptation,
but deliver us from the evil one: for
yours is the kingdom and the
power and the glory for ever.
Amen

8 Ideas and ideals

Introduction

What is an 'idea'? What is an 'ideal'? What's the difference? One dictionary definition of 'idea' is: 'a belief or viewpoint or opinion'. In contrast 'ideal' is defined as: 'a conception of something that is perfect.'

In other words the word 'ideal' suggests something which is much harder to secure or attain, because it is the perfection of an idea.

Can you think of your own ideas, as distinct from any 'ideals' you might have?

Nelson Mandela is recognised to be a man of ideas and ideals.

Back in 1964 he was imprisoned for the ideas he held about the interests of Africans in South Africa. In this final speech of defence from the dock he also set forth his *ideals* for a free South Africa.

Reading

Evidence from the Dock

The lack of human dignity experienced by Africans is the direct result of the policy of white supremacy. White supremacy implies black inferiority. Legislation designed to preserve white supremacy entrenches this notion. Menial tasks in South Africa are invariably performed by Africans. When anything has to be carried or cleaned, the white man will look around for an African to do it for him, whether the

African is employed by him or not. Because of this sort of attitude, whites tend to regard Africans as a separate breed. They do not look upon them as people with families of their own; they do not realise that they have emotions – that they fall in love like white people do; that they want to be with their wives and children like white people want to be with theirs; that they want to earn enough money to support their families properly, to feed and clothe them and send them to school. And what 'house-boy' or 'garden-boy' or labourer can ever hope to do this?

Pass laws, which to the Africans are among the most hated bits of legislation in South Africa, render any African liable to police surveillance at any time. I doubt whether there is a single African male in South Africa who has not at some stage had a brush with the police over his pass. Hundreds and thousands of Africans are thrown into gaol each year under pass laws. Even worse than this is the fact that pass laws keep husband and wife apart and lead to the breakdown of family life.

Poverty and the breakdown of family life have secondary effects. Children wander about the streets of the townships because they have no schools to go to, or no money to enable them to go to school, or no parents at home to see that they go to school, because both parents (if there be two) have to work to keep the family alive. This leads to a breakdown in moral standards, to an alarming rise in illegitimacy and to growing violence which erupts, not only politically, but everywhere. Life in the townships is dangerous. There is not a day that goes by without somebody being stabbed or assaulted. And violence is carried out of the townships into the white living areas. People are afraid to walk alone in the streets after dark. Housebreakings and robberies are increasing, despite the fact that the death sentence can now be imposed for such offences. Death sentences cannot cure the festering sore.

Africans want to be paid a living wage. Africans want to perform work which they are capable of doing, and not work which the Government declares them to be capable of. Africans want to be allowed to live where they obtain work, and not be 'endorsed out' of an area because they were not born there. Africans want to be allowed to own land in places where they work, and not to be obliged to live in rented houses which they can never call their own. Africans want to be part of the general population, and not be confined to living in their ghettos. African men want to have their wives and children to live with them where they work, and not be forced into an unnatural existence in men's hostels. African women want to be with their men folk and not be left permanently widowed in the tribal reserves. Africans want to be allowed out after 11 o'clock at night and not be confined to their rooms like little children. Africans want to be allowed to travel in their own country and to seek work where they want to and not where the Labour Bureau tells them to. Africans want a just share in the whole of South Africa; they want security and a stake in society.

Above all, we want equal political rights, because without them our disabilities will be permanent. I know this sounds revolutionary to the whites in this country, because the majority of the voters will be Africans. This makes the white men fear democracy.

But this fear cannot be allowed to stand in the way of the only solution which will guarantee racial harmony and freedom for all. It is not true that the enfranchisement of all will result in racial domination. Political division, based on colour, is entirely artificial and, when it disappears, so will the domination of one colour group by another. The African National Congress has spent half a century fighting against racialism. When it triumphs, it will not change that policy.

This then is what the African National Congress is fighting for. Their struggle is truly a national one. It is a struggle of the African people, inspired by their own suffering and their own experience. It is a struggle for the right to live.

During my lifetime I have dedicated myself to this struggle of the African people. I have fought against white domination, and I have fought against black domination. I have cherished the ideal of a democratic and free society in which all persons live together in harmony and with equal opportunities. It is an ideal which I hope to live for and to achieve. But if need be, it is an ideal for which I am prepared to die.

From 'Evidence from the Dock' by Nelson Mandela

Reflections

* After 25 years in prison Nelson Mandela was released, never having forgotten those final words about being prepared to die for the ideal of equal opportunities. A man of ideas and ideals, he has become a symbol of freedom in the 20th century.

* Ideas are important to us in our daily lives – they are interesting to play with in learning and can be exciting when we debate them with other people. Ideas are viewpoints. But *ideals* take the human spirit further, in search of perfection. Because we are human we never quite achieve our ideals, but we need them to guide us. It's important never to lose sight of our ideals.

9 Equal before the Law

Introduction

What do you understand to be the difference between 'justice' and 'the law'? Can you think of examples where they are and are not the same thing? For example, what about a case of wrongful imprisonment – is 'justice' or 'the law' weakened in such a case?

Countries with an established judicial system pride themselves on the fact that all people are equal before the law. The problem comes if ever someone appears to be *more* equal than others.

The following reading is taken from the novel *To Kill A Mockingbird* by Harper Lee. It is set in Alabama in the 1930s, where a black worker – Tom Robinson – is accused of raping a white girl, Mayella Ewell. Atticus Finch, a lawyer, decides to take on the accused's defence in a climate of local hostility. These events lie at the heart of the novel.

In this extract Tom Robinson's trial has reached its climax; Atticus Finch is summarising his defence case for the jury.

Reading

To kill a mockingbird

'And so a quiet, respectable, humble Negro who had the unmitigated temerity to 'feel sorry' for a white woman has had to put his word against two white people's. I need not remind you of their appearance and conduct on the stand – you saw them for yourselves. The witnesses for the state, with the exception of the sheriff of Maycomb County, have presented themselves to you gentlemen, to this court, in the cynical confidence that their testimony would not be doubted, confident that you gentlemen would go along with them on the assumption – the evil assumption – that *all* Negroes lie, that *all* Negroes are basically immoral beings, that *all* Negro men are not to be trusted around our women, an assumption one associates with minds of their calibre.

'Which, gentlemen, we know is in itself a lie as black as Tom Robinson's skin, a lie I do not have to point out to you. You know the truth, and the truth is this: some Negroes lie, some Negroes are immoral, some Negro men are not to be trusted around women – black or white. But this is a truth that applies to the human race and to no particular race of men. There is not a person in this court-room who has never told a lie, who has never done an immoral thing, and there is no man living who has never looked upon a woman with desire.'

Atticus paused and took out his handkerchief. Then he took off his glasses and wiped them, and we saw another 'first': we had never seen him sweat – he was one of those men whose faces never perspired, but now it was shining tan.

'One more thing, gentlemen, before I quit. Thomas Jefferson once said that all men are created equal, a phrase that the Yankees and the distaff side of the Executive branch in Washington are fond of hurling at us. There is a tendency in this year of grace 1935 for certain people to use this phrase out of context, to satisfy all conditions. The most ridiculous example I can think of is that the people who run public education promote the stupid and idle along with the industrious – because all men are created equal, educators will gravely tell you, the children left behind suffer terrible feelings of inferiority. We know all men are not created equal in the sense some people would have us believe – some people are smarter than others, some people have more opportunity because they're born with it, some men make more money than others, some ladies make better cakes than others – some people are born gifted beyond the normal scope of most men.

'But there is one way in this country in which all men are created equal – there is one human institution that makes a pauper the equal of a Rockefeller, the stupid man the equal of an Einstein, and the ignorant man the equal of any college president. That institution, gentlemen, is a court. It can be the Supreme Court of the United States or the humblest J P court in the land, or this honourable court which you serve. Our courts have their faults, as does any human institution, but in this country our courts are the great levellers, and in our courts all men are created equal.

'I'm no idealist to believe firmly in the integrity of our courts and in the jury system – that is no ideal to me, it is a living, working reality. Gentlemen, a court is no better than each man of you sitting before me on this jury. A court is only as sound as its jury, and a jury is only as sound as the men who make it up. I am confident that you gentlemen will review without passion the evidence you have heard, come to a decision, and restore this defendant to his family. In the name of God, do your duty.'

From 'To Kill a Mockingbird' by Harper Lee

Reflections

* If you want to find out the verdict and what subsequently happens to Tom Robinson, read the novel.

What this memorable passage brings out is the issue of equality for all before the law. In 1940s Alabama, as Atticus Finch realises, equality could not be taken for granted. It had to be fought for.

We need to value the ideal of equality in law. Such an ideal lies at the heart of a safe and democratic society. And where we see the Law being enforced at the expense of justice, questions should always be asked.

* At the end of George Orwell's famous novel *Animal Farm* when the pigs have taken over from the humans and are running the farm on behalf of the other animals, we learn that justice and the law have been corrupted by the pigs. They create a single commandment for the running of the farm: 'All animals are equal, but some animals are more equal than others'.

In this case, the principle of equality before the law has been sadly lost.

10 Animal Rights

Introduction

A subject which concerns many people is that of animal rights. As human beings we believe strongly in our rights and go to great lengths to defend them. But do we treat other members of the animal kingdom with the dignity they deserve? What about fieldsports and bloodsports?

Listen to the following passage which clearly expresses the view that we do not treat animals at all well. Then we'll hear a poem which offers a slightly different viewpoint.

Reading

Animal Rights

Many people in the so-called civilised western world are by no means happy about the conditions under which our food is produced. Factory farming proves to be a very profitable business which offers more freedom, less responsibility and a much shorter working week. In Britain, a farmer can do much as he pleases with his animals, and the police and RSPCA inspectors cannot be in every field or barn to watch what he does with his own property . . . Factory farming enables just one person to look after ten thousand hens in a battery house which is fully automatic. Food is measured, each bird getting just the correct amount, the eggs are clean, uniform and unbroken. There is some wastage among birds, which have become virtually egg-laying machines, but the production numbers are so enormous and the turnover so fast that a certain percentage of birds are expendable. In order to turn hens into even more efficient laying-machines, wings are cut to save space in the battery system cages, and beaks are cut to avoid feather picking and cannibalism (brought on by boredom and immobility).

Pigs are kept in similar disgusting, inhuman conditions. One person can feed, water and clean out hundreds of pigs, which in old-type houses with outside runs would be impossible. The pigs convert their food to pork or bacon at an economic ratio. The food conversion can be controlled, and the pig can be graded at just the desired weight required by the market. The pigs know no change of atmosphere and at birth are liable to iron deficiency. It is cruel to keep pigs in a temperature of eighty degrees and to limit their movements. A pig born into a factory farm can never experience the freedom to roam about, no, this luxury is impossible because pigs are practically immobilised from birth to the bacon factory. Some American farmers, however, do not even wait for the moment of birth, because hysterectomy is now widely practised in the United States of America. The whole uterus is removed from the sow with piglets inside it, and they are then kept in sterile incubators to form the basis of disease-free herds, perfect for human consumption.

It could be said that the worst aspect of battery farming lies in some of the production of battery veal. Calves are taken from their mothers at birth and are then immobilised either by tethering or by being put into crates. The aim is to keep them anaemic so that the whitest possible meat can be produced. The calves are unable to groom themselves and are kept on slatted floors which are extremely uncomfortable for cloven-hoofed animals and result in deformed and swollen joints. These calves are given a maximum of fifteen weeks to live. After this the extreme anaemia introduced by the way of living and diet would cause death in any case, if they were not slaughtered first. Antibiotics as an aid to growth and to prevent an early death are also frequently employed.

Those who defend these inhuman methods point out that the animals are quite happy – they eat well, and either lay well or put on weight, and this is supposed to be an indication of the lack of cruelty. Unhappy animals, it is argued, would not respond in these ways. I do not think that this is a conclusive argument at all. In my opinion it is a pathetic attempt to justify cruelty.

Tanya Nyari

The Early Purges

I was six when I first saw kittens drown.
Dan Taggart pitched them, 'the scraggy wee shits',
Into a bucket; a frail metal sound,

Soft paws scraping like mad. But their tiny din
Was soon soused. They were slung on the snout
Of the pump and the water pumped in.

'Sure isn't it better for them now?' Dan said.
Like wet gloves they bobbed and shone till he sluiced
Them out on the dunghill, glossy and dead.

Suddenly frightened, for days I sadly hung
Round the yard, watching the three sogged remains
Turn mealy and crisp as old summer dung

Until I forgot them. But the fear came back
When Dan trapped big rats, snared rabbits, shot crows
Or, with a sickening tug, pulled old hens' necks.

Still, living displaces false sentiments
And now, when shrill pups are prodded to drown
I just shrug, 'Bloody pups'. It makes sense:

'Prevention of cruelty' talk cuts ice in town
When they consider death unnatural,
But on well-run farms pests have to be kept down.

Seamus Heaney

Reflections

* What rights do you believe animals have?
  Can or should anything be done to prevent the sort of farming practices described in the first passage?
  Do you agree with the poet that 'pests have to be kept down' and that 'living displaces false sentiments'?
  The topic of animal rights is a live one in society today as more and more people become aware of wider environmental issues. In some contexts, we hear of people taking quite extreme actions to liberate animals which are kept in captivity for experimentation or intensive farming. As with all controversial subjects, we have a duty to inform ourselves as fully as possible – through reading, watching television programmes and discussion – before we reach conclusions and make judgments. *Simple* answers to complex questions are often the wrong ones!

11 Holy Wars

Introduction

Throughout history wars have been fought over religion. Both sides claim that God is on their side and that their cause is just. Sometimes both sides are fighting in the name of the same God – there have been many wars between Protestant and Catholic, although both are Christians.

Religious wars often seem to inspire young, idealistic soldiers (boys and girls) who are prepared to fight and die for their faith.

The following poem sharply captures the fanaticism of a Holy War. It was written by a 15-year-old Syrian student.

Reading

Unsung heroes called fanatics

Ten thousand men would gather there
Each Friday until late
To hear the Imam's fiery tongue
Stir up their blood and hate

'Our faith is like a tree,' he'd say,
'Don't think that I am wrong.
The flowing blood of martyred mess
Will make its boughs grow strong.'

His speeches were hypnotic drugs,
His war was being fought,
His words made men lay down their lives,
Without a second thought.

Not only men would listen there,
But often children too,

Young boys of less than seventeen,
For whom the words rang true.

So to the schools the soldiers went,
To see if they could try
To find some boys to volunteer
To come with them to die

And from a school of eighty boys
Baseej weren't hard to find,
And when the trucks left the gate
Not one was left behind.

So through the desert sands they drove,
Beneath the scorching sun.
Each boy dressed in a uniform,
Each carrying a gun.

Each boy received a plastic key,
And learnt you can't live twice.
But if you're killed, the key'd unlock
The gates of paradise.

Their trainer said, 'This war's Sihad,'
A cold, powerful voice,
'That means it's a holy war,
And so you have no choice.'

Then eighty figures all knelt down
To face the holy city
And each boy prayed as he knelt down
For Allah's peace and pity.

The desert night was quiet,
The morning silent too,
The slaughter when would it commence?
Only the Generals knew.

At last the final order came:
'Tomorrow's the big day,
So clean your weapons, little ones
And for the last time pray.'

Some boys died in the minefields
The others in their trench.
Pathetic torn bodies,
The battle's sickly stench.

All eighty school boys died that day
All eighty eighties more.
Whilst in their bunkers
Priest and despot added to their scores.

That day no positions were seized,
But neither were they lost.

The Generals plan a new campaign,
The mothers count the cost.

Yet on the streets and in the mosques
They'll recruit many more.
Their slogans: If it lasts for twenty years,
We'll fight our holy war.

For five years now the blood has flowed.
No sign that it will stop.
The worst crime of the whole thing is
That both sides fight for God.

Darius Bazergan

Reflections

* 'The worst crime of the whole thing is
  That both sides fight for God.'
  These closing lines focus on the horrid futility of a Holy War.
  The second verse, with its talk of 'martyred mess' emphasises how vital and
  unavoidable war is in the eyes of the religious leaders.
  The poem also brings out the unquestioning involvement of schoolboys, prepared to sacrifice themselves for what they see as a holy cause. It is difficult for
  non-believers to understand this fanaticism, yet it has been a feature of holy wars
  throughout history. During the Crusades, even young children were prepared to
  march to the Holy Land to fight the Turks.
  Although we may try to understand why people are prepared to die for their
  ideals, we can probably never persuade them that war is not right, if they see it
  as the only way to secure justice.

* Our prayers and thoughts should extend to all – soldiers and civilians – who are
  caught up in Holy Wars.

12 Persecution

Introduction
When people stand up to be counted for an ideal in which they passionately
believe, they are likely to face opposition. In a civilised country, argument and
debate will follow and, if some kind of judgment is needed, then the legal framework
of courts and lawyers will try to resolve the issue.

On a broader front, when whole peoples rise up in defence of an ideal – say for
the survival of their territory – they may well be opposed with military force. And
once that military force gains the upper hand, persecution often follows. We see
this around the world today where minorities are persecuted by majorities. In the
1930s in Germany the Nazi persecution of the Jews led them to flee to other
countries or sent them into hiding. And those who did not escape died in Nazi
concentration camps. One victim of Nazi persecution was Anne Frank, a girl who
went into hiding with her family and who kept a diary all about those years of

suffering. She later died in a German concentration camp, but *The Diary of Anne Frank* remains to this day one of the most powerful accounts of what it is to be the victim of relentless persecution.

Reading

The Diary of Anne Frank

Saturday, 20th June, 1942

I haven't written for a few days, because I wanted first of all to think about my diary. It's an odd idea for someone like me to keep a diary; not only because I have never done so before, but because it seems to me that neither I – nor for that matter anyone else – will be interested in the unbosomings of a thirteen-year-old schoolgirl. Still, what does that matter? I want to write, but more than that, I want to bring out all kinds of things that lie buried deep in my heart. There is a saying that 'paper is more patient than man'; it came back to me on one of my slightly melancholy days, while I sat chin in hand, feeling too bored and limp even to make up my mind whether to go out or to stay at home. Yes, there is no doubt that paper is patient and as I don't intend to show this cardboard-covered notebook, bearing the proud name of 'diary', to anyone, unless I find a real friend, boy or girl, probably nobody cares. And now I come to the root of the matter, the reason for my starting a diary: it is that I have no such real friend.

Let me put it more clearly, since no one will believe that a girl of thirteen feels herself quite alone in the world, nor is it so. I have darling parents and a sister of sixteen. I know about thirty people whom one might call friends – I have strings of boy friends, anxious to catch a glimpse of me and who, failing that, peep at me through mirrors in class. I have relations, aunts and uncles, who are darlings too, a good home, no – I don't seem to lack anything. But it's the same with all my friends, just fun and games, nothing more. I can never bring myself to talk of anything outside the common round. We don't seem to be able to get any closer, that is the root of the trouble. Perhaps I lack confidence, but anyway, there it is, a stubborn fact and I don't seem to be able to do anything about it. Hence, this diary. In order to enhance in my mind's eye the picture of the friend for whom I have waited so long, I don't want to set down a series of bald facts in a diary like most people do, but I want this diary itself to be my friend, and I shall call my friend Kitty. No one will grasp what I'm talking about if I begin my letters to Kitty just out of the blue, so, albeit unwillingly, I will start by sketching in brief the story of my life.

My father was 36 when he married my mother, who was then 25. My sister Margot was born in 1926 in Frankfort on-Main. I followed on 12th June, 1929 and, as we are Jewish, we emigrated to Holland in 1933, where my father was appointed Managing Director of Travie N.V. This firm is in close relationship with the firm of Kolen & Co. in the same building, of which my father is a partner.

The rest of our family, however, felt the full impact of Hitler's anti-Jewish laws so life was filled with anxiety. In 1938 after the pogroms, my two uncles (my mother's brothers) escaped to the US. My old grandmother came to us, she was then 73. After May, 1940, good times rapidly fled: first the war, then the capitulation, followed by the arrival of the Germans. That is when the sufferings of us Jews really began. And Jewish decrees followed each other in quick succession. Jews must wear a yellow star, Jews must hand in their bicycles, Jews are banned from trams and are forbidden to drive. Jews are only allowed to do their shopping between three and five o'clock and then only in shops which bear the placard 'Jewish shop'. Jews must be indoors by eight o'clock and cannot even sit in their own gardens after that hour. Jews are forbidden to visit theatres, cinemas, and other places of entertainment. Jews may not take part in public sports. Swimming baths, tennis courts, hockey fields, and other sports grounds are all prohibited to them. Jews may not visit Christians. Jews must go to Jewish schools and many more restrictions of a similar kind.

So we could not do this and were forbidden to do that. But life went on in spite of it all. Jopie used to say to me: 'You're scared to do anything. because it may be forbidden.' Our freedom was strictly limited. Yet things were still bearable.

From 'The Diary of Anne Frank'

Reflections

* Here we see Anne cut off from her friends but using the Diary as her companion, with whom she could share her feelings. What shines through her writing is the sense of optimism that, though she and her family are in hiding and having to live very cramped lives, things would eventually turn out well: the belief that life is bearable even under difficult conditions *because* deep down there is a belief in the ideal of justice.
  As she concludes: 'Our freedom was strictly limited. Yet things were still bearable.'

* In schools we may encounter persecution in other forms – victimisation or bullying. Bullying harms the victim, and it can also damage the bully, as a person. We all need to look out for this kind of persecution and try to expose it.

* Persecution of any kind – verbal, mental or physical – has no place in a caring and civilised community, as Anne Frank's moving Diary should always remind us.

* *Corinthians I, 13: 11–13*
  When I was a child, I talked like a child, I thought like a child, I reasoned like a child. When I became a man, I put childish ways behind me. Now we see but a poor reflection as in a mirror; then we shall see face to face. Now I know in part; then I shall know fully, even as I am fully known. And now these three remain: faith, hope and love. But the greatest of these is love.

The Media

1 The world of Doublespeak*

Introduction

Language is power. It is our major means of communication as human beings. We can use it to tell the truth or to lie; to be honest with a friend, or dishonest; to be pleasant or unpleasant – and so on. In the hands of the media – television, film, newspapers – words are manipulated with equal power, accompanied by still or moving images. One of the developments of recent years has been the emergence of what is sometimes called 'Doublespeak', language which makes the bad seem good, the negative appear positive.

Listen to the following fascinating essay by American journalist William Lutz.

Reading

The world of Doublespeak

Farmers no longer have cows, pigs, chickens, or other animals on their farms; according to the US Department of Agriculture farmers have 'grain-consuming animal units' (which are kept in 'single-purpose agricultural structures,' not pig pens and chicken coops). Attentive observers of the English language also learned recently that the multibillion dollar stock market crash of 1987 was simply a 'fourth quarter equity retreat'; that airplanes don't crash, they just have 'uncontrolled contact with the ground'; that janitors are really 'environmental technicians'; that it was a 'diagnostic misadventure of a high magnitude' which caused the death of a patient in a Philadelphia hospital, not medical malpractice; and that the President wasn't really unconscious while he underwent minor surgery, he was just in a 'non-decision-making form.' In other words, doublespeak continues to spread as the official language of public discourse.

Doublespeak is a blanket term for language which pretends to communicate but doesn't, language which makes the bad seem good, the negative appear positive, the unpleasant attractive, or at least tolerable. It is language which avoids, shifts, or denies responsibility, language which is at variance with its real or its purported meaning. It is language which conceals or prevents thought. Basic to doublespeak is incongruity, the incongruity between what is said, or left unsaid, and what really is: between the word and the referent, between seem and be, between the essential function of language, communication, and what doublespeak does – mislead, distort, deceive, inflate, circumvent, obfuscate.

When shopping, we are asked to check our packages at the desk 'for our convenience,' when it's not for our convenience at all but for the store's 'program to reduce inventory shrinkage.' We see advertisements for 'preowned,' 'experienced,' or 'previously distinguished' cars, for 'genuine imitation leather,' 'virgin vinyl,' or 'real counterfeit diamonds.' Television offers not reruns but 'encore telecasts.' There are no slums or ghettos, just the 'inner city' or 'substandard housing' where the 'disadvantaged,' 'economically non-affluent,' or 'fiscal underachievers' live. Nonprofit organizations don't make a profit, they have 'negative deficits' or 'revenue excesses.' In the world of doublespeak dying is 'terminal living.'

We know that a toothbrush is still a toothbrush even if the advertisements on television call it a 'home plaque removal instrument,' and even that 'nutritional avoidance therapy' means a diet. But who would guess that a 'volume-related production schedule adjustment' means closing an entire factory in the doublespeak of General Motors, or that 'advanced downward adjustments' means budget cuts, or that 'energetic disassembly' means an explosion in a nuclear power plant in the doublespeak of the nuclear power industry?

The euphemism, an inoffensive or positive word or phrase designed to avoid a harsh, unpleasant, or distasteful reality, can at times be doublespeak. But the euphemism can also be a tactful word or phrase; for example, 'passed away' functions not just to protect the feelings of another person but also to express our concern for another's grief. This use of the euphemism is not doublespeak but the language of courtesy. A euphemism used to mislead or deceive, however, becomes doublespeak. In 1984, the U.S. State Department announced that in its annual reports on the status of human rights in countries around the world it would no longer use the word 'killing.' Instead, it would use the phrase 'unlawful or arbitrary deprivation of life.' Thus the State Department avoids discussing government-sanctioned killings in countries that the United States supports and has certified as respecting human rights.

The Pentagon also avoids unpleasant realities when it refers to bombs and artillery shells which fall on civilian targets as 'incontinent ordnance,' or killing the enemy as 'servicing the target.' In 1977 the Pentagon tried to slip funding for the neutron bomb unnoticed into an appropriations bill by calling it an 'enhanced radiation device.' And in 1971 the CIA gave us that most famous of examples of doublespeak when it used the phrase 'eliminate with extreme prejudice' to refer to the execution of a suspected double agent in Vietnam.

Jargon, the specialized language of a trade or profession, allows colleagues to communicate with each other clearly, efficiently, and quickly. Indeed, it is a mark of membership to be able to use and understand the group's jargon. But it can also be doublespeak – pretentious, obscure, and esoteric terminology used to make the simple appear complex, and not to express but impress. In the doublespeak of jargon, smelling something becomes 'organoleptic analysis,' glass becomes 'fused silicate,' a crack in a metal support beam becomes a 'discontinuity,' conservative economic policies become 'distributionally conservative notions'.

Lawyers and tax accountants speak of an 'involuntary conversion' of property when discussing the loss or destruction of property through theft, accident, or condemnation. So if your house burns down, or your car is stolen or destroyed in an accident, you have, in legal jargon, suffered an 'involuntary conversion' of your property. This is a legal term with a specific meaning in law and all lawyers can be expected to understand it. But when it is used to communicate with a person outside the group who does not understand such language, it is doublespeak. In 1978 a National Airlines 727 airplane crashed while attempting to land at the Pensacola, Florida, airport, killing three passengers, injuring twenty-one others, and destroying the airplane. Since the insured value of the airplane was greater than its book value, National made an after-tax insurance benefit of $1.7 million on the destroyed airplane, or an extra eighteen cents a share. In its annual report, National reported that this $1.7 million was due to 'the involuntary conversion of a 727,' thus explaining the profit without even hinting at the crash and the deaths of three passengers.

A final kind of doublespeak is simply inflated language. Car mechanics may be called 'automotive internists,' elevator operators 'members of the vertical transportation corps,' and grocery store checkout clerks 'career associate scanning professionals,' while television sets are proclaimed to have 'nonmulticolor capability.' When a company 'initiates a career alternative enhancement program' it is really laying off five thousand workers; 'negative patient care outcome' means that the patient died.

'The world of Doublespeak' by William Lutz

Reflections

* This article is itself very persuasive on the subject of how language is manipulated to serve certain ends. One of the most disturbing sentences is: 'It is language which conceals or prevents thought'.
  In the nightmare world George Orwell created in his novel *1984* (written in 1948), he depicted language as one of the most important tools of the totalitarian state. Newspeak, the official state language of 1984, was designed not to extend but to *diminish* the range of human thought, to make only 'correct' thought possible and all other modes of thought impossible. In other words, it was a language designed to create a reality which the state wanted.

* When we read newspapers and watch tv and film we need to be alert to the way language is being manipulated for certain purposes. Citizens of the late 20th century are bombarded by media images – it is vital to be able to discriminate between fact and fiction, truths and untruths. Being 'media-literate' is a contemporary challenge and necessity.

* Think about this example of Doublespeak, used by a politician:
  'Capital punishment is our society's recognition of the sanctity of human life . . .'

2 New media: information devices*

Introduction
We live in a world which is rich beyond our ancestors' dreams in *information*. Information technology is the most powerful aspect of the new media in our society. Should we accept it without question? How can we help shape these new information devices so that they *serve* us rather than *direct* us?

We are poised at a very interesting point in history, as the following reading highlights. It is taken from a book significantly titled *Goodbye Gutenberg*. Gutenberg was the German printer who, in the early 15th century, invented movable type and thus transformed manuscripts into early printing.

Reading

Goodbye Gutenberg

The new media and information devices that are currently being tried out or discussed around the world are additional evidence of a wholly new stage through which the economies of the West are passing. A great shift is taking place from producer to consumer sovereignty in Western democracies, a shift that is bringing in its train a change in values and in systems of economic management. In the field of information such devices as teletext, viewdata, cassettes, cables, and videodiscs all fit the same emerging pattern: they provide opportunities for individuals to step out of the mass homogenized audiences of newspapers, radio, and television and take a more active role in the process by which knowledge and entertainment are transmitted through society.

So far no new medium has actually become powerful enough to challenge any existing incumbent in its traditional roles. Indeed, despite a host of problems, the newspaper, radio, and television industries are in many countries enjoying historic heights of prosperity, profitability, and circulation. What people are waiting for is the first sign of a traditional medium moving out of a traditional function, abandoning a piece of its territory to new technology. They wait to see whether pay-TV via coaxial cable will replace the movie theater as the means for distributing major films; they wait to see whether the computer-assisted print systems such as viewdata will take over part of the function of selling classified advertising; they wait to see whether community media based on electronic or video technology will replace some of the functions of local newspapers.

This era is a fascinating one in which to observe the way that technology interacts with human society: for each new device that is taken up, several are lost in experiment and in the marketplace. The moment may be more decisive than the method. For it is imagination, ultimately, and not mathematical calculation that creates media; it is the fresh perception of how to fit a potential machine into an actual way of life that really constitutes the act of 'invention.' Sarnoff's separation of mouthpiece from earpiece helped to turn radio-telephony into radio in the 1920s and turned a person-to-person medium into a means of mass entertainment. British radio engineers in the 1960s turned a new subtitling device for the deaf in television into the new medium of teletext. Both of these examples developed from a conception of a market, the idea of a possible relationship between a device and an audience.

Invention consists of skillful development plus social insight. We now all know that by the year 2000 or 2010 systems of information will be far more interactive and abundant, based more upon electronic transfer than physical carriage, upon individual selection than generalized transmission. But we don't know which transmission system (coaxial cable, optic fiber waveguide, microwave, or some combination of all) will finally emerge, nor which functions will be served by which set of audience devices (screen, telephone, facsimile, home computer). We cannot sit back to wait and see, for it is precisely the process by which societies 'guess' the likely outcome that actually creates the outcome.

A culture grows out of its tools. The hand, the eye, the voice, and the memory were physical functions that gave rise to the arts, crafts, and literatures of mankind. The extension of the limbs into material tools reduced the pain of construction, enabled physical energy to be transferred, increased, stored. Tools separated mind from body, diversified the range of skills and therefore the genres within which human cultures were expressed. The hand-based and mind-based arts and sciences proliferated. New technologies are extensions of old ones. Each mental revolution produced in the era of a new technique (created by the interaction of old needs and new opportunities) is an addition to human experience. The communication revolutions have therefore been cumulative rather than completely substitutive. Each new technology has been summoned into being to cope with an existing and perceived inefficiency or inadequacy and has gradually released its wider potential into society, working out its own peculiar implications. What we have to observe next is the first stage of the journey of computer-based information into our culture, which is taking place more publicly in the newspaper industry than in any other area of society. There it is changing the industrial base of a medium that had already been changing its economic and financial base. It is changing the relationships between all the crafts, professions, and management cadres in what is the basic information industry of Western society.

Anthony Smith

Reflections

* The writer highlights how new technologies inevitably affect value systems, and change the relationship between crafts, professions and management groups.
  We need to take a critical look at how our lives are being affected and ensure that we harness the new media for human good, to improve the quality of our lives.
  Information technology is there for us to shape to our own ends – we must not let it dictate our attitudes and values.

3 From papyrus to information technology

Introduction

Knowledge is one of the cornerstones of civilised society. *How* knowledge is passed from one person to the next or from one generation to the next helps shape our society. In the Middle Ages across Europe scribes copied out scripts by hand – this took time, and so the passing on of knowledge was slow and geographically limited. With the coming of printing in the Renaissance period, information could suddenly be passed around quickly, and the printed word became more powerful.

Now, in the late 20th century, new technologies spread news and information with incredible speed. That inevitably changes attitudes towards knowledge, as the following passage indicates. It comes from a book called *Goodbye Gutenberg*.

Reading

From papyrus to information technology

The development of printing in the fifteenth century was inextricable from the whole social and cultural process known as the Renaissance. Gutenberg's printing press was partly a product of the new thinking, partly its instigator. It is easy to see certain patterns also evident in our own time, when new ideas about the nature of information are arising precisely at a moment when new methods for creating and disseminating the written word are being adopted. The Japanese have given wide currency to the 'Information Society,' and the phrase has now become popular in the United States. The French have added a new set of words to the vocabulary to indicate different aspects of this same phenomenon; they speak of the 'informatisation' of society, the process by which new systems of information are being slotted into new roles; sometimes they use the terms 'informatique,' 'telematique,' and even 'typotique' to refer to the electronic extensions of traditional print media into the new technologies of the 1980s.

Certainly we are moving into a period where entirely new devices are being marketed for disseminating the printed word and where at the same time traditional systems of printing are being transformed by the use of the computer and the reorganization of the industrial aspects of the newspaper. But inevitably the first uses to which new machines are put are traditional ones; the new printing technology is brought into use to resolve inefficiencies and dislocations that have occurred in the mechanical systems inherited from the Victorians. However, even at the moment of their installation it is possible to see ways in which this new technology can serve altogether new functions and change the environment of information in fundamental ways. The new printing presses of the fifteenth and sixteenth centuries were brought in to ease the pressure of demand on the European system of manuscript copying, but they then changed the way in which ideas circulated and facilitated new *national* cultures based upon the printed word.

The switch from stone inscription to papyrus and handwriting signaled new patterns of thought and social organization. The switch from a scribal society to a printing one changed the whole focus of knowledge in the West and created new locations for information in society. The transition from paper to telecommunications systems can hardly prove to be less important, necessitating the development of new skills and new equipment, a new kind of text and a new method of text storage. As with the other great parallel transformation of history, the change is becoming evident in government before is impact reaches society in general. The defense and intelligence communities in the United States have already undergone a thorough changeover, and well over half of all documents relating to intelligence work are now transmitted, filed, and indexed electronically, passing through specialized networks without generating paper copy. The text is generated in video terminals and passed into data storage, to be retrieved and read by those concerned on other video terminals. Even in this and other comparable microsystems a host of moral, organizational, and economic problems are raised by the phenomenon of paperlessness.

Technical librarianship is one of the next fields likely to undergo substantial transformation, and from there the change of system cannot but spread outwards throughout the education system to society as a whole. Banking and monetary systems are meanwhile undergoing parallel and simultaneous transformation, and the work of conceptualizing mass systems of electronic funds transfer (creating a moneyless society?) is well underway. When governmental and financial communities adopt a new technology, they inevitably drag the rest of society between them, however inconceivable it may still be to nonspecialists that they should acquire this totally novel information skill and conduct the basic transactions of civil life via computer.

Today a major break with the past is clearly at hand, and with it will come an important shift in the way we treat information, the way we collect and store it, the way we classify, censor, and circulate it. People will regard the process known as education in a quite different light in a society in which human memory will be needed for different purposes than in the past; we shall think of librarians, journalists, editors, and publishers as different creatures from those of today, since they will be involved in different mutual relationships, using a different technology.

In a sense the only choice which history does not make for us is that between optimism and pessimism. Whether we have 'big' or 'little' government, whether we become a gregarious or a lonely society, individualistic or regimented, is largely a result of the way we choose to use the technology.

From 'Goodbye Gutenberg' by Anthony Smith

Reflections

* Anthony Smith poses some interesting challenges in the final paragraphs of this extract. He argues that education as we know it will change, and that the very organisation of society cannot escape the effects of the new media.

It will be for the current generation of school students to determine in their working lives what exactly these changes will mean for our daily existence. We certainly need to decide whether we shall work optimistically to harness the new technologies and/or resist some changes they force upon us.

By the time all of you are working, these changes will be taking effect. It's up to all of us to decide whether we will happily welcome *all* new technological developments, or whether we will resist some of the changes they force upon us.

4 Power of the press; 'never let the facts get in the way of the story'

Introduction

Newspapers have a strong influence over public opinion. You can probably think of many examples of headlines (particularly in the tabloid press) designed to shock and attract the reader's attention.

Sometimes headlines and reports go too far in their attacks on individuals and organisations. But sometimes newspaper articles can help fight for a just cause, or expose corruption.

The power of the press can be a force for good or ill – a lot depends on your point of view.

The following extract is taken from a book called *The Art of the Deal* written by an American called Donald Trump. He is a very wealthy land-owner and developer who made millions out of property in New York.

Reading

The art of the deal

Get the Word Out

You can have the most wonderful product in the world, but if people don't know about it, it's not going to be worth much. There are singers in the world with voices as good as Frank Sinatra's, but they're singing in their garages because no one has ever heard of them. You need to generate interest, and you need to create excitement. One way is to hire public relations people and pay them a lot of money to sell whatever you've got. But to me, that's like hiring outside consultants to study a market. It's never as good as doing it yourself.

One thing I've learned about the press is that they're always hungry for a good story, and the more sensational the better. It's in the nature of the job, and I understand that. The point is that if you are a little different, or a little outrageous, or if you do things that are bold or controversial, the press is going to write about you. I've always done things a little differently, I don't mind controversy, and my deals tend to be somewhat ambitious. Also, I achieved a lot when I was very young, and I chose to live in a certain style. The result is that the press has always wanted to write about me.

I'm not saying that they necessarily like me. Sometimes they write positively, and sometimes they write negatively. But from a pure business point of view, the benefits of being written about have far outweighed the drawbacks. It's really quite simple. If I take a full-page ad in the *New York Times* to publicize a project, it might cost $40,000, and in any case, people tend to be skeptical about advertising. But if the *New York Times* writes even a moderately positive one column story about one of my deals, it doesn't cost me anything, and it's worth a lot more than $40,000.

The funny thing is that even a critical story, which may be hurtful personally, can be very valuable to your business. Television City is a perfect example. When I bought the land in 1985, many people, even those on the West Side, didn't realize that those one hundred acres existed. Then I announced I was going to build the world's tallest building on the site. Instantly, it became a media event: the *New York Times* put it on the front page, Dan Rather announced it on the evening news, and George Will wrote a column about it in *Newsweek*. Every architecture critic had an opinion, and so did a lot of editorial writers. Not all of them liked the idea of the world's tallest building. But the point is that we got a lot of attention, and that alone creates value.

The other thing I do when I talk with reporters is to be straight. I try not to deceive them or to be defensive, because those are precisely the ways most people get themselves into trouble with the press. Instead, when a reporter asks me a tough question, I try to frame a positive answer, even if that means shifting the ground. For example, if someone asks me what negative effects the world's tallest building might have on the West Side, I turn the tables and talk about how New Yorkers deserve the world's tallest building, and what a boost it will give the city to have that honor again. When a reporter asks why I build only for the rich, I note that the rich aren't the only ones who benefit from my buildings. I explain that I put thousands of people to work who might otherwise be collecting unemployment, and that I add to the city's tax base every time I build a new project. I also point out that buildings like Trump Tower have helped spark New York's renaissance.

The final key to the way I promote is bravado. I play to people's fantasies. People may not always think big themselves, but they can still get very excited by those who do. That's why a little hyperbole never hurts. People want to believe that something is the biggest and the greatest and the most spectacular.

I call it truthful hyperbole. It's an innocent form of exaggeration – and a very effective form of promotion.

From 'The Art of the Deal' by Donald Trump

Reflections

* Trump highlights how he made use of the power of the press to promote his own ideas. He has also been the subject of some very adverse press reporting in American newspapers.

  In the passage Trump says you should always be straight with journalists, though he recognises that words can sometimes be twisted. His words call to mind an old journalists' saying 'Never let the facts get in the way of the story.'

  It is useful to remember these words when you watch TV reports or read newspapers. Sometimes you will find that what you see does not always do justice to the facts as you know them.

  Sometimes, too, we may feel that we have been misreported or misrepresented. And this can happen in everyday incidents and conversations, as well as in media reports. At such times it is very important to hold on to our own values.

* *Romans 14: 1–8*

  Accept him whose faith is weak, without passing judgment on disputable matters. One man's faith allows him to eat everything, but another man, whose faith is weak, eats only vegetables. The man who eats everything must not look down on him who does not, and the man who does not eat everything must not condemn the man who does, for God has accepted him. Who are you to judge someone else's servant? To his own master he stands or falls. And he will stand, for the Lord is able to make him stand.

5 Advertising and consumerism (1)

Introduction

One of the most powerful influences on our lives today is advertising. It bombards us from all sides, whether we're driving down the road, sitting on a bus or underground train, in front of the television or reading a magazine. Advertisers – particularly television advertisers – have begun to change the way we look at things around us. The impact of television advertising should not be underestimated.

The following piece of journalism from writer Michael Ignatieff makes just this point. As it's being read, think about your own reaction to adverts.

Reading

The three-minute culture

Something strange is happening to our attention spans. Most of us no longer watch television: we *graze*, zapping back and forth between channels whenever our boredom threshold is triggered. Grazing and zapping are becoming the way we attend to everything. No one does anything one thing at a time. A new culture has taken shape which caters for people with the attention span of a flea.

We are used to being sold four different products in a three-minute advertising break. We have become so used to the quick-cut style of the pop video that the feature films of the 1930s seem quaint and slow. Some hit singles churned out of 24-track recording studios contain as many layers of sound as a classical symphony.

Politicians no longer address us in speeches, but in 30-second sound bites and photo opportunities. The world's news comes to us in 90-second bits, each one disconnected from the last. The most popular television form – situation comedy – serves up so many 'situations' that as you laugh, you can't remember what you are laughing about.

In a culture of amnesia, messages are imprinted, not by narrative enchantment, but by repetition. The 'hook' of pop songs, the cut line of the ads, the slogans of the parties din their mantras into our cerebral cortex. The more polluted our visual and aural worlds become, the greater the reward if they manage to freeze-frame their brand names in the hectic collage of visual images that stream across our visual field.

What we appreciate in this culture of repetition is not catharsis but cleverness. The traditional emotions awakened by art are too strong for the age of advertising. The ads are the masterpiece of the three-minute culture, and they are so clever we sometimes forget that all we can admire is their cleverness. The levels of involvement are too deep. What we admire – especially in the ads – is ingenuity in the packaging of time. Cleverness is all.

Who is this culture for? Who are its messages beamed at? The masters of the three-minute culture – the advertising, marketing and design specialists – all say it is for everyone, for the consumer. Yet modern marketing is premised not on inclusion but on exclusion. Markets are fragmenting, the ad men say, into even smaller segments; it is point of art among advertising men to target ads to these segments so precisely that other people will not ever understand them. A good campaign is like a good in-joke: it makes those who get it feel included.

The market tells us we are all included in the rites of consumption, yet the *raison d'être* of marketing is to convince us that what we buy gives us membership of an exclusive club. The suit which the jaundiced eye might see as the uniform of every fashion-conscious male under 30 is sold to each of those males as the expression of their own rugged individuality.

Who are these individuals, these sovereigns of taste? People in advertising say the key social distinction today is between those who spend time to save money and those who spend money to say time.

In the old class culture, it was the poor who had no time, the rich who cultivated their leisure. The logic of exploitation in the industrial age was overwork and underpay. It was the poor who used to rise at dawn and work till dark. Now these orders of time have been reversed: the rich rise at dawn; the poor sleep late. In the new order of exclusion in the post-industrial Welfare State, we pay people to do nothing, to sit watching the screens that broadcast the feast of other people's consumption.

This new system of exclusion is creating two time zones in our cities. In one, there are the harried few careering down the motorway fast lane, dialling New York from the carphone, while the Brandenburg Concertos play on the car stereo.

In this zone, the new technology of carphones, lap-tops, modems and Walkmans enables anyone with the money to double their time, to replace sequentiality of tasks with blurred simultaneity. In this zone, doubling your time is much more than a matter of efficiency: it is a question of honour. Keeping busy is to display moral worth in a culture where everyone wants to be seen to be pressed for time. In this zone, the harried and divided attention spans of the wealthy are the creation, not of technology, but of belief. They are not imprisoned by the gadgetry – since they only have to pull the plug and go for a silent country walk. They are imprisoned by what they think is best about them, that wish to live every second of life to the fullest.

The other time zone is that of the inner-city poor: the viscous time of the excluded, measured out in cups of coffee, cigarette stubs, the drip of a leaking roof the council has not fixed. Time always at someone else's beck and call: waiting in the queue at the DHSS, in the waiting rooms of the casualty wards of the hospitals, take your number, take a seat, and wait – for the wheyfaced young doctor who has no time. There is usually television in these waiting rooms, and in the fantasy worlds of hyperactivity that flicker across the screens the patients can measure their poverty not just in terms of income, but in terms of times they cannot have, time they cannot save. They are not spoken to or for: the three-minute culture has nothing to say to them. The songs speak of a world of love which for them means teenage pregnancy in a council flat, of a world of consumption which means rummaging for discarded bell-bottoms in the Oxfam shop. The ads invite them to holiday in Marbella, to drive their Audi through the mountains, to fax their latest contract to the New York office. The advertising they watch in those waiting rooms and the programmes themselves are addressed almost entirely to those who use money to save time, not to those like them whose life is an unending search for ways to use time to save money.

A culture of mass consumption believes, above all else, that it is a democracy of taste, presided over by the sovereign consumer. In fact, the democracy of taste only has votes for those with disposable income. Mass culture talks the language of social inclusion: everyone is a consumer, everyone drinks Coke, everyone can afford Levi's jeans. It is an agreeable fantasy but it is a fantasy whose effect is to make the facts of exclusion invisible. The poor are there all right, at the dark edge of the shoplight's shadow, but the time-harried rest of us are moving too fast to see them.

Michael Ignatieff

Reflections

* The author clearly sees here an increasingly divided society – divided by wealth and by the ability to pay (or not) for those things which adverts push in front of us. 'People in advertising say the key social distinction today is between those who spend time to save money, and those who spend money to save time.'
Think about this phrase and how it relates to your own lives – and those of people around you.
Where does that lead us as a society?
Where does that lead us as a community? Does it lead to a more selfish, less caring community?
This is something we need to be aware of as we see advert upon advert. Perhaps gradually, they do change our values and our sense of community.

* *Deuteronomy 8: 10–20*
When you have eaten and are satisfied, praise the Lord your God for the good land he has given you. Be careful that you do not forget the Lord your God, failing to observe his commands, his laws and his decrees that I am giving you this day. Otherwise, when you eat and are satisfied, when you build fine houses and settle down, and when your herds and flocks grow large and your silver and

gold increase and all you have is multiplied, then your heart will become proud and you will forget the Lord your God, who brought you out of Egypt, out of the land of slavery. You may say to yourself, 'My power and the strength of my hands have produced this wealth for me'. But remember the Lord your God, for it is he who gives you the ability to produce wealth, and so confirms his covenant, which he swore to your forefathers, as it is today.

If you ever forget the Lord your God and follow other gods and worship and bow down to them, I testify against you today that you will surely be destroyed. Like the nations the Lord destroyed before you, so you will be destroyed for not obeying the Lord your God.

6 Advertising and consumerism (2)

Introduction

'Advertising is simply a mirror upon the world as it is. It is the voice of the people. If it doesn't speak what the people want to hear then it doesn't work, and if it doesn't work then it doesn't run. If your problem is with the world as it is, then advertising will always offend.'

This is the conclusion to a newspaper article written by a very successful creator of advertisements. Do adverts shape us, our attitudes and values? Or do they only 'hold the mirror up to nature'? Listen to what this advertiser has to say.

Reading

Advertising

At base, advertising is simply about disseminating information; information about products that, by and large, people want. There was once a time when manufacturers made what they made and advertising agencies were sent out to sell it. But things have changed.

In today's competitive market-place, customer power has grown to match that of the manufacturer. Nowadays people have choice; they buy what they want and manufacturers only make what they will buy.

Which means we advertising people start out with something of an advantage compared to our forbears. We know before we start the process of devising our campaign that out there somewhere, waiting for our message, is a group of people who are likely to be receptive to what we have got to say.

Yes, they're busy, with a lot on their minds, so we'd better make our pitch short, sharp and memorable; and yes, there are a lot of other similar products out there to choose from, so we've got to make sure we explain why ours is somehow better, smarter, different. But, basically, they're open to persuasion. We don't need to adopt mind-bending techniques – assuming we knew any – to achieve our ends.

Despite this fact, advertising is still regarded with consummate suspicion by many. Which is probably sensible. After all, we are trying to sell something and, with so much to choose from, you need to keep alert to be sure you make the right choice.

Curiously, however, our staunchest critics criticise us not so much for selling products people don't want – at which we might try but won't succeed – but for selling, instead, lifestyles and attitudes that they consider anti-social.

To such people advertising is, at best, an agent for misinformation, at worst for social unrest. Even more curious perhaps is the fact that these are invariably the same people who also believe that advertising is remarkably ineffective in selling products, particularly to them. To themselves, they confer the sophistication to ignore the siren's call; to others, they offer protective concern; a patronising attitude that is predicated on the belief that ordinary members of the public are not capable of making informed decisions about how they care to lead their lives.

Any dispassionate, analytical examination of the advertising that appears in the papers, appears on the hoardings, is heard on the radio or seen on the screen, will confirm that the rumour that advertisers have suddenly lost sight of what they are selling is totally unfounded. The great majority of advertising is still in the business of disseminating straightforward information about what a product does, how it is made, and how it differs from its competitors.

In most instances the only thing that has changed compared to yesteryear – about which the critics are wont to eulogise – is the context within which the message is delivered. As affluence grows, as choice abounds, as markets become more complex and audiences for products fragment, it is only sensible that advertisers should aim to use as a backdrop to their advertising, people, places, predicaments, to which their target purchaser is likely to relate. In so doing, the advertiser is not selling the viewer the lifestyle, he's simply selling him the product in the way most likely to attract his attention.

Of course, there are instances where it is appropriate for allusion to lifestyle to come out of the background and into the foreground of the proposition. As everyone knows, the potential customer for a luxury car isn't just buying something to get him from A to B; he's also buying a sense of status and, with that, undoubtedly a sense of superiority.

Accepting that it is a fact of life that such products and such base emotions exist, it would be ludicrous for advertising not to acknowledge the entirety of the reason for purchase. It would be equally ludicrous, however, to pretend that without the advertising the snobbery that is currently expressed through cars – and, for that matter, through so many material possessions – would significantly diminish. Likely as not, all that would diminish would be the level of sales. The extreme critic might think this a good thing. Those whose jobs depend upon the reverse would not.

Advertising is simply a mirror upon the world as it is. It is the voice of the people. If it doesn't speak what the people want to hear then it doesn't work, and if it doesn't work then it doesn't run. If your problem is with the world as it is, then advertising will always offend.

Brian Astley

Reflections

* These are clearly the words of someone who feels that advertising is a force for good in shaping the society we have. For those who have very little, perhaps the answer is a little different?

We are often told that choice is a good thing. But some people – because of poverty – don't have any choice. What do adverts do for them?

This is just one of the aspects of modern society that we need to question and consider when we are trying to define and hold on to what we believe are the right values for a healthy and thriving community.

* *Timothy 6: 3–10*

If anyone teaches false doctrines and does not agree to the sound instruction of our Lord Jesus Christ and to godly teaching, he is conceited and understands nothing. He has an unhealthy interest in controversies and quarrels about words that result in envy, strife, malicious talk, evil suspicions and constant friction between men of corrupt mind, who have been robbed of the truth and who think that godliness is a means to financial gain.

But godliness with contentment is great gain. For we brought nothing into the world, and we can take nothing out of it. But if few have food and clothing, we will be content with that. People who want to get rich fall into temptation and a trap and into many foolish and harmful desires that plunge men into ruin and destruction. For the love of money is a root of all kinds of evil. Some people, eager for money, have wandered from the faith and pierced themselves with many griefs.

7 Advertising in schools

Introduction

Is there too much advertising in the world around us? Or do you feel that it has a proper place? What would you say if programmes shown on schools' television carried commercials? This is exactly what has been trialled recently in some American schools.

Listen to the following article about some reactions to this experiment.

Reading

Wooing a captive audience

Christopher Whittle has a high-tech answer for the problem of cultural illiteracy among American students. Whittle Communications firm will beam *Channel One*, a slick news program for teenagers, directly into schools for a seven-week test period. Whittle has provided each of the six pilot schools with $50,000 worth of television sets and satellite equipment to use as they wish. The only requirement: each day students will have to watch a twelve-minute *Channel One* broadcast – including two minutes of ads.

Whittle's plan to introduce commercial television into the classroom has sparked considerable controversy. 'I think it's appalling and greedy,' says Arnold Fege of the national PTA. Whittle counters that the venture will not only inform students about current events but also provide schools with valuable hardware to increase learning opportunities. 'The equipment we install has enormous secondary benefits,' he claims.

Few educators object to the idea of the news program itself. Modeled on the *Today* show and *Good Morning America*, *Channel One* will be a fast-paced montage of news headlines, facts and features, along with a focus piece examining one story in depth. The young announcers, who include Kenny Rogers Jr., son of the country-and-western singer, will even spring pop quizzes on their viewers. Example: Which of these two is older, the pyramids or the Great Wall of China? (Answer: the pyramids.)

However, each program will also carry four 30-second ads, causing some educators to worry about the encroachment of commercialism on the classroom. 'Do we want our young people to get the idea from school that buying fast food is as important as learning when Columbus discovered America?' asks Patricia Albjerg Graham, dean of the Harvard Graduate School of Education. Adds Bella Rosenberg, an official at the American Federation of Teachers: 'By showing commercials, schools are implicitly endorsing the product.' Others charge that principals are selling their students' souls for a pile of high-tech hardware. Says Peggy Charren, who heads Action for Children's Television: 'They see stars in their eyes in the shape of television sets.'

Administrators at some pilot schools admit that the lure of free equipment influenced their decisions to air the program. But other officials insist that they chose *Channel One* primarily on its merits. 'Some people assume we're mindless dolts and victims of rampant commercialism,' says Thomas Sharkey, principal of Billerica Memorial High School in Billerica, Mass. 'I consider this the best form of corporate-school partnership.' David Bennett, superintendent of the St. Paul school district, cites lack of public funds as a key reason why schools would accept the offer.

If the $5 million pilot succeeds, Whittle will open *Channel One* to schools nationwide. He hopes to have signed up as many as 10,000 schools by the mid-Nineties, giving the program an audience of up to 7 million. The estimated cost to Whittle Communications, half of which is owned by Time Inc., would be $100 million dollars. Already 70 per cent of the pilot's ad time has been sold, with the rest likely to be gone by next month. While Whittle will not release sponsors' names, product categories include sneakers, food and toiletries. Whittle pledges there will be no ads for alcohol, tobacco or contraceptives.

Whether *Channel One* will succeed with its captive audience is yet to be seen. Early reviews from students who saw a prototype program were generally favorable. 'I thought it was very interesting and informative,' said Hajir Ardebili, a seventh-grader at Eisenhower Middle School in Kansas City, Kans. He had one familiar reservation: 'Too many commercials.'

By John E. Gallagher

Reflections

* Advertising clearly enables the schools to have better tv and video equipment, so from that point of view it would probably be welcome. On the other hand, should knowledge be coming into schools courtesy of a car or toothpaste manufacturer?

There are some challenging moral questions here. In a society which has a wealth of advertising the important point is to be critical and selective in viewing. Facts and opinions should not be confused – the media should serve our lives, not direct them.

8 Power of television

Introduction

Television plays an important part in most people's lives today. Our ideas, knowledge and values are influenced by programme makers and advertisers. Many people feel there is too much television, and that it gets in the way of people doing other useful things, or pursuing interesting hobbies.

Teachers and parents often feel that television gets in the way of children's study and homework.

Others feel that television has so much to offer in terms of spreading useful general knowledge about the world around us. What do you think?

The following newspaper article is about the power of television, particularly its influence on Sundays – traditionally, the Christian day of rest.

Reading

Imagine Sunday without TV

What should be done about Sunday?

We expect trains and buses to run on Sunday. We go to concerts, the cinema, fairs and pubs. We watch football, cricket, tennis and show-jumping. Most citizens want to shop on Sunday as they please.

Perhaps the greatest hypocrisy of all is our use of television as a means of escape from the fettered lifestyle demanded by our Sunday laws. With the box in our living room, we can indulge in a wealth of cultural, social and political activities. We feel no guilt about denying a day of rest to the broadcasters, sportsmen, actors, politicians, commercial hucksters and bombast merchants of all kinds who jostle for our attention on the most popular viewing day of the week.

Indeed, it could be said that it is the very boredom of Sundays that drives people to television like the administrators in colonial outposts used to be driven to drink. The addictive nature of TV has been well recognized by anyone who has bothered to investigate the social impact of the electronic media. And the Sabbath is the day of the big fix.

I once received a letter from a woman who worked in a TV rental shop. 'When the TV develops a fault,' she wrote, 'you would think it was the end of their world and that there was nothing to live for. Some of them react like monsters if we cannot repair the set immediately. "What am I going to do?" they moan. "I cannot be without my TV set for another evening".'

Present viewing statistics indicate that the average Briton who reaches the age of 65 will have spent nine years of his life watching television. Children of 16 will have devoted more than twice as many hours to TV than to their schoolteachers. In Chigago there are special clinics aimed at weaning children off the box. In West Germany 184 habitual viewers were paid a substantial sum per week if they would give up TV for a year. Within five months every one of them was back on the electronic nipple.

Every experiment conducted about the nature of TV addiction shows that with the small screen out of the way, people adopt a dramatically different approach to their leisure time. In the German experience, the subjects increased their visits to the cinema threefold; they spent twice as much time playing games and reading; they saw friends and relatives twice as often and, most important, 93 per cent admitted they were more concerned with what their children were doing. Back in 1973–74 when the three-day week caused TV to be shut down at 10 pm, even this short curtailment of hours produced in Britain a significant increase in the sale of paperbacks, a rise in cinema-going, a boost to the theatre box-office, an increase in the sale of chess sets, Monopoly and knitting patterns.

It is certain that decades of TV has not produced wiser, kinder, more humane, more articulate, more concerned societies than we had before. Only broadcasters and home secretaries resist the overwhelming evidence that TV has been a major contributing factor in the increase of violence. Other consequences of too much TV are a decline in learning levels, less communication between parent and child, difficulty in expressing ideas logically, a disinclination to be involved and exercise choice.

The old, the lonely and the handicapped, of course, find TV a great boon. It can stretch the imaginative horizons of children. No one would want to eliminate it. But it is its insidious ability to monopolize our time that constitutes its danger. It is as much the activities it discourages as the behaviour it stimulates that justifies the indictment of TV.

To make life fuller, more active, more involved, the TV addicts must kick their habit. Gradual abstinence is not likely to work.

Since the cold turkey treatment of total withdrawal is hardly practical, the Government could help by using Sunday to break the need for constant television. If the screens were blanked out every Sunday and, as a compensation, Sunday was turned into the fun day of the week, when everything was open to be enjoyed, experienced and shared, millions might find that the family, books, hobbies, plays, walks in the park, gardening, the cinema, conversation were activities more fulfilling than the images on the small screen. They might even be induced to switch off the box on some other day of the week.

Miles Kington, 1982

Reflections

* Do you feel Sunday should be special – reserved for activities that don't take place during the rest of the week? Is television having a bad effect on family life? Does television encourage people to be lazy and prevent them taking up hobbies, or enjoying each others' conversation? Or does TV prompt more people to take up sport and promote a better awareness of life around the globe?

It is surely true, as the writer says, that 'The old, the lonely and the handicapped find TV a great boon'.

In the end, we would probably conclude that it is OK to watch television, but not in excess. As a society, we should be aware of its power for good and for ill.

* **A Nameless Fate**
  Sitting, watching,
  goggling at the box.
  His legs begin to shrink.
  His bottom grows fatter and
  fatter filling the armchair he sits
  in, slowly at first, then faster
  and faster. His eyes grow square
  instead of round.
  His head slowly turns to jelly
  from sitting in front
  of the telly.

Abigail Woodman Age 11

* *Genesis 1: 31; 2: 1–2*
  God saw all that he had made, and it was very good. And there was evening, and there was morning – the sixth day.

Thus the heavens and the earth were completed in all their vast array.
By the seventh day God had finished the work he had been doing; so on the seventh day he rested from all his work. And God blessed the seventh day and made it holy, because on it he rested from all the work of creating that he had done.

9 What makes news?

Introduction

There's a saying that nothing is more useless than yesterday's newspaper. News has to be fresh and up-to-date – the latest major accident, earthquake, crime, sporting event, political conference and so on. But what we actually see as 'news' also depends on someone selecting what they think is newsworthy. Teams of newspaper, radio and television journalists are employed to do just that.

Do we and should we believe all that we read, hear and see in the news? What makes us turn to one channel rather than another, or buy a particular newspaper? Some people accuse journalists and newscasters of sensationalising news items, so that we will follow their coverage, rather than someone else's. And journalists may experience pressures from advertisers to do just this.

Listen to this article, which surveys the current news scene.

Reading

Broadcast News

On 15th April, 1989 when nearly 100 football spectators were crushed to death at Hillsborough, BBC cameras happened to be present. *Grandstand*, scheduled to feature World Professional Snooker during the afternoon, became the focus for news of the tragedy as its scale and intensity developed through the afternoon. It is clear from that afternoon's ratings that, as news began to spread by radio and word of mouth, people increasingly turned to their television sets for information.

From 3 o'clock, when it was first appreciated that something was gravely wrong, numbers rose inexorably throughout the afternoon. On a less dramatic Saturday, ratings only start to rise from 4.15 as interested sports fans tune in for soccer, rugby and horse racing results. On that afternoon, both the pattern and weight of audience flow demonstrates how television was exploited as a means of keeping abreast. Figures for evening news bulletins are equally conclusive. On the same night, 13 million watched BBC's 9.15 News compared to 11 million in the preceding week following an identical programme. And on 21st December 1988, the night of the Lockerbie plane crash, both BBC and ITN bulletins attracted audiences in excess of 13 million, compared to 7 million the previous week.

Major news stories such as these, involving domestic tragedy on a massive scale, will always create a huge upsurge of national interest and concern. People will want to know what is happening, sometimes out of concern for friends or relatives who might be involved, more usually out of a straightforward 'need to know'. What is less certain is how that need is fulfilled by various news sources, and the basis on which they are selected.

Why should people reach for their television sets in times of major disaster or crisis? Is it simply the existence of pictures which serve to underline the drama, pandering a little to ghoulish appetites? Or does the full impact become somehow more real and immediate when conveyed by another human being with whom the viewer can identify? For many people who watched the full horror of Lockerbie unfold, it is the authority and gravity of commentator Michael Buerk's first accounts, rather than the delayed pictures, which are permanently engraved on the consciousness.

It is clear that television is easily the main source of world and national news, newspapers of local news. Why the difference? Three possible explanations suggest themselves. First, there is inadequate local news provision on television; second, newspapers are somehow better or more appropriate for conveying local news; third, any news will be derived from the source most easily available. If the latter proved to be true, television's elevation for world and national news may only be a function of the easy accessibility of peak-time news.

If it were scheduled at less convenient times, news-seekers might simply look elsewhere as they appear to do for their local news. We simply cannot conclude that less peak time news will leave large proportions of the population ignorant or uninformed.

Survey research can also tell something about the value placed on different news sources. A recent IBA survey asked which of the media were trusted to give the *most accurate* news, with the following responses:

Which Media Trusted to Give Most Accurate News
(Base = 1,433)

Newspapers	8%
Television	67%
Radio	11%
All equally	7%
None of them	4%
Don't know	2%

An overwhelming vote of confidence in television overshadows both newspapers, which are subject to no impartiality or accuracy requirements, and radio, which certainly is. On the one hand, removing one source of trusted reporting from easy access may create some hostility; on the other hand, as long as there is a requirement for news provision at more flexible hours it is quite conceivable that those committed to television news will simply make more effort to watch at the rescheduled times. Again, we can only speculate until we known more about how deliberately selection is made between available information sources.

Any terrestrial service determined to maximise ratings may be forced to adopt the more sensationalist and widely excoriated news values of Britain's best-selling tabloid newspaper, the *Sun*. Evidence from abroad suggests that this might be most accurately described as the American legacy. In a paper to the Home Office Jay Blumler outlined some findings from his two year study into the evolution of multi-channel television in the US. This enquiry provides a possible glimpse of the future of television journalism. A general finding concerns the nature of audience behaviour when confronted by a multiplicity of channels. Increasingly, it seems, viewers are prone to use remote controls to skip between programmes, with younger viewers especially liable to watch two programmes or more simultaneously. Broadcasters, increasingly concerned to maintain their audience share, are responding with 'programming strategies of immediate attention-gaining and qualities of pace, impact, brevity, the arresting, and the dramatic'.

This strategy directly impinges on news and information programming which is increasingly dominated by the tenets of good entertainment rather than good journalism: 'American experience suggests that in a more competitive marketplace ... entertainment criteria are increasingly applied to non-entertainment programmes'. The most damning evidence about the impact of these pressures comes from the mouth of a retired CBS reporter in evidence to a Congressional Committee:

'We were ordered to add glitz. We were told to feature a celebrity interview at least every half-hour and if we did offer issue-oriented segments, the watchword was to give more heat and less light, the idea being that a noisy shouting match was a much better ratings draw than any reasoned debate'.

Under this kind of pressure, a compulsory peak-time news service loses all value. We cannot say whether similar glamourising pressures would apply to British news services, and it is certainly possible that the news 'gratifications' afforded by newspapers and television in the UK are entirely different. But it is also possible that an increased diet of salacious stories, crime stories, and showbiz stories will more effectively draw the crowds which a peak-time commercial broadcaster must maintain. The result could be an insidious trivialisation process which would both undermine professional journalistic values in broadcasting and create additional pressures on other media influenced by television's agenda. Far from a better informed citizenry being served by a multiplicity of accessible and accurate news sources, we could emerge with news programmes which inhibit rather than enhance a proper understanding of social and political issues.

From 'Broadcast News' by Steven Barnett in Journalism Review 1989

Reflections

* 'Journalists never let the facts get in the way of the story.' As the article suggests, we turn increasingly to our TV screens for world and national news, to newspapers for local items. TV journalists have a responsibility to present as accurate a picture as they can of people and events in the news. At the same time, broadcasters are aware of the need to compete for audience ratings. 'American experience suggests that in a more competitive marketplace, entertainment criteria are increasingly applied to non-entertainment programmes.'
The values of an accurate and objective news service are under threat. As a society, we need to make sure that we are aware of this, so that we can have a proper understanding of social and political issues, not distorted by pressures of the 'entertainment culture'.

* It is always worth remembering that someone else has selected what makes the news. Your own choice might be different. And just because, for example, the plight of starving or persecuted people ceases to make the headlines, it does not mean that the problem has gone away – simply that other items have been chosen to attract our attention. News is a perilously perishable commodity in the media – and sometimes, so is truth.

10 Heroes and heroines

Introduction

From an early age we each have particular heroines and heroes. They can come from books, films, the world of pop and rock music or the latest toy craze. Hero and heroine-worship are part of growing-up; and indeed many adults continue to remember vividly their childhood heroes and heroines.

Even as an adult, we need people to look up to and model ourselves upon. But if we begin to worship someone, we sometimes become blind to their faults.

In the following extract, a young boy first meets the cowboy Shane, as he rides into his Wild West valley.

Reading

Shane

He rode into our valley in the summer of '89. I was a kid then, barely topping the backboard of father's old chuck-wagon. I was on the upper rail of our small corral, soaking in the late afternoon sun, when I saw him far down the road where it swung into the valley from the open plain beyond.

In that clear Wyoming air I could see him plainly, though he was still several miles away. There seemed nothing remarkable about him, just another stray horseman riding up the road towards the cluster of frame buildings that was our town. Then I saw a pair of cowhands, loping past him, stop and stare after him with a curious intentness.

He came steadily on, straight through the town without slackening pace, until he reached the fork a half-mile below our place. One branch turned left across the river ford and on to Luke Fletcher's big spread. The other bore ahead along the right bank where we homesteaders had pegged our claims in a row up the valley. He hesitated briefly, studying the choice, and moved again steadily on our side.

As he came near, what impressed me first was his clothes. He wore dark trousers of some serge material tucked into tall boots and held at the waist by a wide belt, both of a soft black leather tooled in intricate design. A coat of the same dark material as the trousers was neatly folded and strapped to his saddle-roll. His shirt was finespun linen, rich brown in colour. The handkerchief knotted loosely around his throat was black silk. His hat was not the familiar stetson, not the familiar grey or muddy tan. It was a plain black, soft in texture, unlike any hat I had ever seen, with a creased crown and a wide curling brim swept down in front to shield the face.

All trace of newness was long since gone from these things. The dust of distance was beaten into them. They were worn and stained and several neat patches showed on the shirt. Yet a kind of magnificence remained and with it a hint of men and manners alien to my limited boy's experience.

Then I forgot the clothes in the impact of the man himself. He was not much above medium height, almost slight in build. He would have looked frail alongside father's square, solid bulk. But even I could read the endurance in the lines of that dark figure and the quiet power in its effortless, unthinking adjustment to every movement of the tired horse.

He was clean-shaven and his face was lean and hard and burned from high forehead to firm, tapering chin. His eyes seemed hooded in the shadow of the hat's brim. He came closer, and I could see that this was because the brows were drawn in a frown of fixed and habitual alertness. Beneath them the eyes were endlessly searching from side to side and forward, checking off every item in view, missing nothing. As I noticed this, a sudden chill, I could not have told why, struck through me in the warm and open sun.

He rode easily, relaxed in the saddle, leaning his weight lazily into the stirrups. Yet even in this easiness was a suggestion of tension. It was the easiness of a coiled spring, of a trap set.

From 'Shane' by Jack Shaefer

Reflections

* The rest of this story tells how Shane becomes the young boy's hero – a person to be looked up to and upon whom he can model himself. Having a hero or heroine fulfils a basic human need; but there can be dangers.

  There are many stories of people who try to copy the exploits and adventures of their film heroes – and put themselves and others at risk as a result. Sometimes we can forget that what can happen on the cinema screen can't necessarily be recreated in our own backyards. Modern heroes and heroines have responsibilities to those who follow or worship them. Very often society – in the shape of the media (TV and newspapers) – is quick to criticise film and pop stars who break the law in one way or another.

  Yes, we all need heroes and heroines – we just have to exercise a little care in blindly copying or seeking to emulate their every step, because the images which the media can present to us are often very powerful and unquestioning.

11 'Things were not supposed to turn out this way'*

Introduction
One effect of the media's presentation of images of success is that people's everyday expectations are constantly being raised. We expect success. We find failure altogether unexpected and very difficult to cope with.

The following passage highlights the position of a successful American businessman suddenly faced with a situation he cannot buy himself out of, and which challenges his belief system.

Reading

Things were not supposed to turn out this way

NEW YORK – At the age of 35, Charlie was one of the top 'merger and acquisition guys' on Wall Street and raked in a cool $750,000 a year for his pains. And – as he told me over a glass or three of Chivas in a bar near his office – in the 15 years since we'd both graduated from the same small college in New England, the secret of his success had been to adopt a 'take no prisoners' philosophy in his professional life.

'You don't survive in my game', Charlie said, 'unless you believe in playing to win; in maintaining an edge over everyone else around you.'

Maintaining an edge. To Charlie, there was something quasi-spiritual about this statement. It didn't simply explain his business strategy; it also defined his credo, his world-view. Maintaining an edge wasn't only about pulling in big bucks ('I'm aiming for seven figures next year, Doug'); it also meant living in the right house in the right beau monde suburb with his wife Sally and their three children. And it meant being able to fund such leisure-time activities as managing a couple of up-and-coming professional boxers, or driving himself at 160 mph in one of his Ferraris.

But while his part-time flirtation with racing and fighting hinted at the escapist side of his character, Charlie was, at heart, simply a high-octane version of that classic American figure – the man who had embraced corporate culture with a vengeance, and had flourished within its confines. Or, at least, I thought Charlie had flourished on Wall Street, and I told him so.

His reply was a little bemusing: 'My life is crap.' Then, after a substantial pause and an even more substantial gulp of Scotch, he said: 'Two of my kids have just been diagnosed with muscular dystrophy.' And for the next half-hour, he spoke non-stop about the battery of medical specialists who had seen his kids, and who had all reached essentially the same prognosis: unless there was a major break-through in the war against the disease, they would have little chance of surviving beyond their mid-twenties.

Charlie, of course, did his best to sound controlled when speaking about the catastrophe that had hit his family. But as we talked I sensed that behind his unexpressed (but evident) anguish was a deep sense of confusion at the random nature of this disaster; at the fact that things were not supposed to turn out this way.

After all, Charlie was someone who had worked hard at getting all the components of his professional and emotional worlds just right. It's a deeply American trait – this widely-held notion that, to succeed in the world, you must have a *game-plan*; a clearly defined *agenda* through which you will strive to achieve your very own set of goals. And listening to Charlie speak about the way in which his carefully ordered universe had been undermined by a couple of faulty chromosomes put me in mind of something about the American mind: that the major legacy of our Puritan heritage is 'the belief that you can build your life and work it out, con-scientiously, bit by bit. The task is enormous; it is often dulling; but that is the price you pay for the perfectibility of Man. There is no conception of tragedy; something just went wrong.'

Something had gone seriously wrong in Charlie's life, and what gave his crisis even greater poignancy was his realisation that he couldn't 'fix' the problem. No wonder he felt so helpless. Like all Americans of his class and educational background, he had been taught that the pursuit of excellence was a noble one, and that an essential part of this pursuit was learning how to be a handyman when it came to keeping your life in order. But whereas Charlie was fully capable of, say, repairing a contractual flaw when negotiating a takeover bid, he could do nothing to remedy the genetic accident that had befallen two of his children.

This sense of powerlessness not only kindled his grief and frustration; it also had Charlie thinking long and hard about the subject of money. For money plays a central role in the American quest for perfectibility. It is looked upon as the fuel which propels us forward in our search for a small patch of Utopia to call our own. In short, money and self-fulfilment are truly inseparable companions in American society – which means that, when circumstances beyond our control wreak havoc with our so-called life strategies, we often find ourselves suffering from a grave crisis of faith in an ethos which equates the getting of wealth with the getting of happiness.

Things were not supposed to turn out this way. The longer I listened to Charlie, the more I sensed that this hard-nosed corporate raider believed that his children's illness had rendered his life a failure. His pursuit of wealth had been bound up in the pursuit of an ideal family life – and that dream had now been devastated by the random malevolence of disease. It was, in many ways, like listening to a latter-day Puritan who had toiled so hard to create his own little City Upon A Hill, only to then have it ravaged by plague. Had this been the Massachusetts of 1638, Charlie would have begged that angry, no-nonsense God hovering over colonial Boston for forgiveness, promising to atone for whatever sin had brought this curse upon his house. But as this was the Manhattan of the 1990s, all Charlie could do was sip more Scotch and talk about the need to work harder; to make more money. Money would buy his kids world-class medical treatment. Money, he desperately hoped, would eventually buy them a cure.

For, like so many of his compatriots, Charlie still wanted to believe that money could fix things. And he dreaded being proved wrong.

The Independent Magazine 21 April 1990

Reflections

* Charlie in this passage is a product of an American society which fuels people's beliefs and dreams that money can buy anything and everything. When he discovers that his children have muscular dystrophy he can only say 'things were not supposed to turn out this way'.

  Human beings are shaped by both nature and nurture: by their genes and by the world around them. Our society today is rich in images of success: television, film and advertising can lull us into thinking that the streets are literally paved with gold; we have only to step outside and grab it.

  Another celebrated American writer Tom Wolfe described the 1980s as the 'Me-Decade'. Charlie in this passage is very much a product of that decade.

  His story should help us question such a value system as necessarily the one to follow. It should certainly encourage us to resist being absorbed into media images which present life without failure.

  Charlie's story reminds us that success is not the only goal. It should certainly encourage us to question the media's insistence on achievement and success.

12 The year 2000*

Introduction

As the year 2000 approaches, articles appear in the media about what human beings have achieved and how the human race is preparing for that special date – the millennium.

Why is it so special? Dates seem to be significant to most of us. Millennia have held almost mystical significance for writers and thinkers, and 'a millennium' is also seen as a convenient time slot for charting human achievements.

What would you say are some of the key trends in our world as the year 2000 approaches? According to a book with the grand title *Megatrends 2000*, they include the following:

1 The global economic boom of the 1990s
2 Renaissance in the arts
3 The emergence of free-market socialism
4 Global lifestyles and cultural nationalism
5 The privatisation of the welfare state
6 The rise of the Pacific Rim
7 The 1990s: decade of women in leadership
8 The age of biology
9 Religious revival of the third millennium
10 Triumph of the individual.

The following reading comes from the conclusion of the book ...

Reading

Megatrends 2000

On the threshold of the millennium, long the symbol of humanity's golden age, we possess the tools and the capacity to build utopia here and now.

Yes, there are major obstacles to overcome – from the economic development of the Third World to healing the environment and finding a cure for cancer and AIDS. To a large extent, however, the direction of today's megatrends strengthens society to confront its worst social ills throughout this great deadline decade.

The developed world's economic boom will be the foundation for higher evolution and global affluence.

Wealth has not led to increased greed, as conventional cynicism would have us believe. The hierarchy of needs theory expressed it simply and well: As basic needs, such as shelter and safety, are met, higher needs, such as those for belonging, achievement, and self-actualization – that is, transcendence – rise in their place. It is as valid for societies as for individuals. The satisfaction of basic needs has stimulated the search for meaning exemplified by the renaissance in the arts and the revival of spirituality.

As more countries grow prosperous, they must identify new areas for investment. Less developed countries, where labor is cheaper, become more attractive areas for that profitable investment. Once the Four Tigers achieved developed status, investment in Thailand (from Japan, the Tigers, and others) soared. It also increased in Malaysia, while some observers argued the better-educated Philippines would have been a better target. Now Hong Kong and Taiwan are pumping capital into China.

The Pacific Rim has rewritten the history of economic development, jumping right over the industrial period and into the information economy, where the most important resources do come not from the ground but from people.

Throughout the Third World there is a growing consensus that small enterprise, not central planning, is the road to real prosperity. The spectacle of the Soviet Union and China reaching for market mechanisms will only accelerate the Third

World's shift from a Marxist model of economic development to an entrepreneurial model sanctioned by the Communist superpowers. That will invigorate the quest for economic self-sufficiency.

Prosperity and democracy are what will finally end deadly regional conflicts. As Bob Dylan put it, 'When you got nothing, you got nothing to lose.' Wealth is a great peacemaker. The forty-four richest nations have been at peace for more than forty-five years. When developing countries make peace with their neighbors, a great proportion of their resources can be invested in economic development.

The scourge of AIDS and the suffering it has wrought symbolize our ignorance of our bodies and their priceless immune systems. Yet today, as we learn more about the role of positive visualization and imaging in health, we are on the brink of being able to see into the very nature of the human cell, even the DNA code itself.

We have just begun to use a wide array of new imaging technologies such as nuclear resonance to peer into living tissue. We have just begun to apply biophysics to the relationships inside the cell, as in DNA. We will soon be able to fight viruses and bacteria even before we identify them.

The rapprochement between the superpowers reduces the chance of a regional conflict escalating into a world war. Furthermore, the United States and the USSR have less of an incentive to inflame their client states in order to gain political or military advantage. That creates a more fertile climate for resolving conflicts, which in turn, blunts the effectiveness of terrorism. Developing countries that succeed in preserving their cultures remain stronger and find it more difficult to justify striking out against the West.

The end of the cold war has shifted the world's attention to the environment. Though some would argue it is too little too late, never before has there been *competition* among heads of state for global leadership in the environment.

The post–cold war era will see the United States and the Soviet Union collaborate on the environment and on new nonideological approaches to ending poverty.

The meaning of that great symbol the millennium depends entirely on how it is interpreted. It can mark the end of time or the beginning of the new. We believe the decision has already been made to embrace its positive side. Within the hearts and minds of humanity, there has been a commitment to life, to the utopian quest for peace and prosperity for all, which today we can clearly visualize. Humanity is entering a decade-long race to confront the great challenges remaining in hope of making a fresh start in the year 2000.

The 1990s will be an extraordinary time. The countdown – 1992, 1993, 1994 – is here. Get ready. You possess a front-row seat to the most challenging yet most exciting decade in the history of civilization.

From 'Megatrends 2000' Naisbitt and Aburdene

Reflections

* This style is characteristic of much of the media's current presentation of the approaching millennium. Whether we believe this particular view of the 1990s is for each of us to decide. It is your generation who will decide whether the year 2000 marks 'the end of time or the beginning of the new . . .'

  'The utopian quest for peace and prosperity for all' seems worth embracing, though we should not allow media images to pretend that such a goal is easily attained. It won't be – but the challenge is there.'

* *Matthew 6: 25*

Therefore I tell you, do not worry about your life, what you will eat or drink; or about your body, what you will wear. Is not life more important than food, and the body more important than clothes? Look at the birds of the air; they do not sow or reap or store away in barns, and yet your heavenly Father feeds them. Are you not much more valuable than they? Who of you by worrying can add a single hour to his life?

And why do you worry about clothes? Look at the lilies of the field, how they grow. They do not labour or spin. Yet I tell you that not even Solomon in all his splendour was dressed like one of these. If that is how God clothes the grass of the field, which is here today and tomorrow is thrown into the fire, will he not much more clothe you, O you of little faith? So do not worry, saying, 'What shall we eat?' or 'What shall we drink?' or 'What shall we wear?' For the pagans run after all these things, and your heavenly Father knows that you need them. But seek first his kingdom and his righteousness, and all these things will be given to you as well. Therefore do not worry about tomorrow, for tomorrow will worry about itself. Each day has enough trouble of its own.

Being Human: Two

1 Being reliable

Introduction

Possibly one of the best things other people can say about you is that you are reliable.

Reliability counts for a great deal in our everyday lives. But it is something which – by its very nature – depends upon consistency over a long period of time. You won't be known as a reliable person overall, if your friends and family can rely on you every *other* month, or only when you're in the right mood.

The following episode from Jerome K Jerome's novel *Three Men In A Boat* offers a witty view on consistent reliability – in this case someone who could be relied on to do the wrong thing!

Reading

Three Men In A Boat

You never saw such a commotion up and down a house in all your life, as when my Uncle Podger undertook to do a job. A picture would have come home from the frame-maker's, and be standing in the dining-room, waiting to be put up; and Aunt Podger would ask what was to be done with it, and Uncle Podger would say:

'Oh, you leave that to me. Don't you, any of you, worry yourselves about that. I'll do all that.'

And then he would take off his coat, and begin. He would send the girl out for sixpenn'orth of nails, and then one of the boys after her to tell her what size to get; and, from that, he would gradually work down, and start the whole house.

'Now you go and get me my hammer, Will,' he would shout; 'and bring me the rule, Tom; and I shall want the step-ladder, and I had better have a kitchen chair, too; and Jim! you run round to Mr Goggles, and tell him, 'Pa's kind regards and hopes his leg's better; and will he lend him his spirit-level?' And don't you go, Maria, because I shall want somebody to hold me the light; and when the girl comes back she must go out again for a bit of picture-cord; and Tom! – where's Tom? – Tom, you come here; I shall want you to hand me up the picture.'

And then he would lift up the picture, and drop it, and it would come out of the frame, and he would try to save the glass, and cut himself; and then he would spring round the room, looking for his handkerchief. He could not find his handkerchief, because it was in the pocket of the coat he had taken off, and he did not know where he had put the coat, and all the house had to leave off looking for his tools, and start looking for his coat; while he would dance round and hinder them.

'Doesn't anybody in the whole house know where my coat is? I never came across such a set in all my life – upon my word I didn't. Six of you! – and you can't find a coat that I put down not five minutes ago! Well, of all the –'

Then he'd get up, and find that he had been sitting on it, and would call out:

'Oh, you can give it up! I've found it myself now. Might just as well ask the cat to find anything as expect you people to find it.'

And when half an hour had been spent in tying up his finger, and a new glass had been got, and the tools, and the ladder, and the chair, and the candle had been brought, he would have another go, the whole family, including the girl, and the charwoman, standing round in a semi-circle, ready to help. Two people would have to hold the chair, and a third would help him up on it, and hold him there, and a fourth would hand him a nail, and a fifth would pass him up the hammer, and he would take hold of the nail, and drop it.

'There!' he would say, in an injured tone, 'now the nail's gone.'

And we would all have to go down on our knees and grovel for it, while he would stand on the chair, and grunt, and want to know if he was to be kept there all the evening.

The nail would be found at last, but by that time he would have lost the hammer.

'Where's the hammer? What did I do with the hammer? Great heavens! Seven of you, gaping round there, and you don't know what I did with the hammer!'

We would find the hammer for him, and then he would have lost sight of the mark he had made on the wall, where the nail was to go in, and each of us had to get up on the chair beside him, and see if we could find it; and we would each discover it in a different place, and he would call us all fools, one after another, and tell us to get down. And he would take the rule, and remeasure, and find that he wanted half thirty-one and three-eighths inches from the corner and would try to do it in his head, and go mad.

And we would all try to do it in our heads, and all arrive at different results, and sneer at one another. And in the general row, the original number would be forgotten, and Uncle Podger would have to measure it again.

He would use a bit of string this time, and at the critical moment, when the old fool was leaning over the chair at an angle of forty-five, and trying to reach a point three inches beyond what was possible for him to reach, the string would slip, and down he would slide on to the piano, a really fine musical effect being produced by the suddenness with which his head and body struck all the notes at the same time.

And Aunt Maria would say that she would not allow the children to stand round and hear such language.

At last, Uncle Podger would get the spot fixed again, and put the point of the nail on it with his left hand, and take the hammer in his right hand. And, with the first blow, he would smash his thumb, and drop the hammer, with a yell, on somebody's toes.

And then he would have another try, and, at the second blow, the nail would go clean through the plaster, and half the hammer after it, and Uncle Podger be precipitated against the wall with force nearly sufficient to flatten his nose.

Then we had to find the rule and the string again, and a new hole was made; and, about midnight, the picture would be up – very crooked and insecure, the wall for yards round looking as if it had been smoothed down with a rake, and everybody dead beat and wretched – except Uncle Podger.

'There you are,' he would say, stepping heavily off the chair on to the charwoman's corns, and surveying the mess he had made with evident pride. 'Why, some people would have had a man in to do a little thing like that!'

From 'Three Men in a Boat' by Jerome K Jerome

Reflections

* Clearly Uncle Podger has a reputation for unreliability in DIY. How we each earn a reputation for reliability will depend on:

  – are we reliable with friends?
  – are we reliable with members of our family?
  – are we reliable with our teachers?
  – are we reliable with our employer/customers, if we have a job?

  It is worth thinking about our behaviour each day and whether our words and actions are those which will lead people to think of us as 'a reliable person'. A reputation for reliability is worth having – and it doesn't mean being boring and predictable.

* The following poem by Seamus Heaney offers a moving and thought-provoking view on reliability and true partnership in marriage.

Scaffolding
Masons, when they start upon a building,
Are careful to test out scaffolding;

Make sure that planks won't slip at busy points,
Secure all ladders, tighten bolted joints.

And yet all this comes down when the job's done
Showing off walls of sure solid stone.

So if my dear, there sometimes seem to be
Old bridges breaking between you and me

Never fear. We may let the scaffolds fall
Confident that we have built our wall.

Seamus Heaney

2 Knowledge and learning

Introduction
A basic human characteristic is to want to acquire knowledge. If you think about something you enjoy doing, you probably want to find out more about the subject and get better at it. This would be true of swimming, model making, singing, canoeing, gardening or whatever.

Indeed, the number of books and videos sold each year on different hobbies shows how keen we are to want to increase our knowledge.

The pursuit of knowledge – whether book learning or applied, practical matters – is usually seen as 'a good thing'.

Schools are based around *learning* and exist to promote it. But the following extract from *1066 And All That* is a cautionary reminder that merely learning facts – and stereotyped facts at that – can be rather misleading, albeit rather amusing.

Reading

1066 and all that

CHAPTER 1
CÆSAR INVADES BRITAIN

The first date in English History is 55 BC, in which year Julius Cœsar (the *memorable* Roman Emperor) landed, like all other successful invaders of these islands, at Thanet. This was in the Olden Days, when the Romans were top nation on account of their classical education, etc.

Julius Cæsar advanced very energetically, throwing his cavalry several thousands of paces over the River Flumen; but the Ancient Britons, though all well over military age, painted themselves true blue, or *woad*, and fought as heroically under their dashing queen, Woadicea, as they did later in thin red lines under their good queen, Victoria.

Julius Cœsar was therefore compelled to invade Britain again the following year (54 BC, not 56, owing to the peculiar Roman method of counting), and having defeated the Ancient Britons by unfair means, such as battering-rams, tortoises, hippocausts, centipedes, axes and bundles, set the memorable Latin sentence, 'Veni, Vidi, Vici,' which the Romans, who were all very well educated, construed correctly.

The Britons, however, who of course still used the old pronunciation, understanding him to have called them 'Weeny, Weedy and Weaky,' lost heart and gave up the struggle, thinking that he had already divided them All into Three Parts.

CULTURE AMONG THE ANCIENT BRITONS

The Ancient Britons were by no means savages before the Conquest, and had already made great strides in civilization, e.g. they buried each other in long round wheelbarrows (agriculture) and burnt each other alive (religion) under the guidance of even older Britons called Druids or Eisteddfods, who worshipped the Middletoe in the famous Druidical churchyard at Stoke Penge.

The Roman Conquest was, however, a *Good Thing*, since the Britons were only natives at that time.

Reflections

* This passage is from a famous book that simplifies English history to an absurd level – into either *Good things* or *Bad things*. It reminds us that 'a little learning is a dangerous thing'. The pursuit of knowledge is important; but equally important is first *applying* that knowledge, and second, recognising when you don't know or are not sure about something.

* The following quotations might help us think further on the place of *knowledge* in our lives.

  – 'Knowing what thou knowest not
    Is in a sense, omniscience'.

– 'The Greek circle of knowledge describes the more you know, the more you can see that you don't know'.

– 'Give someone a fish, and you've fed them for a day. *Teach* someone *how* to fish, and you've fed them for life'.

(*Chinese proverb*)

– He who knows not and knows not that he knows not
Is asleep – Wake him.
He who knows not and knows that he knows not
Is ready to learn. Teach him.
He who knows and knows not that he knows
Is a fool. Shun him.
He who knows and knows that he knows
Is wise. Follow him.

3 Disability

Introduction
It might be fair to say that we can judge whether or not a society is 'humane' by the way it treats those with some kind of disability. Do people react differently to those with, for example, a mental handicap or a mental illness? What are our social attitudes towards children and adults who are physically handicapped?

Listen to this extract from an autobiography.

Reading

Mental handicap

I was told within minutes of the birth of my first child that he was a mongol. The young doctor made a genuine and honest attempt to deal with the problem; what he actually said was 'I can tell you because you are intelligent'; it must have seemed to him that intelligence is good protection in the case of news of a disaster. But what should the poor man have said? I can't find a good formula even ten years later. I suppose that bad news is bound to be a shock even if it is broken tactfully and gently; when I was told I rushed to the library and looked for some guidance. The symptoms were all shown, but I was not reassured by pictures of hanging tongues furrowed the wrong way across, strange slit eyes, hanging bellies to illustrate a lack of muscular tone, and cross-sections of brain cells. I wanted to pour out my fears and apprehensions and I wanted to know too much at the same time. The symptoms were all outlined clearly enough; what was lacking was any information of what it would be like for me and my wife. What did we have to face, and who would help us? Could we taken the strain? Why had it happened, and to us? Was there possibly a cure?

It was a great help to me to know that nothing we had done or not done could possibly have made any difference. The feeling of guilt was at first almost unbearable. I felt an almost Old Testament sense of having somehow done wrong and that this was a punishment. We had married when we were more than thirty-five years old, we wanted to have a child, so there was no question of having made a 'mistake' and then pretending that it was all intentional. It seemed to me that in that case we 'deserved' a perfect child and if it was not, there must be a reason for it. I am an ambitious person, more competitive than I care to admit, and I value my own successes however moderate they seem to outsiders. Having a mentally handicapped child made me feel that I had failed. Somehow the earliest bits of morality welled up: I should have tried harder, this was not good enough. A friend arranged that I should see a psychiatrist and I talked to him before I tried to tell my wife that the child was abnormal. At that time I must have projected some of my fears on to my wife. Perhaps when I asked 'Will it drive her to breaking point?' I was really asking 'Have I reached my breaking point?' The psychiatrist was calm and sympathetic and I regained enough control to listen. I heard that the child would make progress, however slow it might be. The child would have a personality and would be educable in a limited sort of way.

Most important for me was that at last I could express my feelings of guilt, resentment and disappointment. Increasingly I thought that I must kill this child. This seemed to be a simple solution and all our troubles would be over. I was quite cool about this at first; I had to be alone with him and then I could do it. Before I went to see my wife that evening, I asked to see him and the sister wheeled him to me in his cot. I could see the signs of mongolism clearly, the shape of his eyes, the tongue that was hanging out. I had been present at his birth – a tremendous experience – and, without knowing it then, I had diagnosed his mongolism. I remember going over to him and seeing a tube in his mouth to drain away the saliva. When his nurse took the tube out, his tongue was hanging out, and I called out to my wife 'Look, he is sticking his tongue out already.' I was terribly elated and excited at that time. We had done it, a boy, immortality had been achieved! I thought him rather ugly but then I had never seen a newly-born baby before and they are supposed to be ugly. Now I wanted to kill him and it was a very frightening thing even to think about. Here was I devoting my life to the problems of educating children of all abilities, having campaigned for the abolition of the death penalty in the past, and the moment my own child did not come up to my expectations I was ready to reject him and even prepared to consider killing him. When I expressed these feelings to the psychiatrist he asked me whether we had given him a name. When I told him we had chosen David he said 'You may be able to throw 'it' out of the window, but you can't do that with someone who is already a person with a name.' I remember feeling relieved and more secure after that interview: I had been able to listen to what had been said.

Later in the evening I was able to tell my wife and this was the greatest relief. She realized that something was terribly wrong with the child but for some time did not completely absorb what had happened. At the time when I told her about the child she had a new perfume on and was happy and radiant, having coped with the birth and having produced a child that she had really wanted to have. Neither of us can bear that perfume any more. If I smell it anywhere I am immediately reminded of that time. After leaving the hospital our friends rallied round, visited us and let us talk endlessly, but did not tell us what we ought to do. Sympathy by itself is useless. It is good to know that others feel for you, but it took me no further with my own need to deal with the shock. We made jokes to each other. It happened at Christmas and we made frivolous collage Christmas cards and sent them to all our friends. I remember being greatly amused that the only film on at the local cinema that week was 'The Mongols'. We needed a chance to express our outrage and resentment at the disaster and when we felt like that it was not much use pretending that everything was going to be easy and lovely. Some of the comfort we had offered to us is still good for a laugh: 'He will never grow up and leave you', the implication being that other 'nasty' children will persist in growing up and being people in their own right! Another crumb of comfort that was offered: 'Well, you didn't want your child to be a genius like Einstein, did you?' Equally unhelpful was the advice 'You must remove the child from the family because the other children will imitate him and become abnormal'.

From an autobiographical essay by Charles Hannam

Reflections

* – 'a sense of having somehow done wrong and that this was a punishment.'
  – 'Having a mentally handicapped child made me feel that I had failed.'
  – 'Sympathy by itself is useless.'

These phrases focus on the guilt felt by the father, a guilt fuelled, of course, by the kind of unthinking comments which concluded this passage.
Physical and mental health are precious to us. Equally, disability is a fact of human life, and it is important that we understand the impact it has on individuals and their families.

* Our thoughts should be with those who have to struggle against disabilities – more importantly, social prejudices of the kind Charles Hannam encountered here need to be challenged.

4 Problems and pain

Introduction

It would be a rare human being who claimed never to have suffered pain or encountered problems which they felt might overwhelm them. Illness, family upset, school work mounting up, falling out with a close friend – each of these can cause us to feel weighed down inside ourselves.

Listen to the following passage from a psychologist about human attitudes to problems and pain; it begins with the reminder that the first of the Four Noble Truths which Buddha taught was 'Life is suffering'.

Reading

The road less travelled

Problems and Pain
  Life is difficult.
  This is a great truth, one of the greatest truths. It is a great truth because once we truly see this truth, we transcend it. Once we truly know that life is difficult – once we truly understand and accept it – then life is no longer difficult. Because once it is accepted, the fact that life is difficult no longer matters.

Most do not fully see this truth that life is difficult. Instead they moan more or less incessantly, noisily or subtly, about the enormity of their problems, their burdens, and their difficulties as if life were generally easy, as if life *should* be easy. They voice their belief, noisily or subtly, that their difficulties represent a unique kind of affliction that should not be and that has somehow been especially visited upon them, or else upon their families, their tribe, their class, their nation, their race or even their species, and not upon others. I know about this moaning because I have done my share.

Life is a series of problems. Do we want to moan about them or solve them? Do we want to teach our children to solve them?

Discipline is the basic set of tools we require to solve life's problems. Without discipline we can solve nothing. With only some discipline we can solve only some problems. With total discipline we can solve all problems.

What makes life difficult is that the process of confronting and solving problems is a painful one. Problems, depending upon their nature, evoke in us frustration or grief or sadness or loneliness or guilt or regret or anger or fear or anxiety or anguish or despair. These are uncomfortable feelings, often very uncomfortable, often as painful as any kind of physical pain, sometimes equaling the very worst kind of physical pain. Indeed, it is *because* of the pain that events or conflicts engender in us all that we call them problems. And since life poses an endless series of problems, life is always difficult and is full of pain as well as joy.

Yet it is in this whole process of meeting and solving problems that life has its meaning. Problems are the cutting edge that distinguishes between success and failure. Problems call forth our courage and our wisdom; indeed, they create our courage and our wisdom. It is only because of problems that we grow mentally and spiritually. When we desire to encourage the growth of the human spirit, we challenge and encourage the human capacity to solve problems, just as in school we deliberately set problems for our children to solve. It is through the pain of confronting and resolving problems that we learn. As Benjamin Franklin said, 'Those things that hurt, instruct.' It is for this reason that wise people learn not to dread but actually to welcome problems and actually to welcome the pain of problems.

Most of us are not so wise. Fearing the pain involved, almost all of us, to a greater or lesser degree, attempt to avoid problems. We procrastinate, hoping that they will go away. We ignore them, forget them, pretend they do not exist. We even take drugs to assist us in ignoring them, so that by deadening ourselves to the pain we can forget the problems that cause the pain. We attempt to skirt around problems rather than meet them head on. We attempt to get out of them rather than suffer through them.

From 'The Road Less Travelled' by M Scott Peck

Reflections

* This, then, is a call to us to recognise that life *will* present problems; it is unrealistic to believe otherwise. If we can learn to *learn* from a problem, then we shall cope better when the next one comes along and our lives will be more fulfilled. We need to remember, too, that friends are there to help us and learn with us.

There is also an important lesson to be learned about putting problems in perspective. As the passage says, 'problems are the cutting edge that distinguishes between success and failure'. As if in evidence of this, a character in one of Graham Greene's novels says, slightly tongue-in-cheek:

'In Italy for thirty years under the Borgias
they had warfare, terror, murder, bloodshed – they
produced Michaelangelo, Leonardo da Vinci and the
Renaissance. In Switzerland they had brotherly love,
five hundred years of democracy and peace, and
what did that produce . . .? The cuckoo clock.'

* Two final thoughts:

'Problems worthy of attack
prove their worth by hitting back.'

'Losing one glove is certainly painful,
but nothing compared to the pain
of losing one,
throwing away the other,
and finding the first one again.'

5 Childhood and adolescence*

Introduction

When your great-grandparents were your age, there was no such thing as a 'teenager' or 'adolescence'. Until about the middle of this century you were either a child or an adult. When you left school and started work you were suddenly 'grown up'. Even as late as the 1930s most young people started work at the age of 13.

Adolescence is seen as a time of change and development. But the question is often asked, 'Do children grow up too soon . . .'

The following passage focuses our thoughts on this subject and moves on to raise important questions about parenting and why adults bother to have children at all.

Reading

Into the dangerous world

'Truly it is not easy to bring up a family.'   *King Babar*

Do children grow up too soon? Or are we only asking them to stay young to preserve an illusion for us of a better world? The separation of the states of adulthood and childhood is vital to the maintenance of the innocence about which we care: yet again, the market force child cannot be kept apart unless huge investments are made – in the case of children, in their education, in housing, in outdoor space, in entertainment, and television, the electronic baby-minder for all those out of school hours.

Child abuse is the crime our decade has diagnosed because a crisis exists, beyond the immediate victims and their assailants, suspected or otherwise, about the decay of goodness; when a child a week is dying as a consequence of family violence, we are looking at a reality that magnifies all doubts about human nature. Children are like the planet, they bear the imprint of our deeds, they embody our hopes – and our transgressions. It isn't a coincidence that the enrolment in Green groups of one kind and another is growing apace, that obsessive – and probably justified – anxiety about polluted food and water has dominated recent politics; the search is on to find something – and someone – uncontaminated and preserve their innocence. Children could be in this respect the repository of adult fantasies and illusions; it is possible we have it all wrong, and they would prefer to grow up at thirteen, leave school, work, smoke, marry and so forth, and they know better (and some child psychologists agree). It is possible that the desire to preserve an ideal of innocence, of learning, of unharmed apprenticeship to living, of love, is another arbitrary imposition grown-ups make upon children. But I for one believe in children's rights to their childhood, and childhood means freedom from pain, from coercion, from violence, the enjoyment of confidence and security and safety, access to food, shelter, and the development of skills.

Much has been done over the last ten years to make life hard for parents – and for parents, read above all, mothers. And everything that makes life hard for parents makes it harder for children. In the era of the market force child, children are suffering, and with them, all of us are being damaged. The privatised baby does not belong in the fantasy family of Fifties suburbia, for which some of the present government thinking seems to yearn, because, in the account book of the dying welfare state, the columns won't balance. When your mother is at work, her situation will not be eased: she will hunt for adequate care that she can afford and anxiety will gnaw her that she has not found it. You, her children, will suffer, and she will suffer for you and because of you, which will add to your sum of suffering. The low consideration of motherhood clashes with the ascribed value of children: the job of child-care, by parents and others, must be given its due.

The reality of children collides with their idealisation in more abstract ways too: children are loved for not being like adults, and when they begin to develop, with human failings as well as strengths, they are blamed for falling short of the ideal of child-likeness. In the words of Adam Smith, 'The qualities needed to advance are in children the reprehensible ones.' Children cannot be expected to be better than people; to be different from the people among whom they live.

Given the problems parents and children face, given the failure to thrive the decade has overseen, the simple response would be to stop making families altogether. Maybe however, as children aren't actually dying out, self-interest isn't the over-riding motive of human conduct. It's a wonder – perhaps even a remaining trace of a deep, buried capacity for love – that people continue to have them at all.

From 'Into the Dangerous World' by Marina Warner

Reflections

* A few interesting lines here:

   'Are we only asking them to stay young to preserve an illusion for us of a better world?'

'Children are loved for not being like adults.'

'The qualities needed to advance are in children the reprehensible ones.'

This last quotation, in particular, pinpoints the fact that child development is all about a loss of innocence, and challenging of the adult world and its values.

The passage is perhaps not very positive about the act of parenting – it certainly should make people think carefully about this subject. And Marina Warner's words should also help us to see more clearly what childhood, adolescence and adulthood stand for. It may help to pause and reflect on this for a while when you are in the midst of adolescence – a major crossroad in life, and a time of change which can be both exciting and stressful.

6 Family life

Introduction

As everybody knows, family life has its ups and downs – being part of a family means we experience a whole range of emotions and situations. And one thing we learn as we get older is that different members of a family need support at different times.

In all families we experience moments of great happiness and sadness, moments of loss, disappointment, success. All are an integral part of family life. Being human is being able to live through the more difficult times as well as enjoying the high points.

The following reading comes from Robert Leeson's novel *It's My Life*. This passage focuses on teenager Jan's coming to terms with a certain loss.

Reading

It's my life

The next day as she bent over her desk, she saw the face of Miss Maudesley, her tutor, eyes anxious behind large glasses, close to her own, asking some questions she could not quite catch. But she answered.

'I'm quite all right thank you.' She must have spoken loudly for several of her classmates turned and stared. Miss Maudesley walked away as though offended. Jan knew she ought to say something, to put things right. But the heaviness in her held her back. Only by the greatest strength of will did she go from day to day, and each word she must speak to others was a burden.

She had gone into a tunnel with no end in sight and no view to left or right – school, home, shops, kitchen, stairs, bedrooms, books, work, sleep. She moved so from day to day, from place to place, and did not know how she reached each point in her familiar round. She saw people but did not look at them, spoke to them, but did not hear what they said. Nothing was real and nothing could be felt, but the heavy ache deep inside her.

On the fourth day, she found herself in the early evening with women from the works, picking up bits and pieces in the supermarket. The cash lady was thin and sharp-nosed with china-blue eyes.

Every six months the supermarket changed hands and she swapped overalls, bright green, dark blue, candy stripe. But she was always there, dipping her head like a sparrow, exchanging genteel backchat with the plump manager, quizzing the customers. She knew everyone, knew all that was going on.

'Not seen your mother lately, love. Is she poorly?'

Jan looked and did not see her, picked up her bag and walked out.

Each night as she came home, Jan would fetch Kevin from next door, looking past the woman there with her broad, handsome face, hard hairdo and low neckline, into the cluttered kitchen with it's glaring TV, its haze of cigarette smoke, to call Kev from where he sat between her boys, pushing chocolate into his mouth.

'Mother poorly love?'

'Away.'

'Anytime you'd like me to pick up some shopping for you . . .'

'It's all right, thank you very much. We can manage. Kev are you coming?'

She did not know why she dragged her brother away. She did not even know why she rushed home, just to get his tea. But rush home she did, and dragged Kev away, for all his sullen looks and sometimes open grumbling. And she made him get undressed and into bed in good time, every night. Mum was 'away' for a while and everything was going on as though she were still here.

She would make cups of tea for Dad as he sat over his books. He did not drink them. But neither did he look at his books. He stared out of the window. And she returned to her room and opened her books and stared out at the darkening street below.

On Saturday as she stepped out of the front door, someone called her. It was old Mr Elsom from next door on the other side. A retired railwayman, he still wore a shabby, black waistcoat and collarless, flannel shirt. His crab-apple face was seamed and weathered, and when he stood close you could smell old man's sweat in his clothes.

He took her sleeve.

'Not seen your mother lately, love. I usually give her some potatoes at this time of year. We've got plenty, Edie and I. Always help people, I say, never know when you may need it yourself.'

Help? What for? Jan thought she saw an inquisitive gleam in his eye.

'No thanks, we can manage.'

(The picture of his offended face went into the collection in Jan's head: Sharon, Miss Maudesley, other classmates, the supermarket lady, the woman next door – hurt expressions, raised eyebrows, half-open mouths. Sometimes, when she slept, these faces came and crowded round her, saying nothing, only staring, until she woke up in desperation.)

As the days passed she was aware that the burden of running the house had slipped on to her, that Dad was doing nothing but his course, coming home, eating a little, letting cups of tea go cold. He was doing nothing, allowing the days to pass, growing more silent, jumping when the phone rang. And it came into her mind that she should complain, speak to him, ask him what he was going to do. But she could not bring herself to throw off this heaviness, to lay herself open to things that might be worse.

One day, at break time, she leaned on the wall in the schoolyard. The faint warmth of the April sunshine comforted her somehow. Someone was talking to her. She stared. Tina Ellis was there bending close and speaking quietly:

'You all right, Jan?'

'Eh?' Tina Ellis and she had never spoken to one another. They'd shouted at each other, and once in the third year, they'd fought in the formroom, spilling stuff from the desks while the others cheered them on.

'Are you all right?'

'Course I am, what do you mean?'

Tina Ellis was silent, as though weighing up Jan's mood. Then she said: 'Our Mum cleared off – six months back.'

Jan pushed up from the wall.

'What are you talking about?' Her voice was hard. Tina's eyes widened.

'Nothing. Forget I said ought. Snob.'

She walked away, leaving Jan staring.

Robert Leeson

Reflections

* The rest of the novel goes on to follow the further implications for Jan and her family that result from her mum's disappearance.

  What Jan is living with is 'the heavy ache deep inside her' as she thinks constantly about her mother. Those around her notice something is wrong but Jan rejects their questions and their offers of support. Even someone who doesn't know her at school asks if she's all right.

  In our school community many hundreds of families are represented. At any one time one family or another will be experiencing joys and sorrows. We should enjoy and celebrate other families' successes and be understanding and tolerant of their problems and, in particular, the effects those problems might have on members of the family.

  Friendship and love lie at the heart of family life.

* **The Heart of Friendship**

  Friends are patient and kind,
  they are not jealous or boastful,
  they are not arrogant or rude.

  Friends do not insist on having their own way,
  they are not irritable or resentful,
  they do not rejoice at wrong,
  but delight in what is right.

  Friendship bears all things,
  believes all things,
  hopes all things,
  endures all things.

  Friendship
  never ends.

  Adapted from: *Corinthians I*

7 'How others see us: how we see ourselves'

Introduction

How do you see yourself – your character, your appearance, your habits?

Now a more difficult question. How do you think *other* people see you? As positive, happy, honest? Or as pessimistic and rarely smiling?

Someone once said that you never *really* understand a person until you consider things from their point of view – until you 'climb into their skin and walk around in it'.

The following very short story might help us to reflect on this difficult question of self-image, and how other people view us.

Reading

The ugliest of them all

She was the ugliest creature I had ever laid eyes on. I wouldn't have minded, but she just wouldn't change for the better. She tried to wear different cosmetics to look nice; it didn't work so she insisted on staying with me, to spoil my image too.

She was silent and would only speak when I spoke. She did everything I did, and worst of all, she always chose to wear the same clothes as me. She was with me everywhere I went, to school, church, discos and parties.

Even when we were apart, she still seemed to haunt me. She was a trespasser on my conscience, and she often turned my dreams into nightmares. One night, with a wicked smile on her ugly face, she told me in my dream that I had to either love or hate her.

By morning, my mind was made up. I looked into the mirror, and told her how much I hated her.

Stella Ibekwe

In contrast, this passage talks about *true* friendship. It was written by Sir Walter Raleigh in the 16th century. (At this time, it was customary to use the word 'man' to mean both women and men.)

Flattery is no Friendship

Take care thou be not made a fool by flatterers, for even the wisest men are abused by these. Know therefore, that flatterers are the worst kind of traitors; for they will strengthen thy imperfections, encourage thee in all evils, correct thee in nothing, but so shadow and paint all thy vices and follies as thou shalt never, by their will, discern evil from good, or vice from virtue. And because all men are apt to flatter themselves, to entertain the additions of other men's praises is most perilous.

Do not therefore praise thyself, except thou wilt be counted a vainglorious fool, neither take delight in the praises of other men, except thou deserve it, and receive it from such as are worthy and honest, and will withal warn thee of thy faults: for flatterers have never any virtue, they are ever base, creeping, cowardly persons.

It is hard to know them from friends, they are so obsequious and full of protestations; for a wolf resembles a dog, so doth a flatterer a friend. Thou mayest be sure that he that will in private tell thee thy faults is thy friend, for he adventures thy mislike, and doth hazard thy hatred; for there are few men that can endure it, every man for the most part delighting in self-praise, which is one of the most universal follies which bewitcheth mankind.

Sir Walter Raleigh 1552–1618

Reflections

* Growing up is all about coming to terms with yourself as you are – the good points and the bad points. If you are not happy with one aspect of your personality you may try to change it. Or you may go on deceiving yourself about your good points, although deep down you know it is not really true.

* Being honest with ourselves is very difficult. *Real* friends are those who are honest enough to tell us the truth. Flattery is not friendship, as the second passage tells us.

8 Patience and frustrations

Introduction

Patience is seen as one of the great virtues in life. But there are occasions when frustrations and impatience build up inside us until we want to scream, or let off steam in some other way. Can you think of an occasion when you reached that point? How did you deal with it? Would you handle it any differently next time?

If you want a tale of frustration listen to the following amusing extract from the novel *Lucky Jim*. In this passage a man called Dixon is on a bus, and in a desperate hurry to catch a train in order to meet up with a girl-friend whom he is afraid of losing. His frustrations just grow and grow . . .

Reading

Lucky Jim

The conductor now appeared and negotiated with Dixon about his ticket. When this was over, he said: 'One forty-three we're due at the station. I looked it up.'

'Oh. Shall we be on time, do you think?'

'Couldn't say, I'm sorry. Not if we keep crawling behind this contraption we shan't, I shouldn't think. Train to catch?'

'Well, I want to see someone who's getting the one-fifty.'

'Shouldn't build on it if I were you.'

'Thanks,' Dixon said dismissively.

They entered a long stretch of straight road, with a slight dip in the middle so that every yard of its empty surface was visible. Far ahead a brown hand appeared from the lorry's cab and made a writhing, beckoning movement. The driver of the bus ignored this invitation in favour of drawing to a gradual halt by a bus-stop outside a row of thatched cottages. The foreshortened bulks of two old women dressed in black waited until the bus was quenched of all motion before clutching each other and edging with sidelong caution out of Dixon's view towards the platform. In a moment he heard their voices crying unintelligibly to the conductor, then activity seemed to cease. At least five seconds passed; Dixon stirred elaborately at his post, then twisted himself about looking for anything that might have had a share in causing this halt in his journey. He could detect nothing of this kind. Was the driver slumped in his seat, the victim of a faint, or had he suddenly got an idea for a poem? For a moment longer the pose continued; then the picture of sleepy rustic calm was modified by the fairly sudden emergence from a cottage some yards beyond of a third woman in a lilac costume. She looked keenly towards the bus and identified it without any obvious difficulty, then approached with a kind of bowed shuffle that suggested the movements of a serviceman towards the pay-table. This image was considerably reinforced by her hat, which resembled a Guardsman's peaked cap that had been strenuously run over and then dyed cerise.

The bus nosed its way on to the crown of the road, and the gap between it and the lorry began to diminish. Dixon found that his whole being had become centred in the matter of the bus's progress; he couldn't be bothered any longer to wonder what Christine would say to him if he got there in time, nor what he'd do if he didn't. He just sat there on the dusty cushions, galvanized by the pitchings of the bus into the appearance of seismic laughter, sweating stealthily in the heat and the apprehension – thank God he hadn't been drinking – stretching his face in a fresh direction at each overtaking car, each bend, each motiveless circumspection of the driver.

The bus was now resolutely secured again behind the trailer, which soon began to reduce speed even further. Before Dixon could cry out, before he'd time to guess what was to happen, the lorry and trailer had moved off to the side into a lay-by and the bus was travelling on alone. Now was the time, he thought with reviving hope, for the driver to start making up some of the time he must have lost. The driver, however, was clearly unable to assent to this diagnosis. Dixon lit another small cigarette, jabbing with the match at the sandpaper as if it were the driver's eye. He had, of course, no idea of the time, but estimated that they must, by now, have covered five of the eight or so miles to their destination. Just then the bus rounded a corner and slowed abruptly, then stopped. Making a lot of noise, a farm tractor was laboriously pulling, at right angles across the road, something that looked like the springs of a giant's bed, caked in places with earth and decked with ribbon-like grasses. Dixon thought he really would have to run downstairs and knife the drivers of both vehicles; what next? what next? What actually would be next: a masked holdup, a smash, floods, a burst tyre, an electric storm with falling trees and meteorites, a diversion, a low-level attack by Communist aircraft, sheep, the driver stung by a hornet? He'd choose the last of these, if consulted. Hawking its gears, the bus crept on, while every few yards troupes of old men waited to make their quivering way aboard.

As the traffic thickened slightly towards the town, the driver added to his caution as psychopathic devotion to the interests of other road-users; the sight of anything between a removal-van and a junior bicycle halved his speed to four miles an hour and sent his hand, Dixon guessed, flapping in a slow-motion dance of beckonings and wavings-on. Learners practised reversing across his path; gossiping knots of loungers parted leisurely at the touch of his reluctant bonnet; toddlers reeled to retrieve toys from under his just-revolving wheels. Dixon's head switched angrily to and fro in vain search for a clock; the inhabitants of this mental, moral, and physical backwater were too poor, and were also too mean . . . Dixon, seeing the hulk of the railway station thirty yards off, returned painfully to reality and rattled along the aisle to the stairs. Before the bus had reached the station stop he plunged down, out, across the road, and into the booking-hall. The clock over the ticket-office pointed to one forty-seven. At once the minute hand stepped one pace onward. Dixon flung himself at the barrier. A hard-faced man confronted him.

'Which platform for London, please?'

The man looked at him as if trying to gauge in advance his fitness to hear a more than usually improper joke. 'Bit early, aren't you?'

'Eh?'

'Next to London's eight-seventeen.'

'Eight-seventeen?'

'No restaurant car.'

'What about the one-fifty?'

'No one-fifty. Haven't got it mixed up with the one-forty, by any chance?'

Dixon swallowed. 'I think I must have done,' he said. 'Thanks.'

From 'Lucky Jim' by Kingsley Amis

Reflections

* We have probably all experienced this kind of journey ourselves, with the frustrations that build up. Some people are naturally patient, others impatient – it's part of their character. What is important on occasions is to understand how others are feeling, and also to learn how to deal with our own frustrations and other people's impatience.

Sometimes impatience and frustration can lead people to lash out verbally or physically, to lose their temper and thus behave badly towards others. Yes, we might understand their reactions, but we should not condone any resulting violence. If you find yourself in a position of extreme frustration, try to take a deep breath, pause ... or even walk away from the situation for a few moments to try and regain composure.

Losing your temper can be a healthy and necessary outburst; but if it's aimed aggressively at someone else it needs to be kept in check. Impatience can be destructive in certain situations and needs controlling – maybe in the style that Dixon on the bus *just* manages!

9 Hope and despair

Introduction

Would you describe yourself as an optimist or a pessimist? Do you, for example, see a glass of water as half-empty or half-full?

Are you confident about the future of our world – are you hopeful about to-morrow?

These are important human questions. They are skilfully addressed in a short play entitled *In the Dock*, written by a 12-year-old pupil. In this play, we have to picture a courtroom in which two people are on trial: one is Hope, the other is Despair.

Reading

In the Dock

The Trial of Tomorrow
Witness for the Prosecution

JUDGE.   Call Despair.

DESPAIR.   My Lord, you must surely understand that this Tomorrow is but a
figment of the imagination,
an illusion, nay, a delusion
on which the souls of weak worms feast
but grow no fatter, and starve, and die,
That tepid mass in one's stomach
when reality breaks, as a wave,
and you know, yes my lord, you know
that despite all your strivings
you cannot change the world in which you live.
Therefore surely Tomorrow is
cause for worry, cause for uncertainty, cause for jealousy?
Cause, no less, for misgivings, for useless preparations,
cause even for Hope? And for the belief that tomorrow brings more
and better than today?
All the trees bear fair fruit tomorrow,
But in reality – they are bitter.
Great flowers bloom tomorrow –
But in reality, they wither.
My lord, I rest my case.

JUDGE.   Call Typical.

TYPICAL.   My Lord, I represent all the ordinary thousands.
My case is one of false pretences,
of an inexplicable urge not to differ,
Not to break new ground,
but to tread the same mill until we drop.
My witnesses are smog, old warehouses
now abandoned, and patched with plastic,
And the knowledge that day after day
Is the same.
If a life consists, M'Lud, of days alike,
then surely Tomorrow is no novelty?
Tomorrow must give way to Today.
My Lord, I rest my case.

JUDGE.   Witness for the prosecution, do you call any more speakers?

WFTP.   But one, M'Lud. Call Reality.

REALITY.   My Lord, the populace is under the impression
that all one's worries will vanish
should one but wait.
This, My Lord, is untrue.
Left unattended, worrying matters grow
as a canker. Surely then,

with the abolition of Tomorrow
All these aspects will be attended to today?
My Lord, look around you. See the threats,
Pollution, the slow death of the environment
That increase tomorrow?
See the extinction of species, the imminent danger
of Nuclear War, that could break out tomorrow?
That tomorrow, we may be no more?
My Lord, I rest my case.

Witness for the Defence

JUDGE.	Call Tomorrow.
CLERK.	Absent, M'Lud. The trial is to be conducted in his absence.
WFTD.	Call Hope.
HOPE.	Gentlemen of the jury, Tomorrow is wonderful.
	Sometimes there is the happy knowledge that Tomorrow is a day of rest.
	Sometimes you may have Tomorrow to finish
	that which you have begun.
	Tomorrow is a day to start anew, to start afresh.
	To forget what is done today and just to live.
	Tomorrow is a comfort, a refuge.
	'It will all be all right tomorrow,' people say,
	and they are right.
	For what, M'Lud, could be worse than today?
	Tomorrow is for seeing flowers, for hearing birds,
	For not caring, for loving.
	Tomorrow is an aid to help us through now.
	We all need Tomorrow.
	M'Lud, I rest my case.
JUDGE.	Are there any more witnesses for the defence?
WFTD.	Only Hope, My Lord. Only Hope.
JUDGE.	Then let the jury consider their verdict.

From 'In the Dock' by Guy Burt

Reflections

* What is your verdict? Are you persuaded by Hope or by Despair about the future?

In times of personal worry and adversity, hope in and for the future – looking on the bright side of things – is an important way of coming through that state of worry. Despair is certainly something to be avoided, if at all possible, though we would not be human if we did not at some point in our lives feel desperate or despairing about something or someone. As with so many human situations and feelings, what we must seek to do is live through and learn from our experiences and emotions.

* A final reflection and perspective on this subject – a poem which seeks to place humans, and their lives and emotions, against the backcloth of eternity:

Ozymandias

I met a traveller from an antique land
Who said: Two vast and trunkless legs of stone
Stand in the desert. Near them, on the sand,
Half sunk, a shattered visage lies, whose frown,
And wrinkled lip, and sneer of cold command
Tell that its sculptor well those passions read
Which yet survive (stamped on these lifeless things)
The hand that mocked them and the heart that fed:
And on the pedestal these words appear:
'My name is Ozymandias, King of Kings:
Look on my works, ye Mighty, and despair!'
Nothing beside remains. Round the decay
Of that colossal wreck, boundless and bare
The lone and level sands stretch far away.

P B Shelley

10 Envy and enthusiasm

Introduction

We all live and work alongside others, at home, at school, in the workplace. When we watch someone else doing or achieving something, we sometimes begin to wish that we could be as successful as they are, or have what they have – good grades at school, fashionable clothes, lots of spending money or exotic holidays.

Envy is a natural and understandable human emotion. But it can be both positive and negative.

Reading

Envy

I envy.
This secret
I have not revealed before.
I know
there is somewhere a boy
whom I greatly envy.
I envy
the way he fights;
I myself was never so guileless and bold.
I envy
the way he laughs –
as a boy I could never laugh like that.
He always walks about with bumps and bruises;
I've always been better combed,
intact.

He will not miss
all those passages in books
I've missed.
Here he is stronger too.
He will be more blunt and harshly honest,
forgiving no evil for any good it may bring;
and where I'd dropped my pen:
'It isn't worth it . . .'
he'd assert:
'It's worth it!'
and pick up the pen.
If he can't unravel a knot,
he'll cut it through,
where I can neither unravel a knot,
nor cut it through.
Once he falls in love,
he won't fall out of it,
where I keep falling in
and out of love.
I'll hide my envy.
Start to smile,
I'll pretend to be a simple soul;
'Someone has to smile;
someone has to live in a different way . . .'
But much as I tried to persuade myself of this,
repeating:
'To each man his fate . . .'
I can't forget there is somewhere a boy
who will achieve far more than I.

Yevgeny Yevtushenko

Reflections

* The person in the poem keeps his envy secret, but goes around thinking that
  whatever he does someone else will do better. And the closing lines will inevitably
  be true for every human being, at some time in their lives:
  'I can't forget there is somewhere a boy [or girl]
  who will achieve far more than I.'

If we go through our lives aware only how others are doing better than ourselves, thinking only about someone else's achievements, then envy becomes
destructive. Envy turns to covetousness and jealousy and becomes more negative, we make ourselves less and less content with what we have.
On the other hand, if envying someone else's achievements prompts us to admire them and seek to match them, then envy becomes a positive emotion. As
the poet suggests, each person can shape her or his own fate. It is important to
look up to people and follow good examples, in a spirit of positive envy and,
importantly, with the *enthusiasm* to achieve something yourself.

* **Enthusiasm**

You can do anything if you have enthusiasm.
Enthusiasm is the yeast that makes your hope
rise to the stars. Enthusiasm is the sparkle
in your eye, it is the swing in your gait, the
grip of your hand, the irresistible surge of
your will and your energy to execute your ideas.
Enthusiasts are fighters. They have fortitude.
They have staying qualities. Enthusiasm is
the bottom of all progress! With it there is
accomplishment. Without it there are only alibis.

Henry Ford's Fireplace Motto

11 Revenge

Introduction

If someone attacks us – mentally or physically – our natural human instinct is to seek revenge. This is understandable, but it's also potentially dangerous.

The following short story, written by a 15-year-old student, won a writing competition. It presents an unusual side to the subject of revenge.

Reading

The lives and deaths of Edward Lysle

Jessica turned on both taps full and closed the curtains. She discarded her clothes, removed the large white towel from the towel-rail, and draped them over the rail. She then stepped on the heavy scales and, having waffed away the warm steam, peered down: they read nine stones and two pounds. 'Not bad,' she thought to herself, 'for a thirty-four-year-old woman of average height.' Having turned off the taps, she proceeded to climb into the bath.

Then, reclining in the warm, soothing luxury of the scented foam-surfaced water, she lowered her eyelids and became oblivious to the world around her. Soon Jessica snoozed quietly and contentedly, forgetting about the chipped plug which was allowing the ever-thirsty pipe to refresh itself continually.

The spider sat hunched behind one of the many 'bouteilles de parfum', waiting patiently. It stretched its short, thick, hair-covered legs and cautiously, in a crab style, manoeuvred itself from behind 'les bouteilles'. The spider hunched its black, button body and slowly, on arched legs, proceeded forwards, towards the bath. It reached the side and looked at the motionless body whose nakedness had begun to be exposed by the descending water level.

The spider had climbed up the bath's waterpipe the day before. Now, gazing down at the almost completely revealed naked body in its fat, black orb of a head, it realised the perilous journey had not been in vain. It gazed down; eight tiny, round shiny eyes, with what seemed to be almost human characteristic – a scheming glare from the glinting, black-baubled eyes.

In the tiny head of the spider, compared to that of a human's, a well-balanced mind was contained. This was no freak of nature – it was Jessica's husband.

Edward, Jessica's husband, had awakened after what he thought was a long and uneventful dream, in the subterranean depths of the soil. Having dismissed the shock that he was buried alive, he could not see, but could feel, and began feeling, until he discovered, on his emerging from the dark grave that he was in his back garden. But everything seemed way out of proportion – the buildings towered hundreds of feet; the garden gnomes stood like statues of liberty and the smallest flowers were the height of redwoods. Then, Edward discovered he had been underground in the soil. He looked down at himself in order to see what state his clothes were in – only to be greeted by seeing long, thick and extremely hairy legs projecting from his round, fat and jet black body. He closed his eyes, one at a time, expecting to awaken in bed next to Jessica. But adding to his horror, one by one, the lids of his eight eyes lowered and raised again. To his amazement he remained quite calm, accepting the fact that he was a spider.

As he could not view all his body, he cast his mind back to former rememberances of spiders. In his mind they were black, hairy, ugly things that he often crushed underfoot solely for their grotesque appearance. He wanted to cry! – No, he wanted to scream! As he was about to test his new vocal chords, if any, he was unaware of the great danger that was above him ...

A speckled thrush, discontented because of his meagre meal of worms, had spotted him. Without hesitation the thrush began to fly directly towards Edward. But some built in warning, which mother nature had kindly invented and bestowed, sent Edward scuttling back into his dark lair. A thought flashed through his mind – he wished he had been buried alive after all ...

Waiting for the cover of dark brought Edward to his senses. The last thing he remembered was another argument with Jessica about her lover ... he vaguely remembered her standing there ... her eyes ... the way he had never seen them before ... filled with fear ... a knife in her hand ... with blood ... blood? ... yes blood! ... dripping on the floor forming little red pools ... her lover at the door shouting ... 'No, Jessica, no!' ... then he remembered a warm sensation tingling all over his body, soothing and relaxing him ... Jessica and her lover talking ... quarrelling? ... no, talking ... but he could not hear ... he could see their mouths move ... but he could not hear ...

After Jessica had murdered him he could vaguely think what she and her lover had done; or was it a hazy, unclear memory? They carried him out into the back garden in the middle of the night ... Jessica exclaiming 'His eyes are open! His eyes are open! Close them quickly, they're horrid.' ... then he was dropped into a pit of about four feet in depth and soil was shovelled all over him ... he was helpless; paralysed; unable to move. 'He'll be a good fertilizer,' he heard her lover joke ... and Edward realized the next thing he remembered was thinking he was buried alive.

Edward had always dismissed reincarnation as 'poppycock!' being a church-going Catholic all his life. But now, faced with his metamorphosized body, he instantly realised he had the chance to revenge upon Jessica. He did not honestly know why he had been reincarnated, whether it happened once, twice or millions of times. He was not sure he was reincarnated for the sole purpose of revenge. What mattered to him was he had the chance of revenge upon Jessica and he was going to use it ...

It had not taken him long to decide he would pursue Jessica and frighten her out of her wits as she detested and feared spiders. This was the purpose of his long and laborious journey.

He began to creep down the enamel quite fast, making towards Jessica ...

The water had drained, leaving Jessica stranded on an island of foam bubbles, which were easily overcome by a determined spider like Edward.

He reached her foot first. Then he slowly climbed up her sole and over her toes, and began to creep down the slope towards her ankle; Jessica remaining in the depths of slumber ... In no time at all Edward had crept slowly and rhythmically up to her knee ... and proceeded up her white thighs, softened by water and foam ... Brian's fate or the punishment of Jessica had not yet really been finalized ... Maybe the punishment of Jessica would satisfy Edward ... in which case Brian, her lover, would remain unharmed ... Edward's heart was beating faster and faster ... his head throbbed as the blood pumped around his fat, furry body ... he passed over her thigh top ... her hip ... he began to move faster in his excitement ... faster ... faster ... he was home and dry he told himself ... eventually ... her navel ...

Jessica awoke unexpectedly; eyes bulging grotesquely and mouth agape as she saw the spider creep, softly but swiftly, with the gentle pad of its feet against her skin. She tried to scream; it still advanced. Her throat was tight and dry; Edward was half-way up her stomach. He had almost reached her breasts when she leapt unsteadily onto her feet; her face contorted in horror and fear. She swung one foot out of the bath (Edward clinging on for his dear little life) and was about to do so with the other, but she lost her pelican pose and keeled over backwards. Jessica's head cracked against the bathroom scales and she emitted a short gargling sound from her throat.

Jessica lay still. She was dead. Edward, who was flung off onto the bathtowel and was still there, knew this. She lay propped up against the bathside; head on one side; mouth and eyes open; legs spreadeagled on the floor; one arm hung over the bath where it oscillated for a long time.

Edward was extremely pleased. He now thought how he could remain with Jessica's corpse until Brian, as neither Edward or Jessica had much family, had seen her. He crawled back onto her hip and made his way towards her head. Edward crawled over her chin and over to the gaping mouth where he had planned to be concealed for a while, even to feed off Jessica – he smiled inwardly at this thought. He hoisted himself over her bottom lip and teeth and padded onto her still warm and spongy tongue. He turned around and looked outside at the thought of the funny situation he was in. Edward was very happy with himself indeed. But being without food for days made Edward feel hungry. He began to explore Jessica's mouth, and soon discovered several food particles which he devoured quickly. Yes, Edward was very pleased with himself indeed; he was even quite thrilled about embarking on his new life. In fact, he had never been as happy for quite a while.

In several sudden jerked movements, Jessica rolled onto the floor into a slumped heap – slamming her mouth tight shut. Edward was jolted backwards quite unexpectedly, and before he knew what was happening, he rolled down her throat and was gone forever.

David John Connor 15

Reflections

* This is a cleverly-written tale of revenge in the context of a love story, with several strange twists.

Children and adults alike can feel strongly tempted to take revenge. But if we act in the heat of the moment, we may get carried away. Think ... pause ... and then act if you have to. Of course, this is easy to say and much harder to do. But by taking some time to think before we act, we may be able to respond more cautiously and wisely.

* *Matthew 5: 38–42*
You have heard that it was said, 'Eye for eye, and tooth for tooth'. But I tell you, Do not resist an evil person. If someone strikes you on the right cheek, turn to him the other also. And if someone wants to sue you and take your tunic, let him have your cloak as well. If someone forces you to go one mile, go with him two miles. Give to the one who asks you, and do not turn away from the one who wants to borrow from you.

12 Living with your actions

Introduction
Perhaps one of the most difficult things about being human is learning to live with the actions you have taken. Children are usually forgiven for their mistakes – it is accepted as part of growing up. But as a young adult we learn that we have to take increasing responsibility for our actions. As we get older, family and friends are less and less likely to bail us out at every mistake.

Listen to the following piece about a man called Albert Pierrepoint, a hangman who changed his mind after 25 years of hanging people, including household-name murderers, Nazi war criminals, and an ex-customer from his own pub.

Reading

Albert Pierrepoint

Albert Pierrepoint, the Yorkshire publican who from 1931 to 1956 also had freelance employment breaking the necks of living human beings on behalf of the rest of us, is still alive.

In 1956, eight years before the last execution in Britain, he resigned. He has never said precisely why, but in his autobiography, *Executioner: Pierrepoint* (published in 1974), he outlined the reasons that led to his change of heart. First, there was the courage of most of his hundreds of victims. 'If death were a deterrent,' he wrote, 'I might be expected to know. It is I who have faced them at the last, young lads and girls, working men, grandmothers. I have been amazed to see the courage with which they take that walk into the unknown. It did not deter them then, and it had not deterred them when they committed what they were convicted for. All the men and women whom I have faced at that final moment convince me that in what I have done I have not prevented a single murder.'

Not only was the death penalty ineffective; it was also, in Pierrepoint's view, unjust, because of the inconsistency with which it was applied. Reprieves were granted or withheld on arbitrary political grounds. 'The trouble with the death sentence has always been that nobody wanted it for everybody, but everybody differed about who should get off.' Executions, he wrote, 'are only an antiquated relic of a primitive desire for revenge which takes the easy way and hands over the responsibility for revenge to other people.' As one of the people to whom it had been handed, he gravely handed it back, calling the bluff of those who approve of executions as long as they can be carried out by somebody else.

Another noted opponent of capital punishment, Albert Camus, wrote in 1957, 'If society justifies the death penalty . . . society must display the executioner's hands.' Executioner Pierrepoint displays his own and leaves you speechless. He was 11 when he discovered that his father and his uncle were both hangmen, and conceived, 'with a thrill of pleasure', an ambition to follow in their footsteps. After leaving school, he applied to the Home Office, was called for an interview ('Why do you want to be a public executioner?') and sent on a training course. This covered such topics as how to calculate the right drop, how to hang two people simultaneously, and what to do if the prisoner was upset or uncooperative.

Once a new hangman had passed the course, his name would be place on a Home Office approved list. He must then await an invitation from a prison governor to attend on such-and-such a date (railway warrant supplied) and hang someone. It was a strict rule that hangmen, like nice girls at a dance, must wait to be asked. To volunteer to hang a particular individual was officially regarded as objectionable conduct, and, if there was one thing that the Home Office would not tolerate in its hangmen, it was objectionable conduct.

Other Pythonesque characteristics of the hanging profession as described by Pierrepoint included the problem of double-booking (like airlines and hoteliers, hangmen were reluctant to lose a fee just because somebody didn't turn up, so some of them would accept two engagements on the same day as an insurance against a last-minute reprieve), and the mandatory holding of an inquest on a body to find our what it had died of.

When the state turns murderer, things must be done properly. Pierrepoint claimed to have acted as properly as the job allowed. He claimed a clear conscience. For years following his execution of Nazi war criminals, Pierrepoint used to receive a regular Christmas box of £5 from an anonymous person who simply wrote 'Belsen' on the accompanying note. Suddenly the gifts stopped. Pierrepoint assumed the giver had died, but nevertheless he went on wondering about the motives and feelings of this unknown person: 'Did he find peace?'

One might ask the same about the executioner who changed his mind.

Reflections

* This is both an amusing and a serious piece!

    Here was a man who spent much of his working life hanging people, in the name of the state. Finally, he decided to resign because he no longer believed that hanging acted as a deterrent.

    The writer of this piece of biography asks whether Albert Pierrepoint could have found peace of mind after executing so many people. Certainly he would have had to live with the actions he had taken, and he might well have agreed with the person who once said that 'if you haven't got a mind to change then you probably haven't got a mind at all!'

* In our own daily lives, we take decisions, change our minds or actions. As we grow up, we learn to accept the results of those actions. Being human is all about accepting responsibility for what we say and do.

* *Matthew 5: 43–46*

You have heard that it was said, 'Love your neighbour and hate your enemy.' But I tell you: Love your enemies, bless those who curse you, do good to those who hate you, that you may be sons of your Father in heaven. He causes his sun to rise on the evil and the good, and sends rain on the righteous and the unrighteous. If you love those who love you, what reward will you get? Are not even the tax collectors doing that? And if you greet only your brothers, what are you doing more than others? Do not even pagans do that? Be perfect, therefore, as your heavenly Father is perfect.

Acknowledgements

With especial thanks to Janet Spencer and Marion Casey, for preparing the text for publication.

The author and publishers would like to thank the following for permission to reproduce copyright material.

All Scripture quotations in this publication are from the HOLY BIBLE, NEW INTERNATIONAL VERSION. Copyright © 1973, 1978, 1984 by International Bible Society. Used by permission of Hodder & Stoughton Ltd.

Aitken and Stone Ltd/the author for 'In good faith' by Salman Rushdie. Bernard Ashley for 'Equal Rights'. *The Bicestrian* for 'Recollections' by Mr Howson. *British Journalism Review* for 'Broadcast news'. Bugle Songs Ltd for 'Russians', lyrics by Sting, © 1985 Magnetic Publishing Ltd. Jonathan Cape Ltd for songs by Bob Dylan. Jan Carew for 'The Outside Chance'. Linda Cookson for 'Fireflies'. The Co-workers of Mother Teresa* for 'Mother Teresa'. The *Daily Telegraph* plc for 'Different values', 'The Interrogation' and 'A nameless fate' © The Sunday Telegraph Ltd/Alan Sutton Publishing. Judy Daish Associates Ltd for *Whose life is it anyway?* by Brian Clark, published by Amber Lane Press. Richard Dawkins for 'The blind watchmaker'. Andre Deutsch Ltd for *Sour Sweet* by Timothy Mo and *Shane* by Jack Shaefer. Faber and Faber Ltd for 'Late' by Judith Nicholls; extracts from *Waiting for Godot* by Samuel Becket; 'Prayer before birth' by Louis MacNeice; extracts from *The Mouse and his Child* by Russel Hoban; 'The early purges' by Seamus Heaney. Victor Gollancz Ltd for *Lucky Jim* by Kingsley Amis. Charles Hannam for *Parents and Mentally Handicapped Children*. Harper Collins Publishers for 'The endless variety' from *Life on Earth* by David Attenborough. Harper Collins Children's Books for *It's my life* by Robert Leeson. William Heinemann/The Octopus Group for *To Kill a Mocking Bird* by Harper Lee. David Higham Associates for 'Reunion' from *The Wind from the Sun* by Arthur C Clarke. Hodder and Stoughton Ltd for 'Do men survive death' by Bertrand Russell and 'Christian beliefs about heaven and hell' by Dorothy Sayers from *The Great Mystery of Life Hereafter*. International Creative Management Inc for 'Challenger' from *What I saw at the Revolution* by Peggy Noonan. The *Independent* for 'When disaster strikes' by Dorothy Rowe; 'Dancing on the ghost of the infamous wall' by Adrian Bridge; 'Out of India' by Tony Allen-Mills; 'Out of the USSR' by Rupert Cornwell; 'Three-minute culture' by Michael Ignatieff; 'Advertising' by Brian Astley; 'News from elsewhere' by Douglas Kennedy and 'Heroes and villains' by Zoe Fairbairn. Michael Joseph Ltd for *Walkabout* by James Vance Marshall; 'Parents' rights' from *Mondays, Thursdays* by Keith Waterhouse. Gene Kemp for 'The rescue of Karen Arscott' from *School's OK* published by Unwin Hyman. H Lewin for Bandiet. Methuen Ltd for *The Life of Galileo* by Bertholt Brecht. John Murray Ltd for 'The Planster's Vision' by John Betjeman. Richard North for 'The price of freedoms'.